MW00378272

St. Louis

The Evolution of an
American Urban Landscape

In the series

Critical Perspectives on the Past

edited by Susan Porter Benson, Stephen Brier,
and Roy Rosenzweig

St. Louis

*The Evolution of an
American Urban Landscape*

Eric Sandweiss

TEMPLE UNIVERSITY PRESS

PHILADELPHIA

Temple University Press, Philadelphia 19122
Copyright © 2001 by Temple University
All rights reserved
Published 2001
Printed in the United States of America

♾ The paper used in this publication meets the requirements of the
American National Standard for Information Sciences—Permanence
of Paper for Printed Library Materials, ANSI z39.48-1984.

Library of Congress Cataloging-in-Publication Data

Sandweiss, Eric.
   St. Louis : the evolution of an American urban landscape /
Eric Sandweiss.
     p.   cm. — (Critical perspectives on the past)
   Includes bibliographical references and index.
   ISBN 1-56639-885-1 (cloth : alk. paper) — ISBN 1-56639-886-x (pbk. :
alk. paper)
       1. City planning—Missouri—St. Louis—History.   2. Cities and
   towns—Missouri—St. Louis—Growth.   3. Urban landscape architec-
   ture—Missouri—St. Louis—History.   4. Landscape changes—Govern-
   ment policy—Missouri—St. Louis.   5. Public spaces—Missouri—
   St. Louis—History.   6. St. Louis (Mo.)—History.   7. St. Louis (Mo.)—
   Social conditions.   8. St. Louis (Mo.)—Environmental conditions.
   I. Title: Saint Louis.   II. Title.   III. Series.
   HT168.S79 S36 2001
   307.76'09778'66–dc21   00-053674

Contents

Part I: Laying the Groundwork

Part II: Building the Fenced-Off Corners

List of Illustrations

Acknowledgments

Like a great city, a successful book merges into one whole and coherent experience the disparate sources and points of view that attend its creation. Whether this particular volume succeeds in such manner will be a decision best made by its readers as they turn its final pages; the one thing for which I can safely vouch from the outset is that this book's completion would not have been possible without the help of a number of individuals, many of them unaware of one another or of the larger project in which they played a part. If I take pleasure in bringing those individuals' names together in one place and expressing my gratitude to them as a group, it is without in any way asking that they bear responsibility for those matters of content, style, and interpretation on which an author must inevitably stand or fall alone.

For their assistance in granting me access to vital records not normally accessible to the public, I owe a debt to Joe Hamilton of the Associated General Contractors, the late Clyde Martini of Bricklayers' Union Local 1, Bob Busch of Carpenters' Union Local 5, Roy Leimberg at the Pitzman's Company of Surveyors, Father Richard J. Bockskopf of St. Francis de Sales Church, Mark Schaefering and Rev. Dr. Samuel Goltermann of Trinity Lutheran Church, Bob Thomas at the Church of St. John Nepomuk, and especially to Bob Meckfessel and Bob Lutz of the First American Title Company. Equally important to the project's success was the access I gained to the vast collections of printed and archival resources that have been assembled over the years in St. Louis. For their guidance through this material, I am grateful, in particular, to the staff of the City of St. Louis Archives, to Glen Holt and Ann Watts at the St. Louis Public Library, and particularly to Martha Clevenger, Emily Troxell Jaycox, Duane Sneddeker, Ellen Thomasson, and all of the reference librarians and archivists at the Missouri Historical Society.

Much of the information needed to complete this book was contained not in storage boxes and library shelves but in the streets and buildings of

St. Louis. The following residents, real estate agents, and building owners allowed me—with more alacrity than I would have mustered in the same situation—to traipse through their houses with clipboard and tape measure in hand: Terry Jo Bishell, Bob Brandhorst, Patricia Colpitts, Wayne Huber, Paul LaFlam, Mark and Shelly Lincoln, Jim Lutz, Jeff Milan, Liz Oldham, Robert and Judith Phelps, Jim and Ellen Summa, Lou Suzick, Lou Tippett, and Judy Wallace.

For financial support during early stages of my research, I am grateful to the University of California, Berkeley, and the American Historical Association. An additional and more general acknowledgment is due to the Missouri Historical Society (MHS), which helped to support the project in the years that followed. I have been privileged in my years at MHS to work among many fine historians and valued colleagues from whose ideas I learned and on whose support I depended; among them, I will single out Robert Archibald, Katharine Corbett, and Karen Goering for their contributions to the completion of this study.

The pages that follow reflect the influence of a number of scholars from whom I have been fortunate enough to learn over the years. Portions of this work were completed under the auspices of a fellowship from the Buell Center for the Study of American Architecture at Columbia University. There, I benefited in particular from my conversations with Elizabeth Blackmar, Daniel Bluestone, and Gwendolyn Wright. At the University of California, Berkeley, where this study first took shape as a doctoral dissertation, Dell Upton's critical comments improved the quality of my work immeasurably; it was further refined through discussion with the late James Vance, Paul Groth, Lawrence Levine, Roger Montgomery, and the late Spiro Kostof. More recently, in St. Louis, Andrew Hurley, Eric Mumford, Joseph Heathcott, and Mark Abbott have all helped me to see a familiar city through fresh eyes and a scholarly perspective.

For their helpful comments on earlier versions of portions of the work contained herein, I thank Christopher Silver, Mary Corbin Sies, Bernard Herman, Lu Ann DeCunzo, David Schuyler, Zane Miller, Elizabeth Blackmar, and Susan Porter Benson. I am grateful, as well, to several publishers for granting me permission to reproduce material already published in similar form in the following volumes: Christopher Silver and Mary Corbin Sies, eds., *Planning the Twentieth-Century American City* (Baltimore: Johns Hopkins University Press, 1996, pp. 76–97); Lu Ann De Cunzo and Bernard Herman, eds., *Historical Archaeology and the Study of American Culture* (Winterthur, Del.: The Henry Francis du Pont Winterthur Museum, Inc., 1996, pp. 319–57); and Andrew Hurley, ed., *Common Fields: An Environmental History of St. Louis* (St. Louis: Missouri Historical Society Press, 1997, pp. 90–106). Finally, I gratefully acknowledge my editor at Temple University Press, Janet Francendese, whose support and patience helped ensure this book's timely completion.

Friends and family are more responsible than anyone for what has been, in the end, a labor of love. For equal parts moral support and technical assistance, I thank Gen Obata, Mark Brack, Michael Corbett, Dan Feldman, Jeff Norman, Michael Samuel, and the late Stuart Moore, each of whom played a distinct but critical role in this work. For their years of unquestioning support, I owe my parents and sisters far more than these words. Finally, to my sons, Noah and Ethan, and especially to my wife, Lee: Thank you for giving me more reason to look forward than back.

CHAPTER I

Introduction

*Fenced-Off Corners,
Wider Settings, and the
New American Landscape*

Edwin Reller Jr. will never occupy the place in the annals of American urban history that is reserved for such luminaries as Frederick Law Olmsted and Daniel Burnham. But in September 1994, when he and the Cotton Building Company announced their plans for a new subdivision in the far western reaches of St. Louis County, the developer found himself playing a small but key part in the changing way that Americans look at cities.

Reller enthusiastically described his $50 million project as a complex of five adjacent "villages," each characterized by common lot sizes and similar housing values. With its range of densely developed housing, its curving streets and its carefully separated land uses, the project was bigger than—but not categorically different from—many others launched by developers in the suburban area known as "West County" in the boom years of the 1980s and 1990s. But before the first surveyor had arrived on the wooded site, before the first load of dirt was hauled away, this particular developer found his project mired in legal difficulties and public criticism; the development ultimately stumbled amidst a transformation of public attitudes in St. Louis County not unlike the transformation already at work in large cities across the country. That transformation saw the widespread decline of a century-old article of faith: that aggressive public and private development should serve as tools in enhancing a "wider setting" of shared civic values across the metropolitan landscape. In the place of this assumption has come a growing acceptance of a phenomenon once dismissed, in this particular city, as that of the "fenced-off corner": small communities inspiring localized political loyalty and promising to their residents a life distinct from that enjoyed by residents of the surrounding region.

This book is written in an effort to understand how such concepts as these first developed in urban America, and how they have subsequently served or misled us in our efforts to guide or adapt to the changes that continually face our communities. The book's focus is St. Louis, a city that is unique in many ways, but typical in far more. St. Louis's story stands for the story of all those cities whose ambitions and civic self-image, forged from the growth of the mercantile and industrial eras, have been dramatically altered in the years since. More dramatically, perhaps, than most—but in a manner shared by all—St. Louis's shifting economic base, population, and altered landscape have forced scholars, policymakers, and residents alike to acknowledge the transience of what were once assumed to be inexorable metropolitan trends: concentration, growth, accumulated wealth, and generally improved well-being among them.

To understand the source of these changes, I have chosen specifically to look at the "urban landscape"—a term that encompasses buildings, parks, streets, and infrastructure—both the grand and deliberate variety, shaped by architects, planners, and engineers, and those ordinary, allegedly "unplanned" spaces that equally form a part of the daily experiences of city-dwellers. I take as axiomatic not only that these structures and spaces are inherently social in their origin and effect (and that the landscape is, therefore, a vital document in which to "read" urban social history), but that, to a more striking extent than other social productions, they are key factors in triggering the dynamic and often unsettling changes that have characterized our society over time.

The second point bears some elaboration, for it informs much of what follows. Cities are concentrated sites of an inherently unstable tension between persistent physical environments and fleeting social change. The fit between intent and realization in the urban landscape is rarely perfect or long-lasting. Instead, as Lewis Mumford once wrote, "the rhythm of life in cities seems to be an alternation between materialization and etherialization: the concrete structure, detaching itself through a human response, takes on a symbolic meaning . . . while subjective images, ideas, intuitions, only partly formed in their original expressions, likewise take on material attributes, in visible structures, whose very size, position, complexity, organization, and esthetic form extend the area of meaning and value, otherwise inexpressible."[1]

The elements of the urban landscape are at once the product of countless previous decisions, and the instigator of many yet to come. The "materialization" of needs and desires, of which Mumford writes, projects those ephemeral wants far into the future. The cost and sheer scale of effort involved in building even a single home ties up labor and money for months or years at a time. Once built, that structure is then implanted in the land-scape, in all likelihood, for generations to come. The circumstances under which others will then see, use, buy, or sell it will, of course, change enor-mously over time. Yet its physical persistence serves, literally, as a touch-stone, uniting socially and temporally disparate experiences around a com-mon, palpable reality. In such manner does a relatively intractable landscape forever restrain and reorder the otherwise more fluid migration of people, cap-ital, and ideas—all of which concepts have tended, incidentally, to be treated in the scholarly record as being either independent, or determinant, of their physical surroundings.

Mindful of these assumptions, I want to look again at the urban landscape as both repository and catalyst of Mumford's "images, ideas, intuitions." More specifically, I will focus on the ways in which St. Louisans defined their indi-vidual and collective identities through the processes of dividing, trading, improving, and dwelling upon land—acts that, as I will argue, not only reflect but actively shape social relations. This focus, which takes us back as far as the city's founding in 1764 and forward to the present, concentrates on the critical period between 1850 and 1910, when the notion of a clear opposition between fenced-off corners and wider settings was articulated, in form and in word. We will see how a convergence of political intention and geographic hap-penstance during that period was vested with an aura of inevitability. We will see, too, how that aura gained sufficient power to direct future political and financial capital toward the maintenance of a city form that had long since ceased either to reflect or to serve the interests of the majority of the city's residents.

For this reappraisal to work, we need to look anew at both the fenced-off corner—the small, closely limited spaces of the home and the street—and at the wider setting, or the city itself. Much of the book will refer back to the streets in a two-mile-square area that includes the heart of what is commonly referred to as South St. Louis (Illustration 1-1). In addition to the fact that much of this portion of the city looks today as it did eighty years ago, the South Side (as it will alternately be called in the pages that follow) survives as a recognizable, distinct entity within the changing whirlwind of neigh-borhoods and communities that make up contemporary St. Louis. While its problems today are legion, the area has suffered fewer of the social and phys-ical ravages that have plagued much of the rest of this shrinking city in the last half-century. The reasons for this relative good fortune will concern me later; for now, it is the fact that South St. Louis opens a window on America's urban past that makes it such an appropriate place on which to focus our his-torical gaze.

If looking at a distinct, small area helps us better to understand the city as a whole, the reverse is true as well: to know these neighborhoods, we had bet-ter track the changing city of which they are a part. Like any urban area, the

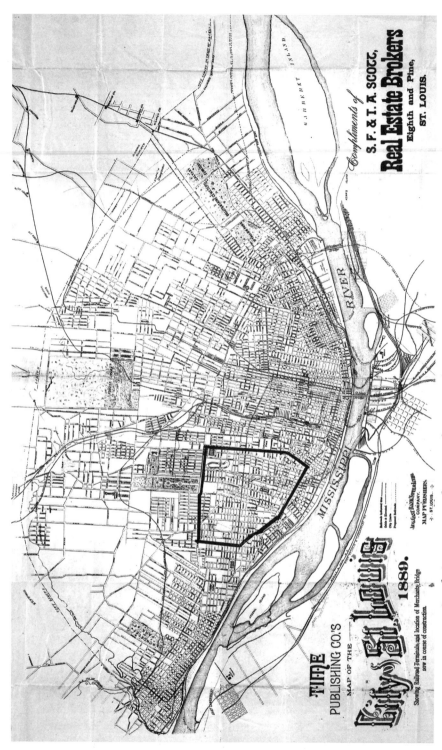

ILLUSTRATION I-I. *South St. Louis Study Area.* The two-mile-square area indicated by the outline is bounded on the west by Grand Avenue (the westernmost limit of the city from 1855 to 1875), on the east by South Broadway (known through most of the nineteenth century as Carondelet Road), on the north by Lafayette Avenue, and on the south by Chippewa Street. This area, which constitutes a large part of what St. Louisans know generally as "South St. Louis," forms the focus of much of the research in this book. South St. Louis's built landscape still looks much as it did when the area was developed in the nineteenth and early twentieth centuries. (Original map, A. Gast, 1889, courtesy of Missouri Historical Society)

South Side has historically been defined, conceptually and physically, in terms of its relation to the rest of the city; as the city changes, so too does the neighborhood. I will, therefore, steer a course between the city and the study area in the pages that follow. This shifting focus can help us recapture the ceaseless, shifting imbalance between fragmentation and unity, between shared or clashing notions of what is private and what public, between evolving definitions of what is "ours" and what "theirs," between the wider setting and the fenced-off corner.

The best place to begin, however, is here and now, in a situation that is familiar to most of us in type, if not necessarily in its particulars. Those who want to know, more specifically, how it is that an inert landscape can take on such charged meaning in people's lives should consider Wildwood. This newest of St. Louis County's ninety-one municipalities is dedicated specifically to regulating projects like the one that Edwin Reller proposed in 1994. Tired of a county planning commission that, in one neighbor's words, "allowed builders to just come in and do what they damn well please," the residents of this formerly unincorporated area voted in February 1995 to create a city of their own on land that included the proposed construction site. Reller's development proposal came just as the Committee for the Incorporation of Wildwood was attaining its highest public profile and reaching the peak of its political effectiveness. Rather than signal the beginning of another major West County development, his announcement simply helped to fan the secessionist flames that five months later resulted in the chartering of the new city.[2]

In its first years of existence, this town of some 17,000 people—spread thinly across 67 square miles of land at St. Louis's suburban fringe—has struggled with the challenges that any municipality faces, such as taxation, infrastructure, and provision of police and emergency services. Unlike their counterparts in other newly incorporated towns across St. Louis County, however, Wildwood's residents have placed a rather different priority at the top of their list: the self-conscious pursuit of "community."

"There comes a time," wrote the Committee for Incorporation in their Plan of Intent, filed with the St. Louis County Boundary Commission late in 1992, "when everyone must choose to find a better way." Staking their right to "control their own destiny," the committee asserted that "we seek a government which is of, for and by the people to protect their interests and not that [sic] of others, to ensure their values and not those of others."[3] The rhetoric of the Plan of Intent balanced inclusion with exclusivity—a desire to build one community with a complementary wish to reject all others.

In the brief time since Wildwood's highly public battle for incorporation, the pursuit of this complex mission has been most clearly manifest in one particular aspect of civic activity: the design of the municipal landscape. Just as the initial election was characterized partially in environmental terms ("a victory for the trees," as one supporter dubbed it), so too was the early course

of the new city defined largely by decisions about land use and physical appearance. City officials spent the bulk of their first years in office crafting zoning
ordinances and building codes, all in an effort to make a place that would be
distinct from its suburban surroundings. To guide them in their work, they
engaged preservationists, ecologists, and the "neotraditional" Florida-based
planning firm of Andres Duany and Elizabeth Plater-Zyberk, which recommended among other things that the city adopt a "Jeffersonian grid," within
which small neighborhoods ("the optimal size . . . is ¼ mile from center to
edge") would give physical definition to the community's social goals.[4]

In their quest to preserve political and architectural control within their
newly defined community, the citizens of Wildwood, Missouri are not alone.
Throughout North America, and amidst great media attention, Wildwood and
towns like it have arisen in common reaction against the growth that encir-
cles not only big cities like St. Louis but most of America's small towns as
well.[5] Politically, Wildwood's citizens have attempted to carve a sympathetic
niche out of the monolith of St. Louis County. They have set about to make
a place that will function as our cities and small towns used to function, a
place where the values and interests of "others" outside the community need
not interfere with their own, a place where—to borrow from television vernacular—"everyone knows your name." Their efforts to give shape to this
vision through urban design reflect not only a desire to set themselves apart
from the surrounding sprawl, but also an earnest belief in the power of physical planning to aid them in realizing their broader social goals.

The suburban landscape against which Wildwood's residents chose to react
in 1995 is familiar to most of us. Across west St. Louis County, along arterial
roads that once brought truck produce into the city, mansarded shopping centers enframe spacious parking lots; in adjacent residential subdivisions, frame-
and-veneer houses with gabled roofs and pedimented entries rise on concrete
platforms surrounded by new-laid turf. The names of these new subdivisions,
like the styles of the homes within them, belie their almost-urban density.
Motorists cruising Manchester or Clayton Road pass gateways and billboards
announcing all manner of "creeks," "oaks," and "estates," not to mention
enough "meadows," "summits," and "trails" to make this mostly low-lying
region sound like a Swiss canton.

Despite the disapproval with which Wildwood's citizens—echoing a growing number of social or architectural critics—might view such familiar landscapes, they are the products of developers who operate from motives and
means essentially similar to those employed by their predecessors for more
than a century. While it is tempting to join the ranks of writers who dismiss
the outcome of those developers' efforts today as a "geography of nowhere,"
an irredeemable "empire wilderness," the quality of this contemporary metropolitan landscape concerns me less, in the pages that follow, than the long
history—most of it unseen—that frames our current reluctance to claim it as

our own, to acknowledge the order and the historical patterns that lie within its apparent chaos. This is, after all, *our* city; it has developed neither (as the earliest city planners once believed) through autonomous, almost biological tropisms, nor (as revisionist critics maintained in more recent decades) through decisions forced down our throats, but through the highly responsive—if flawed—mechanisms of free-market capitalism and representative government.[6]

The passion with which Americans debate the appearance of their cities reflects a common recognition, beneath our differences, that the urban landscape is an inherently social product. Developers of subdivisions like Summit Heights or The Meadow at Cherry Hills (to name just two of the current crop in St. Louis County) know that too—which is why they choose names that correspond more closely to idealized images of the nearby landscape than to its actual appearance. So, for that matter, do Duany and Plater-Zyberk, when they flatter their client's revolutionary spirit with talk of the "Jeffersonian" grid, as though a community of sturdy husbandmen were only awaiting the arrival of front porches and four-way stop signs to make its presence known.

Given the charged social meaning of urban space, then, it does not require a tremendous stretch of the imagination to find in the controversies surrounding communities like Wildwood a larger tension at work than simply the conflict of trees versus highways. This book presumes instead that the seeming contradiction so evident today in American cities like St. Louis—their expansion into broad metropolitan regions, and their simultaneous atomization into small municipalities and fragmented neighborhoods—is one symptom of a particularly American tension. It is a tension that has dogged American culture since this nation ceased to be the commonwealth of small villages and yeoman farmers envisioned by men like Jefferson; a tension that lurks between the often conjoined terms of "liberty" and "justice"—between the rights of individuals and the responsibilities of citizens. It is the tension of fenced-off corners and wider settings.

According to the ideals to which most Americans would still subscribe (whether they live in Wildwood or in the impoverished city of East St. Louis, Illinois, across the Mississippi River), these poles must hold each other in check. As long as they are balanced—as long as society functions collectively to protect the liberties of each of its members—then democracy works. When that delicate balance is broken—when political bodies run roughshod over the rights of their constituents, or when the liberties accorded society's "factions" (to borrow from James Madison) threaten the overall social compact—then, it is said, either anarchy or tyranny beckons.

It is this larger, underlying dynamic that makes the politics of everyday urban development seem so urgent to its participants. Our choices about whom we will associate with and whom we will ignore, about which responsibilities and privileges belong to "the people" who deserve them and which to the "others" who do not, do more than reflect the happenstance of political boundaries. Wildwood is but one more reminder that those boundaries are themselves products of our decisions about how to tie together or break apart the elements of our social fabric. The city is not only a political entity but a *place*, and we engage in the political process largely in order to manage our conflicting claims on that place. The patchwork of streets and survey lines etched across the land becomes in this way a blueprint for mediating between the larger, corporate interests of abstract institutions like cities and counties, and the more particular interests of the citizens who go about their daily lives there. It diagrams the limits of private rights and public responsibilities—and it does so in ways that we seldom notice until we find ourselves on the wrong side of a "No Trespassing" or "End County Maintenance" sign.

To judge from the evidence that the urban blueprint presents today, the difficulty that American cities face is not necessarily that either extreme—the fragmented pursuit of liberty or the overweening maintenance of order—threatens to overwhelm the other. The "unified service area" and the consolidated metropolitan government are as much artifacts of our time as are fragmented political landscapes like those of St. Louis County, Missouri or Cook County, Illinois. The problem rests more in the difficulty that we seem to have in negotiating between these extremes. The trouble that we have comprehending our contemporary metropolitan landscape is both cause and symptom of that difficulty. The citizens of Wildwood talk about restoring a sense of community, yet they reject the claims of an existing community, St. Louis County, which served area residents' interests for nearly two hundred years. To which community is the greater loyalty owed? City planners speak of downtown as though it still served uniquely as the region's hub, while developers treat it as simply another cluster of commercial and office functions—another "edge city," in effect, among many. Are St. Louisans somehow responsible for maintaining a single symbolic and financial center that represents the entire region? Many of the neighborhoods close to the urban center, where we expect to find the greatest density, are empty; the suburban fringe—for all of its "glens," "trails," and "creeks"—is often more densely populated. Are we obligated, as some maintain, to repopulate the central city before spreading out along its edges? Such questions force us to reconsider not only the look of the city but the traditional social, cultural, and political expectations that we bring to the urban landscape. It is perhaps because they are so hard to answer today that the current form of our cities is so easily dismissed as a geography of nowhere.

This book is dedicated to the dissenting proposition that everywhere is somewhere, no matter what it looks like. To find that "somewhere" is to do more than recognize the new order of the metropolitan landscape; it is also to see more clearly the conflicting ways in which we construct relations between individuals and their communities. In the process, we stand at least a chance of finding fresh ways to reconcile the tensions inherent in our culture generally, and in our metropolitan areas particularly.

To make somewhere out of nowhere, however, we must take the trouble to do two things: first, to understand how our cities came to look as they do, and second, to examine why we have such a hard time making sense of them. As it happens, those challenges—tracing the changing form of the metropolis and tracing the history of our efforts to articulate that form—are really part of the same task. Both, ultimately, lead us back to a time when the fenced-off corner and the wider setting provided Americans with a seemingly clear set of alternatives for urban growth.

Drawing from the history of St. Louis, this book will demonstrate the proposition that changing urban form, on the one hand, and our changing understanding or expectations of that form, on the other, are mutually impressionable and inextricably intertwined. That simple proposition is by no means universally accepted. Many contemporary critics and architects, ascribing to urban forms an autonomy and a power to determine behavior that they have rarely had, treat the elements of our urban landscape as the unchanging carriers of their original shapers' intent. Others, positing that particular social programs must translate into particular images and designs, shortchange people's remarkable ability to adapt virtually any human landscape to a range of needs.[7] Only by reconnecting the phenomena of form-giving and form-interpreting into a singular, dynamic process—a process whose outcome is far less predictable or clear-cut than historians or policy-makers might wish—can we start to make the contemporary metropolitan landscape look less inevitable and more comprehensible than we have imagined, less like nowhere and more like somewhere.

The difficulty of reorienting ourselves in such a way has been compounded, as I hope to show, by the long historical shadow of the city of fenced-off corners and wider settings, a city that dates roughly from the mid-nineteenth through the early-twentieth centuries. It is upon that city, uncomfortable or unjust as it may have been for many Americans in its time, that we have long depended in our effort to express the differing ways in which Americans can reconcile the tensions between individual liberties and civic responsibilities. As the United States begins a third century and a new millennium, the lingering image of this presumably more orderly place still provides us with many of the terms that inform our discussion of an uncertain metropolitan future.

By way of reconstructing at a glance how such a city differed from the landscape of our own time, let us consider St. Louis more than a century ago. We might begin some twenty-five miles east of Edwin Reller's dream development, in a section of South St. Louis known as Soulard. It is a very different landscape from that of late-twentieth-century suburbia (Illustration 1-2). Like

ILLUSTRATION 1-2. *Soulard Neighborhood, South St. Louis, bird's-eye view, c. 1875.* Late-nineteenth- and early-twentieth-century American reformers pointed to the crowded landscapes of working-class urban neighborhoods like this one as evidence of the growing influence of "fenced-off corners" on the city at large. (Reprinted from Camille N. Dry and Richard J. Compton, *Pictorial St. Louis: A Topographical Survey Drawn in Perspective* [St. Louis, 1876], plate 25, courtesy of Missouri Historical Society)

Baltimore's Fells Point, Cincinnati's Over-the-Rhine, Boston's North End, and dozens of other communities that still stand in America's older industrial cities, the Soulard neighborhood was first peopled by foreign-born immigrants in the mid- to late-nineteenth century. Most of these people were new to the city, eager for work, and willing to live in crowded conditions to get it. The blocks of their neighborhoods were lined with shops and corner taverns, livery stables, small factories, and cheap housing. Under the church spires that punctuated their skylines, the language and the customs of Slovenia and Bohemia, Sicily and Salonika, found safe haven against the unfamiliar world that pressed from without.

In 1900, the city's intellectuals and social reformers were as horrified by aging, poor neighborhoods like this as were their counterparts a century later by the endless tract developments of the suburban edge. The reason for their critical response, however, was quite different. The problem with Soulard and areas like it was not that they lacked a localized sense of community but that they possessed too *much* of one. Separated by cultural and linguistic divides from the rest of the city, congested and at times ridden with disease, home to political bosses who derived their power by distributing favors, these enclaves threatened the welfare of the larger civic community, to which all the city's residents needed ultimately to be attached. To muckraking reporters like Jacob Riis, as to crusading mayors like Cleveland's Tom Johnson or to early city planners like Benjamin Marsh, such quarters would have no place in the city of the future. The task of opening up the "fenced-off corners," as one St. Louisan disparagingly called the Soulard area at the time, and integrating them into a larger civic whole, was one of the chief avowed motives of the professionals, business leaders, and public officials who united under the banner of civic reform in cities across America.

Soulard was not an exceptional case, in this city or any other. While contemporary reformers may have wished to depict them as isolated outposts, such neighborhoods actually comprised much of the American urban landscape in 1900. They ringed the country's downtowns like barrel hoops, constraining once booming centers of commerce and trade from reaching the more affluent neighborhoods that lay beyond. On the other side of town from Soulard, to the north of St. Louis's central business district, German-speaking families crowded the once bucolic streets around Hyde Park, just uphill from the packing houses and lumber yards that lined the north waterfront. Between Hyde Park and downtown, the city's newest immigrants—Jews from Russia and Poland—crowded into aging tenements around the busy Biddle Market. Farther west, past the new city hall on Market Street, stretched the Chestnut Valley and the adjacent Mill Creek Valley: a two-mile–long zone of bars, cheap hotels, pawnshops, and—not least—the homes of a good number of St. Louis's 35,000 African American residents, who enjoyed few opportunities to move to more desirable quarters (Illustration 1-3).

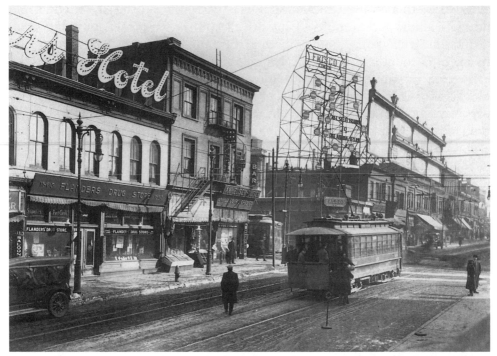

ILLUSTRATION 1-3. *Market Street at Eighteenth Street, c. 1910.* Extending west from downtown St. Louis along some of the city's oldest and busiest streetcar lines, the Chestnut and Mill Creek Valleys were poor and working-class, largely African American neighborhoods at the beginning of the 1900s. This area of small flats, tenements, saloons, churches, and neighborhood retailers would see some of the most dramatic clearance in St. Louis during the decades that extended from the City Beautiful movement of the 1910s to the urban renewal era of the 1950s and 1960s. (Courtesy of Missouri Historical Society)

What solution did enlightened civic leaders offer to the problem of the fenced-off corners that proliferated in America's cities? Not surprisingly, considering the spatial terms by which they defined the problem, their response was conceived in physical ways. If people could be debased by their surroundings, reformers reasoned, surely people could be elevated by their surroundings as well. To that end they offered a series of improvements to the urban landscape, ranging from stricter housing codes to great public building schemes. In place of fenced-off corners, growing in distinct manners across an increasingly diverse city, they promoted (to borrow once again from a phrase coined by a St. Louis advocate of the movement) a "wider setting" of civic commerce, culture, politics, and architecture. To this end, the city would be made into a continuous, interconnected, and accessible system of spaces, closely tied to a prominent core. Its new spatial unity would both reflect and promote a new social unity.

Like the fenced-off corners that linger in American cities to this day, elements of the wider setting remain visible in St. Louis and in cities across the country. They appeared earliest in such grand-scale experiments in landscape engineering as New York's Central Park and Boston's "emerald necklace" of parkways (both conceived, after the Civil War, in the studios of the influential landscape architect Frederick Law Olmsted), and they continued in a variety of forms through the century that followed: in the neoclassical stolidity of San Francisco's and Cleveland's civic centers and the landscaped vistas of Philadelphia's Benjamin Franklin Parkway; in planned industrial zones like Chicago's Central Manufacturing District; in the comprehensive boulevard systems of younger cities like Kansas City and Dallas; in high-speed expressways, like Los Angeles's Arroyo Seco or Detroit's Davison, and in their larger, postwar counterparts, the interstate highways. In these instances and in so many others, planners and investors justified their work in terms of its benefits to the entire city, rather than to the city's constituent parts. Whether focusing on transportation improvements, facilities for business and industry, government centers, or recreational spaces, theirs was the self-delegated task of reconceiving the city as a single organism, each of whose parts worked toward the smooth functioning of the whole.

St. Louis still shows evidence of these Progressive Era efforts to plan for the wider setting. They survive in broad gestures like the landscaped parkway that stretches along Market Street west of Twelfth Street (Illustration 1-4), replacing a good part of the old Chestnut Valley; in small improvements like the market building and the old Carnegie Library that stand at the northern edge of Soulard; and most conspicuously along the downtown waterfront, where the Gateway Arch rises on a landscaped hill once covered by warehouses, factories, and busy wholesaling establishments.

Even to categorize such pieces of the urban landscape, as I have in this quick survey, is to partake less of an objective description than of a powerful metaphor that continues to cast a shadow on our understanding of American urban life. Yet if this metaphor ever accorded with reality, it does so less every day. The image of the city as a battleground between factional interests and a single, common good (an image propagated by planners, public officials, and even historians from the turn of the twentieth century onward) clearly offers an increasingly inadequate explanation for the shifting picture of development and decay, of concentration and dispersal, of localized and regional ties that characterizes not just St. Louis but virtually all American cities. Even to turn that image on its head, as the residents of places like Wildwood have, by valorizing the fenced-off corner at the expense of the wider setting is to partake of the same dated metaphors.

ILLUSTRATION 1-4.
Market Street at Eigh-
teenth Street, c. 1990.
Today, the landscaped
parkway that extends
along Market Street west
from Tucker Boulevard
(Twelfth Street) to Twen-
tieth Street is all that
remains of the Chestnut
Valley—once one of
St. Louis's most crowded
and vibrant, but impover-
ished, neighborhoods.
(Courtesy of the author)

Instead, as this book will argue, the clear opposition of fenced-off corners
and wider settings is itself a historical artifact, a response in both real and
imagined terms to particular patterns of urban growth during a particular
period. It explains neither the tightly limited towns of pre-industrial, early-
nineteenth-century America, nor the fragmented, multi-centered metropo-
lises that characterize our own time. It describes one historical stage of an
ongoing, dynamic relationship between people and the spaces they inhabit in
America's cities. While this stage was not distinguished by tremendous social
harmony, it did represent a momentary clarity of contrasts—contrasts not
simply between different architectural and urban forms, but of a broader sort
as well. The city of fenced-off corners and wider settings—as fact and as
metaphor—both reflected and impelled distinct ways of conceiving the balance between individuals and society, between common rights and individual liberties. Its streets and its buildings provided a clear, if contestable, diagram of the tension between a civil society and its component groups. That
tension is anything but clear today, as it is likely to remain so long as we seek
to explain the city of the present in terms that more closely describe the city
of the past.

In order to reveal that past more clearly, this book proceeds in a manner that combines chronological and thematic logic. Chapter 2 focuses on the peculiar way in which the city's origins as a colonial settlement—first of the French, then of the Spanish Empire—colored its transition to an American community. During the sixty-year interval between St. Louis's founding in 1764 and its legal incorporation as a city in 1823, urban form was largely divested of its initial pretensions of reflecting a God-given, universal social order. While this kind of post-colonial transition is familiar to readers of early American history, the manner in which it took place here was rather surprising. First, for all the textual and cartographic evidence that they left to the contrary, the city's colonial overseers never achieved the kind of union of urban form and social order to which they aspired. Political and economic pressures led instead to a city that was, socially as well as physically, disorderly and fluid. More important to the later growth of the city was their rhetorical legacy—a vocabulary for idealizing the landscape as a coherent social artifact and as a means for social control. While the earliest American officials, after their arrival in 1804, had tried to realize that ideal in a manner consistent with free-market practices and republican beliefs, their efforts were stymied by a wariness of enforcing measures that might be seen as infringing on individual property rights. Even as they failed in their efforts to improve the chaotic streetscape and to organize the haphazard land market, however, they etched more deeply into public discourse the idea of the urban landscape as an image of stable social order.

By the middle of the nineteenth century, the means for realizing that image were at hand. They came both from above—in the increasing refinement of the city's legal power to articulate a "public" interest in the landscape—and from below—in the efforts of a small and influential group of merchants and professionals who seized the initiative in developing property in the fast-growing town. Chapter 3 looks at the convergence of those two approaches in the decades between incorporation and the onset of the Civil War—a period that saw the city's population grow fortyfold. In the seesawing laws that governed assessments for street improvements, in the city's changing approaches to developing the old town Common, and in the development ventures of men like industrialist and politician Thomas Allen, there appeared the outlines of a resolution to the tension of public and private interests. It was a resolution that responded at once to the mandates of republican, capitalist ideology and to the lingering power of the colonial myth of urban order. The city had in a sense come full circle by the 1850s: the imprint that developers like Allen had begun to stamp upon the landscape—a consistent plan, closely maintained by an elite circle of men—was in a way the fulfillment of the failed promise of the original village. Yet if the practical means for making of the city a coherent spatial and social statement had at last been achieved, the political and ideological control needed to maintain it had already been traded away. With the coming fractionalization of the population that resulted from foreign immigration and clashing Yankee and Southern interests, and with the strangling effects of a Civil War that split the city into armed camps, St. Louis would soon lose whatever tenuous union of interests might once have governed the development of its expanding urban landscape.

Part II of this book highlights the subsequent effect of that loss: a splintering of public and private interests in the landscape throughout the late nineteenth century. The development of this city of "fenced-off corners" can only be understood as arising from the interlocking roles of three categorical parties to the shaping of urban space: landscape "producers" (builders, realtors, lenders), landscape "consumers" (residents), and landscape "regulators" (public officials whose job it was to balance the interests of producers and consumers).

Chapter 4 examines the first of these groups. Here I consider the breakdown of the City's efforts to control the Common subdivision as the starting point in the dissolution of the antebellum link of select private interests and public order. From this point on, the various functions of city-building (including the real-estate trade, banking and lending, and construction labor) came to include an ever wider range of such producers within their purview. With little or no guidance from the public sector, separate communities of increasing complexity and distinctiveness formed around the tasks of buying, selling, and developing property. In tangible, visible ways, the urban landscape began to reflect this fragmentation, forcing into public and private discourse new explanations of the city's spatial order that went beyond the simple, static image long maintained by influential St. Louisans. At this point, practical necessity and republican rhetoric converged on the image of the city as the sum of many interchangeable parts, each molded by independent actors working in their own self-interest.

Yet this revised image, too, proved to be only fleetingly applicable to a city undergoing tremendous social and economic change. The production of urban spaces, as we will see in Chapter 4, underwent a second structural change, as the inefficiencies of a development process resting in the hands of an increasing number of specialized and localized actors were overcome by consolidation and simplification. By the 1890s, a new set of rules applied to the city-building game. A smaller group of participants was able to offer economies of scale unrealizable in the previously fragmented industry, and the developers who succeeded by the turn of the century tended to be those capable of the greatest breadth and diversity of function. This generation was quite unlike the developer elite of Thomas Allen's time, for they no longer presided over a simple and relatively undifferentiated urban landscape. Instead, they used their functional and financial capacities to develop a city that was increasingly stratified, socially as well as physically.

In order to understand how these changes in the production of space led to a new articulation of how the city "ought" to look, I consider their effect on the other two parties to the landscape. Chapter 5 turns to the consumers of nineteenth-century urban space—specifically, the people who lived in St. Louis's neighborhoods during the years of their settlement and most rapid growth. Here, I will look at the differing ways in which rooms, houses, blocks, and neighborhoods (the layered sequence of spaces that resulted from the work of our landscape producers) were intertwined in the lives of the residents of four distinct areas of South St. Louis developed between the 1860s and the 1910s—that period in which the techniques of construction and finance changed so dramatically. A close study of who these people were, and how they arranged themselves within the landscape, suggests the extent and the limits of city builders' power to shape the ways that people live. St. Louisans never lacked for creative choices about how to live under less than ideal circumstances. Yet particular configurations of local space—the arrangement of rooms in an apartment, for instance, or of buildings on a block—were instrumental in determining the various ways in which people simultaneously defined themselves as family members or citizens, neighborhood residents or St. Louisans, and even as consumers or producers of urban space.

While representative government was in theory the means by which these simultaneous identities—like the constituent elements of the landscape itself—were negotiated and held in check, it managed then, as it so often does still, to do something quite nearly the opposite: political decisions hastened the separation of landscape producers from landscape consumers, forced individuals to identify exclusively either with a neighborhood or with the city at large, and hardened visible differences between one part of town and another. As I hope to show in Chapter 6, this effect was achieved as much by accident as by design. The political process, which largely followed rather than guided the private development and use of urban space, rationalized the *status quo* under the guise of mediating between public and private interests in the landscape.

To illustrate how this came about, I will focus on the city government's most conspicuous function in the shaping of the landscape: planning and maintaining the city's streets. Streets did more than ease movement from one site to another. They marked, in an actual and a symbolic way, the relation between one place and the rest of the city around it. As such, street-making was an intensely political process with intensely social implications. Yet as we will see, the men who ran the municipal government operated throughout the late 1800s with little clear idea of how this important aspect of the city's growth would be managed. If any principle guided their actions, it was an abiding desire to choose the most expedient and least costly course of action at each turn. By 1900, decades of pay-as-you-go street planning—

a variant of the "segmented system" that historian Robin Einhorn identified in Chicago's public improvements during the same period—had created a particular kind of imprint on the landscape, one that made South St. Louis look quite different from other parts of the city.[8] The inadvertently unequal streetscape that crisscrossed the city (and that served the wealthier neighborhoods of the city's central corridor more efficiently than it did the poorer neighborhoods to the north and south) came at last to be treated as the "proper" streetscape, as government officials and influential citizens rationalized public improvements that favored the perpetuation of existing conditions over a more costly return to a vaguely envisioned, egalitarian grid plan that had been articulated in the mid-nineteenth century. Laws and ordinances brushed a public-sprited veneer across the lopsided landscape of private development.

But public policy had less predictable consequences, as well. Undeniable regional differences in urban public improvements helped foster a growing consciousness among city residents that they lived in distinctive and different areas. By the turn of the twentieth century there arose in South St. Louis, in particular, a sense of neighborhood belonging—and of opposition to the center of the city—that was absent from within the traditional, more fragmented landscape that had developed in the area in years past. This new cohesion grew as much from physical and geographic circumstance as it did from such more familiar factors as class and ethnicity that have long been singled out in the literature of urban social history. The egalitarian ideal of public-improvement distribution that developed after the sale of the town Common had been more a commitment to equality of opportunity than to equality of result; couched in the vague, republican terms that were applied to local public policy through most of the century, that commitment had appealed to a wide variety of citizens. But when even the promise of equal opportunity proved chimerical for large areas of the city, the seeds for regionally based political conflict were sown.

It is in this context that we need to reconsider the often misunderstood civic improvement movement of the early 1900s, which forms the subject of Chapter 7. Rather than being an all-powerful drive for order, rationality, and predictability amidst the chaos of the industrial city (to either good or ill effect, depending on one's viewpoint), city planning represented an expedient codification of existing trends; it was an effort on the part of government and business officials to gain hold of existing conditions in the city and to try, once again, to fuse private and public interest in the landscape as powerfully as they had been tied in the mid-nineteenth century. The specific, physical vision that such well-known planning reformers as Henry Wright, George Kessler, and Harland Bartholomew brought to St. Louis was a systematized adaptation of the tight-knit neighborhood units—or fenced-off corners—already developed through the combined effects of private development efforts and general government noninvolvement. The achievement of the planners was to make this differentiated and hierarchical landscape seem not only natural but good for all of St. Louis's residents, to bring it under the control of a centralized authority, and to describe it as a "wider setting" to be maintained in the interest of all St. Louisans.

South St. Louisans would for several decades resist this vision of a unified city, dismissing it as favoring the interests of other parts of town. By the 1920s, however, it was clear that the South Side would be spared most of the attention of the planning community and, therefore, much of the spatially and socially divisive impact that land clearance and redevelopment would exert on the once wealthy central corridor, which lay just to the north. In that area, more than elsewhere, civic reformers and planners had tried to arrest the continuous and presumably harmful dynamic of urban social and spatial change. They had labored to set into the city's legal and physical infrastructure a particular vision of a hierarchical landscape that derived from the particular point at which St. Louis stood at the time that they began their work. Their own actions would, however, inevitably have unique consequences, and would inevitably set in motion a new sequence of change in the articulation of sectional (and increasingly racial) concerns in relation to municipal interests. This sequence concerns me in the book's Epilogue, which briefly reviews the aftermath of the early planners' agenda in a quickly changing city. If much of the South Side remains today as visible testimony to the landscape of another time, that may be due in large part to the fact that the area escaped the inadvertent consequences of the same controlling urban vision that had earlier consigned it to a marginal corner in the redefined form of the city. If the valued and cherished corner bakery, tavern, dime store, and shoe repair shop stand today where they once did, that fact is no credit to the men and women who tried to make St. Louis a better place to live in 1910. It may, however, offer us clues as to what we have lost and gained in our efforts to reshape the city in the last two hundred years.

Sam Bass Warner, writing memorably of Boston, characterized the turn-of-the-twentieth-century American city as a "divided" place.[9] He described that division as a line between the center and the periphery, between the neglected, aging landscape of the urban core and the fast-developing suburbs. This twofold split in the city has been noted not only by Warner and other urban historians, but by the earlier planners and politicians and chroniclers of the city whose records they discovered and whose viewpoints they interpreted. As this study of the shifting fortunes of one city will show, the turn-of-the-century metropolis was indeed a divided place, and its divisions did indeed have a deeper, more monolithic quality than they had had in the past. But they also fell in unexpected places, and they tended to disappear or to re-form themselves independently of any system that either the people responsible for determining their locations, or the people responsible for explaining their history, have ever been able to contrive. Rather than being a monolithic whole, imposed (with either benevolent or malign intent) upon its disparate parts, the "official" city of early-twentieth-century reformers and commercial elites was never more than one—particularly well-defended—solution, among many, to the problems facing a diverse urban populace.

The city of fenced-off corners and wider settings provided a useful metaphor for one generation of Americans seeking to understand and improve upon the divided city. But, like the man who came to dinner, it stayed with us for so long that we forgot, at some point, that it was a temporary guest rather than a permanent resident. Like it or hate it, we have been reluctant to dismiss it from the table. This book is written in an effort to retrace our steps in the American city, to give full due to the historical accretion of nuances and insinuations and contradictions that too often has rested unheard behind the noise of a clear, grand narrative—a narrative that has always consisted of equal parts analysis and wishful thinking. It is a journey that includes not just the Frederick Law Olmsteds and Daniel Burnhams of the world, but the Edward Rellers, too. There is much to be learned anew on this journey, not just about how our past is diagrammed in brick and asphalt, but about the city's continuing viability to serve as a place where the balance of individual rights and collective responsibilities can be freely debated, openly demonstrated, and readily adjusted for generations to come.

Part I

Laying the Groundwork

CHAPTER 2

Lines on the Land

The Lingering Imprint of Colonial St. Louis

On 27 November 1822, readers of the *Missouri Republican* found a cursory note, buried in the paper's routine review of the proceedings of the new General Assembly, that "Mr. Simpson, pursuant to notice, introduced a bill to incorporate the inhabitants of St. Louis, which was read."[1] The incorporation of St. Louis under the laws of the new state of Missouri, which went on to be ratified by a bare majority of the town's residents the following spring, proved far more crucial to the fate of this wilderness outpost than either the press's nonchalance or the electorate's ambivalence would suggest.

The creation of a municipal, corporate entity lay at the heart of the development of the city of fenced-off corners and wider settings. Considered narrowly, it gave residents of a dilapidated, formerly colonial settlement the legal means to fund and to oversee the improvements on which their future depended. Beyond that basic but vital function, the new charter created a new and in many ways peculiar entity—the City of St. Louis—that was at once defined by, and potentially at odds with, its own inhabitants. The act accelerated an already shifting, often uneasy relation between the private interests of individual residents and property holders, on the one hand, and the public interests articulated by these individuals in the name of the larger urban community, on the other.[2] Between the 1820s and the cataclysm of the Civil War, St. Louisans with a stake in the city's future would experiment with ways of tying their personal interests to the improvement of the public landscape. It was in that landscape—part colonial holdover, part new development—that

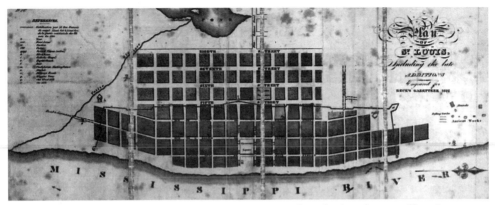

ILLUSTRATION 2-1.   *St. Louis in 1823.* Lewis Beck's idealized map offered eastern readers a glimpse of the newly incorporated city at the edge of the American frontier—a city that had been laid out in accordance with French planning practices, some sixty years earlier. Like New Orleans, St. Louis was planned as a grid of rectangular blocks arrayed parallel to the Mississippi River shoreline on either side of a central public space devoted to military and governmental uses. (Reprinted from Lewis Beck, *Gazetteer of the States of Illinois and Missouri* [Albany, 1823], courtesy of Missouri Historical Society)

the city's economic and political elite modeled their resolution of the growing tension between the urban whole and its constituent parts.

In the years after incorporation, the problem they faced was, more simply, to describe and conceive of such a public landscape in the first place. The city's incorporation, as it happened, was just one of a number of efforts in the early 1820s to define and stabilize this nascent community. At the same time that Missouri's new state legislature clarified St. Louis's legal identity, others were clarifying its status in time and in space. Thanks to their efforts, a series of printed images of the city offered the world graphic evidence of St. Louis's promise.

Lewis Beck's *Gazetteer of the States of Illinois and Missouri,* published in Albany, New York, in 1823, gave Americans their first look at the plan of the new city; its neat, even waterfront grid, echoing that of better-known New Orleans, suggested similar pretensions and perhaps a similarly prosperous future (Illustration 2-1). Three years later, the posthumous publication of Victor Collot's *Journey in North America,* a topographical account of the Frenchman's 1796 journey up the Ohio and Mississippi valleys, included the first published plan of the earlier colonial village (Illustration 2-2). The book's French and American readers would surely have been struck by the orderliness of this place; had they also seen Beck's map, they might likewise have been struck

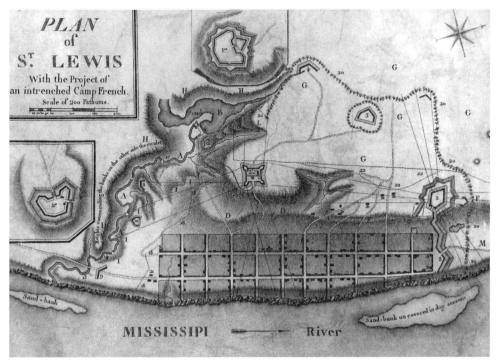

ILLUSTRATION 2-2.   *St. Louis in 1796.* Published just a few years after Beck's plan of St. Louis, Collot's map purportedly showed the village that the military explorer had come to fortify in the 1790s. But the fortifications delineated by Collot's assistant, Charles Warin, were never actually built; even the rudimentary fence that surrounded the town Common (a mile southwest of the central area depicted in this map) had fallen into ruin by the end of the colonial era. The "pond" and "rivulet" shown on the south end of the village formed a geographical barrier that would profoundly affect the eventual growth of South St. Louis, isolating it from the center of town until well into the twentieth century. (Reprinted from G.H.V. Collot, *Voyage dans l'Amerique Septentrionale . . .* [Paris, 1826], courtesy of Missouri Historical Society)

by colonial St. Louis's essential similarity with the contemporary town, only slightly expanded, of thirty years later.

Establishing the formal continuity between colonial village and American city was more than a matter of historical curiosity. It also bore directly on who stood to profit from the new city's growing prospects as a commercial center. In 1825 a St. Louisan named Theodore Hunt was appointed to clear up the morass of conflicting land claims that had, since the American takeover of the Louisiana Territory in 1804, frustrated those anxious for the quick development of St. Louis's property. The most prominent of the citizens called before Hunt's commission was seventy-five-year-old Auguste Chouteau, who,

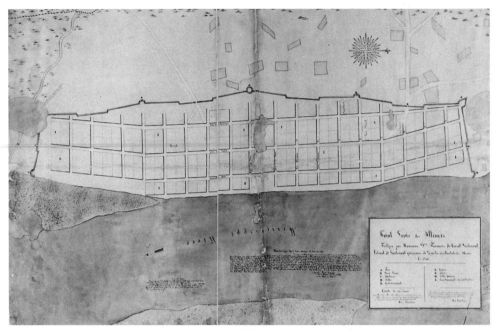

ILLUSTRATION 2-3. *St. Louis in 1780.* The original plan of St. Louis, first drawn by either Pierre Laclède or Auguste Chouteau and redrafted more formally in 1780, was long since lost by the time that Chouteau testified before Theodore Hunt's land commission in 1825. Chouteau then redrew the plan, which has itself since been lost; this 1842 tracing of his work has since come to represent the "original" St. Louis plan to generations of historians. (Courtesy of Missouri Historical Society)

as the thirteen-year-old assistant of New Orleans–based fur trader Pierre Laclède, had witnessed the founding of the village in 1764. His appearance before the commission on an April morning in 1825 became the occasion not just for yet another deposition about the possession and title of one city block or another, but for a celebratory recounting of the city's origins. In July, under Hunt's direction, Chouteau oversaw the preparation of a new copy of the map (since lost) that he had drawn in the 1780s, showing the original town plan as laid out by himself and Laclède (Illustration 2-3).

Chouteau's map was part legal device, part illustrative supplement to the tale that he spun before the land commission, and on which he would continue to elaborate until his death in 1829. Offering at once the first detailed account of the city's origins and a personal claim to its most valuable land, Chouteau recalled that he had selected the site for the new village, and that he had then commenced to "cut down trees, draw the lines of a town, and build the house where this deponent now lives."[3] While his account differed in assigning to himself (rather than Laclède) full credit for the town's plan, it was in other ways an elaboration of a sketchier picture, drafted in 1821, by John Paxton, editor of the town's first published directory. Laclède, Paxton had written, "told his friends that he was commencing the foundation of a town, which might prove with time, to be one of the richest in America."[4] Like Chouteau's long-winded deposition, and like the newly minted maps purporting to show both colonial and contemporary St. Louis, Paxton's account added to the city's claims of physical and historical legitimacy—claims that complemented the new charter in clarifying the city's identity and giving shape to its social order.

But there were problems with these assumptions. The origin story, with its suggestion of a clear vision for the future and a systematic plan for settlement, was further thrown in doubt by the variation between accounts crediting either Chouteau or Laclède—a question that would continue to flair up periodically through the subsequent history of this ancestor-conscious city. Further, the very need for Hunt's land commission, itself a successor to similar committees that had been formed and dissolved for two decades, indicated something of the uncertainty as to just who had settled where, and who held title to what.

As for the shape of the city itself, Beck's contemporary picture notwithstanding, the idea of a neat and orderly urban landscape was little more than a fairy tale to St. Louisans of the 1820s. The actual condition of the city's streets in 1823 was bad enough to prompt Mayor William Carr Lane to appoint a special survey commission to "appeal to the intelligence of the antient inhabitants" of the town in order to determine the "true position, width, and bearing" of those streets—in essence, to figure out where, exactly, they were.[5] The commission reported in July that "as many buildings and other permanent improvements of ancient date have been made so as to encroach on those [original street] dimensions, they cannot now be removed, but ought to be left in the occupancy and possession of their respective owners until they be destroyed by time and accident or removed by the proprietors.... It is impracticable at the present time to make the city conform to the plat made of the same."[6]

Taken together, then, the new-drawn maps and the tentative histories of the 1820s are less useful as sources of historical information on colonial St. Louis than they are as evidence of a wholly new, post-colonial groping toward order, a search for a historical and spatial context within which to place a newly chartered city that was conspicuously lacking in both. Like New York, Boston, and other cities founded as the outposts of colonial empires, St. Louis and its citizens actively engaged the challenge of redefining themselves in the image of the new republic.[7] To understand the peculiar power of idealized maps and twice-told origin myths in meeting that challenge, we must peer into the long shadows cast by the city's origins, some sixty years earlier.

The Landscape of the Early Town

The symbolic appeal of Chouteau and his founding narrative—not just for St. Louisans of the 1820s but for citizens of a hundred or more years later—is one clue to the extensive legacy of the colonial period on the later life of the city. Entwined within this legacy were both the ideal of stability that later St. Louisans yearned for, and the root of the tensions that have forever kept them from attaining that ideal. That contradiction was built into the city's very existence. St. Louis was in its inception both a commercial venture and an ideological statement. It was chartered with the stated purpose of bolstering defense, Christianizing natives, and, not least, furthering trade along one edge of a vast frontier that stretched from the port of New Orleans north to Canada. In 1763 the French governor of Louisiana, Jean Jacques D'Abbadie, granted New Orleans–based merchant Gilbert Maxent exclusive rights to the fur trade along the Missouri and upper Mississippi Rivers. That summer, Maxent's partner Pierre Laclède Liguest led a party north to the Illinois country (an area already established on either side of the Mississippi with villages, missions, forts, and agricultural lots) to establish a permanent base for the firm's operations. Depending on the source, either Laclède or his young assistant, Auguste Chouteau, chose an elevated spot on the west bank of the Mississippi, approximately ten miles south of the mouth of the Missouri. In February 1764, while Laclède gathered supplies and recruited settlers from existing French settlements on the east side of the Mississippi (land that only recently had been surrendered to the British in the Treaty of Paris that followed the Seven Years' War), Chouteau and his party began to build a warehouse and a few cabins at their landing place. In April, Laclède returned and, again depending on the source, either sketched a plan of the town that he expected "to be one of the richest in North America," or witnessed the progress already made in that direction by Chouteau and his men.[8]

Like other settlements throughout colonial North America, St. Louis's origins lay in the launching of an explicitly commercial enterprise; that enterprise was in turn tied by royal charter to the interests of an expansionist government concerned with supporting its global ventures. The landscape created to serve this controlled system of intertwined public and private welfare was remarkably similar across the Spanish, French, and English dominions of the continent. Indeed, it made little difference to the shape of the new village when Chouteau learned that his settlement, along with all of the lands west of the Mississippi, had been secretly ceded to Spain shortly after the signing of the Treaty of Paris. By the time Spanish authority was firmly implanted in Louisiana in 1769, his town plan was five years old. French settlers had been assigned land on an informal basis since 1764; in formal, written deeds since 1766. The Spanish lieutenant governor, Don Pedro Piernas, confirmed these earlier grants and, mindful of the essential similarity between the existing landscape and that mandated by the settlement laws of his own empire, issued no new town-making proclamations after his arrival at St. Louis.[9]

The landscape of the colonial settlement consisted, as it did elsewhere in North America, of several interlocked pieces working together toward a civic whole. Most important was the town itself. Chouteau, as he later recalled, laid three long streets, each 36 French feet in width, parallel to the river bank at intervals of 300 feet.[10] Up the hillside from the river ran a perpendicular set of 30-foot-wide streets, laid 240 feet apart. Chouteau divided the resultant oblong blocks into four equal houselots each. In the center of the grid, three 300-foot-square blocks set off the village's most important public spaces: facing the river, in the same manner as the public *place* at New Orleans, sat the open marketplace; to the west of it was a block reserved for the company headquarters; west of that was the site of the future cathedral.[11] Taken together, the elements of this central, public axis diagrammed a comprehensive social hierarchy that belied the village's ostensible origins as a simple commercial entrepot. Even the names of the three principal streets—the *Rue Royale, Rue de l'Eglise,* and *Rue des Granges*—reflected the perceived unity and mutual dependence of crown, church, and husbandman at the edge of a pagan and uncultivated wilderness.

Immediately beyond this compact settlement, at the top of the hill that climbed west from the river, lay the first of five sets of common fields that would soon encircle the village (Illustration 2-4). These long, narrow fields, which—in spite of their name—were granted for individual use in the same manner as the houselots, followed in their form the example already set by the French in their settlement of the St. Lawrence River valley and, to a more direct extent, in the nearby Illinois settlements of Kaskaskia, Cahokia, and Fort de Chartres. Laid in widths of one or two arpents (an *arpent* measured 180 feet), each field stretched another 40 arpents into the back country—a total size of approximately 30 or 60 acres, depending on the width. When landgrants in the closest common fields, the St. Louis Prairie, were completed, surveyors laid one set of new farmlots a mile south of the village (the Petite Prairie fields), and another to the northwest (the Grande Prairie fields). This latter set came to define the approximate limit of a perimeter of cultivation encircling the village. Along this perimeter, south from the Grand Prairie, were established the Cul de Sac, Prairie des Noyers, and Carondelet Common Fields (the last actually belonging to the village of Carondelet, which lay beside the river just south of St. Louis). Around their outer extent, a communally maintained fence provided St. Louis's only defense until a series of palisades, optimistically christened Fort San Carlos, were constructed by the Spanish in preparation for the British and Indian attack of 1780.

Two other features completed the carefully planned landscape of the original settlement. The Common, a fenced but undivided tract of roughly two thousand acres reserved for communal use as a woodlot and pasturage,

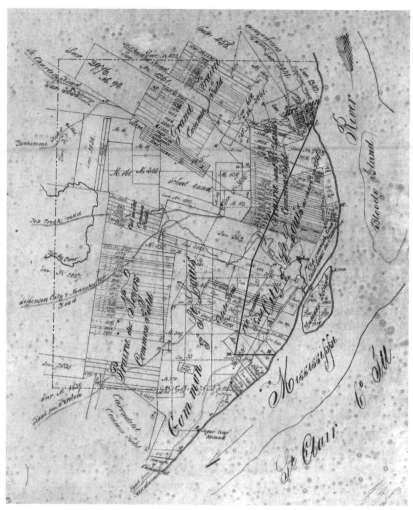

ILLUSTRATION 2-4. *St. Louis Property Surveys, Highlighting Colonial Land Divisions.* The five sets of long, narrow, agricultural lots known as common fields—the Grande Prairie, Petite Prairie, St. Louis Prairie, Cul de Sac Prairie, and Prairie des Noyers—surrounded the village on all sides. Also visible here are the Mill Creek tract, just west of the village, which was held privately by the Chouteau family, and the Common, to the southwest, which was dedicated to the shared use of all St. Louis's inhabitants. (J. Hutawa, 1847, courtesy of Missouri Historical Society)

stretched between the Petite Prairie and Prairie des Noyers fields, beginning a mile southwest of town. The Mill Tract, the largest privately owned parcel of land adjacent to the village, belonged throughout the colonial period to the men whose private fortunes can most accurately be claimed to have been one with the fortunes of St. Louis: first Laclède, then his common-law son, Chouteau. This property extended approximately three miles west from the Mississippi just south of the village, along the valley formed by the *Petite Riviere,* or Mill Creek. It was here that the mill dam and its later, larger successor, Chouteau's Pond, separated the center of town from the lands to the south.

If this landscape of regulated commerce and agriculture, of complementary private and public spaces, of centralized residences and outlying farmlots, ever truly reflected the society of those who dwelt in it, that correspondence had clearly begun to break down within twenty-five years of St. Louis's establishment. By the time that formal Spanish rule came to an end in 1800, a widening gap had opened between the clearly delimited social and physical order that the government struggled to maintain, and the centrifugal force of diversified personal interests among the townspeople. As in other colonial settlements across North America, traditional land divisions endured, even as their original social and ideological context withered under the disparate desires of colonial settlers.

Social pressures had strained the town's tentative order almost from the start. Most were rooted in the basic problem of promoting individual incentive without disintegrating the communal fabric. As the overseers of a new and, in many ways, still tentative settlement on a hostile frontier, St. Louis's Spanish rulers depended on retaining a population large enough to carry out their defensive and commercial goals. There is some evidence that the influx of French settlers fleeing the newly hostile territory east of the Mississippi in the 1760s was shortly offset by an equally strong outmigration that followed the arrival of the Spaniards.[12] We know that by 1778, Governor Bernardo de Gálvez in New Orleans was sufficiently concerned with the population problem in upper Louisiana that he directed his subordinates in St. Louis to offer a 5-arpent-wide strip of farmland, as well as tools, pigs, chickens, and a supply of corn, to any outsider who came to settle in the area. In return, Gálvez made what must have seemed to him the natural demands that these settlers swear an oath of loyalty to the Spanish Crown, and that the local government reserve the right to "take measures" upon any sign of "sloth or abandonment" on the part of its new subjects.[13]

Gálvez operated on the assumption that he could maintain the mesh of privileges and responsibilities that had for hundreds of years kept the interests of Spanish colonists inextricably tied to those of the Spanish government. This assumption proved highly contestable as the eighteenth century drew to a close. St. Louisans were simply not the tillers of the soil that the framers of the sixteenth-century Laws of the Indies had presumed in their prescriptions for colonization. The fur trade, with the commerce that grew up around it, was by 1800 a far more attractive option to local residents. Many were, by this time, husbandmen solely by virtue of their landholdings. The French trader Charles Larpenteur later recalled one such resident, William Sublette, as "a farmer near St. Louis, but [one who] was more trapping beaver than farming."[14] Captain Amos Stoddard, who arrived in 1804 to take control of the Louisiana Territory for the American government, noted that St. Louis's Creole settlers "had no disposition to resort to agriculture, at least so long as they were able to navigate the rivers, pursue the chase, or the Indian trade."[15] While such comments were typical of Anglo-Americans arriving in French or Spanish colonial territory, their veracity in this case was supported by the dilapidated condition of the fence that had once surrounded the Common, protecting nearby common fields from the damage wrought by free-roaming animals.[16] Even before the collapse of this Common fence some time in the 1790s, the common fields were apparently far less well-cultivated than their neat appearance on contemporary maps would suggest. According to the recollection of at least one early settler, those strips which were covered with trees or brush had simply lain unused, rather than being cleared for planting.[17] That this violation of the carefully planned self-sufficiency of colonial settlement vexed Spanish officials is obvious from the reply drafted by one unnamed functionary in New Orleans to a group of St. Louisans who, in 1799, unsuccessfully petitioned the government for a chance to enter the fur trade. The respondent suggested that his petitioners instead pursue farming. "It is now 150 years," he wrote, "during which you have been sowing wheat, and you have not yet had even the little ability to furnish your capital with that grain." As justification for his decision to bar the complainants from the fur monopoly, he relied on the simple, circular logic of habit and tradition. "To the government alone," he reasoned, "does it pertain to understand the most effective means for the prosperity of its subjects."[18]

If the government at New Orleans was able to maintain the exclusive character of the prosperity derived from fur trading in St. Louis, it was less successful in controlling the static system of land allocation that had long represented the most fundamental means it possessed for keeping social mobility in check. Where inhabiting and improving the land had, as late as Gálvez's rule, been theoretically inviolable conditions of settlement, later settlers would recall that by 1800 "habitation of one's concession was impossible or incidental to Spanish law, usage, and custom."[19] Where the colonists of New Spain had traditionally been forbidden to release their lands except with the express permission of the government, real estate now changed hands on a regular basis.[20] Where the landholding patterns of St. Louis had once provided an index of social status, American observers noted that "grants were now made to all who chose to apply for them, without condition, to any extent, and of course, without regard to the means of the applicant."[21] Finally, where traditional land allocation practices had been designed to bring the area's population together into the close, defended space of the central blocks of the town, the streets of Laclède's original village housed less than half of the people of the administrative district of St. Louis by 1800.[22]

The maintenance of a clearly delineated, closely controlled social and physical landscape had ceased to be a practicable condition of the town's existence even before American rule came to Upper Louisiana in 1804—the year after Jefferson and Napoleon concluded the United States' formal purchase of the vast territory. After that date, the city's new overseers had little opportunity to mold the division and sale of land according to a consistent set of rules in the way that the town's founders had. Indeed, one of the most troublesome problems faced by the territorial government in its first years was that, unlike most places on the western frontier, St. Louis had no land available for public sale. Instead, the entire area was enmired in conflicting claims of private ownership that effectively prevented the establishment of a new and comprehensive system for dividing and distributing land. As it had been to the Spanish governor, the issue of control over land became vital to the assertion of general governmental control at the onset of the American period; as such, the settlement of the land question was a key goal of the town's new overseers.

In theory, St. Louis should have been one interchangeable piece of a vast landscape administered in the name of the enfranchised American public by their elected representatives. The law that annexed the lands of Upper Louisiana to the Indiana Territory in 1804 called for the continuation in those lands of the section-and-township system first encoded by the Continental Congress some twenty years earlier. Across the prairies and woods, Missouri River floodplains, and rocky Ozark uplands that stretched west from the Mississippi, the Congress ordered an unvarying grid of mile-distant survey lines, evenly subdivided by a finer grid that marked the 160-acre quarter-sections reserved by the government for the westward-moving populace.[23] There were impediments to that vision, of course, chief among which was the vexing fact that tens of thousands of people, long settled on this land, considered it to be their own. From his council room beside the St. Louis levee, William Clark, federal Indian agent, began applying himself to the land issue in 1808—a job that would occupy him until his death three decades later. Around the forty-year-old settlement of St. Louis, however, the problems were of a different and in some ways less tractable nature. Here, the land was overlain with a pre-existing patchwork of privately owned tracts. Amos Stoddard noted that there seemed to have been, in St. Louis, a suspicious rush of land grants given in the year prior to his arrival. The captain's suspicions were not far off the mark. A frenzy of claims and purchases had in fact preceded American takeover, elevating and consolidating the status of a handful of powerful Creole settlers like Louis Labeaume, whose acquisition of twenty-six separate claims left him with more than 14,000 arpents of land to his name before Stoddard and his troops set foot in St. Louis.[24]

In 1805, with the formation of an independent Louisiana Territory, Congress ordered the appointment of a board of land commissioners at St. Louis to ascertain the validity of all pre-1804 land grants. Clearly, the reclaiming of land for the public domain (an act of potential economic as well as symbolic import) was one of Congress's primary intentions; to this end, the act nullified all claims made between 1800, when the Spanish had returned nominal control of Louisiana to the new French republic, and 1803, when Napoleon sold it to the United States. The fact that St. Louis had remained, during this interval, under the actual control of Spanish officialdom, and that all land grants had consequently been made in the name of a sovereign who no longer had true power over the territory, was taken by the Americans as sufficient grounds for invalidating those grants and returning them to the government's control. Further, the Americans stipulated that all claims dating *prior* to 1800 be substantiated with full, formal documentation as well as proof of possession and inhabitation. Such formalities had become, as we have seen, increasingly rare in the final days of Spanish rule. Land claimants protested that the letter of the law had rarely been applied to colonial-era grants; Stoddard himself later admitted that no more than one-half of the titles dating from this earlier period had been properly surveyed, and that fully nineteen out of twenty were "incomplete," by the Americans' criteria.[25]

More than any other, the issue of land grants polarized the St. Louis political scene in the first decade of American rule. On one side stood the so-called "junto" of wealthy and powerful Creole landowners like Chouteau, Labeaume, and Bernard Pratte Sr., all of whom served as judges in the newly formed Court of Common Pleas, as well as Antoine Soulard (who in his continued position as official surveyor was capable of exerting a unique influence on the solution to the land question). On the other side were more recently arrived settlers, led by John B.C. Lucas (himself French born), the Pennsylvanian appointed by Jefferson as land commissioner and, not incidentally, an aspiring land developer in his own right.[26] Eventually, Lucas's hard-nosed interpretation of the law won out over the more lenient terms promoted by his rivals. In spite of the conciliatory passage in 1807 of an act conceding claims to settlers who could prove simply that they had inhabited their land for ten years or more, Lucas's commission had confirmed fewer than one-third of the roughly three thousand claims that it considered before its dissolution in 1812.[27] In the same period, Soulard was replaced by Americans Silas Bent and William Russell—surveyors presumably less apt than their predecessor to verify questionable, pre-1804 claims.

But the land commission was unsuccessful in its efforts to return great numbers of disputed claims to public control. When the Missouri Territory was organized in 1812, voters elected a territorial council dominated by members and sympathizers of the junto. Under their guidance, the council reversed the ban on claims made between 1800 and 1803, at the same time dropping the earlier requirement of proof of actual habitation. As substantial an effect as these new rules had on the continuation of problems surrounding private land claims, they were soon augmented by yet another catalytic event—this one rooted not in the protests of the older, Creole settlers but in the claims of some of those same American investors who had lobbied for public land sales.

In 1811, an earthquake shook the land along the New Madrid Fault, in southeastern Missouri. The quake, felt as far away as Pennsylvania, was the largest recorded in the continental United States, before or since. It leveled many of the buildings of southern Missouri and Illinois and caused the Mississippi to change its course, inundating towns and farmlands alike. In 1815, Congress passed a law entitling owners of land ruined in the earthquake to a free grant of public land elsewhere.

The New Madrid act coincided with a time at which growing numbers of American immigrants were finding their way to St. Louis; once there, they found none of the cheap federal lands that had facilitated the settlement of other western pioneers. Instead, those who could afford to do so, like William Russell, purchased property from private owners (many of the latter group now realizing handy profits on land once granted them at no cost), on an open market. St. Louis land investors, not surprisingly, heard about the New Madrid law before the farmers of rural southern Missouri did. They traveled south and bought up property for pennies on the dollar, intent either on converting their new titles into valuable land around St. Louis or on selling them on the open market. For two decades, openly advertised New Madrid claims, good "on any of the United States lands, title indisputable," were a commonplace in St. Louis newspapers. Three-quarters of the more than five hundred such claims made around the city came, according to one study at the time, from people who had resided in St. Louis, not New Madrid, in 1811.[28]

Not surprisingly, then, urban growth in the early years of American rule was concentrated on private property. In its initial stages, however, that growth actually maintained the outlines of the landscape first dictated by Chouteau and Laclède. That landscape, once reflective of the government's power to control and preserve order, by now stood for something else. It had come to serve the speculative interests of a small group of individuals who by 1803 effectively controlled the city's property and dictated its public policy. The most visible land development of the period came from the team of J.B.C. Lucas and Auguste Chouteau (cf. Ill. 2-1). In 1816, they subdivided a combined portion of their St. Louis Prairie property—a move that pushed the urban landscape beyond the confining limits of the town boundaries and, at the same time, presaged the future importance of the central corridor that stretched west along the gentle northern slopes of the Mill Creek Valley. Between what eventually became Fourth and Seventh Streets, Lucas and Chouteau extended and doubled the width of the old east-west streets of the village. Conscious of the need to tie this speculative foray into the familiar, settled portion of the town, the developers not only continued the existing street pattern but donated a full block of their addition to the county for the erection of a new courthouse. This public square, north of Market between Fourth and Fifth Streets, was only one block off the public axis of Chouteau's original village.

Three years later, Jeremiah Connor's subdivision of a 2-arpent common-field tract just north of Chouteau's and Lucas's land continued their precedent of establishing compatible but improved streets west of town. At the edge of Connor's narrow addition, an uncommonly generous 80-foot strip (today's Washington Avenue) was deeded to the county as a public thoroughfare. What Connor sacrificed in privately held acreage, he planned to recoup in the improved land values of lots fronting his spacious, neatly laid street. His gamble, unfortunately, coincided with a financial crisis in St. Louis that saw the collapse of inflated real estate values and the failure, in 1821, of the once reliable Bank of Missouri.[29] Faced with the instability of private capital, and lacking the political means to provide for their well-being with public funding, the townspeople of St. Louis stood in peril of losing whatever strides had been taken by entrepreneurs like Chouteau, Lucas, and Connor toward the improvement of their settlement. It was at this precarious point that incorporation took place, and it was at this point that Chouteau's testimony and his accompanying map, along with Paxton's "Notes" and the maps of Beck and Collot, all appeared. In retrospect, they might as likely have eulogized the town's demise as they did foretell its ascent to the rank of the largest city in the American West.

CHAPTER 3

"The Inhabitants of St. Louis" and Their Land

Redefining Urban Order in the Antebellum City

St. Louis's future in the years following incorporation depended on equal parts luck, money, and geographic fortuity. As much can be said for any city, anywhere. But coloring St. Louis's transition from hamlet to thriving urban center was the peculiar commingling of colonial memories, capitalist opportunity, and republican ideals that had already made itself apparent by the 1820s. If lingering aspirations toward an imagined colonial order provided St. Louis politicians and developers with a framework for working out some of the thornier problems that lay ahead, the hard business of trading, regulating, and improving land would soon dictate the outlines of a less stable and more difficult balance between individual liberties and common good; this balance ultimately would give way to the tensions of the city of fenced-off corners and wider settings.

The city's streets offered a template for reconceiving a new community in the traces of the old. St. Louis's first mayor, the Pennsylvania-born William Carr Lane, passed an act authored by street commissioner Joseph Laveille, also a Pennsylvanian. The law renamed the city's north-south streets according to a simple ordinal system, and it gave to east-west streets the arboreal names (Spruce, Pine, Locust) of Philadelphia's renowned grid.[1] In the process, Lane recast the simple, orthogonal plan of St. Louis—first laid and maintained in accordance with the Roman-based tradition of French and Spanish colonization—clearly in the image of the American speculative city. In a polyglot frontier town whose population, as St. Louis city directory editor John Hogan admitted at the time, "is much diversified, and has no *general* fixed character," the Americanization of street names was a simple but vital step toward the establishment of a new, readable social and physical order.[2] As the eighteenth century's *Rue Royale, Rue de l'Eglise,* and *Rue des Granges* became First, Second, and Third Streets, the city shed the anachronistic symbols of an encompassing social and religious system and established instead a conceptual system for accommodating limitless growth.

How was this conceptual system to become actuality? Certainly not through the direct efforts of the central authority that had brought those streets into being. In the first years after incorporation, Lane and the city's aldermen instead found political and financial advantage in charging the city's residents with responsibility for municipal improvement. The city charter anticipated the survey commission's resigned attitude about streets, formally limiting public responsibility for their grading or paving. Instead, the charter required abutting property owners to pay paving costs and, further, forbade such paving without the written application of two-thirds of the affected landholders.[3] The City's legislated exemption from the primary costs and responsibilities of the streetmaking process was also reflected in the charter rule that governed the means by which private land was appropriated for new streets. The charter had called for the appointment of a twelve-man jury to decide, in such cases, the damages and benefits incurred to the owners of land around the proposed street. Depending on the nature and location of the improvement, the jury might find that the owner of confiscated land had either suffered a material loss, benefited from the improved accessibility of his property, or as was most often the case, experienced some combination of the two. The jury was also free, in theory, to assess the cost of confiscated land against others in the general vicinity who might derive greater commercial gain, or higher property values, from the new street. Nowhere in this early articulation of a "segmented system," as Robin Einhorn has termed it, was the city at large presumed to be a potential beneficiary of the public improvements taking place in its midst. Instead, the public treasury was liable only for that amount of damages that remained (if any) after individual beneficiaries had already been assessed.[4]

Simple financial calculation was, of course, not absent from the 1822 charter's logic. Its provisions for street paving and opening represented one logical approach to the improvement of a city whose public revenue was limited by a scant, half-percent property tax. But they also indicated that, beyond vesting the municipal government with the power to establish and repair public rights-of-way, the charter's framers considered that much of the responsibility for—and many of the benefits of—the city's street system rested with individual landowners.

This reluctance to frame a sphere of public responsibility that transcended the simple encouragement of individual initiative was not, however, long-lived. Mayor Lane and others realized that the orderly city of Lewis Beck's map and Auguste Chouteau's history could never be maintained by a radically democratic (or, to be more accurate, politically squeamish) system of dispersed decision-making. What individual would voluntarily foot the bill to improve streets that were, in John Paxton's words, "so extremely muddy as to be rendered impassable"?[5] In mid-August 1823, Alderman James Kennerly introduced an ordinance conferring on the aldermen the power to order street paving, at the abutting owners' expense, "whenever the board of street commissioners shall deem it expedient and of urgent necessity."[6] The necessity was deemed sufficiently urgent that, on that same day, the board used its new powers to order the improvement of a number of downtown streets.[7]

In 1826, the aldermen's public efforts to promote street improvement accelerated into a full-scale governmental commitment to transform St. Louis into a proper city. Beyond simply cleaning up public thoroughfares, this commitment represented a new assertion of a shared public interest, protected and overseen by the municipal government rather than by individuals. Abandoning their earlier policy of allowing existing impediments and obstructions to wither away in time, aldermen voted for the first time to begin levying a $100 fine against anyone responsible for obstructing the streets.[8]

Despite the legal progress toward establishing a centralized authority beyond even that which the French or Spanish had maintained, St. Louis's lawmakers were no match for the overwhelming reality of overstrained public services and diversifying human needs in the frenzied atmosphere of the Jacksonian frontier. The area's population, which increased by nearly half in the 1820s, would in the following decade more than double, reaching a total of over 52,000 by 1840.[9] The combination of a greatly expanded trade with the Southwest and ever-increasing steam-powered river traffic with New Orleans and the Ohio Valley in the 1830s had begun to lend credence to the familiar boast of local businessmen that their city was "by nature the best point for the distribution of the commerce, intelligence, and forces of the West."[10] But to the weary traveler disembarking at the levee or riding in from the prairie, the streets of St. Louis proved a far cry from anything promised by the hyperbole of land promoters or the tall tales of traveling companions. Frederick Steines, one of a growing number of German immigrants attracted to the Missouri River valley at this time by Gottfried Duden's glowing *Report of a Journey to the Western States of North America*, recalled picking his way around mud puddles and between the carcasses of horses and pigs in what he described—perhaps charitably—as "a very insignificant place," distinguished only by its "sad and unattractive appearance."[11] Edmund Flagg, traveling west from his home in New England in 1836, confirmed what the city's surveyors had reported thirteen years earlier: "There are," wrote Flagg, "but few of those rectilinear avenues cutting each other into broad squares of lofty granite blocks, so characteristic of the older cities of the North and East." Instead, he found "much in St. Louis to remind one of its village days."[12]

The lackluster appearance of the old city center aggravated (and was, in turn, aggravated by) a tendency that has continued in St. Louis to the present day: a constant, centrifugal growth. Long before streetcar tracks or highways, before industrialization or redlining, city residents spread themselves far from the heart of the city. The colonial period had already seen the official establishment of separate, adjacent villages like Carondelet, to the south, St. Charles to the west, and St. Ferdinand (later Florissant) to the north. Between 1800 and 1810, when the population of the district of St. Louis (which included these outlying communities) jumped by 132 percent, the population of the town itself grew by only 34 percent.[13] In the early decades of American rule, after the physically conservative additions of Chouteau, Lucas, and Connor, the city's colonial landscape began to be obscured by the work of a variety of essentially self-interested land speculators. Privately held urban developments spilled out of both ends of the city limits, along the riverfront (Illustration 3-1). The town of North St. Louis, in 1816, was the first such addition. Significantly, its grid was based not on the old city grid, as Lucas and Chouteau's addition had been, but on the curve of the shoreline. North St. Louis was designed to offer an earlier, alternative landing point for cargo originating upstream from the city—particularly for the lumber that was arriving in ever greater quantities from the forests of Minnesota and Wisconsin. Two decades later, with the practice well-established adjacent to the city limits and beyond, former mayor Lane wrote to his children: "Everybody in the West nowadays make towns—I do as others do—and have laid out 'St. George' below the powder-mill tract [the new federal arsenal two miles south of the city center]."[14] Lane's development was part of a boom in South Side property speculation that also saw the dedication of "South St. Louis" (like St. George, oriented to the river rather than to the old city), as well as the first subdivisions of the property once belonging to Antoine Soulard, the man who had served as city surveyor from 1795 to 1805. The precedent of these riverine suburbs continued into the next decade, with the establishment of the towns of Bremen and Lowell beside the old North St. Louis addition. All benefited, as surely as did the city itself, from the successful efforts of a young army colonel, Robert E. Lee, who was posted to the site in 1837 with the mission of deepening the Mississippi's channel along the Missouri shore, thereby enhancing the commercial prospects of the growing community. Indeed, the area's population was becoming sufficiently scattered by this time that in 1843 one thousand unincorporated St. Louis County residents petitioned the state house of representatives to separate the

ILLUSTRATION 3-1.   *St. George Addition.* Early St. Louis land developers like William Carr Lane found advantage in opening up their own
new additions along the river, beyond the crowded and decaying center
of the city. Lane's St. George Addition was located more than two
miles south of what were then the formal city limits of St. Louis.
(Reprinted from E. Dupre, *Atlas of the City and County of St. Louis,
by Congressional Township* [St. Louis, 1838], courtesy of Missouri
Historical Society)

city from the county, requesting that the offices of the latter then be removed
to a location more convenient than downtown.[15]

Like these dissatisfied exurbanites, the owners of early outlying developments did not necessarily intend to join the city itself. South St. Louis was at
least a forty-minute walk from city hall in these pre-streetcar days; to walk

from downtown to Lowell would have taken close to an hour. These distances were all the more forbidding at a time when the population of the city proper was largely concentrated within a one-mile radius of city hall, and when even the relatively central corner of Sixth and Locust Streets was considered too far from the business center to merit serious consideration as a real estate investment.[16] In advertising their new lots to the public, the riverfront developers consistently described their sites as distinct urban centers; South St. Louis was promoted as a "manufacturing community," while the Soulards proclaimed their First Addition "unsurpassed in beauty and eligibility for a town."[17] Clearly, these early speculators either had unusually long-range plans for the eventual incorporation of their properties or, like Lane, saw themselves as Western "town-makers," shaping separate, privately governed domains.

In fact, extraterritoriality offered considerable advantages to property owners. Untouched by the burden of municipal regulations and property taxes, these men and women exercised a *de facto* governmental authority over their landscape nearly as complete as that enjoyed by the village's former colonial overseers. When they dedicated their additions to the county, developers were free to set conditions that, in effect, linked their newly public landscape with their own private interests in perpetuity. Lane, for instance, who saw his St. George addition as the potential site of a railroad line to the iron mining region of southeastern Missouri, stipulated that he and his heirs should forever enjoy the right to operate such a line through public streets at no cost.[18]

In this manner, Lane and others like him came to constitute a new landholding elite, one whose authority was based less on traditional social status than on their ability to take advantage of the opportunities provided by a capitalist land market. To maximize these opportunities, they invested outside of the legally defined city, which was already largely subdivided and which had seen the tentative development of land-related laws that subordinated private discretion to the newly strengthened public authority that came with incorporation. Instead, they seized on lands whose locations—beside the arsenal or at an advantageous docking point—offered an alternative source of economic security, away from the crowded but decaying streets of a seventy-year-old downtown.

The city government, aware of the potential benefits that such developments represented for municipal coffers, did what it could to encourage annexation in the 1830s.[19] It was evident, however, that developers required further incentive before they would be willing to submit to the additional burdens represented by annexation. In 1835, a revised city charter gave residents the power to petition for new streets; if every landowner along the proposed route consented, the city was obliged to open a right-of-way through their property.[20] Further, in those instances where the City itself chose to open a street on private property, a new and more favorable set of financial calculations applied.

Previously, property owners had been subject to an assessment of benefits that offset the damages they received from the city in payment for their confiscated land. The new charter removed this benefit assessment and made the city liable for the entire value of the appropriated property.[21] The following year, in yet another concession to potential developers, the board of delegates voted to finance the full cost of street paving with existing public funds rather than individual paving assessments.[22]

There was indeed a subdivision boom after 1835; while, in the previous five years, eight subdivisions had been dedicated in and around the city, the period 1836–40 saw the dedication of fifty-two.[23] Virtually all, however, were outside the city limits, and none of those were proposed for annexation. Within the city, meanwhile, the government had failed to use its new powers to order the pavement of a single block.[24] In desperate need of a means for improving the city's fiscal and physical condition, and bereft of a combination of power and persuasion as compelling as that enjoyed by their imperial predecessors, they continued to enlist the support of private landowners by whatever means were most expedient. As they struggled toward that goal through the 1830s and 1840s, lawmakers swung back and forth, from one ordinance to the next, between their conflicting inclinations to sweeten the carrot or to sharpen the stick.

In 1839, the responsibility for paving costs was returned to abutting property owners. At the same time, however, the government maintained its right to order streets paved. The effect was immediate; in the three years after the new law was passed, paving, previously at a three-year standstill, was ordered for ninety-three city blocks.[25] This prodigious jump in paving activity reflected, in part, the city's new release from the financial burdens that had previously slowed its role in this fundamental activity. But it also indicated larger changes at work. The 1841 expansion of the city limits, ordered by the state assembly, had increased the city's area nearly sevenfold (Illustration 3-2).[26] These expanded limits extended on the South Side to include St. George and the Soulard additions, and west to the line of Second Carondelet Avenue—today's Eighteenth Street. A vast area suddenly awaited improvement. Opening costs were supported in this area by a one-sixteenth percent tax increase earmarked solely for new-limit improvements. Soon, the city further enhanced its powers by raising property tax rates yet again, this time to 1 percent of assessed value—double the longstanding statutory maximum.[27]

Along with the *faits accomplis* of boundary expansion and tax increases came a string of conciliatory laws designed to ease the burdens of city landowners. Among the most significant was the relaxation of the law requiring unanimous consent for street openings. The City began to approve openings first on the petition of two-thirds, then one-half, of the affected property owners.[28] These loosened requirements helped to contribute to an explosion in the number of street-opening ordinances in the enlarged city. In the two

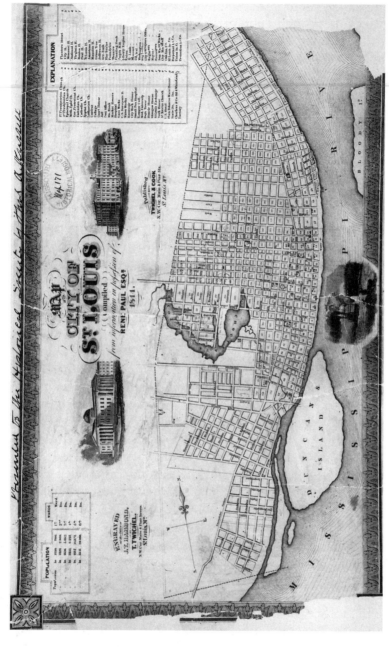

ILLUSTRATION 3-2. *St. Louis City Limits, 1844.* The 1841 boundary expansion, which increased the city's area by a factor of seven, also posed greater challenges in the continuing struggle to balance personal incentive and public responsibility in the task of developing urban land. The blocks of the originally incorporated town lie at the center of the map, just above the steamboat image. (T. Twichel, 1844, courtesy of Missouri Historical Society)

years before the passage of the two-thirds rule, four blocks had been opened; the following two years saw the opening of 393 blocks. Then, in the two years that followed the reduction of required signatures to one-half, that number shot up to over nine hundred.[29] Sacrificing still more of its former authority, the government in 1843 relinquished its right to order and tax pavement without the adjacent owners' consent.[30] Rather than allowing this virtual ban on paving assessments to force new-limit improvements to a halt, however, the City found a means to finance those improvements without special assessments. The aldermen set aside one-quarter of the 1 percent property tax now received from new-limits residents and reserved it for street improvement in the area. Two years later, without a single newly paved street to show for their new system, they raised this fraction to one-half.[31] Newly incorporated subdividers like the Soulards were in a sense paying for the pavement of their streets as they would have under the old system, but with two differences: first, this assessment was now included in their basic taxes, rather than being levied separately, and second, the cost was shared by other landowners throughout the new limits. Street improvement had gone from being an entirely segmented service, offered on a case-by-case basis to those willing to pay, to being a public responsibility in which a large part of the city shared a stake.

St. Louisans thus experienced, into the 1840s, two apparently divergent trends that transformed the idealized, post-colonial city into an arena of conflicting interests: first, the steady strengthening of governmental means for controlling the urban landscape; second, a proliferation of individuals fashioning the landscape according to their own interests. How did this apparent contradiction resolve itself? The question becomes less problematic the minute we realize that principle landowners and government, far from being opposing interests, were effectively and increasingly the same. What appeared to be deepening conflict was really the search, by a limited number of St. Louisans, for a variety of means by which to exercise influence in the city—to join the interests of the whole and its parts.

While decisions about municipal governance putatively rested in the hands of all of St. Louis's enfranchised citizens, they were in fact exercised by a highly selective cross-section of those citizens. Wealth and power were distributed unequally in the young city, particularly since the influence that rested with families of the city's Creole elite persisted long after the arrival of American government. Yet with the development of a democratic political machinery, as well as of a republican outlook that treated land ownership as a self-obtained reward rather than a government-granted entitlement, such convergence could no longer be justified with the dismissive high-handedness of a Bernardo de Gálvez. Instead, city officials struggled to substitute a new legal and ideological framework for the authoritarian, theocratic glue that had held together the landscape of early-colonial St. Louis.

A brief look at the individuals involved in the process of shaping the city reveals more about the relation of land laws and subdivision practices in the 1830s and 1840s (Illustration 3-3). The men and women who subdivided lands on the south side of the expanded city in these early years epitomized the changing social profile of power in mid-nineteenth-century St. Louis. Descendants of the Creole elite were conspicuous among their number; the largest developer, Julia Soulard, was not only the widow of the former French surveyor, but the daughter of colonial St. Louis's wealthiest inhabitant, Gabriel Cerre. Sophie Chouteau, the widow of Auguste Pierre Chouteau and granddaughter-in-law of Pierre Laclède, dedicated one subdivision, as did Joseph Papin, who was related by marriage to the Chouteaus.[32] Other French-descended developers included a few among that segment of the Creoles that would go on to gain the greatest prominence in the business interests of the American city: Bernard Pratte Jr., like his father a fur trader, who was elected mayor in 1844; Louis LaBeaume, whom we have already encountered as an early land speculator, and who went on to become one of the chief investors in the Pacific Railroad; and Louis Bogy, the banker, attorney, and later Senator whose interests included the Pilot Knob iron works and the profitable Wiggins Ferry, which dominated river traffic to Illinois before the completion of the Eads Bridge in 1874.

In addition to the members and descendants of the colonial elite was a significant number of prominent Anglo-Americans. Some, like land surveyor William Russell, were long-established in the city; others, like his son-in-law Thomas Allen, were more recently arrived. A few, like Larkin Deaver, who had married the granddaughter of Joseph Papin and Marie Chouteau, were tied to the earlier French families. Most, however, represented a new breed of St. Louisan who would eventually supplant these families in their financial and political—if not always social—prominence. This new group included British immigrants like John Withnell, whose land-developing activities were supplemented by his work as the contractor for major buildings like the St. Louis Cathedral and the state capitol at Jefferson City. The group also included successful, American-born merchants and professionals like John Daggett, who parlayed his drygoods business into a prominent political career, and Charles Dickson, who would become one of the most active promoters of the Eads Bridge. Of the twenty-six people who dedicated subdivisions within the area on which this study will focus before 1854 (a year whose significance will become clear shortly), sixteen can be definitely linked to a vocation, as listed in the St. Louis city directories. Of those with identifiable occupations, six were merchants, four attorneys, two physicians, one a notary, one the secretary of the city gaslight company, one a city tax collector, and one a member of the board of delegates.[33]

That the subdividers of land in South St. Louis represented a kind of transitional group from the city's landed elite to a rising class of speculators and

A. Subdivision of Lot 5, Block 15, St. Louis Common (1844)
B. Louis Labeaume and John Withnell's Subdivision of the St. Louis Common (1845)
C. Soulard Additions (Julia Soulard) (1838–1848)
D. Thomas Payne's Addition (1852)
E. Thomas Allen's Additions (1848–1852)
F. Devolsey Addition (Joseph Charless) (1848)
G. Edward Haren's Addition (1848)
H. Julia Cabanne's Addition (1849)
I. Fairview Addition (Charles Dickson, J. J. Murdoch, David H. Armstrong) (1848)
J. Isaac Taylor and Edwin R. Mason's Addition (1848–1852)

K. Joseph Papin's Addition (1844)
L. Barsaloux Tract (John Daggett et al.) (1839)
M. Fairmount Addition (William Price, John Ivory) (1850)
N. Shirley Place (John Ivory, J. J. Clark) (1852)
O. H. C. and F. J. Lynch's Addition (1840)
P. John Daggett's Addition (1849)
Q. Labadie's Addition (John Daggett) (1845)
R. Larkin Deaver Estate Addition (1850)
S. Honore Picotte's Addition (1849)
T. Arsenal Addition (Isaac Taylor, Edwin R. Mason, J. R. Dougherty) (1850)
U. Laclede Addition (1846)
V. School Land Subdivision (City of St. Louis) (1849)

ILLUSTRATION 3-3. *South St. Louis Subdivisions, 1838–53.* The earliest subdivisions in South St. Louis were concentrated, not surprisingly, closest to the city center. Early South Side developers came from an elite class of influential merchant and professional families; they lived almost exclusively in the wealthier blocks west of downtown. For an understanding of how this and other study-area detail maps fit within the landscape of the larger city, see Ill. 1-4. (Courtesy of the author; information drawn from Norbury Wayman's St. Louis subdivision maps in the collections of Missouri Historical Society, and from subdivision deed books in the office of the Recorder of Deeds, St. Louis) professionals is corroborated by the relation between the location of their subdivisions and the location of their residences. Only five of the twenty-six developers mentioned above actually lived south of Chouteau's Pond, the meandering mill pond that separated South St. Louis from the center of the city; of these, only Julia Soulard and Thomas Allen resided within the limits of their subdivisions. In this sense, Soulard and Allen were the last representatives, on the South Side, of a tradition of landholding that stretched back to feudal times; while both sold their lots in the context of a free, capitalistic land market, and both did so for the purpose of economic gain, each retained a personal, rather than a purely financial, tie to their property.

Increasingly, such local and personal ties were being replaced by more strictly commodified relationships between land owners and their property; relationships shaped more by the political and economic framework of city life than by generations of family tradition. Unlike Soulard and Allen, the other subdividers of South Side property during this period lived downtown—normally within a few blocks of their stores or offices. The interest that they retained in their land was strictly that of the salesman in his product; the lots that they sold were functionally equivalent to the pelts or the patent medicines that passed across the counters of their shops and warehouses. As merchants and professionals, however, they participated in transactions whose procedures were already well-established, and whose values might depend upon weather conditions or market fluctuations in Boston, New Orleans, or the Oregon Territory.[34] As major landowners in the fast-growing city of St. Louis, they were in a position to exert far greater influence on the parameters of their trade. As we have seen, political decisions made at the state and municipal levels had a basic impact on the city's landscape in the early decades of American rule. It is not surprising, therefore, that a significant portion of the group of developers profiled above held some public office at or around the time that they subdivided their land. Nine of the pre-1854 developers in the study area—just over a third of their total number—served in the state house of representatives, the mayor's office, or on one of the city's representative bodies (the council, the board of aldermen, or the board of delegates) within a period of five years before or after the date of their subdivision.[35]

This marked convergence of political and landholding interests was encouraged by the passage of an ordinance in 1839 requiring elected office holders to be landowners.[36] The law in itself, however, cannot fully account for the close correlation of the two groups in the 1840s. The explanation lies more in the fact that the city's political institutions were at last capable of exerting a significant impact on the shape and extent of the urban landscape. In the first thirty years of American rule, the citizens and government of St. Louis had essentially worked with an existing urban form. Real changes and additions took place outside of the geographic and political limits of the city itself.

As the estates of the French families were divided and sold, and as expanding boundaries brought ever more land into the city, opportunities for investing in and developing city land multiplied. A greater number of those men who, like William Carr Lane, had pursued political careers added to their influence by becoming land developers, and a greater number of land developers, like Thomas Allen, sought to protect their interests by pursuing political office. The result was the creation of a new landed political elite, and with it, new possibilities for fusing public and private interest in the landscape.

That fusion took on several forms in these early years of urban growth. Two episodes in the subdivision and development of land, both of them based on the city's South Side, illustrate the differing ways in which republican-era St. Louisans fashioned a system for explaining and maintaining a spatial order that was in effect little more democratic than that established under French and Spanish rule. So long as the people who governed the city were effectively the same as those who developed its property, both developments worked toward the same ends. But as soon as that equation between public and private interest broke down, these two episodes would stand as models for the divergent approaches to ordering urban space that ultimately resulted in the city of fenced-off corners and wider settings.

The Whole Defines Its Parts

The event that, more than any other, crystalized the government's eagerness to encourage and incorporate private developers in the development and maintenance of the urban landscape was the City's subdivision and sale of the roughly 2,000-acre expanse of the St. Louis Common. Here, on the one significant piece of land in St. Louis that remained in the public domain, was the opportunity at last to stamp upon the landscape a uniquely American form. The development of the Common was not only necessary for the growth of St. Louis; it would also serve for two decades as a testing ground on which to adjust the still-uncertain relationship between public rights and private privileges in the shaping of urban space. While the sale of the Common would eventually help to direct development away from the exclusive province of individual estates and toward the more familiar, more rationalized landscape of the modern city, it served at first as another magnanimous gesture, in the name of the public interest, to precisely that limited group of landowners whose cooperation had always seemed necessary to furthering the public interests of the city.

St. Louisans in the 1830s thought of the common land not as useful agricultural property, nor even as the logical site of the city's future growth. It was, instead, a "waste," a no-man's land whose chief value was as a shelter for the "desperate, lawless vagabonds" who preyed upon unsuspecting travelers.[37]

ILLUSTRATION 3-4. *View of the St. Louis Common, 1840.* Artist John Caspar Wild depicted the Carondelet Road, leading south from St. Louis to the colonial-era settlement of Carondelet, at a time when the land around it (including the old Common, which lay just to the west, along the right-hand edge of this view) was largely undeveloped. (Reprinted from J. C. Wild, *The Valley of the Mississippi Illustrated* [St. Louis, 1840], courtesy of Missouri Historical Society)

It is difficult, now, to picture this land, at once so useless and so close to the thriving city. Because of its relatively wild state, the Common was seldom depicted by the artists and printers who had begun to sketch the busy water-front and the downtown skyline. We can glean some idea of its appearance from John Caspar Wild's 1841 view of the southeastern corner of the Common, looking south to the town and common fields of Carondelet (Illustration 3-4).[38] Wild's view actually shows what would have been the busiest and most developed portion of this land—along the Carondelet Road, close to the river. Even here, however, the artist focuses on the picturesque dilapidation of the scene to suggest an area that is betwixt and between, a place more often passed through than stopped at. Farther west, away from road and river, where even the occasional lumber cart never rolled, the Common of the 1830s was simply a forty-year-old version of the already neglected and rundown Common of the 1790s. After three decades of American rule, it remained the ostensible, but not the usable, property of the citizens of St. Louis. The ethic by which it could be considered truly communal land, by which "public" property could be, in and of itself, productive and useful property, had long since died a quiet death in the private city. The Common was, to the municipal government of the 1830s, simply money gone wasting.[39]

The decision in 1836 to conclude the land-claims inquiries that had dragged on for over thirty years may have contributed to the rush of subdivision activity that occurred after that date. It also made possible the commencement of the sale of land in the Common, which would eventually constitute the greater part of South St. Louis. As with other street- and land-related laws of this period, official pronouncements regarding the Common sales reflected a marked ambivalence in the attitudes of St. Louisans toward the public and private utility of the urban landscape. While state and local authorities effectively granted to explicitly private interests the opportunity to develop property there as they saw fit, they did so in the name of the public good. With some creative manipulation of legal and historical precedent, this new equation of public and private interest could be made to seem entirely logical and unsurprising. The Committee on the Common, in order to reiterate and strengthen the public claim to this land, had cleared the way for its sale by declaring as trespassers all those who "take possession of cultivate improve or cut wood or quarry stone" there.[40] To "cut wood" was, of course, precisely one of those uses for which the Common had originally been reserved. Guided by the logic of committee chairman Wilson Primm—a prominent Whig who was himself the recent author of the most comprehensive history yet published of the young city—the municipal government was now reasserting its historical authority over the land in order to *deny* the historical uses once protected by that same authority. To use the common land for personal ends—to cut wood or graze cattle there—was no longer to participate in that network of mutual rights and obligations that had once come with membership in the urban community. Such acts were, instead, inimical to the newly defined public interest, which entailed turning over as much property as possible to individuals who might then seek to make it productive.

Rhetorically, these individuals became a collective body: they constituted the community itself, and the community in turn acted to protect their interests. In such manner could the Committee on the Common declare that, "whatever show of claim may be exhibited by any person to a portion of said Commons, that of the inhabitants of St. Louis is at any rate the eldest and most meritorious."[41] No difference of birth could separate one person from another in the republican city, but those who defied the will of the government ("any person") could be portrayed as having less of a legitimate claim to power than those who followed it ("the inhabitants of St. Louis"). In this turn of logic, individuals represented something akin to the "factions" of James Madison's *Federalist* No. 10: theirs were the special interests that stood in the way of absolute liberty for all. Primm's reasoning represented an expression of republican indignation, not at the tyranny of the group over the single person, but at the tyranny of the single person over the group. There was,

however, something disingenuous about this seemingly incontestable sentiment. First, the rights to cut wood or graze cattle had themselves once been
granted to the collective "inhabitants." Second, the inhabitants for whom the
committee spoke were themselves a collection of individuals. A look at the
details of the survey and sale of common lands reveals a good deal about just
what a tightly constituted collection they were.

In March 1835, the legislature authorized a city election to approve the survey, subdivision, and sale of parcels of common land to the highest bidder.
The election took place early in the following year, and the sale was approved
by a majority of the electorate.[42] The nature of city surveyor Charles DeWard's
Common subdivision ensured that those private citizens who did bid on
common lands would come from a fairly rarefied stratum of the city's overall population, and further, that their plans for their new property had no necessary bearing on the timely or logical development of the city. This was a
sale not of houselots, nor even of city blocks, but of large land tracts, the scale
of which was more in keeping with that of public lands being sold across the
northern Missouri prairie than with the crowded blocks of the young city
(Illustration 3-5).

Using as his base line the eastern border of the Prairie des Noyers common
fields (the future location of Grand Avenue), DeWard laid out the very picture
of the republican landscape: an even grid of 40-acre lots (each further divided
into four 10-acre blocks). Running through the grid, one mile to the east of
its western border, he planted the 120-foot-wide path of "the principal or Jefferson's Avenue," which ran south from Chouteau Avenue (the southern edge
of the old Mill Tract) to its termination at the river.[43] Aligned at right angles
to this broad avenue were fifteen 40-foot-wide streets, spaced at even quarter-mile intervals and numbered consecutively from north to south. In the far
northeastern corner of the Common, at the crest of the hill that sloped down
to the Mill Creek, DeWard laid Second Carondelet Avenue—soon to mark the
western border of the city—as well as four 120-foot-wide avenues: Missouri,
Mississippi, Park, and Lafayette. These short but intentionally impressive
streets described the perimeter of the "public square" reserved in the Common ordinance—soon known, as it is today, as Lafayette Park.[44] Aside from
that single embellishment in the section of the Common closest to existing
urban settlement, nothing in DeWard's map indicated more than the barest
hint of how the minimal grid should translate into urban space. Its relation
to the ragged fringe of the old Petite Prairie fields, which formed the eastern
boundary of the property, remained sketchy and tentative. The simple plan
was based as much on the need to facilitate property sales as to devise a logical plan for the city's growth; in this sense it was not entirely different from
the extraterritorial private subdivisions laid out along the riverfront at the
same time.

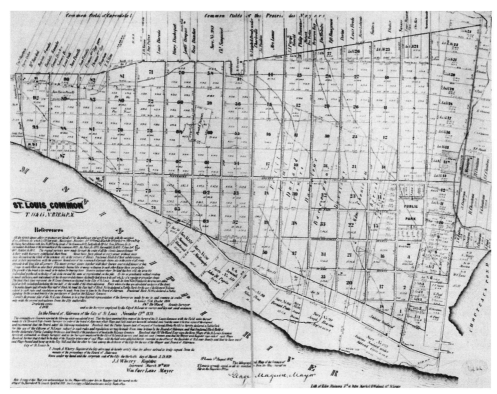

ILLUSTRATION 3-5.   *St. Louis Common Land Divisions, 1838.* Surveyor Charles
DeWard's 40-acre grid helped to transform the Common land from its earlier identity as communal property into a template for free-market land speculation. Jefferson Avenue, then as now one of South St. Louis's principal north-south thoroughfares, runs through the center of DeWard's survey; the western edge would
eventually form the route of Grand Avenue. (C. DeWard and J. Hutawa, 1838,
courtesy of Missouri Historical Society)

If they had no clear preference as to how exactly the Common development should fit into the existing fabric of the city, the state and city governments did share one basic goal in their effort: they looked forward to reap-
ing an enormous profit—far more than any private developers were then
earning from their more limited land offerings. To entice buyers, the legislature had devised a lump-sum payment plan, typical of the property sales
of the period, that called for the annual payment only of 5 percent interest
on the purchase price for ten years, after which time the principle would
finally come due. With these incentives in place, sales began promisingly.
After a month the Committee on the Common could confidently predict total
profits of $400,000.[45]

The Parts Define the Whole

The Common subdivision showed policymakers waking up to their power to define the components of urban space. More typically, those component parts were shaped from below—that is, through private initiative. The experience of one especially prominent—but by no means unique—South Side developer provides a case in point. Thomas Allen was thirty-four years old in 1847; a native of western Massachusetts, he was a prominent attorney and, thanks to his five-year marriage to Ann Russell, a wealthy man. Allen and his bride lived just east of the St. Louis Common in the house built by her father, William Russell. In 1804, Russell had been dispatched by Thomas Jefferson to St. Louis, where he was given the title of deputy surveyor for the new American territorial government, replacing Antoine Soulard; in the years that followed, he had managed to buy up many of those lands whose boundaries he charted, leaving his son-in-law with a substantial dowry of land and money. Before the wedding, Allen had signed an agreement with Russell that committed him to providing his bride, for the remainder of her life, with the income earned on his newly inherited property.[46]

In January 1847, Allen himself had extended the grounds around the Russell house by buying from John Cabanne more than 30 acres of surrounding common field lots. This ground, first granted to Pierre de Volsay, one of the original settlers of the upper Louisiana territory, became Allen's for a down payment of $1,500 in cash. In two years he would be expected to pay Cabanne the remainder of the $6,289 purchase price. In the meantime, he had to keep up regular interest payments set at the unusually high rate of 8 percent.[47] Somehow, Allen needed to find a way to make the land pay him back before his own final payment came due. He called on William Cozzens.

Cozzens, the city engineer, met Allen beside the house on a December morning. For four dollars a day, he had agreed to measure the property, divide it into even, salable parcels and straight streets, and draw up a plat with which Allen might entice prospective buyers. Behind Cozzens, three assistants prepared to stretch a long chain, at his direction, to mark the projected edges of the streets, alleys, and houselots that would soon cover the old French land grant. Their measurements were precise and consistent; in the weeks that followed, imaginary 60-foot streets, 16-foot alleys, and 25-foot lots soon stretched inexorably across the irregular tract, which in at least one place was "deep under water." Corners were marked, first, with wooden stakes driven into the hard ground, then, as the stakes continued to be stolen at night by nearby "Dutch" residents foraging for fuel, with stones.[48]

In April 1848, Allen rode two miles north to the courthouse, where he filed a copy of Cozzens's plat, then signed a statement vowing that the streets shown on it would be "released and declared highways for the use of the public." Before conceding these rights of way, Allen exacted a return promise from the city. In words that sprang easily from the lawyer's pen, he obligated the city to enforce his rule that "there shall be no slaughter house, no bawdy house, soap and candle factory, tannery, distillery, nine pin alley, or any other offensive business or occupation set up or carried on" within the limits of what he christened his First and Second Additions to the City of St. Louis.[49]

A week before his trip to the courthouse, Allen had taken steps to ensure both the future character of his developments and the security of his investment. On April 4, he sold to Peter Kenrick, the Catholic bishop of St. Louis, a single block of the First Addition for $4,809—three-quarters of the entire cost of his original purchase from Cabanne. In deference to the cleric (if not to the unquestioned resources of the Church), Allen demanded only $100 in down payment; for the payment of the remainder he allowed the generous period of ten years. For his part, the bishop saw the site as an advantageous location for what would become the first parish church catering to the city's growing German population: Sts. Peter and Paul. Allen gambled that his leniency with Kenrick would reap its own rewards. It did. Three years after his strategic first transaction, Allen had earned over $25,000 from land sales and rents in his two additions. By 1853, that figure had doubled. His investment had increased in value by 800 percent.[50]

These, then, were the converging means for shaping urban space in republican-era St. Louis: in one case, the government controlled the dispersal of land among a select group of citizens; in the other, citizens developed their land piece by piece, folding their separate projects into one collective, *de facto* public landscape by means of their subdivision deeds. In either case, the players had become much the same, and in either case, monetary profit proved a more effective medium for sealing the public-private partnership than had earlier ideals of civic obligation. The emerging capitalist city was captured nowhere more vividly than in a remarkable annotated map published by a North St. Louis printer named J. H. Fisher in 1853—the year that Allen calculated the profits of his South Side additions (Illustration 3-6). In sharp contrast to the neatly contained city that Lewis Beck had portrayed thirty years earlier, Fisher's map showed dramatically the accumulated effect of the converging approaches to developing public and private space in the former fur-trading outpost. The map documented a city that was at once physically complex and undeveloped—a city spilling into, yet still contained by, the vast lands around it. Fisher captured St. Louis in the midst of an urban explosion that would leave its population enlarged by nearly one-third in the space of the coming decade.[51] His map offered irrefutable evidence that around the entire city, as around Thomas Allen's estate, the line between city and countryside was capable of changing from one day to the next.

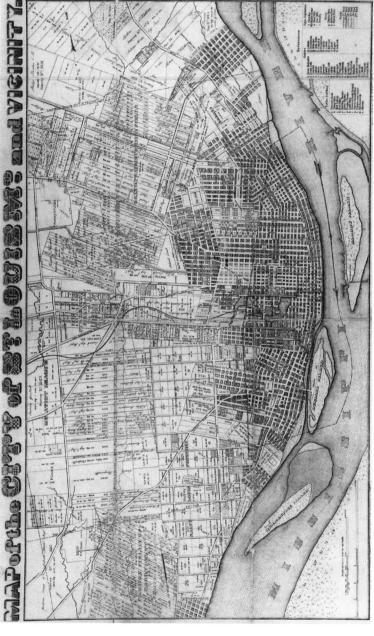

ILLUSTRATION 3-6.   *St. Louis, 1853.* J. H. Fisher's map documented a city that was at once spilling into, and still contained by, the lands around it. As the map illustrates, the old Petite and St. Louis Prairie fields have become templates for street growth west from the river, and Chouteau's Pond is undergoing the drainage that would improve sewage drainage in the center of the city and provide space for the city's new rail yards. Farther west, existing agricultural property lines and longstanding rural roads such as Gravois (which cuts diagonally through the Common toward the upper left-hand corner of the image) still define the landscape. (J. H. Fisher, 1853, courtesy of Missouri Historical Society)

For all its apparent complexity, however, Fisher's map spoke as much to the past as it did to the future. More meaningfully than the idealized images offered by the chroniclers of the 1820s, it portrayed the overwhelming influence of the past upon the choices of the present. Fisher showed a city still clinging to its waterfront; its westernmost blocks could be reached in less than a half-hour's walk from the levee. Street and property lines vividly showed the city's once agricultural landscape in the process of its transformation into the armature of an urban streetscape. The common-field boundaries that radiated out from the old village provided a template for the streets and blocks of the newly laid subdivisions of wealthy land developers like Allen. On the south side of the city, the outlines of the old Common contained the 10-acre grid of the city's 1836 land offering; just to the north of it, the newly drained mill pond still showed like a phantom beneath the new-laid tracks of the Pacific Railroad. The remarkable fact about Fisher's map was not that it showed such great transformation in St. Louis, but that it showed so little. In the endurance of earlier systems for dividing and ordering property, as in the converging interests that now joined those who governed and those who developed that property, St. Louis's landscape in 1853 in a way fulfilled the ideal that had eluded colonial governors and earlier American capitalists alike: it signified a historically and politically explicable city, the predictable future of which was built into the very ground from which it rose.

In the years that followed, Fisher's map would be revised again and again. With each new printing it lent itself ever more readily to a quite different reading. The second half of the nineteenth century would witness the growth of St. Louis into the nation's fourth most populous city and, with it, the development of an increasingly complex and diffused system for improving and maintaining the city landscape. Dispersal of the responsibility for, and ownership of, land and buildings would make one part of the city increasingly different from another, creating changing social and political alignments among various groups through their shared roles in developing or experiencing urban space. But the reassuring memory of those times in which the face of the city was forcefully imprinted with the image of a simple mesh of private and public interests—the memory of the stable colonial village or the antebellum town—would never sink far below the troubled surface of the explosive period to come.

Part II

Building the
Fenced-Off Corners

CHAPTER 4

Producers

The Evolution of the Private City-Building Process

Finishing the Old City

By 1853, the year that J. H. Fisher first printed his map, St. Louis presented the appearance of an Eastern city. Even as other Missourians were pinning their economic future to the agrarian, slaveholding economy of the South, the residents of St. Louis were by now firmly linked by commercial ties to financial centers like Boston and New York.[1] The blocks of the original village, politely dismissed a dozen years earlier by Charles Dickens as "quaint and picturesque," had acquired the unmistakable appearance of a successful urban business district, not unlike those of the cities from which St. Louis's capital flowed. In the wake of the disastrous waterfront fire that destroyed buildings along some twenty city blocks in 1849, a new and more substantial streetscape now arose: the classical facades of the Merchants' Exchange, Barnum's Hotel, and the United States Post Office punctuated the impressive rows of new, cast-iron-front warehouses waiting to receive goods unloaded from the crush of steamboats lined up cheek-by-jowl along the levee. On the crest of the hill overlooking the downtown bustle, facing the river in one direction and the westward-stretching prairie in the other, the aging courthouse was being transformed by the first of the extensive renovations and additions that would preserve its position as the city's most prominent building in the decades to come[2] (Illustration 4-1).

It was in this impressive structure that the three justices of the Missouri supreme court convened in October of the same year. Their caseload for the

ILLUSTRATION 4-1. *View of St. Louis, 1854.* In the wake of the 1849 fire that destroyed much of the city's waterfront district, St. Louis's skyline soon acquired a more monumental and permanent character. The courthouse dome rises at the center of the image; westward growth has advanced most quickly in the relatively flat, unimpeded terrain that stretches directly behind it. (E. B. Krausse, after G. Hofmann, 1854, courtesy of Missouri Historical Society)

fall 1853 session seemed far less consequential than the docket of a year earlier, when the judges had turned down the petition of a slave named Dred Scott, who sought to gain in slaveholding Missouri the freedom denied him during his earlier travels into the free state of Illinois. In this session, the court was called on to rule on the question of whether another slave, known only as Joe, was entitled to appeal his earlier conviction for stealing a fiddle (he was not); on another day, they decided if a downtown merchant was responsible for the cost of a mule that had died falling into a homemade sewer in front of the man's warehouse (he was). Buried in the middle of this eclectic docket was one case that seemed, at a passing glance, to center solely on the arcana of municipal taxation procedures. But in the matter of *Benoist v. The City of St. Louis*, the Court did no less than to confirm the end of an era: St. Louis, they decided, had become a genuine city as of the third week in October 1850.[3]

It was on this date, as Judge Hamilton Gamble (incidentally, the lone dissenter in the *Scott* decision) wrote in his majority opinion to *Benoist*, that the streets leading out from the center of town through the expanded 1841 limits had been sufficiently improved, according to the conditions of Article 7, Section 17, of the city charter, that the City could assess residents of the outlying "New Limits" at the full 1 percent tax rate then levied against other city residents. Gamble's decision confirmed in statutory prose what St. Louisans thought they could tell from a simple walk around town: the city's urban landscape had begun to extend beyond the crowded and prosperous streets of downtown, onto land that had only recently been untouched countryside. If that process did not yet seem entirely complete, locals in any case had little trouble by this time closing one eye and summoning up their powers of imagination. Like city engineer Samuel Curtis, describing in his journal the "quite open and beautifully rolling" land around the city's southwestern boundary at Second Carondelet Avenue (later Eighteenth Street), they shared a faith that "the day is not distant when [outlying lands] will be covered with the hordes of the city."[4] The time had come for St. Louis's boundaries to comprehend a city, not only in name but in fact.

But the city that local residents perceived as being somehow finished by 1850 was, as the Fisher map suggested, a city of the past. Limited in scale and physical complexity, its landscape was the product of decisions made by a small number of individuals sharing similar backgrounds and common interests. The history of its growth to that date had in large measure been the story of a struggle to define and balance the demands of public and private interest, in a place whose origins had been justified in the name of the former and whose subsequent development had depended on the encouragement of the latter.

Mid-century St. Louis was a city whose leaders were still as anxious to rehearse the past as to plan for the future. In a period of tremendous change that included the press of refugees from the failed revolutions of Germany, the paired crises of the 1849 fire and the cholera epidemic that followed closely on its heels (a scourge that claimed the lives of roughly 7 percent of the city's residents), and the unexpected swell of trade and population that attended the California gold rush and the resolution of the Mexican War, established St. Louisans once again turned to a remembered or imagined past for their bearings. In 1847, the city had chosen to celebrate the unlikely occasion of its eighty-third anniversary with an elaborate historical pageant and banquet—an opportunity, as it turned out, for another ceremonial retelling of the Chouteau/Laclède origin story, this time by the prominent politician and amateur historian Wilson Primm. A few years later, with party and ethnic factionalism beginning to reach full boil in this border city, yet another version of the tale would appear to great fanfare—the long-missing written account left by Chouteau himself, "discovered" by his son Gabriel among some old papers. The staff and subscribers of the prestigious Mercantile Library, under whose imprint the narrative eventually appeared, were evidently little troubled, in these uncertain times, either by the text's uncanny resemblance to John Paxton's 1821 account or by its contradictions with Chouteau's own testimony before the land claims commission in 1825. Sufficient, it seemed, was a chance to remind the citizens of St Louis—an increasingly unpredictable place—that they owed a common civic debt to the foresight of one man.[5]

The urban landscape had by this period been disposed of in a manner that seemed to respond more to the ideals of an earlier day than to the press of contemporary events. By the 1850s, with most of the outlying additions incorporated, with the Common divided into a grid of 10-acre lots, with seesawing street laws at last on fairly solid footing, and with land developers typically active in city government alongside their own entrepreneurial pursuits, a kind of balance had been attained between public and private interests. That balance was, however, momentary at best. In retrospect, neither the physical form of the city, nor the division of public and private property, nor the urban social order itself appeared likely to remain stable for much longer in St. Louis.

The resolution, years later, of the Civil War—a period that had seen bloody rioting in the city's streets, martial law imposed upon the entire population, and a robust urban economy brought to a standstill—seemed for many St. Louisans an adequate explanation for the transformation of a dynamic but backward-looking city into a heterogeneous, industrial metropolis. Among historians, the war has provided fodder for one of the most durable truisms of St. Louis history-writing: Wyatt Belcher's 1943 thesis that South-facing St. Louis, ill-prepared for the economic reorientation required after the war, lost out to Chicago capitalists who were better-positioned to dominate western rail development.[6]

The trauma of Civil War in this border city, however, was more symptom than cause of changes already set in motion by the diffusion of social and economic resources among a growing and diversifying population. The challenge St. Louisans faced in making sense of those changes was undoubtedly set in high relief by the battles over slavery and secession, which pitted Southerner against Northerner, German against Irish, black against white—all within the streets of St. Louis. But those conflicts comprised only the most acute subset of a larger set of chronic divisions in the crowded city, including those that had long been catalyzed by the most basic acts of negotiating space. Bridging either side of the events that forced St. Louisans to choose sides in a contest for the nation, the arduous process of shaping and developing land left a subtler but in ways just as deeply ingrained mark on the shifting line between private interest and public good. The transition in this particular city from a relatively simply defined social and political order to one that was complex and highly factional—from "republican liberalism" to "pluralist liberalism" (to borrow the phrases that historian Philip Ethington chose to apply to another American city, San Francisco, in the same period)—took on many dimensions.[7] But the experience of shaping and using the landscape—something all St. Louisans shared—was perhaps the most ubiquitous.

The changing structure of real estate sales, home lending, land development, and building construction in St. Louis between 1850 and 1910 played a vital part in the development of the contrasts between what some St. Louisans would later call the city's "fenced-off corners"—places that seemed to detract from an idealized landscape of political, cultural, and spatial unity—and its "wider setting"—places that brought that ideal closer to reality. Like the manner in which people went on to use the urban landscape in their daily lives (discussed in Chapter 5), or to shape it through regulations and public policies (the subject of Chapter 6), the city-building process gave structure to a particular set of relationships among St. Louisans, and between those St. Louisans and the spaces they inhabited. Far from being steady and unchanging, that structure was inherently unstable. Spatial and social relationships locked into a wobbling feedback loop that saw each changing in response to the other, then provoking new changes in response. In each of the structuring frameworks under consideration in the three chapters that follow—that is, in the production, consumption, and regulation of space—social change nevertheless assumed a common trajectory in the decades that separated the "finished" city of 1850 from the restless metropolis of 1910.

The first stage of this evolving social order, which lasted roughly up to the time of the Civil War, was marked by unity, simplicity, and a lack of specialization among the key players. The next—which continued into the building boom of the 1880s—was characterized by multiplicity, diversification, and specialization; and the last, which persisted well into the twentieth century, by a renewed unity, this time derived not from a return to earlier habits and practices but from the regulation and control of the more complex means developed in the previous years. In this chapter I want to consider those three idealized stages as they manifested themselves in the work of the "producers" of St. Louis's urban landscape: developers, realtors, contractors, tradespeople, and money lenders whose efforts set the city-building process in motion. How did the evolving urban landscape reflect transformations in these men and women's professional practices, and in their own relations to one another? How, on the other hand, were those relationships and practices molded by the realities of shaping urban space in St. Louis? In the chapters that follow, the focus of such questions shifts both to landscape "consumers"—the people living in St. Louis's neighborhoods—and to "regulators"—the lawmakers and public officials who sought to control development of public space. In each case, I will continue to use South St. Louis as a focus area for understanding changes taking place across the city. Together, these three overlapping groups—on the South Side and around the city—altered the illusory equipoise of the city of 1850. By the turn of the twentieth century they represented competing claims on a landscape once presumed "finished" in its shape and fixed in its social import. Those claims, then, would demand either reconciliation, or a convincing new explanation, by a new generation of St. Louisans seeking to shape the city.[8]

The City Takes a Stand: Public Land Sales and the 1855 Expansion

The story of the city-building process in the late 1800s properly begins with the biggest development venture in the city: the attempted urbanization of the scrubby prairie of the St. Louis Common. Here the particular public-private balance of the mid-nineteenth century, as we saw it develop in the previous chapter, was most precarious. From its first subdivision in 1836 to the real estate boom of the 1850s, the Common went from being a symbol for the simultaneous promise of municipal revenue, widespread urban growth, and investment opportunity for a few prominent citizens—all with minimal government involvement—to being the trigger for a new pattern of social and spatial relations in the city.

It became clear soon after the initial sale that the easy windfall that city officials expected might not be as quick to arrive as they had hoped. As the early notes of Wilson Primm's Committee on the Common indicate, the problem of nonpayment quickly established itself as their principal occupation. In June, a group of purchasers, in danger of defaulting on their first payments, petitioned the committee to allow them to turn their properties over to "secondary claimants" (presumably, friends or relatives) rather than be forced to give such lands back to the city for resale.[9] By January 1837, the members of the committee were inviting overextended buyers to file "a proposal in writing setting forth the terms on which they wish to compromise"; a few months later, they ordered the city attorney to determine what legal recourse they had in prosecuting those purchasers who were, in spite of the City's compromises, still delinquent. Defaults were by then so common that the attorney simply suggested that the committee stop suing for nonpayment.[10] By mid-1842, former mayor William Carr Lane, a major investor in Common lots, reported to his wife that "I am about as hard pressed as I can possibly be," thanks to the series of local financial crises that fell in the wake of the nationwide depression of the late 1830s. Lane was hardly alone in, as he put it, "having been so overreached"; in addition to his seven lots, the City had foreclosed on more than 120 separate purchases. The list of delinquent buyers was an impressive one; in addition to Lane, it included such prominent citizens as South Side alderman and developer George Morton and aldermanic president (and former street commissioner) Joseph Laveille.[11] The City's attempt to enter the lucrative land development game had, by almost any measure, failed.

In the summer of 1843, a second sale of Common lots was authorized, this one subject to many more conditions than the first. Rather than loosen the restrictions that had forced earlier buyers to default, the City now instituted a series of moves designed to specify more firmly the parameters that best served the "inhabitants of St. Louis." This time, Primm's committee imposed a minimum bid of $25 per acre on all properties. Buyers were required to put down one-fifth of the purchase price; the remainder of the principal was payable in four annual installments, each of which included a steep, 10 percent interest charge. Not only financial details were subject to this kind of careful preplanning; there was, for the first time, an effort made to dictate the placement of the lots offered for sale. The committee listed at first only one-third of the total number of available lots; the remainder were to be offered in increments over the next two years. The location of these initial parcels was determined by an effort to "leave, if possible, alternate lots unsold."[12] Like the eventual system by which federal lands were ceded to railroads across the West, the new sale was intended to leave across the Common a neat checkerboard of developed land that would spur an evenly dispersed pattern of subsequent growth. Once again, however, the operation yielded less than they had hoped for. By fall 1845, the City suspended its land sale one more time; vast areas of the Common now remained in the possession of the municipal government, whose only real plan for the land was to be rid of it.

The failure of the early Common sales owes itself to a number of colliding factors. One problem faced by the committee was, unquestionably, the relatively great distance between Common lots and downtown—although the city was beginning to demonstrate signs of the decentralized, dispersed growth that characterizes it to this day. The financial panic of 1837, already mentioned, hit St. Louis as hard as it did anywhere, and leveraged, speculative investments like real estate were among the first to falter. In the midst of this nervous climate, the City's role in the Common sales remained that of the cautious middleman, rather than of the brash developer. Instead of offering small lots on a grid of closely spaced streets, the City sold large, undivided parcels, with streets spaced a quarter-mile apart. Some of those Common lots returned by default were as large as 32 acres; none was less than an acre and a half. By far the majority were quarter-sized (10-acre) divisions of the 40-acre sections that surveyor Charles DeWard had laid across the land in 1836. The high number of defaults on these lots might have suggested that those St. Louisans able to afford such large parcels had, to a great extent, already purchased them. But state and local officials, badly pressed for funds with which to improve the city's infrastructure (especially after the 1841 expansion, which took in far more acres of land than it did taxpayers), continued to try to sell large, open lots to a small class of buyers rather than creating small, pre-surveyed lots for purchase by a large number of buyers. Governmental reluctance to become more actively involved in shaping and selling public land had ironically had the effect of ensuring the government's continued role in maintaining that land, and of slowing the private land-development process on the South Side.

The failure of so many of the purchasers of the Common land to pay for their properties had left much of the vast tract an undeveloped burden on the city, a useless financial liability rather than a productive source of income. It remained that way until 1854, when the city government abandoned its earlier and relatively more passive role and began to act like a developer. In February of that year, the state legislature had authorized local authorities to form a new Board of the City Common, responsible for "subdivid[ing], prior to their sale," the remaining parcels of Common land.[13] Inherent in the language of this simple mandate for the Second Subdivision of the City Common, as it was called, was an unprecedented commitment on the part of St. Louis's representatives in Jefferson City actively to create—rather than simply to promote—the kind of urban landscape that wealthy citizens around town had begun to develop on their own lands. With the new attention to a smaller scale of development came a new concern for the place of that development in the larger urban landscape. Rather than offer the entire extent of the Common for sale, as it had in 1836, or even limiting the sale to large, alternating lots, as it had in 1843, the City was now authorized to sell only those few portions already divided into smaller blocks and lots.[14]

The form taken by those blocks represented a reconciliation of the existing agricultural scale of the Common divisions with contemporary ideas of the proper scale of urban development. The units of that newer scale—the individual blocks, lots, and streets of the new subdivisions—resembled not the old square city blocks laid out by Laclède and Chouteau, but the more complex larger land divisions of contemporary developers around the city.

The nascent streetscape of the Second Subdivision suggested a number of preconceived ideas about the future shape of city development that were absent from DeWard's original survey. In particular terms, it established a more complex hierarchy, within each block, of public thoroughfare and internal service alley; it confirmed the sanctity of the 25-foot building lot already prevalent in more-developed cities like New York (the original lots of St. Louis had been more than twice that width); and it suggested that the primary flow of traffic through the area would be along north-south streets that headed toward the central corridor, rather than east and west, within the South Side. Just as important, if less concrete, the new subdivision represented two broad shifts in the social-spatial order of the landscape. First, it suggested a landscape not only of equal opportunity but of equal result, a landscape whose final appearance was more clearly conceived than it had been in the past. Second, and related, it demonstrated the use of public power to turn land back into private hands—not the hands of a few investors who happened also to run the city, but of a wide number of the "inhabitants of the city" in whose name the land had first been sold twenty years before.

On the morning of October 24, 1854, curious St. Louisans gathered at the English Cave beer garden, on the South Side, to watch the commencement of bidding on hundreds of lots scattered across some two dozen neatly platted blocks in the central portion of the Common. The City had, of course, auctioned houselots before, but in the past these transactions had consisted of isolated, probated properties, and they took place downtown, on the courthouse steps. Now the auctioneer was bringing his wares directly to the people. He offered title not just to a few parcels of scattered land, but to an entire neighborhood spread over dozens of acres just a minute's walk from where his audience stood, a neighborhood that promised soon to feature streets, alleys, houselots ready for immediate improvement, even a public market. On each one of the auction's four days, the city sold more than two hundred lots at an average of $8 per square foot—far less than property in the heart of the city, but considerably more than undeveloped land nearby.[15]

The Second Subdivision of the Common was a success. In the following spring, the City offered a Third Subdivision, this one consisting of twelve blocks scattered about the western half of the Common, around the far edges of the old Petite Prairie fields (Illustration 4-2). This time, the Board of the Common acted with the acumen of a seasoned real estate agent: on May 2, local citizens awoke to an advertisement in the morning newspaper announcing the "Great Sale of the City Commons To-day"; free horse-drawn omnibuses running throughout the day carried them from downtown and from the Soulard Market to the auction site at the corner of the Gravois and Arsenal Roads. As with the Second Subdivision, Common-land bidders tended to be craft workers and small-time shopkeepers—much the same population that already inhabited closer-in districts on the south side of town. These were not the men who settled their business in the saloon of the Planters' Hotel or in the drawing rooms of Lucas Place, but rather a new class of real estate investors, for whom a 25-foot houselot was an affordable—but not insignificant—gamble. In the course of the day, they had picked up $45,000 worth of property. Within a week, bids were taken for every lot of the Third Subdivision; their total value amounted to $160,000.[16] Unlike purchasers of Common land in decades past, Second and Third Subdivision purchasers owned pieces of the city, not unimproved tracts. If their means for shaping their newly owned space were limited, they nevertheless benefited from a system that made that space accessible, which it had not been before.

The success of the Second and Third Common Subdivisions was both a symptom and a cause of the continued growth and improvement of the city during the 1850s. New Limits street improvements mandated in the 1841 charter had, as the supreme court affirmed, been completed in 1850. Two years later—still before the Common auctions—St. Louisans had already begun to take note of the general rise of property values, particularly in the less-developed southern half of the city. The City's 1854 sales elevated prices within

ILLUSTRATION 4-2.   *Locations of the Second and Third Subdivisions of the St. Louis Common, 1854–55.* The second and third subdivisions, far more limited in scope than the initial offering of Common lands, emulated the scale and marketing techniques of nearby subdivisions. (Courtesy of the author)

the Common itself to a level over ten times that of the previous decade, according to city booster John Hogan's enthusiastic (though not necessarily inaccurate) estimation.[17] Hand in hand with the optimistic vision of the Common Subdivisions came a new momentum in private land sales, in South St. Louis and around the city. Hogan pointed excitedly to a growing general "desire to have a spot, no matter how small, which one may call his own," and reported that, like Thomas Allen, "many large holders of land adjacent to the city have been induced to divide them [*sic*] into lots and sell them at public auction."[18]

A strengthened public commitment to shaping and selling land, then, had worked to diminish the amount of land for which the City was responsible and to catalyze a new pace of development in the private sector. A practical concern for dispensing with unsold land had led city officials to seek the help of a new set of "inhabitants." As Common property left the control of the government, the meaning of the public-private balance of responsibilities and benefits of urban land began to shift. Thanks to a new commitment to exercising public prerogative, the landscape of this large section of the city became more clearly delineated and better prepared for particular uses. At the same time, the new purchasers of Common lots, no longer a small, familiar group of well-off merchants and professionals, embodied the republican ideal of a citizenry embarking on the pursuit of prosperity from an even footing of opportunity, far better than had their counterparts of twenty years earlier. The city was growing, but City control of that growth would not keep pace for long.

The early 1850s were years of grand territorial ambition for Americans. Accompanied by the imperial rhetoric of leaders like Missouri senator (and St. Louis land speculator) Thomas Hart Benton, the nation's recent acquisitions of California, Texas, and the Oregon Territory all signaled Americans' eagerness to see their sovereignty expand across a politically uninterrupted continental landscape. In St. Louis, as in the country at large, territorial expansion could be taken either as an opportunity for social leveling or as a means for securing for the future the advantages derived from existing inequities. Already, before the state supreme court's decision in the *Benoist* case had officially heralded the "closing of the frontier" in terms of earlier expectations of the city's growth, men who stood to benefit from expansion had raised their voices in favor of realizing a kind of manifest destiny for St. Louis. Why not, they argued, anticipate the inevitable growth of the region and incorporate still more of the empty land that lay west of the city limits? As early as 1850, real estate pioneers Hiram Leffingwell and Richard Elliott had proposed the construction of a great road that would ring the city at a radius of roughly four miles from the courthouse; three years later their idea was incorporated into a bill introduced into the state senate by Isaac Sturgeon (a St. Louis land developer), calling for an election on the expansion of the city limits to a line just beyond this projected "Grand Avenue," as it was by now called.[19] Sturgeon's proposal visualized an improbably scaled, 300-foot-wide avenue laid along the gentle ridge line at which the City Common met the eastern border of the former Prairie des Noyers common fields (Illustration 4-3). The road would continue southeasterly from this line to a point on the Mississippi River just north of Carondelet, and northerly to meet the river once again, below the new town of Bremen.

While local boosters like John Hogan agreed that the 1841 city boundary had by this time become little more than an "ideal line," beyond which urban

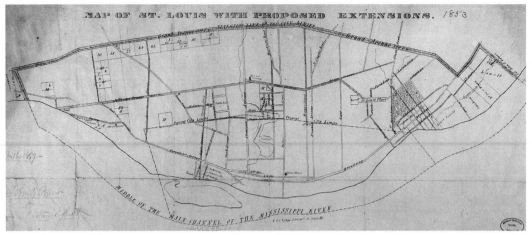

ILLUSTRATION 4-3.   *Proposed Route of Grand Avenue, 1853.* While some St. Louisans opposed the expansion of the city limits to the new line of Grand Avenue, a majority of voters viewed the new street as an opportunity for the city to profit from the growing press for property west from downtown. The proposed Grand Avenue route corresponded with a ridgeline that had formerly defined the eastern limits of the Prairie des Noyers and Grande Prairie common fields. (E. and C. Robyn, 1853, courtesy of Missouri Historical Society)

growth had already crossed, Sturgeon's idea to recognize the political implications of that growth received a mixed reception.[20] Support for Grand Avenue and the expansion of the limits came from a circle of citizens increasingly distant from the Creole and early-American Whig elite who were previously so instrumental in the shaping of the city. Writing to former mayor Jonathan Darby shortly before the election, James Mullholland predicted that "the voice of the plebeians will be for the extension of the City Limits, and the Aristocracy a little opposed to it."[21] Among those "a little opposed" were wealthy landowners like P. Dexter Tiffany, who feared that the City's damage/benefit calculation, by which private lands were appropriated for street rights-of-way, could never compensate them fairly for the lands they stood to lose in the making of this wide thoroughfare.[22] But other landowners, as Mulholland realized, felt differently. To them, the expansion and development of the city carried the promise of cheaper and more plentiful land, of better services and greater convenience to downtown. Like the immigrant brothers Henry and Alexander Kayser, solid Democrats who would before long succeed in entrenching themselves in the city's political machinery, many of this group were relative newcomers, looking for a way to enjoy some of the power and wealth that had accrued to successful developers with deeper roots in the city.[23] The Kaysers, and others like them, lobbied hard for expansion. Their efforts first met with defeat in an 1853 city referendum, then at last proved successful when St. Louisans voted on the matter for a second time, late in the following year, after the successful Second Common Subdivision sale.

In spite of the reservations of the "aristocracy," the expansion had a broad-based appeal that helped to strengthen new ties between the public and private sectors. It constituted a victory not only for aspiring landowners but for the men who ran the machinery of municipal government: they broadened their tax base and increased their power over a large area that had belonged, economically and geographically, to the fast-growing city but had remained under the foreign control of the county. Nevertheless, the price of conquest was great. The city's hard-pressed system of infrastructural improvements, which had barely caught up with the 1841 expansion, was suddenly faced with nearly ten additional square miles of broken, untouched land. As of the morning after election day, the city was, once again, an unfinished place. The task of seeing to its improvement would inevitably fall, once again, on private developers with private agendas.

The Shape of the Development and Construction Process After 1854

Through the Common subdivisions and the expansion of the city limits, the municipal government of the 1850s demonstrated its power and desire to play an active role in the development of urban space—a desire embedded in St. Louisans' continually reconstructed memory of their colonial past. Yet the organs of public power at the time were limited—as they were in every growing American city—in the degree to which they could control or direct power in a highly fluid social and economic environment. The City's public-space initiatives in this period were therefore largely limited to throwing open additional public land for private development. The presumed beneficiaries of that strengthened role were, by mid-century, not the self-described "aristocracy" but a newly diversified class of landowners and developers who had not before played a significant part in the physical growth of the city. The landscape envisioned by the government officials who set that process in motion was, perhaps as much by virtue of the lack of any clear plan as by some clearly felt ideology, a landscape of equal opportunity and of uniform growth. It presumed a simple and straightforward partnership between government (which conferred the benefits of private property) and citizens (who returned the favor through improving the landscape and paying the City for their benefits).

But the more the city grew, the more the task of developing its spaces returned from the province of the municipal government to that of the individuals who bought, sold, subdivided, and built and dwelt on its land. Private initiative, rather than public regulation, held the upper hand in determining the city's form into the twentieth century. The job of first taking unimproved property and making it ready for development, then of developing that property and making it ready for habitation, involved a number of separate stages. City-building activities not only reflected but actively shaped the ways in which St. Louisans related to one another during a period of rapid growth and change. In the pages that follow, I review some of the most important of those stages: subdivision, lending and finance, the real estate business, and construction labor.

Common to all of the segments of the city-building process in this period is the three-way shift described above: from a period marked by a relatively simple delineation of activities and agents, through a time of breakdown and fragmentation, to a final stage of consolidation and centralized control. As city-building diverged increasingly from the purview and control of city government (which lent an encompassing sense of community, or "public interest," to anything carried out in its name), the matter of defining communities through land development grew more complex. The key to understanding that complexity lies in the overlap between the general, structural dynamic of the city-building process, on the one hand, and the particular constraints and opportunities offered by the local landscape of St. Louis, on the other. Both of those levels—structural and specific—operated to transform the seemingly completed city of 1850 into a city of unreconciled extremes and unanswered questions in 1910.

Stage One: Simplicity

Private subdivision activity, depending as it did upon the traditionally socially exclusive privilege of land ownership, was perhaps the clearest example of the simplicity and homogeneity that characterized the private city-building process at mid-century. Considered from the standpoint of the social profile of developers and their relation to the lands that they dedicated, it is apparent that, outside of the Common subdivisions, such activity continued through the 1850s to maintain basically the same character as in previous decades: it was carried out by representatives of a relatively narrow cross-section of the city's population, most of whom lived far from their actual subdivisions (Illustration 4-4). Of the forty-three names connected with subdivision deeds in South St. Louis between 1854 and 1865, over half resided north of the area, within the more densely populated central corridor (which extended north from the railroad tracks that covered the former site of Chouteau's Pond to Morgan Street—later Delmar Avenue), at the time of their subdivision. Only three lived directly on the property that they dedicated for subdivision, five lived south of the railroad tracks but outside of the core of South St. Louis, and two lived on the north side.[24] The typical developer was either a merchant or an attorney who lived downtown. Overall, the developers of the 1850s and 1860s retained a conspicuous connection to city office: six (John Sarpy, Henry Lynch, Edward Haren, John Corcoran,

Lafayette Ave.

A. South Compton Hill Addition (Ariadne Miller) (1859)
B. James B. Eads Subdivision (1854)
C. Thomas Targee Estate Subdivision (1860)
D. Sol Smith's Subdivision (1865)
E. Lafayette Addition (C. Gibson) (1859)
F. Nicholas Durand Estate Subdivision (1859)
G. (City of St. Louis) (1860)
H. Franklin A. Dick's Subdivision (1860)
I. Third Subdivision of the City Common (1855)
J. Kingsbury's Addition (Jules Kingsbury, Alfred Waterman) (1856)
K. Julia G. Cabanne's Second Addition (1855)
L. Oliver Quinette, James Eads, William S. Nelson Subdivisions (1857)
M. Baldwin Estate Subdivision (1865)
N. John McNeil and Charles E. Hart's Subdivision (1859)
O. Labadie and Lynch's Addition (Henry, George Lynch; Nicholas Demenil) (1856)
P. Corcoran's Addition (Robert et al. Corcoran; Ellen Gorman) (1861)
Q. Hardage Lane Estate, First Subdivision of the Lami Tract (1863)

R. Thomas Nelson, Nathan Holmes, Thomas McMartin Subdivision (1859)
S. Ida Warren's Addition (1864)
T. Arsenal Addition (J. S. Dougherty, Joseph B. Wells) (1855)
U. Continuation of Arsenal Addition (Julia Walker, Gilbert Spier, George W. Bull) (1854)
V. Second Subdivision of the City Common (1855)
W. Edward Haren's Addition (1854)
X. Oakland Addition (Peter Camden, Samuel C. Davis, Elihu Shepherd) (1864)
Y. Adam Lemp and August Kaeckel's Subdivision (1855)
Z. William Wible's Subdivision (1855)
AA. Martha Bank's Subdivision (1860)
BB. Henry Belt and John Priest's Subdivision (1859)
CC. Henry T. Blow's Subdivision (1856)
DD. Alex Kayser's Subdivision (1859)
EE. Elihu Shepherd's Subdivision (1860)
FF. Louis Bogy, Eugene Miltenberger, and ( )Sarpy's Addition (1855)
GG. Edward Delano's Addition (1859)

ILLUSTRATION 4-4. *South St. Louis Subdivisions, 1854–65.* Early South Side subdivisions were developed as investments by a socially and politically prominent group of developers who tended to live close to downtown. (Courtesy of the author)

Henry Belt, and Lewis Bogy) served at some time in either the city council or the board of delegates.[25]

With the continued spread of subdivision came a growing need to organize and promote the sale of land, and with that organization would eventually come the means for spreading land sales beyond the narrow limits of the community that dominated land development in the city's early years. The practice of selling property in a systematic way, and of relying on it as a source of income, rather than simply as one method for accumulating capital outside of wages or other investments, did not have deep roots in St. Louis. While property sales and purchases had often had a frankly speculative character even prior to the American takeover in 1804, the idea of the city as a commodity— a collection of parcels waiting to be bought and sold—was not widely shared before the 1850s. The nascent real estate industry was the province of a handful of well-financed operators. The first office explicitly devoted to buying and selling real estate appeared in 1849, when the partnership of Hiram Leffingwell and Richard Smith Elliott opened for business.[26] The most salient change represented by this largely nominal event was the beginning of an effort to coordinate local property transactions and to provide a common forum in which they might be made. Until Leffingwell and Elliott's short-lived *Real Estate Register* appeared in 1850, the only way for a potential property buyer to discover what land might be available was to scour the daily newspapers or to show up at the door of the courthouse, where land auctions were held. The *Register* purported to condense this information into one source—a public service that promoted private profit, since it served primarily as an advertisement for Leffingwell and Elliott's own ventures. Such blurred lines between advertisement and public service were not uncommon in the early years of the local real estate industry; in like manner did Richard Goodwin, advertising his new Real Estate Exchange in 1859, offer a less than altruistic solution to the alleged problem "of going from one agent to another" in search of property. Goodwin's Exchange was, like Leffingwell and Elliott's, a means of encouraging more business for himself. It offered customers a service that would become increasingly necessary in the fast-growing city. The fact that only a few men ventured to provide that service before the Civil War, however, speaks both for the continued ease of direct transactions made between buyers and sellers and, perhaps, for the slow development of a more abstract sense of land as a marketable commodity with an identity extricable from that of the particular person who offered it for sale.

As real estate became increasingly well-developed and regulated, so too did the banking and lending system to which it was tied. Here, too, the formalization or elaboration of the trade initially resulted in the emergence of an extremely constricted industry, managed by a small number of people who handled a wide range of problems. For years, only one bank, the Bank of Missouri, was legally chartered by the state; its constitutionally mandated conservative lending policies had driven borrowers to a small number of private banking houses that operated independently of state limitations. Legislation at last caught up with practice in 1857, when St. Louis representatives in the state senate pushed through the General Banking Law, which granted charters to ten independent banks, totaling thirty branches. While the new law seemed to promise a widening of the publicly regulated sources of credit available to St. Louisans, it turned out to be an experiment whose time had not yet come. Just as the reins were loosened on state banking, economic panic hit Missouri; a number of private houses were forced to close, and the state-chartered banks were suspended three years after their inception.[27] The credit industry remained the domain of a small group, operating largely free of regulations.

Like real estate and finance, the ultimate stage of property development—building construction—was slow to leave behind the early-nineteenth-century legacy of a handful of active agents handling a wide range of tasks. The principles of cooperation and non-specialization in the construction industry still prevailed in the South Side in the 1850s. The account books of Henry Hagan, a St. Louis house carpenter, show that he regularly contracted a number of jobs beyond basic framing, including laying finished flooring and making doors. Hagan performed in a variety of roles, not only for his employers but for his crew: he sold them their supplies, their food, and their tobacco.[28] Orsemus Robinson, a carpenter hired by the Soulard family to build a row of houses on their property in 1842, was likewise responsible for far more than basic framing: he built stairs, hung doors and windows, and painted the rooms. Like other carpenters of the time, his labor was rewarded through in-kind payment. Instead of cash, he was paid in the form of deeds to other lots on the Soulard property, an arrangement that allowed Robinson the opportunity to expand the scope of his services still further, becoming a developer as well as a builder.[29]

By the time Robinson went to work for the Soulards, however, local building practice was beginning to be transformed in St. Louis, as elsewhere, by specialization, by an increasingly pronounced division of labor, and by the growing acceptance of a cash economy. The local signs of this change were still isolated, but they were nevertheless prophetic. In May 1840, for example, the newly formed Journeymen Carpenters' Society voted to strike for a ten-hour day. The carpenters expressed a view of labor relations in the building industry that belied the seeming simplicity of Hagan's or Robinson's operations: "there will, as a matter of course, always be a struggle," they announced in a published report, between laborers and bosses. The relation between those two classes was too abstract, and too deeply entrenched, to be altered within the existing structure of construction work. It was instead at root a monetary relation, based on the necessarily unequal distribution of wealth. Since wealth, as the society's spokesmen wrote, "creates to itself an artificial basis of power, both in a social and political point of view," their only path to greater rights lay in the fundamental redistribution of wages between boss and worker.[30] The very idea of seeing construction as something other than a simple and relatively cooperative process—or of seeing labor unrest as something other than a basic resistance to hard work—was anathema to most St. Louisans—particularly before the arrival of the "'48'ers"—German radicals who later exerted a marked effect on the city's political and cultural life. The editors of the *Missouri Republican* responded vehemently to the journeymen's radical stance, calling them "mere adventurers—men who know not what toil, either corporeal or mental, is." They went on to warn of the consequences once "the principle be established, that the relation between the contractor and his hands is a political one, and that their interests are antagonistic to the man who has the work to do."[31] The new union's failure to establish a stable organization in the coming years testified to the fact that that principle was as yet far from established. As was the case with other aspects of the development process during the antebellum period, construction was perceived not as an activity dictated by abstract relationships or governable by public regulations, but as a concrete task carried out for particular ends, by men who knew one another and whose separate interests worked toward a common goal.[32]

Stage 2: Specialization

The sheer rapidity with which the city was growing made some kind of breakdown in this simple formula inevitable. Important changes in the municipal government's own role in cultivating private development, beginning in the mid-1850s, heralded the arrival of a period of increasing complexity and specialization in the development process. The decision to try a new approach in selling the Common lands, combined with the extension of the city limits to encourage the development of those lands and the property around them, had had the effect of multiplying the amount of space available to a wide cross-section of the city's population. With this renewed public commitment to surveying and opening land came an accelerated development in the private means of improving it.

Although the Second and Third Common Subdivisions and the 1855 expansion helped to speed the rate at which South Side lands were subdivided, they did little in the short term to alter the general character of the community of people responsible for those nearby developments. In the following decade, however—between the end of the Civil War and the city's separation from St. Louis County in 1875—the social profile of South St. Louis subdividers began to change. Thirty-one subdivisions were dedicated between 1866 and 1875 (Illustration 4-5); the most striking feature of the list of forty-two names discovered in connection with these developments is the end of the overwhelming preponderance of central-corridor addresses among this group;

ILLUSTRATION 4-5. *South St. Louis Subdivisions, 1866–75.* After the Civil War, as the development process dispersed among a larger group of agents than had characterized earlier decades, subdivision developers were far likelier to actually live on the property that they opened for development. (Courtesy of the author)

A. Compton Hill Place (Felix Coste, Chas. Hornbostel, Rbt. Heinrichs) (1868)
B. City Subdivision (1870)
C. Southeast Compton Hill (Julius Pitzman) (1873)
D. Partition of Chambers Estate (Jane, Mary, B. M. Chambers) (1872)
E. Mullanphy's Subdivision of Block 12, City Commons (1866)
F. Thomas Allen's Western Addition (1869)
G. Mary Bingham's Subdivision of City Commons (1866)
H. Nicholson Place (David Nicholson) (1875)
I. Thomas Allen's Central Addition (1869)
J. City Subdivision of the Durand Tract (1866)
K. Reilly's Summit (William Switzer, John Platt) (1869)
L. Peter Weizenaecker Estate Subdivision (1872)
M. O. M. Tucker's Subdivision of the Barsaloux Tract (1869)
N. John Daggett's Second Subdivision of the Barsaloux Tract (1870)
O. Joseph J. Clark's Subdivision (1867)
P. J. B. Bowlin's Subdivision (1866)
Q. City Subdivision of the Durand Tract (1866)

R. Charless Garden Subdivision (Charlotte Charless, Louis LeBourgeois) (1873)
S. Eva Muegge's Subdivision (1866)
T. Jacob J. and Jesse G. Engel's Subdivision (1869)
U. Ferdinand Provenchere's Addition (1866)
V. Gustave Wiebert's Addition (1871)
W. Schild's Subdivision (William Schild et al.) (1872)
X. Oakland Addition (Nathaniel Cole, Ephraim Obear) (1872)
Y. John Withnell's Subdivision of the City Common (1870)
Z. John F. Homann and Co.'s Subdivision (1867)
AA. City Subdivision of Block 70, St. Louis Commons (1871)
BB. Elbreder Estate Subdivision (George, Henry, Catherine Elbreder) (1875)
CC. Betts' Subdivision (William Betts et al.) (1875)
DD. Francis A. Quinette's Subdivision (1869)
EE. Zepp and Wolff's Subdivision (Philip, Henry Zepp; Louis Wolff) (1866)
FF. Adolph Heinicke's Subdivision (1875)
GG. Peter Kenrick's Subdivision (1867)
HH. Henry A. Clover's Subdivision (1869)

barely one-third of them lived north of the railroad tracks. A few lived south of the tracks, north of the heart of South St. Louis (generally in the wealthier neighborhoods north of Lafayette Avenue), while half of the total lived directly within the area—five of them on the property that they dedicated for subdivision. If the decade included the huge Central and Western Additions of Thomas Allen (extensions of his earlier developments of the 1840s), it also saw the dedication of single-block subdivisions made by men like Adolph Heinicke, a china maker, or Henry Elbreder, a truck farmer, on the land surrounding their own homes. Professionally, a similar transition was evidenced; merchants now numbered in the minority, and in marked contrast to earlier South Side developers, there were no attorneys. By contrast, the group included a bricklayer, a teamster, and two gardeners. Direct links with city government also began to dissolve in the post-1865 period. Only two of the subdividers (Allen and John Daggett) held an elected city office at any time in their life. Increasingly, it was a connection to the land itself that formed the primary common bond between these disparate developers.[33]

In the 1876–85 decade, as subdivision was slowed considerably by the nationwide economic depression, the changing social profile of subdividers continued in the direction set after the Civil War. Ten subdivisions were dedicated during this period (Illustration 4-6); seven of the ten individuals identified in connection with those subdivisions resided on the property that they dedicated. In summary, then, significant portions of the landscape of South St. Louis were beginning once again to bear a personal, rather than strictly commodified, relation to the lives of the people who developed them. That connection was now less likely to be seen in the inherited estates of men like Thomas Allen than it was in the small tracts, sometimes consisting of only a handful of houselots, of former Common land, now owned by a wide cross-section of South St. Louisans. The structure of the land-development community had loosened considerably from its earlier highly defined character to include a range of men and women that more closely resembled the population of the area at large.

As St. Louis's population continued to multiply, and as subdivision activity proceeded apace (not only on the South Side but throughout the city), real estate activity assumed an ever-greater role in the city's economy. The period between the Civil War and the depression of the 1870s had been marked by a steady rise in the ratio of the value of personal property to that of real property. After the mid-1870s, however, the direction of the ratio reversed: the depression damaged citywide real estate values less, proportionately, than it did personal property values, and real property value proceeded to climb back at a faster rate to its earlier level. Growth in real property valuation continued to outstrip growth in personal property until after the turn of the twentieth century.

With the increasing importance of property investment, and the growth of opportunities spurred by the city's continuously expanding population, greater

A. Roe Place (Ephraim Obear, James Sands, Julius Pitzman) (1885)
B. Richard Graham Estate Addition to Compton Hill (James Graham et al.) (1877)
C. Boyce's Lafayette Avenue Addition (John O. Delany, Mary Boyce) (1879)
D. William V. M. Reilly's Subdivision (1883)
E. Tower Grove Park and Grand Avenue Addition (James Russell Estate) (1881)
F. James Macadara's Subdivision (1885)

G. Auguste, Frederick, and Wm. Ewing's Subdivision of the Vasquez Tract (1885)
H. E. W. Meier's Subdivision (1876)
I. Louis Wolf Estate Subdivision (1877)
J. Laura Schroeter's Subdivision (1878)
K. Eloisa Kayser's Subdivision (1885)
L. Eloisa Kayser's Subdivision (1885)
M. Thomas Kerr Estate Subdivision (1876)
N. John C., T. R. H. Smith, Richardson Estate Subdivision (1876)

ILLUSTRATION 4-6. *South St. Louis Subdivisions, 1876–85.* The 1870s and 1880s saw a continuation of the trend toward increasing geographical and personal ties between developers and their subdivisions. (Courtesy of the author) numbers of men turned to the real estate trade as a profession. In contrast to the organizational simplicity that had characterized the profession in Leffing-well's and Elliott's day, real estate investment was now a professionalized and more locally specialized activity, involving dozens of agents around the city. As the number of men going into the business grew, the need for some coordination of their activities became more acute. At last, in 1877, twenty-nine firms united to form the St. Louis Real Estate Exchange, an organization chartered to "extend the scope, multiply the facilities, promote the activity and elevate the tone and character of the real estate business in St. Louis."[34] In the same year, the municipal assembly established licensing fees for real estate brokers and agents, acknowledging their professional legitimacy and bringing them on a legal par with other, more established businesses.[35]

The system of credit that underlay real estate investment was also transformed in a manner consistent with the growing complexity and specificity of property development between the 1860s and 1880s. At first, it seemed that banks would fill the need created by this expanding area of investment, as a postbellum period of lax regulation promised to put money in circulation virtually at the borrower's whim. Although private banking never regained its earlier prominence as a source of credit after the panic of the 1850s, state-chartered savings banks came back more popular, and less restricted in their practices, than ever before. Between 1865 and 1873, forty-eight banks were chartered in St. Louis alone; they were, needless to say, built more on credit than on specie. Only 10 percent of their allowable capital needed to be paid in at any given time, and bankers were allowed to loan money at interest rates of up to 12 percent. The spiraling cycle of credit at last came crashing down in the mid-1870s; this time, a new state law (passed amidst the labor turmoil of 1877) put an end to freewheeling banking practices. Under its terms, banks in big cities like St. Louis were required to begin with a minimum capitalization level of $100,000; of this amount, a full half had to be paid in at the outset. Tellingly, the banks were further forbidden from speculating in real estate. The effect of these measures was marked: sixty banks were operating in Missouri in 1874; only twenty-five were open by 1880.[36]

Was there any alternative for the prospective landowner seeking to finance his purchase, particularly for the great numbers of immigrant working men and women who sought to buy a home in poorer areas like South St. Louis? Even before the crisis of 1877 had precipitated tighter restrictions on capitalization and lending, the bank credit so easily acquired by capitalists and wealthy speculators was often unavailable to poorer borrowers who had little collateral with which to secure a loan. The unavailability of chartered banking services did not, however, leave such homeowners unable to forge their own particular communities around the financing process. The most frequent solution to the problem had been to acquire a mortgage directly from the seller. This might be supplemented with a riskier (and costlier) second mortgage from a relative, neighbor, or local businessman. The potential benefits of organizing this informal system of finance were too great to go unnoticed. Occasional efforts to reach smaller borrowers had been made in St. Louis through the years; organizations like the Citizens' Mutual Savings Fund and Loan Association had advertised in the 1850s to "tradesmen, mechanics, and such as were, from circumstances, excluded from the benefits and advantages of other moneyed institutions."[37] Such businesses allowed workers to acquire the right to borrow cash by investing as little as one dollar a month in "shares"—essentially savings certificates worth a fixed par value, most often $200. Investors earned 6 percent interest on their shares, but paid a steep 25 percent "premium" for the privilege of taking out a loan.

The principle behind such cooperative savings associations was essentially the same as that which underlay an institution that became increasingly popular in St. Louis in the wake of the credit crackdown of the 1870s: the building and loan society. The building and loan systematized the informal communities of borrowing and lending that had sprung up outside of the bank-based lending industry in earlier years. It was essentially a financing instrument set up by men seeking to promote housing development. As one journal of the time noted, these men might be employers working to "obtain homes for men employed in one or two factories, machine shops or railroad shops in the immediate neighborhood," or like the officers of the Park Building and Loan, chartered in St. Louis in 1890, they might represent various elements of the building industry.[38] Frequently, the building and loan was an adjunct of a small real estate business; by providing the developer with a ready pool of capital, it guaranteed him a source of credit with which to entice home-buyers.

In a manner that presaged the imminent consolidation of other areas of the increasingly dispersed city-building process, the building and loan was an enticing investment not only for home-buyers but for others as well. Largely unregulated in their early years, they offered a higher rate of return than government bonds, while their reliance on real property allowed them to project an image of being every bit as safe.[39] Indeed, by 1892, the state Bureau of Statistics of Labor counted more "capitalists" and "professionals" among shareholders than "mechanics" or "laborers." Investors found no shortage of institutions in which to place their cash: in St. Louis alone, more than two hundred building and loans were operational that year, representing an estimated 30,000 investors.[40] Nevertheless, the typical borrower remained a workingman of modest means. The average loan as of the mid-1890s amounted to somewhere between $2,500 and $2,800; if we consider the average size of a first mortgage during this period to have been roughly half the purchase price of a home, then the typical building-and-loan-financed home cost somewhere in the neighborhood of $5,000, a figure considered roughly appropriate to a modest, custom-built house in the late 1800s.[41] Wealthier buyers with sufficient cash or collateral to borrow from a conventional bank would, need-less to say, prefer such premium-free loans to those of the building and loan associations. Increasingly, then, the lending market was split into several tiers, each tailored to fit the needs or means of a different class of homeowner.

As this review suggests, while the numbers and types of people involved in some way in subdivision, real estate, and finance continued to grow, the reg-ulations and institutions that governed their activities were adjusted to lend increasing structure and predictability to the process. Where the gentleman's agreement, the handshake, and the promise may have offered sufficient struc-ture within the world of downtown bankers and lawyers (or, conversely, within the world of the immigrant home-builder and the money-lending cor-ner grocer), the regular interaction of people from different social classes or neighborhood roots demanded order and rules to substitute for that which might no longer be intrinsically understood.

Nowhere was this formalizing tendency truer than in the construction industry, where, as we have seen, an awareness of the potential effects of spe-cialization and diversification was evident as early as the 1840s. Early efforts to establish a firmer division of responsibility in the building process had come not only from the bottom (as in the Journeymen Carpenters' unsuc-cessful strike) but from the top as well. In 1858, thirteen men met in the office of architect Thomas Walsh to "form an organization of the Professional Archi-tects of St. Louis, to protect and assist each other in the elevation of its mem-bers."[42] Like architects in larger eastern cities of the same time, the members of the fledgling St. Louis Architectural Association sought to restrict and reg-ularize the building profession, and to establish the architect, rather than the contracting carpenter, as the principal liaison between a client and the men who built for him.[43] The number of architects practicing in St. Louis was not greatly affected by this tentative promotion before the busy years of the 1880s (that is, around the time that the other aspects of the development process also began to diversify); however, after that time, the local ranks of the pro-fession began to increase at a rate of 50 percent each decade.[44]

While the architectural profession in St. Louis took an increasingly active role in the construction of public buildings and expensive residences in years to come, it remained largely uninvolved in the construction of the vast major-ity of the city's homes—those costing less than $5,000. In the meantime, res-idential construction of even a modest sort acquired a complexity and level of coordination that had been absent in the 1840s. In contrast to the com-prehensive skills offered by Henry Hagan and Orsemus Robinson, the con-tractor of even an inexpensive home in the 1870s and 1880s might have spent the better part of his efforts coordinating the labor of more than a dozen dif-ferent kinds of workers. The account books of the St. Louis builder Charles Jones, for example, are filled with the records of his payment to everyone from excavators and stairbuilders to plasterers, wood grainers, and roofers.[45]

The *Building Trades Journal*, which supplied investors and contractors with news of the local construction scene, warned its readers in 1886 that "the operation of building is of such a character that one man cannot afford to become a professor of all the trades connected therewith." The advertisements that filled the pages of that journal corroborated its editors' advice; they offered the services of glaziers, plumbers, gas fitters, painters, and a variety of other tradesmen.[46]

To the consternation of the editors of the *Building Trades Journal*, one of the consequences of that specialization was the unionization of each level of the construction labor hierarchy, from hod carriers and millworkers up to the more exclusive ranks of bricklayers and stonemasons. In contrast to the first furtive and isolated efforts of the Journeymen Carpenters, unionization had become a powerful and ubiquitous fact of the St. Louis labor scene. Union activity in St. Louis—led by a strong German element—had helped to win the eight-hour day shortly after the Civil War, and to make St. Louis the most heavily affected of all American cities in the labor unrest of 1877.[47] Despite the generally conceded failure of local workers to win significant gains from their successful shutdown of the city that summer, unions—in particular, construction unions—became increasingly active and outspoken. Each May, as building activity was set to roll into high gear, one or more of these groups could be counted on to announce a work stoppage in support of higher wages, reduced hours, or both.[48] Their proliferation after the 1870s, like the contemporaneous appearance of building-and-loan societies or the increasingly common dedication of small, owner-occupied subdivisions, bespoke the continuing trend toward specificity and dispersal among both the agents and the intended beneficiaries of city-building.

A brief look at one of the oldest and most prominent of those unions active on the South Side—the Bricklayers—indicates that the union's originally intended function of codifying and protecting a traditional, skilled trade in the face of a growing labor force shifted somewhat as those larger changes unfolded. Where it had in its earliest years represented well the general, increasing fragmentation of building and development among small groups of like-minded individuals, the union's activities by the turn of the century pointed toward a new paradigm of city-building in St. Louis, one that would become as obvious in other aspects of the process as it was in the construction industry.[49]

Citywide, the Bricklayers' Union was by no means the largest of the many construction unions active in the late nineteenth century; its membership numbered just over one-third that of the carpenters in the busy years of the early 1890s.[50] In spite of their limited numbers, however, bricklayers enjoyed an advantageous position in the labor market. In a city where local soil conditions and strict fire codes combined to mandate brick construction for all but the poorest and most distant residential areas, the skills of a trained bricklayer were in consistently high demand; union members earned a higher wage than did any other construction workers.[51] In addition to protecting working conditions and ensuring good wages, the union's division into a handful of neighborhood-based locals allowed it to serve a social function as well. Early local meetings were as likely to include discussion of an upcoming picnic, or the appropriation of money for a former member's funeral, as they were to address problems at the job site. Local No. 3, the union's South Side branch, had an almost entirely German-ethnic membership. Founded in 1872, the local conducted its business entirely in German until 1879, after which time it used both German and English. After abandoning this badge of ethnic exclusivity, it continued to concentrate on maintaining an equally strong occupational exclusivity; its membership remained intent on keeping their ranks tightly controlled and on separating themselves from the rest of the building trades. In the flush years of the 1880s, the local's minutes reflect an overriding concern with such basic problems as regulating the term of apprenticeship, keeping out stonemasons who wished to join their union, and forbidding membership to any bricklayer who worked in a contracting capacity.[52]

In the 1890s, that exclusivity no longer served as effectively to ensure the well-being of union members. Local No. 3 devoted itself ever less to the task of maintaining bricklaying as an exclusive craft, and ever more to the necessity of keeping its members well-fed in the wake of hard times and an increasingly diversified construction industry. As work became scarce in the wake of the 1893 depression, union members turned in desperation to jobs that paid substandard wages. One walking delegate in 1895 encountered a number of such men working on the South Side; one told him "to tell the Union for him to go to hell," and another announced that "he did not intend to quit and did not care if the Union did fire him."[53] When the "dull times" deepened, members voted to allow themselves to work for whoever would hire them, at whatever wage they could find. Bricklayers like Joseph Hardnacke, who had left the union to become contractors, were allowed to rejoin if their ventures proved unsuccessful.[54] As the local relaxed its rules to meet the demands of the times, it also dropped some of the separatist policies that had characterized its earlier years. In 1897 the union's executive committee ordered it to drop entirely any use of German in its printed materials; in 1898, the three St. Louis locals combined and signed a single agreement with the "boss bricklayers" association (one that forced them to settle for a wage of 50 cents per hour, less than they had earned before the depression), and at last joined the citywide Building Trades Council, which had sought their membership since its formation in 1886.[55]

The local's strength (or at least its security) now came through casting its lot with a wider circle of fellow workers, rather than maintaining its members' exclusive status as a rarefied breed of craftsmen. To say that the bricklayers' shift in practice and emphasis represented the stirrings of a heightened

class consciousness, or the foundations of a new radicalism, would be erro-
neous, particularly in light of the subsequent conservative role taken by the
Building Trades Council on the local political scene. Instead, construction
workers continued, as always, to seek job security by the most effective means
possible. If they chose to band together across the boundaries of their particular trades, that new organizing tactic was at least as much a product of the
increasing consolidation of the building process and the demands of contractors as it was the reflection of an autonomous sense of class solidarity.[56]

Stage 3: Consolidation

With the increasingly powerful boss bricklayers' union and the Building Trades
Council, there appeared in 1895 another construction organization, the Master Builders' Association, whose existence also pointed toward a new level of
coordination and organization emanating from the top of the local building
industry. The Master Builders' Association, which drew its charter membership from the ranks of the city's carpenters, owed its existence to a traditional split within that trade between those who "contracted" directly with
landowners and those who worked under the supervision of other builders.
In the years before the association was formed, that split had grown increasingly wide in St. Louis, and increasingly set in its profile. In addition to coordinating the numerous tasks involved in home-building, contractors were
also charged, after 1882, with providing plans and specifications for all new
buildings to city building inspectors; they therefore had to be conversant with
every aspect of the constantly changing construction process, as well as to be
literate and able to draw according to a common standard.[57]

The legal framework within which building took place tightened considerably in the late nineteenth century. Where early building laws had related
almost entirely to fire safety, they were eventually dictated by a separate building department; meanwhile, major expansions of the building law—in 1882,
1897, and 1905—regulated every aspect of construction from foundations to
chimneys.[58] The attitudinal change that came with these increasing responsibilities was evident in the master builders' original charter, which reflected an
approach to construction that differed consciously and markedly from the practical concerns that preoccupied the carpenters' or bricklayers' unions at the
same time. Rather than begin with a set of rules regarding wages and working
conditions, as the unions were forced to do, the master builders vowed to
develop a code of ethics and to establish a library that might "promote a knowl-
edge of literature, history, and science as relates to building."[59] Like the members of the St. Louis Architectural Association four decades earlier, they
extolled the virtues of a generalized approach to construction. This generalized approach was made possible by their own relative social exclusivity and
by their privileged standing in the hierarchy of the construction process.

Whatever the attraction of gaining new insight into literature, history, and science, there was a steady and dramatic increase in the numbers of men who listed themselves as "contractors" in the city directory through the late nineteenth and early twentieth centuries. Even before the establishment of the Master Builders' Association, the title conferred upon its bearer an occupational status that their previously listed profession (in most cases, carpenter or bricklayer) had not. As the numbers of these self-defined building professionals multiplied, the number of listings for carpenters and bricklayers slowed and eventually decreased.[60] By 1910, to call oneself a carpenter or bricklayer implied a highly specialized skill and a status as a wage earner rather than as one who established his own pay scale according to the work at hand. Listing one's trade as "contractor," on the other hand, indicated that one had joined a newly strengthened stratum of actors in the city-building process: a class of men whose comprehensive approach to development was closely protected from access by great numbers of people (whether by virtue of a new job title or, more concretely, by the necessary possession of greater educational or financial means).

The shift toward the dominance of a better-defined, more professionalized class of developer in South St. Louis during this period was most evident spatially in the handful of enormous subdivisions that began to appear around the area's western edge at Grand Avenue in the final years of the century. These and other similar subdivisions of the time were the products not of long-time property owners but of professional real estate men. In the 1886–1895 decade, six of the twenty developers of new South St. Louis subdivisions (Illustration 4-7) were listed in city directories as real estate agents—a larger number than that represented by any other profession. A substantial tract on the west side of Grand, long the estate of Thomas Allen's wealthy in-laws, the Russell family, offers a clear example of the new developers at work. This vast property was subdivided through the 1880s and 1890s not by the Russells but by the Connecticut Mutual Life Insurance Company, which had long maintained an office in St. Louis but only in recent years extended its interests in any systematic way to real estate development.[61] The company's thirty-block Tower Grove Park and Grand Avenue Addition, laid out upon what had been the Russells' lands, pointed the way to a new scale of subdivision, one made possible through access to corporate capital. The provision of utilities and services, the improvement of streets and alleys, even the appearance of the buildings to be erected and the uses to which they might be put—all were increasingly likely, by the turn of the century, to have been established before a single houselot was sold.[62]

After a subdivision was dedicated, the same phenomena of scale and planning were evident in the manner in which land and buildings were advertised and sold to the public. By about 1893, the success of the real estate trade was reflected in the large, boldface advertisements that realtors placed in the daily

Lafayette Ave.   Lafayette Ave.

Grand Ave.

Jefferson Ave.

Gravois Ave.

S. Broadway (Carondelet Rd.)

Grand Ave.

Gravois Ave.

Jefferson Ave.

Chippewa St.

Pre-1886 Subdivisions

1886–1895 Subdivisions

A. Compton Heights (Henry Haarstick, Julius Pitzman) (1890)
B. Compton Heights First Addition (Haarstick, Pitzman) (1895)
C. Adele Morrison's Subdivision (1887)
D. City of St. Louis (1890)
E. Weiss' Subdivision of City Block 1436 (1892)
F. Shenandoah Place (1891)
G. Gustave Mechin's Subdivision (1893)
H. Wm. H. Gummersell's Subdivision of City Block 1434 (1891)
I. David Nicholson's Compton Hill Addition (Nicholson, Pitzman, John Tracy) (1889)
J. Sarpy's Subdivision of City Block 1379–80 (Armand, Virginia Peugnet) (1889)
K. Sarpy's Subdivision of City Block 1351 (Peugnet) (1889)
L. Sarpy's Subdivision of City Block 1381 (Peugnet) (1886)
M. Switzer Place (Isaiah Steedman) (1892)
N. Wilhelm's Höhe Second Addition (Caspar Vielhaber et al.) (1891)

O. Wilhelm's Höhe (Vielhaber et al.) (1891)
P. Charless Garden Subdivision, Am. Plat (Charlotte Charless, Louis LeBourgeois) (1887)
Q. Arsenal Heights (1892)
R. St. Wenceslaus Subdivision (1892)
S. Gravois Place (George Parker, Charles Russell) (1891)
T. Cherokee Place (Louis Grund, Henry Hiemenz) (1891)
U. Cornet's Subdivision (Henry L., Ann Cornet) (1890)
V. John Scullin's Subdivision of City Block 1511 (1890)
W. Lorenzo E. Anderson's Subdivision (1890)
X. Benton Park Addition (Ernst H. Vordtriede) (1888)
Y. Old English Cave Addition (Herman Stamm) (1888)
Z. Concordia Place (L. T. Hammer, F. Hohenschield) (1890)
AA. Kayser's Subdivision of City Block 1628 (1887)
BB. Adolph Heinicke's Resubdivision (1887)
CC. Coon's Subdivision (Mary Way, Mary Derby) (1888)
DD. Eloisa Kayser's Subdivision (1887)

ILLUSTRATION 4-7. *South St. Louis Subdivisions, 1886–95.* In the 1880s and 1890s, South Side subdivision development reflected the trend toward consolidation and professionalization in the city-building process. (Courtesy of the author) newspapers. These displays bore a greater resemblance to nearby department store advertisements than they did to the simple classified listings that had typified earlier real estate advertisement. More than simply listing available properties and their prices, agents bragged of generous financial terms and pre-arranged conveniences and amenities. Increasingly, real estate sales became the province of a well-coordinated and highly visible trade group. In 1900, real estate auctions were moved from the courthouse door to the floor of the Real Estate Exchange. The year 1899 saw the initial publication of a regular journal for realtors and developers, the *St. Louis Builder.* This journal, rechristened the *Realty Record and Builder* in 1907, consistently advocated the coordination of the building and developing process, and helped to lobby for new laws requiring more systematic preparation of land prior to its subdivision.[63] Its back pages were regularly filled with advertisements from a new breed of South Side real estate investor—men like Wilbur Parker, who offered forty new homes just west of Grand Avenue and appealed not just to home-buyers but to investors of "out of town capital"; or firms like Nichols-Ritter, which announced that it would sell interested investors $100 shares in its 468-acre development on Gravois Road, returning 6 percent interest and a portion of one-half the net profit.[64]

With the consolidation of subdivision and real estate sales, the home mortgage market also lost some of the dispersed quality that it had acquired through the 1870s and 1880s. The chief agent of that dispersal, the building and loan, faded for both intrinsic and extrinsic reasons. The depression of 1893 dampened construction and real estate activity throughout the city. Just before it, the formation of the Missouri Building Association League, a watchdog organization, and the passage of the Missouri Savings Bank Act had already combined to limit the freewheeling activity of the late 1880s. As with banks, the numbers of building and loans in St. Louis dwindled drastically in the last decade of the nineteenth century—from their 1893 peak they were reduced to thirty-two by 1903.[65] Unlike the banks, those institutions that remained did not possess great wealth: local building and loan assets declined from nearly $14 million in 1896 to less than $2 million in 1903.[66] As the initial issues of their shares were loaned out, these institutions were more likely to shut down altogether than to initiate a new series of loans. By the early 1900s, the function of the building and loan was increasingly subsumed by large-scale developers capable of offering easy terms to working-class buyers. The *St. Louis Builder* confidently announced in 1905 that "the buy-ground-at-a-dollar-a-week era has come," and new players in the development game, like the Lincoln Trust Company, bragged that their new $5 monthly payment plan "brings into the market small buyers who otherwise could not have been reached."[67] The participation of trust companies and insurance companies, as well as the increasingly frequent inclination of realtors to sell shares of their developments, gave prospective buyers a source of credit that required less advance planning on their own part—and came more cheaply—than borrowing from a building and loan, and was more readily available to them than bank-originated financing.

The Second and Third Common Subdivisions, together with the 1855 expansion of the city limits, reflected a generalized faith among political leaders in the prospects for St. Louis's future growth. Less explicitly, they suggested a faith that the city—a public corporation—could and should take a more active part than it once had in guiding the ways that the privately managed city-building process developed an expanding urban landscape. If setting that process in motion meant acting temporarily like a developer, and selling land to working-class immigrant families rather than to the small class of merchants and professionals who had traditionally owned property (and who had failed, in the Common, to create a city), then so be it. City officials of the 1850s had one eye on the future; but the other looked longingly back at the faith in the attainability of a stable, capitalist order that had driven public and private development in the 1830s and 1840s.

Thanks in part to this more active role in opening up land for development, and in part to the simple multiplier effects of an expanding population and a growing economy, the improvement of land in St. Louis did indeed pick up after the 1850s. Around the city, and on the South Side in particular, a variety of actors came together to produce livable places where once had been only unsettled spaces. The various stages of that process—including subdivision, land sales, lending, and construction—were sufficiently interconnected that they shared a common trajectory in the second half of the nineteenth century. The purpose of this review has been to illuminate that trajectory in a way that might also begin to shed light on a question basic to this book: how did the growth of cities like St. Louis come to suggest to some a proliferation of "fenced-off corners," against which a presumed "wider setting" of public interest must be developed and strengthened?

The city-building process, which brought together communities of common interest in the task of shaping urban space, is vital to understanding this question. Within the complexities of that broad process, a discernible three-stage shift prevailed in the relation of the actors to their actions. In the antebellum period, when lending, real estate trading, subdivision, and construction were still the province of a relatively limited number of agents, the functions of each field were far ranging and largely unrestricted: the carpenter built stairs, hung windows, and laid flooring; the wealthy private banker used his capital as he saw fit; the realtor functioned both as public clearinghouse and self-interested merchant. In the 1870s and 1880s, neighborhood building and loans, specialized construction unions, and dispersed land ownership all helped to distribute the tasks of city-building across a wider range—and greater number—of individuals. With this dispersal of actors came increasing specialization and regulation of the activities in which each engaged. Finally, control of this increasingly complex process was assumed by a well-defined group of managers: master builders, large-scale developers, diversified realtors able to offer their own financing. Their new diversification was made possible not by a return to the simplicity typical of the mid-century development process, but by conscious professionalization and the mastery of the specialized techniques and myriad public regulations developed in previous decades.

In years to come, the job of shaping the city would grow more complex. But the experience of the decades 1850–1910 had proven that that job could be handled either by many individuals working separately, or by a few working in concert. The consequences of each approach were visible in the changing appearance, habitation, and use of the urban landscape—subjects that will concern me in the chapter that follows. St. Louisans themselves lent meaning and dimension to the structural dynamic of city-building by the manner in which they experienced, or consumed, the city-builder's products. Ultimately, though, it would be the role of the City—the public community to which all of the "inhabitants of St. Louis" supposedly owed a shared sense of belonging—to define more sharply the divergence of these two approaches to shaping space: the one, dispersed and various; the other, controlled and centralized. That public presence in urban space—so intrinsic to our understanding of the early city—will once again occupy our attention in this book's final chapters.

CHAPTER 5

Consumers

Everyday Space in Four Neighborhoods

"The lower end of our city," wrote a correspondent for the St. Louis *Daily American* in 1847, "formerly called Frenchtown, [is] now more emphatically *Dutch town.*" The salient fact of South St. Louis's development, in the eyes of local observers, has always been its marked identity as a German neighborhood. From the 1840s, when the crowded blocks of Frenchtown—as the aging streets just south of downtown were collectively known—began to house a steady stream of refugees from the political and economic turmoil of Germany (Illustration 5-1), St. Louisans have known this section of the city first and foremost in terms of its ethnic character.[1] The persistence of that description and of the reality that lies behind it are so striking that it would seem incumbent on the historian of South St. Louis to make the ethnic experience the primary focus of inquiry.

But as it would be in all of America's Little Italies and Chinatowns and Greektowns, South St. Louis's ethnic identity is a necessary, not a sufficient, clue to understanding the area's history.[2] To some extent, the notion of finding an identifiably "German" character before the late 1800s is an anachronistic application of the legacy of 1848 and the subsequent political changes that brought Hanoverians, Bavarians, and Saxons under common rule. But more broadly, ethnicity—or even the set of behaviors and practices that we call more generally "culture"—arrives not in neatly wrapped packages, fresh off the boat, but through the long and arduous process of reconciling remembered traditions with newly faced challenges. One of the most constant of these challenges, in the lives of St. Louisans or any other city-dwellers, was

ILLUSTRATION 5-1. *Street Scene, South St. Louis, c. 1910.* Thanks to the combined effects of speculative land development, geographical circumstance, and public policy, informal neighborhood gathering spaces like this in South St. Louis would come to be seen by many St. Louisans as distinct from—if not inimical to—the interests of the city at large by the turn of the twentieth century. (Courtesy of Missouri Historical Society)

the negotiation of space—whether within the frame of a house or the grid of a city. The experience of moving from one room to another, out the door, down the street, and across town is so commonplace—and so rarely documented—as to go almost unnoticed; for precisely those reasons, it bears closer scrutiny than historians have generally given it. South Side residents like August Schumke, Gottlieb Schmidt, and Frederick Pape—among the others whom we meet in this chapter—bore enough superficial resemblance to one another that, from the distant perspective of history, they can be conveniently lumped together in any number of common categories. But their homes, streets, neighborhoods—and therefore their lives—were nevertheless distinct, in ways each would have immediately recognized.

This chapter focuses on the intimate level at which these people and others structured their lives within the urban landscape: the places where they sat down to eat, walked to work, talked over the backyard fence. In the overlap of everyday life and the everyday spaces in which it unfolds lies a variety of potential experiences that together lend richer meaning to casual generalizations about "the lower end of our city," or "German ethnicity." In the evolution of that experience across four South St. Louis neighborhoods lies further evidence of the changes that ultimately resulted in a city riven by apparent polarities—by fenced-off corners and wider settings.

I want to focus for the moment, then, on the "consumption" of space—that is, the acts of paying for, living in, and modifying a place. How was the nature of the communities forged within urban neighborhoods related to the changing circumstances under which those neighborhood spaces were first produced? What, in the changing form of domestic spaces or streetscapes, either determined or reflected the boundaries between shared and private lives? How did the changing relations between city-dwellers and city-builders help to impel the deeper social splits that historians have long identified in the early-twentieth-century city?

To the extent that such large questions have answers, they surely begin at a smaller scale of experience than we have yet considered. To approach that scale I will profile four small areas, scattered around South St. Louis and developed at different times between 1870 and 1910, as the line of continuous settlement pushed south and west from its earlier limits around Russell and Second Carondelet Avenues to the area around the intersection of Grand Avenue and Chippewa Street, some two miles away. Each study area is representative, in its architectural forms, of the blocks around it; further, each was developed at a different phase of the city-building process described in the previous chapter. Each consists of five adjacent streetfronts, arrayed across two separate blocks (Illustration 5-2). This particular choice of form allows us to look for patterns that might be evident along one side of a single street that extends for several blocks, on the four streetfronts that comprise a single block, or on facing sides of one street.[3] For the sake of convenience, each neighborhood will be labeled with the name of one of the streets included in its boundaries: (1) "Menard" refers to the west side of the 2000 and 2100 blocks of Menard Street and the east side of the same blocks of Eleventh (originally Rosati) Street; (2) "McNair" is made up of the west side of the 2600–2700 block of McNair Avenue, the east side of the same block of Indiana (formerly Emma) Avenue, and both sides of the same block of Missouri Avenue; (3) "Pennsylvania" consists of the west side of the 3200 and 3300 blocks of Nebraska Avenue and the east side of the same blocks of Pennsylvania Avenue; (4) "Halliday" refers to the south side of the 3300 and 3400 blocks of Halliday Avenue and the north side of the same blocks of Pestalozzi Street.[4]

Each neighborhood profile draws on a range of archival material and material evidence to portray the link between physical forms, the people using them, and the evolving "character" of their neighborhood. In general, my treatment of that elusive concept rests on the basic presumption that the relative concentration or absence of a number of common traits among residents and their dwellings was a significant factor in the formation—and, more

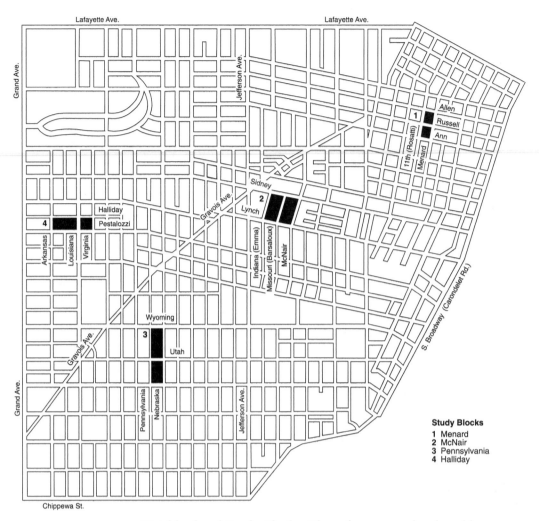

ILLUSTRATION 5-2. *Neighborhood Study Blocks.* These four areas, developed between the 1840s and the 1910s, provide the data for much of the information contained in this chapter. (Courtesy of the author)

vaguely, the perception—of each neighborhood's character. I presume, for example, that a neighborhood populated entirely by first-generation Bohemian laborers felt noticeably closer socially to its residents than a neighborhood where no ethnic or occupational category was more prominent than another. This closeness was reinforced by a number of institutions, such as the ethnic church, the *turn verein* and the *sangerbund*, the benevolent society and the union hall, that celebrated ethnic, religious, or occupational difference.[5] But that clustering of cultural characteristics cannot be understood apart from the landscape within which it took shape.

If this chapter reveals the uniqueness of people's experiences between one neighborhood and another, it also confirms the general applicability of the broad parameters I outlined for the post–Civil War city-building process. Not surprisingly, the production of space, on the one hand, and its consumption, on the other, were intimately related. It is the precise nature of that relation that is surprising, for it reveals the complex and shifting layering of social connectedness in the urban landscape. The early South Side landscape, as exemplified in our first example—Menard—was marked by a wide gulf between the people responsible for the largest units of space—city subdivisions—and those who inhabited and shaped the smallest units, the individual houses. At the same time, however, the relations between these parties were characterized by an informality and a relatively personal cast that would soon disappear in the area. In later-developed neighborhoods, the disparity between subdivider and home-builder narrowed. So, too, did the gap between the character of seller and buyer, or resident. Their relations, nevertheless, took on a more formalized and impersonal quality than that which had typified earlier transactions. It was in combining those two models—preserving the centralized social order of the mid-nineteenth-century city while at the same time retaining the demarcations and differences that separated later social and spatial communities—that civic leaders would eventually try to arrest the continuous cycle of change in the urban landscape.

Menard

The countryside south of the Soulard Additions had, in spite of Thomas Allen's best intentions, developed only slowly in the decades that followed his first land survey. Despite its nominal urbanization in 1855, when it was incorporated within the expanded city limits, Allen's land remained relatively unsettled. To the north, close by the Pacific Railroad tracks, and to the east, beside the river, urban development had advanced more quickly. Here, immigrant families had begun to settle into crowded three-story buildings that filled the decrepit blocks of Frenchtown, blocks once occupied by a gabled cottage or two set back unevenly from an unpaved street. This was South St. Louis until well into the 1860s.

In spite of the relatively undeveloped state of his property, St. Louisans could see that Thomas Allen was headed for greater things than awaited a local attorney and small-time developer. Shortly after the survey of his First and Second Additions, he began to supplement his law practice with new professional interests, chiefly the Pacific (later the Missouri Pacific) Railroad, which he had lobbied hard to finance and incorporate, and of which he had assumed control by 1850. At approximately the same time, Allen and his family left the William Russell estate for a new townhouse on Lucas Place, the two-block-long street west of downtown where the city's most prominent residents were erecting homes under the protection of a set of restrictive covenants designed to preserve the exclusivity of their expensive enclave.[6]

Allen's years on Lucas Place were marked by a steady rise in fame and fortune. After two years on the city council, he gained election to the state senate. In 1867, with the railroad on solid financial footing, he purchased a second major line, the Iron Mountain, which ran from the city to the lead and iron mines of the eastern Ozarks. Reorganized as the St. Louis, Iron Mountain, and Southern Railroad, this route would eventually extend to the Gulf of Mexico. When Allen sold it to Jay Gould in 1881, he turned a 100 percent profit on his original investment. The same year found him residing even farther from the old Russell estate, for it was then that Allen was elected to the United States Senate.[7]

Along his path to corporate and political prominence, Allen's interest in the lands around the Russell house grew less personal and less direct than in earlier years. While he continued throughout his life to provide his wife, Ann, with an income derived from rents on that property, it became an increasingly insignificant portion of his substantial fortune, a stepping-stone before the edifice of power and wealth that he eventually erected for himself. Increasingly, Allen's land served him as a source of potential capital; one commodity to be traded in the quest for others. When the time came to finance the original Iron Mountain purchase, Allen opened up all of his property for public sale. The plat that he registered at the courthouse in 1869 for even one portion of the extensive estate—the land within the old city limits, east of Second Carondelet Avenue—was far more ambitious in its extent than the one registered under his name twenty years earlier. Around the still-undeveloped Russell estate, he laid out some thirty-five blocks, etched in a skewed grid over the obsolete boundaries of the Petite Prairie common fields. These blocks maintained a formal continuity with practices developed in a century of urban growth: they matched the size and proportion of the better-settled Soulard blocks to the north, which themselves echoed the scale of Laclede's original plan.[8] Allen was able to adjust that scale just enough to fit his development into the existing, agricultural scale of the old Petite Prairie fields, the boundaries of which he chose for expediency's sake to preserve. Presumably with the guidance of surveyor William Cozzens, he placed seven rows of blocks (including one adjusted to be slightly smaller) and seven 60-foot-wide streets over the 13-arpent-wide strip of fields (Illustration 5-3). Like the blocks of the Soulard Additions, each of Allen's blocks was bisected by a narrow north-south alley; between alley and street were laid two parallel rows of twelve 25-foot-wide lots.

Nothing in this basic layout of streets and blocks suggested that the Allen additions should develop differently from the already settled blocks beside them, nor that the streetscape itself should form the basis of a visually dis-

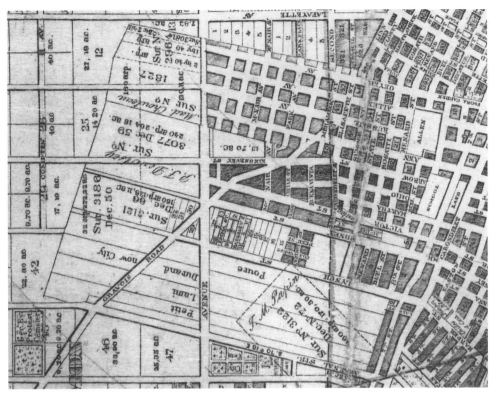

ILLUSTRATION 5-3. *Thomas Allen Additions and Surrounding Land, 1853.*
As this detail from J. H. Fisher's map shows, developers like Allen used preexisting
property demarcations (in this case, the Petite Prairie common fields) as a template
on which to draft the streets and blocks of their subdivisions. Allen's own home is
marked on the upper right-hand side of the map; the streets of his addition (like
Ann, Russell, and Allen, named for the developer's wife) either extended west
along the old property boundaries or intersected those routes at a ninety-degree
angle. The slight cant of the streets north of Geyer Avenue reflects the southern
edge of the earlier developed Soulard family additions, north of the Petite Prairie.
South of Victor Street—beyond Allen's property but still within the former bounds
of the Petite Prairie—other developers would use the colonial survey lines as the
basis for their own subdivisions. (J. H. Fisher, 1853, courtesy of Missouri Historical
Society)

tinct community.[9] In simple physical terms, the development instead reflected
his desire to "continue" South St. Louis as it then existed. It was an additional
piece in the relatively continuous and undifferentiated urban landscape that
Allen and his fellow major developers hoped to sell across the city during the
period of consolidation that fell between the early, disparate waterfront developments of the 1830s and 1840s and the later dispersal of subdivision across
a wide range of developers.

The final stage in Allen's preparation of his land for development depended on the introduction of convenient transit to downtown. Although a horse-drawn streetcar had run along Carondelet Road for a decade, there was as yet no regular transportation serving the South Side west of Carondelet—an area that included the newly opened Common subdivisions and the important commercial route of Gravois Road, which led southwest to the farmlands of the Meramec River valley. In 1867, however, the directors of the new Gravois Rail Road Company had received permission from the city council to run a set of tracks from downtown, through the Soulard and Allen Additions, and out to Gravois.[10] The route led through the last undeveloped portion of Allen's property: the land that lay immediately beside the Russell house itself. The 1869 plat map had shown this area as a final holdout, a last gasp of the personalized landscape, in the even grid that blanketed the Allen property. In the early 1870s, Allen at last opened this final piece (which included the 2000 and 2100 blocks of Menard and Rosati Streets) and paid the city to pave the streets on which the new tracks were being laid. He then began to advertise lots on those blocks for sale or for twenty-year lease.[11]

While Allen's Additions, as they developed in their first decade, were not the hurly-burly and teeming blocks of "old buildings, all brick and all crowded together" that inspired the wonder and repulsion of visitors to the oldest quarters of St. Louis from Charles Dickens to Theodore Dreiser, they were nevertheless a far cry from the orderly, use-segregated landscapes of later, more distant St. Louis neighborhoods.[12] A look through Richard Compton and Camille Dry's 1875 pictorial atlas (Illustration 5-4), combined with an examination of city directories and contemporary maps, gives us an idea of the Menard area as it might have looked to the census enumerator as he made his rounds in 1880.[13] In addition to Sts. Peter and Paul, the German Catholic church erected on the land that Allen had sold to the archdiocese in 1848, several other spires arose in the immediate neighborhood. Among the largest of these new churches were Trinity Lutheran Evangelical, built at the corner of Eighth Street and Lafayette Avenue in 1864, and three blocks west, the Bohemian congregation of St. John Nepomuk.[14] Large factories, while quite close, were for the most part clustered to the east, between the waterfront and the Carondelet Road. The most conspicuous exception, Adolphus Busch's enormous brewery, rose above the low skyline a half-mile to the south, on the site at which it remains today. At a smaller scale, houses on these blocks were built close to one another and to the street, with two of the most common commercial uses—saloons and groceries—thickly intermixed (often several to a block); neighborhood residents often plied such crafts as blacksmithing, wheelwrighting, and coopering not in formidable industrial sites but in jerry-built, backyard sheds (Illustration 5-5).[15] On the site once occupied by the yard of the Russell house was the Union Park, one of a number of privately owned parks and beer gardens that had begun to dot the landscape of

ILLUSTRATION 5-4. *Menard Area, bird's-eye view, 1875.* Judging from comparison with early photographic records and with surviving elements in the landscape, Camille Dry's collected bird's-eye views of each block in the city portrayed the crowded and densely developed landscapes of areas like Menard with remarkable accuracy. (Reprinted from Camille N. Dry and Richard J. Compton, *Pictorial St. Louis: A Topographical Survey Drawn in Perspective* [St. Louis, 1876], plate 28, courtesy of Missouri Historical Society)

the South Side. The streets around the park were noisy with the pounding of horseshoes and the cries of a motley succession of vendors: "book agents, itinerant tintype photographers and grinders of scissors and hand-organs" as one South St. Louisan recalled them years later. Through the alleys, as the same diarist remembered, moved a different class of merchant: "ice-men, coal-men, ash-men, rag-men and the fellow with the animal wagon who gathered up dead cats and dogs."[16] If the street was the setting for a steady flow of human traffic, it was also the site of potential danger, a fact brought home to the Fath family, residents of 2007 Menard, when their son Bernard was struck by a passing streetcar in the confusion that followed a minor street fracas.[17] To the Faths and their neighbors, the street was a place where their own lives intersected in unpredictable ways with those of others whom they might or might not know.

For most of the early residents of Menard, Thomas Allen was the only "outsider"—in terms of his social background or his place of residence—who figured into the all-important function of financing or building their houses. The majority of families living in the area rented their living space from

Major Industrial Sites

1. lumber yard	9. brewery	17. stables	25. brickyard
2. malt house	10. brewery	18. brewery	26. rope walk
3. flour mill	11. brewery	19. cotton mill	27. printing
4. brewery	12. lime works	20. tobacco factory	28. brewery
5. brewery	13. brass works	21. mill	29. lumber yard
6. granite works	14. brewery	22. brewery	30. brickyard
7. lumber yard	15. zinc works	23. brewery	31. brewery
8. lime works	16. brewery	24. brewery	32–37. brickyards

ILLUSTRATION 5-5. *South St. Louis: Saloons, Groceries, and Major Industrial Sites, 1880.* Workplaces, sites for socializing, and everyday retail spaces like groceries were closely mixed into the residential fabric of nineteenth-century South St. Louis. In addition to the expected clustering of saloons and groceries along such busy streetcar routes as Gravois and South Broadway, this map indicates the extent to which they typified the streetfronts of even small streets within the densely settled neighborhoods at the northeast corner of the study area. Industrial sites, on the other hand, typically occupied cheaper and less settled land along the edges of the more heavily inhabited areas. (Courtesy of the author)

Allen's tenants, who were in their social and occupational makeup people much like themselves, and who themselves lived on their properties. Possession of a long-term lease, generally costing $40 to $50 per year, entitled a family to build on their property; the building then became their outright possession, which they were free to sell as they wished, along with the remainder of the lease to the ground on which it stood. This was not a neighborhood developed from afar by speculative builders, relying on distant sources of capital. Of the twelve buildings in the two blocks under study for which permits exist, all but one were built for families that inhabited them; no permit was issued for more than a single building, and all of the contracts were drawn immediately after the date on which the ground lease was signed. For the most part, the money needed to finance construction (up to $1,500 for larger buildings) was raised not from banks or savings institutions, but from neighbors or relatives. Of fifteen mortgages acquired by residents prior to the mid-1880s (that is, during the period of the area's most substantial development), only three came from men involved professionally in real estate or finance. More typical were lenders like Martin Germann, a neighborhood saloon-keeper, or Lawrence Resnitschek, a bricklayer who lived around the corner. More than half of the lenders during this period worked as laborers, and most lived in the immediate neighborhood.[18] Comparable information on the identity of the contractors hired to construct these buildings is, unfortunately, missing from existing city records; however, given the small scale of the contracts, as well as the fact that three of the area's residents were themselves bricklayers, we can make a preliminary inference that the construction process may have been as localized as the lending process was at the same time.[19]

The houses that Allen's new tenants constructed made up the overwhelming portion of the neighborhood's built fabric. Walking down the 2100 block of Menard or Rosati, the census-taker would have seen a nearly continuous wall of brick extending from one corner to the next—each building pushed to the front edge of the lot; most of them butting up against their neighbors to either side, or standing a narrow passageway's width apart from them. The enumerator gained entry to most buildings not through a door fronting the street, but from the side of the house, which he reached through the side walkway. In some cases, that passageway was visible from the street; just as frequently it was hidden behind a front door that appeared to lead into an interior hallway (Illustration 5-6). For Menard residents like the bricklayer Joseph Hardnacke (whom we encountered as a struggling contractor in the previous chapter) and his wife and four children, the side passage functioned as a kind of outdoor hallway; it was covered by the sloping roof and protected from the public world of the street by a one-foot-deep extension of the building's facade, but was open to the private space of the backyard (Illustration 5-7). To reach the second-floor quarters occupied by Hardnacke's neighbors—the Wenzel family, who squeezed nine people into their small apartment—the census-

ILLUSTRATION 5-6.   *2100 Block of Menard Street.* (Courtesy of the author)

taker would have climbed the wooden stairs that opened onto the passage-way, and ascended to the overhanging balconies.

Limited in size by the narrow width of Allen's lots (not to mention the added expense of an additional bearing wall that would have been required of a wider structure), and lacking an interior stair hall, buildings in Menard housed families like the Hardnackes and Wenzels within the most spartan of floor plans: two undifferentiated rooms of the same size (generally 14 to 16 feet in either direction); one in the front of the house, one in the rear (Illustration 5-8). Rather than seeing this interior arrangement as a simplified version of the classic urban rowhouse plan—front entry and side stair-hall flanked by two or three rooms *enfilade*—as it had developed in St. Louis and in other American cities, it would perhaps be more germane to consider it a direct outgrowth of the simple "Creole" house plans long typical of poorer quarters of St. Louis and close in form to houses found throughout the French settlements of the Mississippi valley for over a century. Such homes, usually a single story in height, had generally consisted of two rooms and typically featured a porch or gallery covered by an extension of the sloping roof. Traditionally built with their gables to the sides and the entry and porch along the long front facade (Illustration 5-9), they were in St. Louis more often turned perpendicularly to the street in order to fit onto the narrower houselots typical of city subdivisions.[20]

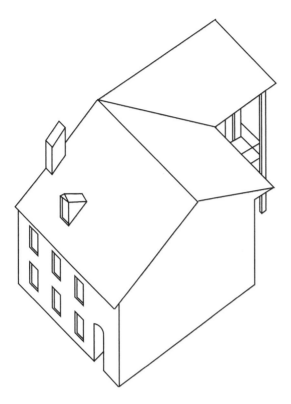

ILLUSTRATION 5-7. *Typical Menard Area Residential Structure, axonometric view.* Early South Side buildings typically restricted entry from the street, instead offering access to their apartments from side entries hidden by the facade. In the case of the buildings represented by this schematic diagram, that passage could be entered through a doorway in the front wall; for other buildings, like those shown in Ill. 5.6, tenants reached their units through a narrow gap that opened between adjacent structures. (Courtesy of the author)

Clustered closely together on narrow lots, their facades unrevealing of the spaces inside, their entrances tucked away from the sidewalk, the buildings in Menard formed a screen between the street and the domestic world within. Behind that screen, the interior plan of each unit—as well as its relation to others in the same building—reflected and encouraged certain basic patterns in the relative organization of private, family, and communal living among area residents. Builders created no separate space for interior circulation between rooms, let alone for cooking, eating, or defecation. No protected corners or light-filled bays punctuated the simple linear structure of the rooms or dictated the placement of particular household functions in one spot rather than another. Like the crowded streets through which Menard residents passed on their way to school, church, market, or work (and from which their buildings symbolically separated them), the interior spaces of these homes were simple and open, easily traversable from one to another. Their shape dictated little intrinsic ordering to the life lived within, but demanded instead that the structures of everyday life (perhaps a wardrobe or dining table within, a corner grocery or peddler's cart without) be superimposed upon—and in the process lend added meaning to—otherwise undifferentiated space. This lack

ILLUSTRATION 5-8.   *2113 Menard Street, plan.* Simple, undifferentiated floor plans made little allowance for privacy, specialized uses, or domestic technology. A subsequent generation of improvements often included a back ell with kitchen and bathing facilities; more recently, rehabbers converting such flats to single-family homes have often sought to open up first-floor living space by removing the wall that originally separated the front and back rooms. (Courtesy of the author)

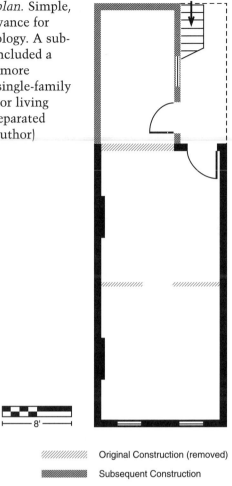

———— 8' ————

////////// Original Construction (removed)

▨▨▨▨ Subsequent Construction

of internal differentiation distinguishes the homes and streets of Menard from those of later-developed South St. Louis neighborhoods.

Also loosely arranged (and likewise tightly protected from the street) were the common spaces shared by the families living in each building. Back yards (paved with stone or brick) were crowded with alley-facing buildings, communal privy vaults, workshops and tool sheds, and wells (at least until water was piped into these blocks in 1878). Washing was most likely done at "slop sinks," located on the side porches, which drained into the yard through pipes tied to the porch posts. Given the crowded condition of interiors and yards, it is not surprising that, as one slum investigator would later discover, "for six or seven months of the year [the porch was] the best living room of the apartment," and that cooking moved from the back room onto the porch during the spring and summer.[21] At such times, the shared experience of

ILLUSTRATION 5-9.
*"Creole" House, South
St. Louis.* Unusually for
late-nineteenth-century
St. Louis, this side-gabled
house carries its portico
(an echo of French colonial
building practices) along
the street-facing elevation.
South St. Louis builders
typically rotated this traditional building form
ninety degrees to accom-
modate narrow city lots.
(Courtesy of the author)

families within single buildings was further expanded from the already considerable interaction encouraged by open porches and shared yard facilities.
On those porches and in those yards, separate paths and individual lives
inevitably overlapped. Here, screened from the relatively uncontrolled sociability of the street (where anyone might pass and anything might happen),
families shared a social experience that was more limited, more controllable,
and more predictable.

Who lived behind those protective facades in 1880? The people of Menard
shared a number of traits in common—the most obvious being the ethnic origin that made St. Louis (with Cincinnati and Milwaukee) one of the nation's
most German cities.[22] Two-thirds of the household heads enumerated in the
1880 census were of German extraction (by birth or parentage); another 20 percent were Bohemian. Only one-quarter had been born in the United States,
and nearly half were under the age of thirty-five. Nine in ten worked as laborers. Most lived in buildings with other families of the same ethnicity. As uniform as the overall population of the neighborhood was, the population of its
individual, limited spaces was even more so. Exceptions to the general neighborhood profile, in particular, tended to live in close proximity to one another.
In the first six buildings south of 2100 Rosati Street, for example, enumera-
tors counted twenty-five separate households. All but six were headed by
Bohemian-born men. As mothers in those buildings leaned over their porches
to chat with the neighbors, or called to their children in nearby yards, they
spoke in a language that was incomprehensible across the street. Within each
building, too, a lack of internal spatial definition usually gibed with a characteristic social closeness. In 1880, two families occupied the building at 2025
Menard: upstairs lived Emil Burckhardt, a French-born (possibly Alsatian)

watchmaker. Sharing the side gallery and yard with him and his wife, and living downstairs, were Mrs. Burckhardt's father, August Schumke, as well as her unmarried brother and sister. The relatively free connection between the units of such buildings lent itself to such close social arrangements. Within the freely arranged space of a single apartment, social ties were tighter still: Menard's households consisted overwhelmingly of nuclear families. Virtually no one took in boarders or lived with relatives beyond the members of their immediate family. While conditions within each building—and even within each dwelling unit—were quite crowded, families remained, within themselves, compact and well-defined. The fact that Menard residents accepted a relative lack of private or differentiated space within each apartment reflected a sense of security (or, at worst, a willing resignation to the paucity of other options) in regard to the others with whom they shared their living quarters.

How did the relationship of residential space and social clustering change as the young neighborhood matured? To some extent, the neighborhood's increasing spatial definition accompanied a declining social distinctiveness. Nevertheless, the original circumstances of its development continued to define it into the next century. By 1900, Menard was fully developed. New buildings that filled what had in 1880 been vacant lots maintained much the same fundamental form as earlier structures, although the fashion for mansard roofs created greater numbers of third-floor units. More common than the construction of entire new buildings was the addition of rear ells onto existing structures, thus creating a narrow third room explicitly for cooking and washing at the back of the building, and leaving the original rooms better defined for use as parlor (in the front) and bedroom (in the center).[23]

With the transformation of existing physical structures came an accompanying transformation of the neighborhood's existing social structure. The ethnicity of the area's heads of household remained substantially the same from 1880 to 1900, although a slightly greater percentage in the latter year were American born. This basic similarity belied, however, a great change across the same period—one common to many aging, core neighborhoods. A sizable number (nearly one-quarter) of the 135 households in Menard were headed by women, most of them widows. With the feminization of the head-of-household population came a marked increase in their median age—from thirty-eight in 1880 to forty-four in 1900. Over one-third were over the age of fifty, and women were far likelier than men to be over sixty-five. This shift also helped to account for a change in the vocational profile of the area: in contrast to the earlier dominance of manual labor, that broad occupational category now accounted for only a little more than half of household heads. The percentage of people with no job at all, most of them older, jumped to nearly one-quarter of the total. While the nearby presence of labor-based employment, then, had perhaps helped to attract the population that first moved to Menard, much of that population remained after its need for such employment had ended.

The aging of the Menard population accounted as well for changes in the structure of families, which suggests that, like occupation, family structure and choice of living space need not have been functionally related to one another.[24] Children had grown and moved on; typically, an older couple or widow lived alone or with one or two children who had not yet left home. Households were twice as likely as before to include relatives from beyond the immediate family—grandchildren, in-laws, and the like. In other words, Menard households consisted of smaller but more extended groups, and they were less likely than they had been previously to include working parents or school-aged children. At 2025 Menard, where Emil Bernhard's and August Schumke's families had lived, Ferdinand and Henrietta Otto now lived with their two grown daughters and a nineteen-year-old nephew. Upstairs (within the same household, as far as the census enumerator was concerned), they rented rooms to two young women unrelated to the family. Elsewhere, widows often gathered within single buildings. Two of the four families dwelling at 2118 Eleventh Street, for instance, were headed by widows (both of whom lived with their grown children) and a third family rented their extra room to a childless widower. These older, smaller, and less closely related households inhabited household spaces that were somewhat larger and more internally self-sufficient, particularly with the introduction of electricity and, more gradually, indoor plumbing, than the spaces typical of the incipient neighborhood in 1880. With the expansion and elaboration of interior spaces at the expense of shared exterior space came a lessening of the most readily identifiable common bond between residents of the same building: a smaller percentage of household heads now shared their address with others of the same ethnic heritage. The notion of the dwelling as a small community, as the shared province of unrelated but similar households, whose domestic functions were carried out within earshot or eyesight of one another, had quietly begun to fade.

By 1910, the scale of the change in Menard's population had become clear. The proportion of German-ethnic households dipped, for the first time, to less than half the total population. In their place came more Bohemians (now more than one-third of the total) and a surprisingly large number of Americans with native-born parents (one in ten). The percentage of laborers was not, as we might have expected, markedly higher than it had been before. Ethnic clustering had decreased: in a sharp shift from previous years, most of the residents of this diversifying neighborhood lived in buildings whose other residents were of different ethnicity than their own. The dominance of first-generation residents also began to crumble; nearly half of those enumerated were American born. Finally, the median age of household heads declined to forty-three—higher than it had been in 1880, but below the figure for 1900.

; of 1910, then, the population of Menard was far more mixed, and less marked by extremes of any given characteristic, than it had been in previous census years. Much of the population of the neighborhood had, in a sense, turned over. In the generation after the area's initial urbanization, families had aged with, and adjusted to, the buildings in which they lived. Traces of that original cohort were still evident in the 1910 population of building owners, who were as a group older and more foreign than the residents of the area at large. Where this group had once closely resembled the general mix of the population, they now stood out in sharp contrast to a younger, less homogeneous group of tenants who now made their homes in Menard.

These newer residents inherited the dense architectural fabric and closely mixed land uses established by their predecessors in the 1870s and 1880s, a fabric that had developed hand in hand with a population characterized by its close common ties and its readily identifiable differences from the population of the city beyond the front wall. By the time of their arrival, however, the wave of remodeling activity begun in the late 1880s, as well as the provision of electricity and plumbing, both of which increased the utility of indoor space, had begun to lessen the degree of space shared by separate units within any given building. Eventually, even the side porches would be walled off and separated as distinct, private spaces. With the definition of dwelling space and the attendant lessening of a shared spatial experience within the home came other signs that the neighborhood was changing. The almost paternalistic connection that the Allen family had maintained to the area had at last begun to dissolve after the death of Allen's widow in 1897; over the next generation, her children sold off all of the family properties (generally, to existing leaseholders).[25] The Union Park, where people had come to picnic, to drink beer on Sunday, to parade on the 4th of July, was subdivided and sold for building lots; the Russell house was soon all but surrounded with three-story flats. Mortgage activity, while considerably less after 1886 than it had been before, was confined to professional lenders, all of whom worked downtown.

In summary, then, Menard was an example of a neighborhood initially developed at close range: most of its property was controlled by a man who had lived on the site, its residents arrived there from adjacent city blocks, and they borrowed money from or rented apartments to others from the nearby area, whom they might have known or lived beside at a previous address. This familiarity between the various actors in the settlement of the area was reflected in its loosely arranged domestic spaces, both internally and between one unit and another. Differentiation, or the drawing of tangible lines between spaces that were shared with others and spaces that were reserved from others, took place neither at the broad level of the city against the neighborhood (we have seen how Allen continued to define a streetscape similar to those of earlier subdivisions) nor at a more intimate level, within the home (where owner-occupants typically shared a loosely organized, spatially unspecific household world with one or more other families). The principal line of demarcated space lay instead between that domestic world and the street, where spaces, while similarly unspecific, were less within the control of Menard's residents. The fluidity of street and transit connections between Menard and the older blocks to the north, and the free intermixing on its blocks of commercial and residential land uses—these were phenomena that remained, for better or worse, beyond the control of the populace of the neighborhood. Their chance to assert a delimited, uniquely private space came in the creation of the individual building. For all of the fragmentation of this construction process, however, the neighborhood exhibited a notable degree of architectural uniformity. Houses in Menard, like the people who built them, were quite similar to one another.

The social transformation evident in Menard by 1910—which included greater variation in the ethnicity, age, and family size of local households—had accompanied a subtler architectural transformation, whereby lines between one dwelling unit and the next became more clearly drawn. This dual change reflected more of a symbiosis than a cause-effect relationship between space and society. Architectural changes, once made, proved more suitable to a new group of residents; those residents went on to continue making more such changes.

More common in the urbanization of South St. Louis were neighborhoods developed at some distance from existing settlement, without the organizing hand of a single developer. Subdivision was as likely to be the inadvertent result of death or bankruptcy as it was a conscious investment decision, and the social profile of a block was as likely to have evolved gradually as it was to have been predetermined by the already established character of the block across the street. A look at three other neighborhoods suggests that the circumstances of Menard's development—which resulted in a particular concatenation of spatial and social divisions among and between its residents, and between them and the city at large—were not exactly repeated elsewhere. In spite of its change through time, Menard always reflected the legacy of the first phase of simplified, localized city-building in which its streets were shaped. The other neighborhoods stood at different points along the continuum of simplicity, specialization and dispersal, and consolidation that underlay the private development process through the late nineteenth and early twentieth centuries. In each, a unique combination of land divisions, building techniques, lending practices, and residential choices resulted in a unique relation between private domestic space, the streetscape, the neighborhood, and the city. As time passed, social and spatial cohesion in St. Louis' neighborhoods was less likely to develop from the most personal level outward, and more likely to grow inward from the level of the neighborhood itself.

McNair

Among Thomas Allen's colleagues in the mid-nineteenth-century South Side political and landholding elite was John Daggett. Daggett had come to the city from his native Massachusetts in 1817, at the age of twenty, and opened a drygoods store six years later. He eventually enjoyed a successful career in public service as mayor in 1841 and as president of the St. Louis Gas Light Company from 1842 to 1849, and he invested some of his mercantile wealth in a portion of the 4-arpent-wide strip of the Barsaloux tract, which lay in the Petite Prairie fields southwest of Allen's lands. In 1852, as Allen was beginning to improve his properties, Daggett dedicated the first portion of the Barsaloux Addition, as he called his property. Neither the site of his home nor an intended source of a conservatively managed steady income, the Barsaloux Addition played a different part in Daggett's fortune than Allen's properties had in his. The absence of a close and continued presence in the land's development would leave a lasting mark on its eventual social and physical landscape.

The timing of the dedication of the Barsaloux Addition was less fitted to the developer's needs, and less opportune in terms of nearby growth, than Allen's 1869 additions had been. Despite the proximity of Gravois Road, already an important commercial route leading out of the city, the subdivision was far ahead of actual settlement. Daggett therefore made no actual plans to dispose of his property until 1866, when he extended its area and petitioned the city to improve Sidney Street, which ran along the boundary between the Barsaloux fields and Allen's Devolsey fields (see Illustration 5-3). A year later the city council granted the Gravois Rail Road Company permission to extend its route southwest through Allen's additions to Sidney Street, and thence west to Jefferson Avenue.[26] At this point, the developer began to sell.

Like Allen, Daggett—presumably with the aid of city surveyor William Cozzens—manipulated the standard St. Louis residential lot size (roughly 25 by 125 feet) to form city blocks whose dimensions accorded with the space available to him. That space had been determined by uses and standards of measurement developed in a quite different context than the one which the developer hoped to create. Daggett's solution to the problem of overlaying a system of blocks and lots upon the predetermined boundaries of colonial common fields contrasted with the more traditional, near-square module employed in the Allen and Soulard Additions (Illustration 5-10). Rather than preserve the form of the standard city block within his allotted space, he sought a way to maximize the amount of salable land on his property and ensure the quick improvement of surrounding streets. In the process, he created blocks that were physically distinct from others in the area, as well as more suggestive in their form of the architectural arrangement that should

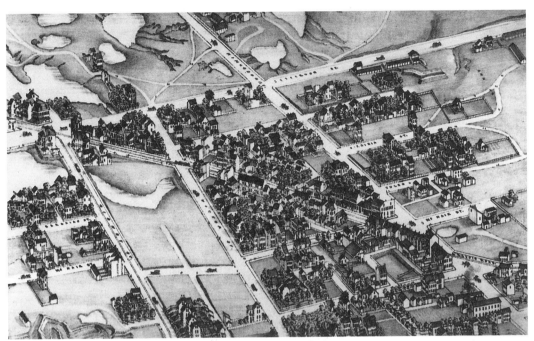

ILLUSTRATION 5-10.   *McNair Area, bird's-eye view, 1875.* More distant than Thomas
Allen's subdivisions from the center of the city, the McNair area was still largely undevel-
oped at the time that Camille Dry sketched its appearance in 1875. The specific blocks of
McNair lie on the left-hand edge of the image, several blocks east of the busy corner of
Jefferson and Gravois Avenues. (Reprinted from Camille N. Dry and Richard J. Compton,
Pictorial St. Louis: A Topographical Survey Drawn in Perspective [St. Louis, 1876], plate
37, courtesy of Missouri Historical Society)

follow. The Barsaloux Addition was an early example of the growing definition of exterior spaces that would typify the South Side's development in the
late nineteenth century.

The 4 arpents of the Barsaloux tract amounted to 770 English feet in width.
Where the developers of earlier subdivisions might have fit two rows of blocks
within this 4-arpent strip, Daggett filled it with single blocks, each more than
twice the length of traditional blocks closer to the center of town.[27] The new
blocks differed in their internal arrangement as well as in their scale. Building lots faced not onto one of two streets but onto one of four; an I-shaped
system of three internal alleys (as opposed to the more traditional single,
central alley) allowed Daggett's surveyor to draw lots facing each side of the
block. Lot and alley dimensions were carefully fitted to the space available
on the old common field tract. The central piece of the long (north-south) side
of Daggett's blocks consisted of fourteen 25-foot-wide lots with a 29-foot-
wide lot at either end, totaling 408 feet. On either side of this blockfront ran

a 20-foot alley; beyond the alleys were lots facing Sidney and Lynch Streets. These end lots, which varied slightly in their actual length, averaged 102 feet at the southern end of the block and 140 feet at the north, giving the block (alleys included) a total length of 690 feet. The dedication of Lynch Street on the southern edge of the property added 50 feet to this length; this extra distance, combined with the 30 feet that composed half of the Sidney Street right-of-way (Allen was responsible for the other half), completed the 770 feet of land available to the developer.

The relatively simple calculus that resulted in the long blocks of the Barsaloux Addition had several effects—intentional and otherwise—on Daggett's investment and on the subsequent development of the neighborhood. First, it gave him more salable land by eliminating the strip midway between Sidney and Lynch Streets that would otherwise have been surrendered to the city for use as a public right-of-way. Second, by placing homesites on all four bordering streets, rather than having just two lots at either end of the block, as in the Allen blocks, Daggett responded to the demands of the public improvement process: his new system ensured that the improvement costs assessed to abutting residents would be divided among a larger number of taxpayers, thus easing the individual burden on each and encouraging the quick improvement of the area. Less immediate but longer-lasting in its impact was the creation of two distinct kinds of streets, as opposed to the relatively undifferentiated grid of the Menard area. In one direction ran Sidney and Lynch— the old borders of the Barsaloux tract—which continued uninterruptedly from Carondelet Road west past Jefferson Avenue. As major routes for east-west through-traffic (and eventually as streetcar routes), these streets would attract more commercial buildings and more highly valued housing stock than north-south streets like McNair Avenue, which were poorly connected to other streets outside of Daggett's subdivision, and which became almost strictly residential in character. Finally, the widening of the more desirable lots that abutted the alley and street corners suggested a slight hierarchy within each block, with larger or more expensive structures anchoring the ends of each street front and narrower, cheaper buildings confined to the middle.

From the start, McNair's development was influenced by a lessening of the kind of personal autonomy with which Allen had organized his own subdivisions. In 1869, Daggett prepared to finance his anticipated sales by acquiring a substantial loan from the local office of the Connecticut Mutual Life Insurance Company: $5,000, repayable in its entirety after five years.[28] The time for making such financial commitments was inopportune; in 1873, Daggett, like investors across the country, experienced a series of setbacks that ended in his bankruptcy. A year later he died, his loan due and still unpaid. It was then that Daggett's executor began to sell the still considerable number of lots platted along streets like McNair, Barsaloux (later Missouri) Avenue, and Emma (later Indiana) Avenue in order to pay off outstanding debts.

There was little to show for Daggett's unsuccessful development scheme in the year following his death. Isolated from existing, extensively settled blocks, the Barsaloux Addition did not benefit from the kind of urban spillover that had helped to spur the quick growth of the Menard area. Camille Dry's view of the area in 1875 reveals only the most scattered evidence of imminent development (see illustration 5-10). What had appeared as sharply cut lot lines and neatly laid alleys on the subdivision map were visible only in the backyard fences of a few disparate houses and a vague rut along the inside of one block. McNair was not paved until the year that Dry prepared his atlas. Missouri Avenue had just been graded and would not be macadamized for another five years. To the west, the alleged route of Emma Avenue lay somewhere underneath one of the area's ubiquitous sinkholes. To the east, the remains of one of the city's several Civil War–era fortifications lay in a crumbling, earthen pile. Businesses and commercial activity were clustered just west, along Gravois Road; there, too, stood the new church of St. Francis de Sales, built in 1867 for a growing number of Sts. Peter and Paul parishioners who had begun to move from Soulard's and Allen's additions farther west, many of them to work on the dairy farms that proliferated on either side of Gravois.[29]

The variety of circumstances under which land in McNair was bought and sold, and the lack of a clear social or physical precedent dictating its growth, resulted in a curious architectural mixture. Because land was cheaper in the Barsaloux Addition than in the more centrally located Allen Additions (25-foot lots fetched around $450, about half of their value in Menard), pressure to yield a quicker return by building densely was lessened. To some extent, this kept away the speculative non-resident builder. Two-thirds of the building permits located for McNair were issued to men or women who went on to live in the houses that they had built. More than half of the households visited by the 1880 census enumerator lived in single-unit dwellings. One story high, these buildings typically featured the same simple floor plan common to early units in Menard. In contrast to that neighborhood, however, the relation of one building to the next was not as strictly dictated by the geometry of street and property lines. Houses were disconnected from one another and set back at varying distances from the sidewalk. The block, for all of the deliberation with which it was planned, functioned less as an independent formal entity, dictating the shape of future construction, than as a site on which to build one's home.

While lots and houses in McNair were fairly cheap, the process of borrowing money for their purchase brought property owners in contact with a wider circle of individuals than their Menard counterparts had experienced. Mortgages were acquired not from friends and neighbors but from professional lenders. Of thirty-three loans obtained before 1886, all but seven were acquired from persons listed in city directories as working in finance or real estate; and all of those persons worked downtown. Not all of those lenders were, however,

ILLUSTRATION 5-11.   *Rowhouses, 2220–26 Sidney Street.* Speculatively built row-houses, typically built in quantities requiring access to a large amount of start-up capital, reflected a new distance between neighborhood builders and neighborhood residents. (Courtesy of the author)

personally uninvolved with the neighborhood; a number actually lived on the South Side. A new class of lender, typical of this period of dispersed responsibility for city-building, they combined personal familiarity with the neighborhood and access to downtown capital.

Despite the scattered single-family homes standing in McNair, a precedent had also been set, by 1880, for the appearance here of a development phenomenon absent from Menard: the speculative construction of attached or closely spaced rows of identical buildings (Illustration 5-11). Their builders—men like Charles Frank or the partners William Outley and John Sellers—were professional real estate developers who, like others involved in financing McNair's development, lived not in the more exclusive blocks of the central corridor but nearby, in South St. Louis. Their construction projects differed from the houses scattered around the block, both in their form and in the manner in which they were built. Rows like 2709–2719 McNair and 2702–2720 Indiana depended for their existence on a scale of organization and interaction between different actors that was absent from single, owner-occupied houses. Both required relatively large sums of capital ($7,000 in each case) to erect—money that could be raised only from lenders who had access to many people's money. Their construction required the coordination of organized work crews under the supervision of a contractor who, like the lender, demanded payment in a timely, regular fashion.

Built as single-family dwellings, the speculative buildings in McNair conformed more to the rowhouse type in their interior arrangements and their relation to the street than to the simple urbanized Creole plan. Interior spaces were more strictly separated from one another, while front doors—the real and symbolic intersection of public and private space—marked a more visible and accessible transition from the street into the domestic world. When William Reisze, his wife, and any of their nine children entered their home on Sidney Street, they came through the front door into a side stair hall flanking a row of two to three rooms (Illustrations 5-12 and 5-13). Their circulation from front to back was thus internalized (through the absence of any side porch) and at the same time separated from the rooms of the house. With one family inhabiting two floors, those rooms became far more particular in their function and less intensively used than they were in the crowded buildings of Menard. In their more specific spatial arrangements, such buildings bore a relation to the urbanized Creole buildings roughly analogous to the relation that the blocks of McNair bore to those of Menard: they offered a more suggestive, specific formal template onto which patterns of family or community structure might be traced. The fact that such suggestions were deemed necessary or desirable suggests that the social order of the neighborhood was either less clear-cut, or less easy to anticipate, than it had been in Menard.

The population of the three streets included in this study was fairly diverse in the early years of their development. This was, as of 1880, primarily a neighborhood of immigrants. Seventy percent of household heads had been born outside of the United States. Beyond that, the differences between McNair's and Menard's population were more striking than the similarities. There was no clear-cut ethnic predominance here of the kind that characterized Menard. If Gottlieb Schmidt and his neighbor Gerhard Kunnemeyer walked down the block, they were as likely to see Patrick Fox or John Dolan as they were to see Peter Wachtel or Joseph Meyer. Of the forty-two household heads in McNair, German ethnics represented only slightly more than one-third; Bohemians accounted for another 10 percent, while members of various other ethnic groups, mainly Irish and English, made up 40 percent. Laborers continued to form the bulk of the population, as they did in Menard, but there were significantly greater percentages here of jobless people and persons employed in a clerical or sales capacity.

The residential units in the neighborhood contained a different kind of household than in Menard. Families in McNair were older and larger. Household heads were somewhat likelier than their Menard contemporaries to live

ILLUSTRATION 5-12.   *2036 Sidney Street, plan.*
Front doors and side stair halls helped distinguish
McNair's rowhouse structures from earlier, simpler
residential architecture of South St. Louis. (Courtesy
of the author)

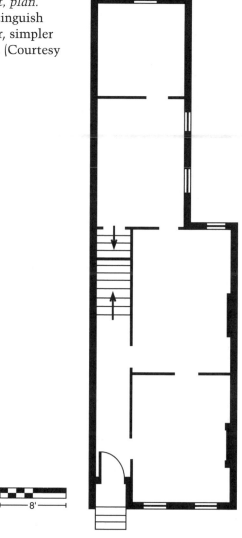

with members of their extended family, and far likelier to take in boarders.
This kind of social extension held between the units of a single building as
well: heads of household were less apt to share an address with others of the
same occupation or ethnicity. In spite of that relative heterogeneity, residents
of some ethnic backgrounds tended to cluster within particular types of buildings, with a correspondence developing between the rowhouses—with their
speculative origins and their more elaborated floor plans—and families that
came from outside of what would become the social norm of the neighborhood. Charles Frank's buildings on McNair, for example, were rented solely
to the families of second-generation American or British heads of household

ILLUSTRATION 5-13. *2030–36 Sidney Street, elevation.* 2036 Sidney is at the right side of the photograph; its plan matches that of its neighbors, all of them built at the same time. (Courtesy of the author)

like Thomas Brooks, a thirty-nine-year-old bookkeeper from Michigan who lived there with his wife, three children, and the family servant. A disproportionate number of their neighbors in the owner-built surrounding structures, in contrast, were men and women of German ancestry.

By 1900, McNair contained three times as many households as it had twenty years earlier. The neighborhood was now nearly as densely populated as Menard. The bulk of the new construction in which this expanding population lived consisted of multi-unit buildings—especially two-family structures, which now made up more than half of the total housing stock. Some speculative building activity continued, although the classic single-family, three-bay, front-entry rowhouse design, such as it was employed by speculators like Charles Frank, lost its currency by the 1880s. Builders experimented instead with designs that combined the simplicity and cheapness of the three-room-*enfilade,* external-staircase plan of urbanized Creole buildings with a more rationalized and complex circulation system, offering a modicum of architectural sophistication for a relatively reasonable price. The four-unit building at 2708–2710 Missouri, for example, consisted essentially of two

ILLUSTRATION 5-14. *2708 Missouri Avenue, plan.* In doubled buildings like this, South Side builders combined the cheapness of the urbanized-Creole tradition with the fashionability of more contemporary rowhouse design features. (Courtesy of the author)

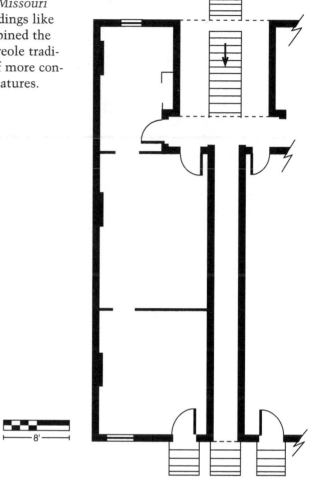

adjacent, two-family structures—each two rooms deep with a rear kitchen ell—connected by an interior hallway that led back to a covered exterior staircase. This configuration represented a doubling of certain buildings in the Allen blocks, which had featured upstairs access by way of porches tucked beside the rear ell, rather than extending along the entire side elevation (Illustrations 5-14 and 5-15).

Like those smaller, single-lot-wide buildings, the plan of 2708 Missouri concentrated shared domestic spaces away from the world of the street; the areas common to its separate units were in the rear, obscured from public view. It also maintained the relatively unspecialized, three-room arrangement long a mainstay of South Side housing. At the same time, however, several details in the building's construction suggested that its occupants shared space more freely with their neighbors up and down the street than with their fel-

ILLUSTRATION 5-15. *2708–12 Missouri Avenue, elevation.* The adjoined units of 2708 and 2710 Missouri appear on the left, with the central passage between them leading to the upper units of each address. (Courtesy of the author)

low tenants: the front facade presented doorways that opened directly onto the street, and the central passage to some extent segregated the occupants of the building from one another as they entered their separate units. In this sense, it grafted some of the characteristics of the early rowhouses onto the urbanized-Creole form, displaying an unfamiliar openness toward the street, with a corresponding lessening of the openness that had once characterized the spaces between units. Behind its separating walls, in 1900, lived an Ohio-born widow and her grown daughter, a young, second-generation-German couple and their infant son, a German carpenter and his wife and children, and an Austrian couple and their three young children.

Just as such buildings subsumed individual dwelling units under the aegis of one encompassing structure, so too had the population of the neighborhood begun to assume a more evident uniformity and homogeneity than in 1880. In the decade following that year, most of the Anglo or American household heads had left the South Side altogether. By 1900, McNair was less of a grab-bag socially than it had been, and more of a well-defined community on the order of Menard. As in Menard, the age of household heads had increased—

from the earlier median of forty years to forty-two. While McNair residents were far less likely than their Menard counterparts to share their address with others of the same ethnicity or occupation, such clustering was more common than it had been twenty years earlier. This was explained in part simply by the increased proportion of multi-unit dwellings (in other words, more people of all kinds shared the same address), but also by the increasing dominance of German ethnics, who now made up nearly two-thirds of heads of household. The proportion of "others" (again, chiefly people of British descent) in the meantime had declined by half. Rowhouse developments like Charles Frank's lost their ethnic and class distinctiveness as German- and Bohemian-descended household heads began to replace the original Anglo-American tenants and as two families filled spaces previously occupied by one.

Despite this trend toward an ethnic mix resembling that of Menard, the population of each of the two areas had maintained some distinct social characteristics: McNair residents were more often native born, laborers there were far likelier to belong to one of the fields that can be classified as "skilled," and a greater percentage of the workforce was engaged in the clerical and sales jobs created by the city's growing importance as a financial and commercial center.

This divergence was reinforced by a different pattern of residential mobility within the neighborhoods. In both, the inertial power of place was strong: household heads who were traceable in city directories ten years prior to their appearance in the census were more likely to have lived at the same address than in any other place. This inertia cut across all of the distinguishing factors of ethnicity, occupation, family size, and the like. In contrast to the Menard pattern, however, there were, among those who came to McNair from other addresses, far more who came from *distant* addresses, elsewhere in the city, rather than from the immediately surrounding blocks. Menard residents who had moved from elsewhere in St. Louis to the location where the enumerator found them tended to have come from nearby. By the same token, if they went on to move in the following decade, they often stayed within a four- or five-block radius of their census address. Furthermore, a significant number moved back to the older, more central blocks of the Soulard Additions, in defiance of the outward, radial vector in which most of the city's mobility took place.[30] McNair residents had come from farther away (if only because there were fewer urbanized blocks in the immediate vicinity where they might have lived), and in turn tended to move farther away once they did move. As though bounding through an invisible gravitational field, their previous residential momentum seems almost to have increased their trajectory as they subsequently moved once again out of the neighborhood. For many, McNair was more of a way-station between one part of town and another than it was a geographic locus around which their lives revolved. To live there reflected a conscious opinion about the advantages of one location over another as much as it did a simple inclination to stay on familiar streets.

By 1910, McNair had acquired a character that diverged still more from that of Menard than it had in previous years. The differences were as clear in the neighborhood's landscape as they were in the social composition of its residents (Illustration 5-16). Groceries and saloons were restricted to nearby corners, leaving the rest of the street exclusively residential. Nearby Gravois Road continued to draw other commercial uses away from the smaller streets of the neighborhood. Factories were, for the most part, a streetcar ride away. In contrast to the new ethnic heterogeneity of Menard, the residents of the area were still more uniformly of German descent than they had been previously and still more apt to have been born in the United States. While the majority continued to work with their hands, sales and commerce represented an even larger percentage of the working population.

From the start, then, McNair had evolved spatially and socially in ways that differed from Menard and suggested the changing form of community in late-nineteenth-century South St. Louis. Where Allen's blocks had represented a formal continuation of the early platting and settlement of the South Side, Daggett's were placed apart from the existing grid and given a form that responded to different needs and different transportation patterns. Where Allen had maintained close control over the subdivision, lease, and sale of his land, Daggett had been unable to control his property, leaving it instead in the hands of his creditors. Where Menard's residents came from the immediately surrounding neighborhood and tended, if they remained in the city, to remain within that same neighborhood, McNair's population was more likely to have come from and travel to distant addresses. Their experiences brought them into contact with a wider cross-section of the city, not because a wealthy landowner had constructed their blocks so as to tie into blocks elsewhere in town, but because their own personal dealings with builders and lenders necessitated going outside of a small circle of personal acquaintances, just as their jobs as clerks or salespeople may have necessitated taking the streetcar downtown to work each day. Their domestic lives were neither as intermixed architecturally, nor as strictly shielded from the street, as those of their Menard contemporaries.

The almost feudal quality of Allen's developments had been marked by the paradoxically close relationship between a landscape "producer" whose financial and personal interests were spread across the city (even, for that matter, across the country) and hundreds of "consumers" whose lives were focused within an area of a few square blocks. This disparity was reflected in the spatial levels at which each imprinted its own sense of identity upon the landscape. Allen's point of reference, or the community that he considered himself to be a part of, was the city as a whole. The spaces that he developed—his combined additions—were closely tied in form and location to that larger community.

Major Industrial Sites

1. brewery	9. lumber yard
2. cordage works	10. brewery
3. malt factory	11. provision company
4. brewery	12. planing mill
5. brewery	13. brewery
6. brewery	14. planing mill
7. brewery	15. lumber yard
8. brewery	16. ice and coal

ILLUSTRATION 5-16. *South St. Louis: Saloons, Groceries, and Major Industrial Sites, 1910.* By the beginning of the twentieth century, South St. Louis reflected the growing separation of retail, work, and residential spaces that was typical of American cities even before formal zoning codes brought such separation into the legal realm. Much of the area's industry (particularly such space-intensive uses as brickyards) had moved away under ongoing pressure from residential development (as well as the improved access to distant points offered by a growing number of streetcar lines). With the exception of the longer-settled blocks of the Soulard and Allen Additions in the northeast, small retail uses like groceries and saloons were increasingly confined to streets with high foot or streetcar traffic. (Courtesy of the author)

Allen did little to keep the world of his particular developments from being wholly absorbed in the life of the city, nor would it have been a smart business decision to do so. The spaces developed by people like Lawrence Resnitschek or Emil Bernhard—the individual buildings that lined Menard and Rosati Streets—articulated the spatial dimension of community at an entirely different scale: they connected the paths of individuals at the micro-level of the room, or of apartments within a single structure. Between these two loosely arrayed spatial levels of building and city was another—the street—which mediated between them. With its houses pushed tightly up against the sidewalk and doorways hidden behind front facades, the Menard streetscape represented a physical and symbolic line between the two radically different levels of spatially defined community that stood on either side of it. In keeping with the lessening gap between the social profiles of its producers and of its consumers, McNair's landscape was less polarized—in comparison with Menard's—between its largest and smallest spatial units. Between them, a middle level of space—that of the streets within the subdivision—began to emerge, almost incidentally, as a shared social realm, distinct from both the household interior and the larger landscape of the city. On either side of that middle realm, space acquired new levels of definition, between subdivision and city on the one hand, and within the walls of the home on the other.

Pennsylvania

For all the differences in their physical and social development, Menard and McNair both came into their own directly following their initial subdivision by a member of the first generation of American-born, Anglo-ethnic land developers. We could follow a clear line between the experiences and intentions of those developers and the later development of the neighborhoods. The property that lay in the western half of Block 55 of Charles DeWard's 1836 survey of the St. Louis Common had first entered the land market during the same busy period of antebellum real estate speculation that had seen Allen's and Daggett's subdivisions come into being. Its urbanization, however, was less immediate. A location distant from existing development, and the lack of a single investor who, whether by choice or default, sold his property shortly after it was laid out in blocks and lots, kept the Pennsylvania area from attaining its present form until close to the turn of the twentieth century. When at last it became a well-populated area, Pennsylvania clearly exhibited the shift in the organization and control of public and private spaces that was hinted at in the contrast between the Barsaloux and Allen Additions. Without drawing a population that was vastly different from that of either of the other neighborhoods, the area nevertheless reflected a growing desire on the part of developers and residents alike to plan for clear demarcations between one neighborhood and the surrounding city, as well as within and between the interior spaces that constituted the domestic environment. To a greater extent than in McNair, these clear demarcations framed an intermediate level of spatial relationships—that which lay between homes and the street—that was consistently and intentionally open.

Despite its location in the evenly divided, publicly sanctioned grid of the Common, Pennsylvania developed its own localized and somewhat autonomous character as soon as it was fully developed. While that character clearly belonged to South St. Louis, the rationalized construction methods and pre-established land-use guidelines that prevailed in the area's development placed it a small step away from a kind of universalized neighborhood-building process, a process that was later embraced by civic reformers as a model for citywide development and as the means for lessening the divisive influence of particular neighborhoods upon the urban region as a whole.

The northwest corner of the western half of Block 55 (an area of roughly 5 acres) was typical of the Common lots that passed through the hands of a variety of local German-ethnic investors after the opening up of the public land sales process. It was initially sold by the city to the farmer Henry Gempp in 1845. Gempp cultivated the land until his death, at which time it passed to his son Benjamin. The younger Gempp made an early effort to develop the rural plot in the 1870s but soon defaulted on his loan, as had John Daggett, during the financial panic of the 1870s. The man who bought the property from foreclosure in 1875 was a thirty-seven-year-old lawyer and investor named Herman Haeussler. He would go on to hold it for more than three decades before selling it (earning a 300 percent profit for his patience) to Diedrich Steimke, who operated a planing mill nearby on Gravois Road. Steimke created a subdivision—called Utah Heights, after the street that ran along its southern edge—in 1907.[31]

The basic formation of the blocks in Utah Heights was determined by the City's experience in subdividing the Common. With the outer block dimensions and the locations of the surrounding streets already determined, the developer's flexibility was limited to determining the size of his lots and the uses to which they might be put. Facing the two long sides of the block, Steimke lined up two rows of fourteen 128-foot-long lots. Each lot was 30 feet in width, with the exception of two 46-foot-wide lots at the southern end of the block. The northern end of the block consisted of a row of eight lots, also narrower on the interior of the block and wider on the corners, which faced north onto Wyoming Street. The deed to Utah Heights carried on in the standard tradition of restricting noxious uses like slaughterhouses and soap factories, but it also reflected an effort to break away from the early pattern of mixed development exemplified by the Allen and Barsaloux Additions. Steimke forbade any business or commercial use on the north-south streets and required all buildings to be two stories in height, with no more than two units to a floor. He also assigned a minimum value—$3,000—to the cost of any structure in the subdivision, and imposed a uniform, 15-foot setback to the building line. These legal restrictions would shape the block's development far more forcefully than either the simple covenants drafted by men like Allen or the formally suggestive block-and-lot layouts attempted by Daggett and other early developers.

South of Utah Heights, the notary and sometime alderman Edward Haren chose to use his share of the Common differently. In 1854, five years after he purchased his 5-acre plot from the city, Haren subdivided his property—just in time, as he must have reasoned, to take advantage of interest aroused by the adjacent, publicly sponsored Second Common Subdivision. The venture was successful: on the day of the subdivision, he was able to sell virtually every one of his spacious, 50-foot-wide lots. The land commanded from $6 to $10 per front foot (roughly the same as land in Allen's Second Addition, sold a few years earlier); most of it was sold in tracts of several lots each.[32]

By the 1870s, the area around Cherokee Street and Pennsylvania and Nebraska Avenues had developed into a small pocket of proto-suburban settlement (Illustration 5-17). Close to Gravois but lacking streetcar access to downtown, it was more suitable for families of some means seeking to live on small estates away from the bustle of the city, or for farmers in need of both adequate land and reasonable proximity to city markets, than it was for laborers or office workers without the means to own their own carriages. The census enumerator of 1880 found eight households living on the block; they ranged from the family of Frederick Pape, a gardener, to that of Charles Hermann, a brewery owner whose fortune was estimated at over $300,000.[33] They owned their own homes, for the most part, and most had lived on the block since the time that Haren had first sold his lots. With little in the way of an established neighborhood around them, they remained tied to downtown for their financial needs; half of the mortgages taken before 1886 came from professional lenders, the remainder were financed by the seller, and nearly all of the lenders lived or worked downtown.

In 1900, the area was only marginally more developed than it had been twenty years earlier. The block that would become Utah Heights remained barely settled, and only eleven families lived on the two blocks combined. The social complexion of the heads of household, however, had begun to change in telling ways. Most of the older families had left. Laborers now outnumbered proprietors. Half of all household heads were first-generation immigrants, and all but one were of German parentage. Most rented rather than owned, and only single-family homes remained. In other words, while the area was, in a physical sense, still beyond the frontier of South Side urbanization, it had already begun to acquire a social character more in keeping with the increasingly well-defined profile of the rest of South St. Louis.

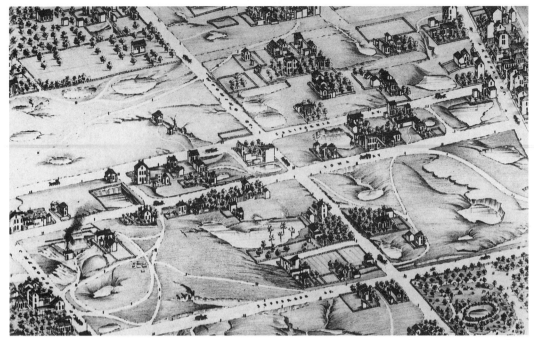

ILLUSTRATION 5-17.   *Pennsylvania Area, bird's-eye view, 1875.* In the 1870s, Pennsylvania—located on either side of Wyoming Street in the top center of this view—was still
an area of small agricultural plots and protosuburban homes. (Reprinted from Camille N.
Dry and Richard J. Compton, *Pictorial St. Louis: A Topographical Survey Drawn in Perspective* [St. Louis, 1876], plate 35, courtesy of Missouri Historical Society)

By 1910, Pennsylvania and Nebraska Avenues were paved and supplied with
water pipes, Cherokee Street and nearby California Avenue each offered streetcar lines and commercial services, and the cost of residential lots had risen
to about $30 per front foot.[34] The years 1905–1910 had marked a period of
wholesale building in the area, as the older homes located there were taken
down and replaced with new multi-family structures. As had been true of
McNair during its own construction boom, housing development was the
province both of future residents seeking a home and, to a lesser extent, of
speculative builders seeking a profit: more than two-thirds of the thirty-two
permits located for the two blocks were given in the name of residents. Even
non-resident homeowners shared a broader tie to the area. Most were South
Siders, and the men and women to whom homeowners turned for their mortgages, while they represented a group made up almost entirely of professional
lenders, lived or worked in South St. Louis as well. Indeed, improved city
record-keeping allows us to identify the contractors hired to build these
homes, and this group, too, was largely made up of residents of nearby blocks.

ILLUSTRATION 5-18. *Front Porches, 3227–31 Nebraska Avenue.* Wide lots, front porches, and prefabricated materials characterized the new homes of the Pennsylvania area in the 1910s. (Courtesy of the author)

Like Menard thirty years earlier, Pennsylvania was developed from "within." In sharp contrast to the earlier neighborhood, however, this localized scale did not equate with an absence of professional building and financial services. Instead, the development industry had diversified enough that "localized" and "professionalized" were no longer mutually exclusive terms.

Thanks to changes in taste, law, and technology, the new streetscape of Pennsylvania was noticeably different from that of older South St. Louis neighborhoods. Wider lots and uniform building setbacks (required in the Utah Heights subdivision, voluntarily followed in Haren's Addition) allowed for a less dense, more spacious scale of development than in the blocks of Allen's Addition (Illustration 5-18). The near simultaneity of the new buildings' construction gave them a stylistic unity lacking in the incrementally developed blocks of the Barsaloux Addition. New roofing materials allowed builders to frame simpler, flat roofs rather than the pitched gables typical of earlier periods; precast decorative brick pieces, marketed in the catalogues of such giant local brickmaking firms as St. Louis Hydraulic-Press Brick and Progress Press Brick, permitted them to adorn their facades cheaply and easily. New building codes mandated indoor plumbing facilities and outlined minimum window exposures and maximum lot coverage. The common building type that responded to and resulted from these exigencies—the flat—formed a third basic house form (after the urbanized-Creole building and the rowhouse) in the vocabulary of South Side residential buildings.

The contrast of the new residential architecture to that of just ten years earlier was obvious to anyone who simply looked across to the east side of Nebraska Avenue. There, buildings erected in the 1890s continued to feature the room-wide, two-to-three-rooms-deep box plan with side entrance—albeit without the side galleries typical of buildings in the Allen or Soulard blocks. The typical two- or four-family flat of 1905–1910, on the contrary, had a prominent front entry (wide enough to accommodate doorways to both upper and lower units, and sometimes further emphasized with a commanding front porch), and a more involved interior plan that featured two basic, interlocking axes within which specialized rooms, circulation space, and storage areas were carefully and specifically arranged. The combination of exterior openness and interior delineation that characterized the rowhouse plan, was here brought into sharper relief.

In 1910, John and Rose Lukas moved their family to a new flat at 3236–3238 Pennsylvania. Here they found a building—among many in the area—substantially different in its design from the apartment where they had previously lived on Eleventh Street, in the Menard area (Illustrations 5-19 and 5-20). Although the internal arrangement was based loosely on the rowhouse plan, builder Frederick Moberg departed from that type largely from a need to adapt it to the needs of a single-floor unit. The front door through which Lukas—a tailor—stepped as he came home from the shop each evening opened into a narrow side hall, to the right of which he might have found his three children, his wife, or his mother waiting in the front parlor or the living room that continued in single file toward the back of the building. Past the living room, where in his previous residence he would have reached either the back wall of the house or the kitchen, Lukas stepped into a median zone comprising an alcove, a pantry, and the bathroom. Behind this zone, at the back of the house, he may have found his wife or his mother preparing the evening meal in the kitchen; beside them was the door leading to the rear stair hall that permitted access to the basement and the upper apartment. For the Lukases, as for their neighbors in this block of new-built homes, internal space progressed in a predictable manner, from public to private, from household display to household production, as they moved from front to back.[35]

The variation in such flats from both traditional rowhouse plans and from the earlier urbanized Creole tradition are worth noting, as are its potential social implications. The inclusion of a room intended solely for cooking and eating was standard on the South Side before this time, but bathrooms and plentiful closets and storage niches were not. This new specialization of space

ILLUSTRATION 5-19. *3236 Pennsylvania Avenue, elevation.* Families like the Lukases found in flats like these a more spacious and highly specialized dwelling space than they had known in older sections of South St. Louis. (Courtesy of the author)

was evident in other ways as well. The side hall, rather than continuing back to the kitchen or to a rear stair, gave onto a narrow and rather dimly lit bedroom—a concession to the desire for a separate, private sleeping space in the absence of a second floor devoted to such private functions. The bedroom broke up the simple, transparent front-back movement of the traditional floor plan, creating a small dead end, a pocket of intimacy, that was clearly removed from circulation or public exposure.

Finally, the relations among tenants within the same building, and between all tenants and the public world of the street, were reflected as well as shaped by the flat plan. Residents of buildings in Menard had shared common areas outside of their doors, and in their back yards, all of it carefully screened (often at extra expense and labor) from the public world of the sidewalk, where women waited for their streetcars, men loitered outside saloons, vendors hawked their wares, and children played ball. The street enforced a different kind of sociability from the kind that inevitably occurred within the outlines of the building lot. Buildings in Pennsylvania, in contrast, opened wide onto a street that had already been cleared of non-domestic uses, a street that

ILLUSTRATION 5-20.   *3236 Pennsyl-vania Avenue, plan.* (Courtesy of the author)

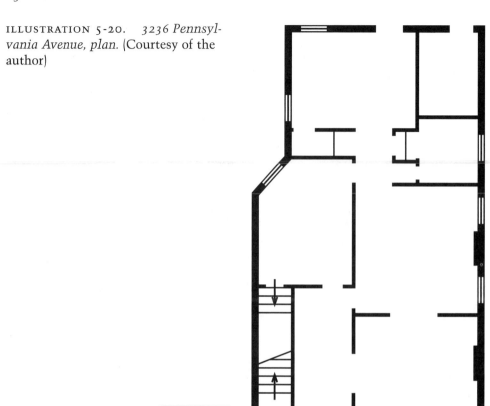

—8'—

already served as a mediate zone between private and public space. Their front doors and porches emphasized the accessibility of interior from exterior space, as though to minimize the difference between household and streetscape. Yet this seeming openness was qualified by a sequence of factors, visible (the small front lawns) and invisible (subdivision deed restrictions), that removed the sights, sounds, and smells of the city from within reach of the domestic world.[36] Among themselves, tenants were similarly screened. The front stair, which would have been open to the side hall in the rowhouse plan, was now walled off to allow upstairs tenants to enter their flats without having to witness the domestic habits of their downstairs neighbors. This separation was loosened somewhat in the less formal rear, where residents of both units had access to the shared back hall; but since the first-floor unit generally had its own private egress to the back yard, its tenants had little need to use the door leading out from the back hall. In architectural terms, the flats of Pennsylvania worked in a direct manner to separate residents of their separate units from one another—in spite of the superficial resemblance that such buildings bore to single-family homes. They worked less directly, as one stage in a sequence of spatial and legal boundaries, to further separate those residents from the public world of industry, commerce, and unpredictable social diversity that lay beyond their own subdivision.

Where eleven households had lived in 1900, nearly one hundred resided in 1910. As a whole, the new population was relatively mixed, and at the same time distinct from the population of older South Side neighborhoods. Three-quarters were American born, although more than half of the total were, like John and Rose Lukas, of German descent. Like Menard and McNair in the first years of their settlement, this was a relatively youthful population; more than one in three heads of household were under the age of thirty-five. Their occupational profile was more diverse than that of either Menard or McNair: half were laborers (but none of them unskilled), while one-quarter worked in clinical or sales jobs, and 10 percent were managers or proprietors. They were less likely, in their well-separated flats, to share a residence with others of the same occupation or ethnicity.

The general social profile of Pennsylvania residents was neither a simple replication of the social order of an adjacent, older neighborhood, as was the case of Menard's early residents, nor an uncertain ethnic hodgepodge destined to be sorted out in later years, as happened in McNair. Residents came there, apparently, knowing the kind of neighborhood that it would be; that is, its "character" (to lean on a necessarily vague term) was established early in its settlement and was not simply a function of the character of an adjacent neighborhood spilling over into it. The people who lived here in 1910 had arrived within a handful of years either from outside St. Louis (in the case of roughly half of all household heads) or from addresses more than a mile distant, lying in a general vector to the northeast. Once arrived, they inhabited a landscape whose physical distinctiveness from the older city blocks nearby offered a common sense of identity to a group otherwise notable for its diversity. The openness of their shared streetscape was contained, on one side, by the careful elaboration of interior spaces and, on the other, by the legally codified restrictions that kept these subdivisions growing according to plan.

Halliday

The Halliday area—the 3300 and 3400 blocks of Halliday and Pestalozzi Streets—grew, like the Pennsylvania area, out of the old Common land; like Pennsylvania, too, it was urbanized only after decades on the land market, during which time it witnessed a series of false starts. But as it finally took shape during the first decade of the twentieth century, Halliday evinced different patterns—socially and to a lesser extent physically—from those that characterized any of the sub-areas examined above. These early differences pointed more firmly toward a new model for development that would redefine the relation of public and private space in St. Louis.

Part of the reason for the eventual distinctiveness of Halliday lay in perceptions rooted in the earlier history of the area. The high ground around the intersection of Grand and Lafayette Avenues, in the northwest corner of the town Common, had from the earliest days of its settlement acquired a rather aristocratic reputation. Among the men who erected their homes in the vicinity were James Eads, whose success in bridging the Mississippi River would soon bring him international fame; wealthy investors like John Roe, who would enhance the value of his own property by chartering the Tower Grove and Lafayette Railroad Company to bring streetcars directly from downtown to his doorstep; and German-born entrepreneurs like Julius Pitzman and Henry Haarstick, who would in 1890 create Compton Heights, to this day the South Side's most exclusive subdivision.[37]

Just south of this enclave, other wealthy St. Louisans had purchased Common lots in the 1840s. One was Wilson Primm, the prominent Whig attorney who had run unsuccessfully to succeed John Daggett as mayor. Like other early Common investors shaken by the financial shockwaves of the 1830s, Primm was forced to mortgage and eventually sell his property. A series of such transactions in the following years left the land in the hands of James Harrison, a co-founder of the Pacific Railroad, owner of vast lands in the iron mining region of southeastern Missouri, and executive of one of the Midwest's largest steel mills.[38] Despite its promising pedigree, this land was not destined to become the kind of seigneurial domain that Thomas Allen had enjoyed. It was not until Harrison's son-in-law, Isaiah Steedman, inherited the property in 1884, forty years after its initial sale, that subdivision began to seem a possibility. The completion of a bridge over the railroad crossing at Grand Avenue, and the conspicuous opening of Compton Heights, both in the later years of the decade, provoked Steedman to dedicate the subdivision of Switzer Place (named for an earlier resident of the property) in 1891. Still, the development languished until 1905, when it was renamed Tower Grove Heights and its lots were at last sold to individual purchasers.[39]

Having passed untouched through the period of early, simplified city-building and the later era of more dispersed development, Tower Grove Heights as it finally appeared was a prime example of the consolidated development industry of the end of the nineteenth century. These blocks were divided in rows of spacious, 40-foot-wide houselots; a long list of deed restrictions, similar to those in Pennsylvania, ensured the construction of two-story homes set back uniformly from the street.[40] The development was financed by the Connecticut Realty Company, a subsidiary of the Connecticut Mutual Life Insurance Company organized specifically for the purpose of "platting, laying off, subdividing, grading . . . improving, developing, and building on" land.[41] Connecticut Realty had already proven its ability to operate at a scale and level of thoroughness not before seen in the area; its vast Tower Grove Park and Grand Avenue Addition, just south of Tower Grove Heights, had consisted of thirty blocks laid out over the former estate of James Russell (brother of Thomas Allen's father-in-law, William Russell). In all of its developments, the company carefully restricted land use and building placement; it laid utility and sewer lines and paved streets, all at its own expense, in advance of land sales. In addition, it provided its own financing to potential buyers, allowing them to buy for the relatively low down payment of 20 percent and annual interest of 5 percent, a point below the common rate at the time. This kind of operation required access to large sources of capital—in the case of Tower Grove Heights, a half-million dollars borrowed from the Mercantile Trust Company just before the developer began auctioning lots in 1905.[42]

A similar chain of unsuccessful early investments in the Common had left the property just east of Tower Grove Heights in the hands of another of the city's financial and political elite: Joseph Charless Jr., son of St. Louis's first newspaper editor, city alderman, president of the State Bank of Missouri, and inevitably, another director of the Pacific Railroad.[43] Again, the progress of the land's development bore little relation to the colorful lives led by its developers. Charless was murdered on a downtown street corner in 1859; his daughter Charlotte married a wealthy Creole and moved to New Orleans, though she held onto the land until her death in 1887. As frequently happened in the history of South Side subdivision, the property was initially subdivided not to carry out the ambitions of an opportunistic landowner but simply to facilitate its distribution among her heirs. Still, the land languished. Not until four years after the younger Charless died was the "Charless Garden" subdivision sold, as one block of land, by those heirs to a group of nearby merchants and businessmen incorporated as the Arsenal and Tower Grove Improvement Company.[44] Their new name for the subdivision, Wilhelm's Höhe, reflected their own ethnicity and that of the investors they sought to attract. These were men, like grocer Caspar Vielhaber or butcher Peter Sartorius, who lived and worked nearby, and who represented the South Side's native population far better than better-heeled outsiders of an earlier era like the Harrisons and the Charlesses. Their involvement in the development would seem at first glance not unlike the activity of the money-lending saloonkeepers and bricklayers in Menard, but they differed from that earlier cohort in fundamental ways. Vielhaber and company were a legally incorporated group, and they were able to offer financing to potential residents by joining forces with the same powerhouse of finance that had handled Tower Grove Heights: Connecticut Mutual.

Lots in Wilhelm's Höhe and Tower Grove Heights sold for roughly $40 per front foot, notably more than elsewhere on the South Side. Houses built in the area were likewise more expensive than the norm, generally from $4,000 to $6,000 for each home or duplex. Roughly half of the area's lenders were employed in the financial or real estate industries; most of the remainder were owners financing their own sale. In the actual process of their construction, buildings in Halliday were likewise distinct from others in South St. Louis. Despite their temporal and stylistic similarity to Pennsylvania's buildings, they represented the efforts of a more widely based group of investors and builders. To a greater extent than any of the other neighborhoods, Halliday existed as an investment opportunity before it was a community. A far greater number of the permits in Halliday (two-thirds of the total found) were issued to speculative developers, men or women who would not go on to reside in the home. A greater number of the contractors whom they employed (one-third of those with traceable addresses) lived outside of South St. Louis. In at least two cases, professional architects were engaged. Occupationally and geographically, then, the men responsible for constructing these homes differed from the eventual population of the neighborhood more clearly than the builders of the other study blocks had.

The evolving stratification evident in the development of Halliday's buildings was mirrored as well in the disposition of household space. In their size, massing, placement on the lot, and general facade treatment, they were similar to roughly contemporary structures being built on Pennsylvania or Nebraska Avenues. Inside, however, they were likely to feature floor plans that reflected a still greater specialization of spaces, as well as a further step away from the basic linear progression from front to rear that flats in the latter area shared with earlier rowhouse plans. Halliday floor plans were relatively "opaque": their organization was not evident at first glance, and familiarity with the interior of the house depended on one's entry through a series of screened spaces. In the flats at 3324–3326 Halliday, one of a number of buildings in the area erected in 1906 by the investor/builder Charles Starck, the hallway passage has all but disappeared (Illustrations 5-21 and 5-22). Instead, one enters through an entry into a vestigial hall that is only minimally distinguished from the front parlor to its left. As one looks into the house from this open and accessible front area, the dimensions of the house seem to contract; further passage is limited by the back wall of the parlor and by the sliding doors that terminate what remains of the hall. In other words, rather than having the option of proceeding straight through to the rear of the house along either a side corridor or a path through the primary rooms, the visitor is screened from all but the front portion of the interior of the house. This public area is, at the same time, made more open and accommodating by its organization as a single, wide space that allows for greeting, acclimation to the interior (a coat closet stands at one side of the room), and sitting.

A second tier of rooms, behind the entry-reception area, serves more private functions. Through the sliding doors lies a living room-dining area, which with its woodburning fireplace (a luxury rather than a necessity in this house

ILLUSTRATION 5-21.   *3326 Halliday Street, elevation.* (Courtesy of the author)

fitted for steam heat) and its symmetrically aligned windows represents the most formal room in the house. Adjoining it to one side, as in 3238 Pennsylvania, is a master bedroom which, thanks to the increased width of the lot, is in this case lit through windows along the side wall of the house. Rather than being a vestige of the side hall, the bedroom is now completely separated from the circulation pattern that commences in the entry of the house. The living room, no longer the center of a three-room, *enfilade* procession, also stands by itself, distinct from the rest of the house. In the far corner of each of these middle rooms, doorways open onto a rear hallway which gives onto the bathroom and storage spaces and finally to the kitchen. In contrast to flats on Pennsylvania, the rear stairs leading from the upper unit to the back yard are pushed into a projecting ell; this addition leaves space in both upper and lower units for an extra bedroom beside the kitchen and reduces the amount of space shared by household members within each unit.

In their careful, hierarchical separation of room uses, in the opacity of their plans, in their tendency to push neighborly interaction to the front of the house, toward the street rather than away from it, Halliday buildings represented a thorough inversion of the spatial organization of older Menard buildings. That inversion had other dimensions as well. Like the residents of Pennsylvania, families who moved to Halliday after the turn of the century

ILLUSTRATION 5-22. *3326 Halliday Street, plan.* Behind their welcoming facades, the residential structures of Halliday presented visitors with a series of carefully screened interior spaces. Porches and parlors, open to neighbors and friends, gave way to the increasing privacy of dining rooms and bedrooms, kitchens and baths. (Courtesy of the author)

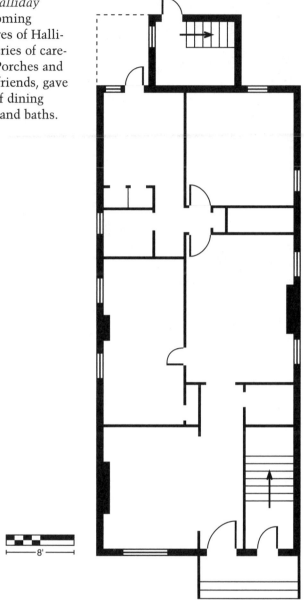

lived on streets that were screened from the commercial life of the city as carefully as the interior spaces of their homes screened sleeping, eating, and social functions from one another. If the transition between street and home, gently modulated by open yards and inviting porches, was unusually open, residents could at least feel secure that their private interiors opened outward onto a "good neighborhood." That perception rested in part on the effect of deed restrictions and on the social makeup of the area's residents. To an even greater extent than Pennsylvania residents, they represented a far more Americanized, middle-class population than that which still characterized the older neighborhoods of the South Side. Only 17 percent of household heads in 1910 were of German parentage, and nearly one-third were the children of American-born parents. Most were under the age of fifty. They were likelier to work in clerical, sales, or proprietary positions than as manual laborers. With this shift toward younger, native-born, white-collar heads of household came a sharply increased tendency, compared with the other study areas, to dwell in extended family groups. One-third of households included relatives beyond the nuclear family, and one in four housed boarders.[45] The idea of the apartment as a source of rent, and not simply the refuge of one nuclear family, was encouraged by the greater size and room separation of the Halliday units. But it also reflected the weakening here of a highly predictable cultural link to home ownership. In contrast to McNair and Pennsylvania at the same time, where owners were far likelier than renters to be older, first-generation German or Bohemian immigrants, the property-owning population of Halliday (about half of the total number of household heads) differed from renters only in the category most purely tied to wealth: occupation. To own a home there implied little about one's ethnic background or age, but much about how one made a living. If home-owning was a cultural symbol, that culture was now defined by paychecks and bank accounts rather than by language, religion, or memories of the old country.[46]

Earlier mobility patterns also suggested that moving to Halliday was the product of a different relationship between people and property than that which we have seen in the other neighborhoods. The study of previous residence in older neighborhoods like McNair and Menard (as well as, to a lesser extent, Pennsylvania) revealed that except for age and home ownership, few social factors significantly predicted earlier location; in general, older homeowners were the likeliest to have lived at or near their current address a decade earlier, while those who moved from elsewhere represented a broad cross-section of the overall neighborhood population. The wholly new Halliday area, however, had had no homeowners a decade earlier; nor were there adjacent neighborhoods from which residents, in keeping with the conservatism of relocation that we have noted, would logically have arrived. To an even greater degree than had been true of Pennsylvania or McNair, a wide variety of people living throughout the South Side made a conscious choice to come here—and not simply because it was close, or because it was where the neighbors moved. While localism—the pull of a South Side neighborhood for existing South Side residents—continued to determine a certain percentage of the neighborhood's population, people with no earlier geographic tie to the area were drawn more than ever from a socially distinct group. That relative newcomers to the city differed, as a group, from earlier St. Louisans indicates that, were it not for the factor of conservative movement, the neighborhood would have acquired a population even more distinct from that of older South Side blocks. Outsiders moved there, not so much in order to be around others like themselves, but to live in a place whose social or physical character, for whatever reason, appealed to them. The new neighborhood created a new social community, rather than reflecting one that already existed.[47]

A review of the interaction of space and social life in Halliday highlights its distinctiveness from the patterns that characterized earlier neighborhoods, and points us toward an understanding of why twentieth-century planning advocates should have found it so attractive an alternative to the earlier, publicly sponsored conceptions of urban order that have been touched on in earlier chapters and will be examined again in the one that follows. In Halliday, where interior spaces were most differentiated (in terms of their specific uses and their spatial arrangement), family structure was at its most diffuse. Similarly, between the units of a given building, where shared ethnicity and occupation were far and away the exception rather than the rule, strict spatial separation prevailed. In each case, the careful delineation of separate spaces allowed or encouraged the close coexistence of different kinds of people. At the next outward levels of spatial experience—the building in its relation to the street, and the street in its relation to the larger neighborhood—the definition of socially identified spaces (and spatially identified people) reversed itself. The families of Halliday, like the families of Pennsylvania, shared a relatively open streetscape: their homes or apartments were entered by way of front porches and stairs facing the street; the fronts and even the sides of each building were fully visible from the public right-of-way; more of the unbuilt portion of each houselot was in the front of the house rather than in the more protected rear. Through this visible permeability between home and street, residents shared a new type of kinship with their neighbors; they dwelt in a common "room," which achieved further definition by its enforced distinctiveness from other exterior rooms (that is, blocks or subdivisions) around it. Missing from the new room was the backyard blacksmithing shop, the corner tavern, the streetcar, the "grinders of scissors and hand-organs." A walk down the street made the boundaries between one subdivision and another, or between the older and newer neighborhoods of the South Side, nearly as clear as the walled, gated borders that separated the more fortunate St. Louisans living on their private streets in the central corridor from the public domain beyond.

The neighborhood experience varied across time and space within the larger bounds of South St. Louis. Wherever it occurred, however, that variation was controlled by an overriding complementarity of spatial and social structure, not unlike that which ordered the city-building process that we saw in the previous chapter. Heterogeneous groups of people interacted within explicitly and highly defined parameters, while within groups already highly defined by blood, class, or ethnicity, those physical parameters loosened or became less explicit. If spaces within a dwelling unit overlapped and if the functions that they served were only minimally defined, then the people who shared those spaces shared common social traits or close blood ties that predisposed them to accept (or to create) open, unspecific dwelling spaces. Conversely, where interior spaces were well separated, more strongly suggestive of particular functions, the households that occupied them more often included extended relatives or boarders. Similarly, where units within a particular building were carefully separated from one another, neighbors were likelier to come from different ethnic or occupational backgrounds. Neither cart nor horse drove this dynamic; instead, people both adapted to, and consciously shaped, the spaces in which they lived.

A second kind of complementarity took place within the spatial realm, between one level of organization and the next. Open domestic spaces (as in Menard) were typically marked off by clear boundaries separating the home from the street; the street in turn connected loosely to the surrounding city. Tightly delineated domestic spaces, on the other hand (as in later neighborhoods like Pennsylvania or Halliday), tended to give onto more open streetscapes characterized by clear, modulated transitions between street and home, and between one home and another. At the next level of spatial connection—that between street, or subdivision, and city at large—the connection was once again carefully defined, as distinctive building patterns and deed restrictions gave to the neighborhood a particular, predetermined character that set it apart from others around it.

These shifting and intertwined relationships—between social and spatial forms of order, and within the varying levels of space through which people moved—offer a framework for understanding the urban experience that diverges from the traditional perspectives of urban and architectural history. Rather than treating the neighborhood primarily as a function of ethnic congregation, or class or occupational segregation, or public works distribution, or architectural character, this suggestive framework rests on the presumption that the neighborhood was a complex phenomenon born in the social intersections formed around the acts of producing and consuming space, and nurtured by the ongoing power of places to relocate and redefine those intersections into the future. Spatial boundaries expressed, and then went on to redefine, the boundaries by which individuals united to form communities.[48]

The very notion of a "neighborhood" experience appears, from this vantage, to be highly contingent and problematic, as does the broad-brushed application of "German" to describe a set of distinctive and changing areas within the larger setting of South St. Louis. In the early years of the South Side's development—a time in which city-building functions were simplified and relatively unspecific—the area's social landscape was atomized and highly personal.

Community was experienced, at one extreme, at the level of the household and the individual building, and at the other in an unfettered connection between the neighborhood and the city at large. The character of space at each of those levels was the product of personalized and relatively informal procedures for claiming, developing, and dwelling upon urban land—whether those procedures were enacted by a developer like Thomas Allen or by a tenant like Emil Burkhard. In the consciously republican terms that defined mid-century development issues like the Common subdivision, Menard might have been considered a landscape that promised both liberty (in the individualized scale at which spatial decisions were made) and justice (in its essential uniformity and its close ties to the rest of the city). That seemingly ideal balance, however, was held together by a tremendous class disparity between the producers and consumers of urban space. By the turn of the twentieth century, the formula was essentially reversed. The social landscape of areas like Halliday was marked by an openness that joined together communities at a level between that of the household and that of the city—that is, something akin to our commonsense definition of "neighborhood."

These communities, in which a greater variety and range of people were brought into contact with one another than had previously been typical, were regulated by a formality and a planned, intentional visual character that served to join diverse individuals in a new common interest. If the class disparity between developer and home-buyer or tenant (producer and consumer) was not so great as it had been, then neither was the opportunity to define a private level of community on the one hand, or a broader, citywide level on the other.

In the next chapter, we will see how this new intersection of landscape order and social control was sharpened further by the intentional and inadvertent actions of the men who shaped public policy in St. Louis. Once it became recognized and accepted, the landscape of distinctive but predictable neighborhoods, of spaces delimited in conscious and specific ways by well-financed private builders, began to suggest to some St. Louisans the model for a newly conceived "wider setting." While this model aided St. Louisans in once again finding a way to articulate the ends of public policy, it would mask the fact that private, rather than civic, pursuits had shaped the landscape to which reform-minded St. Louisans aspired.

CHAPTER 6

Regulators

Public Improvements in the Urban Landscape

We last considered the government's role in shaping urban space during the transitional period of the mid-1850s. With the pre-1841 public landscape technically "completed," with portions of the Common recently subdivided not for the benefit of wealthy land speculators but for homeowners of more modest means, and with the establishment of extended city limits favored by an emergent group of small property holders, the city at that time was perched between two eras in the social organization of space.

On one side of this transitional moment stood the landscape of the old city: a reflection of the simplified public-private partnership forged during fifty years of uncertain experimentation with the government's proper place in organizing space. During that time, the interests and prerogatives of a relatively limited class of private land developers had been increasingly identified with public policies regarding the improvement of property. That identification was made visible, to an extent, in the shapes of subdivisions like the Soulard and Allen Additions, where the estates of long-established families were divided in row upon row of city blocks that connected with—and preserved the essential form of—the older blocks of the colonial village. In terms of the social process of creating and experiencing urban space, community was best defined at the level of the entire city, at one extreme, and within the individual building at the other.

On the other side of that temporal divide stood a landscape organized, by public initiative, for division into an ever greater number of spatial units, controlled by an ever greater number of individuals with unique agendas and unique methods for transforming their property. Henry and Benjamin Gempp's one-block garden plot in the Common, which eventually became Utah Heights, typified this new, fragmented landscape. There, and in other turn-of-the-century subdivisions around the South Side, diverse groups of people were brought together through their common ties to an increasingly articulated and regulated building process, and through their common experience of a visually distinctive, shared portion of the larger landscape.

The story of the transition from one era to the other was, as we have seen, largely the story of the evolving social or spatial structures that lent order and predictability to privately sponsored development and to the neighborhood experience. But in spite of the degree to which the character of nineteenth-century South Side neighborhoods was determined by the kind of "regulation without laws," as Sam Bass Warner put it, that characterized the intertwined aspects of the private city-building process and localized residential patterns, neighborhood growth nevertheless depended as well on the continued development of the kinds of services that could only be provided on a citywide basis: streets, sewers, utilities, and the like.[1] Of these services, streets were at once the most essential and the most problematic (Illustration 6-1). The street was a necessary means for coming and going, a repository for utility service lines, an inducement to real estate investment, and at a more abstract level, a marker of the relation between one particular place and all of the places that surrounded it. Unlike gas supply—which had been entrusted to a chartered corporation as early as 1841—or water service—which required large investments in pumps and reservoirs that clearly constituted a citywide benefit and therefore clearly fell to the city treasury—streetmaking constantly challenged St. Louisans' ability to agree on the relative propriety of providing equal service to all or differential service according to the needs of each.[2]

This chapter returns us to the subject of the urban landscape as a product of public policy, in light of what we already know about the development of city-building and neighborhood culture in the late-nineteenth and early-twentieth centuries. I will focus primarily on streetmaking practices and problems within the South Side, then consider the effects of these specific practices on the larger problem of developing a citywide system of decent public thoroughfares. As in other cities, the relationship between localized and citywide improvements highlighted and eventually reshaped the evolving relation of the city as a whole to its constituent parts.[3] Although there is a straightforward historical continuity to that story, a number of additional questions suggest themselves at each step of the way. How much power did the City have, through its part in planning infrastructural improvements like streets, to control the shaping of space? To what extent did public officials provide a guiding vision for (or follow in the wake of) the private development process? How did decisions made at a citywide level encourage or inhibit social interactions at the localized level, or between one part of town

ILLUSTRATION 6-1.   *Street Paving, St. Louis, c. 1906.* The task of opening and paving streets constituted a major portion of the city government's daily business in the nineteenth and early twentieth centuries. Brick streets, which gained growing currency in St. Louis around 1900, were considered a vast improvement over the city's traditional macadam paving techniques. (Swekosky Collection, 1906, courtesy of Missouri Historical Society)

and another? In answering such questions, we need to turn to the record of the street planning process and to compare that record to the changing manner in which city officials explained or justified their actions through time. Such an inquiry suggests that a clearly expressed "picture" of the city followed from—rather than guided—the rapid development of St. Louis's landscape. The combination of certain basic political predispositions with (a) essential geographical circumstances and (b) the better-articulated private development process dictated streetmaking policy. The physical results of that policy, in combination with the consolidation of the private city-building process, went on to suggest ways of organizing urban space that, in the city of fenced-off corners and wider settings, would become less accidental and more intentional in their nature.

The early vision of an evenly dispersed, simple urban landscape, suggested by the subdivision of the Common, was itself the byproduct of a more fundamental belief that the government's role in regard to public land was to make it available in some systematic and fair way to citizens, each of whom was then free to develop according to his own abilities or needs.[4] The identity of those citizens, or "inhabitants," as they were collectively labeled by the members of the committee on the Common, was less encompassing than such vague, democratic rhetoric might have indicated. Few, for example, could reasonably have afforded the 10- to 40-acre lots in Charles DeWard's original survey, and as it happened, few of those who thought they could afford them were able to. By the time of the Second and Third Subdivisions, however, public land policies in St. Louis had at last begun to serve the needs not just of wealthy speculators but of all those St. Louisans who, as John Hogan had written at the time, "desire[d] to have a spot, no matter how small, which one may call [one's] own." But because the spatial vision embodied in the Common was secondary to the social or political assumptions that underlay it, it had little power in the coming years to prevail over the physical consequences of the essential fiscal conservatism and libertarian leanings of the political culture from which it had sprung.

In part because of the absence of a stronger guiding vision, the improvement and planning of the city's streets in the remainder of the nineteenth century would serve less to smooth the physical surface of the city than to mark the rough and broken places in its social landscape. Streetmaking would remain, in spite of a recurrently expressed desire to the contrary, a reflection of the disjointed social fabric of the city. It would highlight, rather than mitigate, the differences between one section of the city and another. A poorly articulated governmental approach to making streets—one that, for economic and ideological reasons, placed the initiative squarely on citizens—eventually resulted in an increasingly well articulated landscape, quite different from the vaguely imagined, loose grid of the 1850s. Accepting that complex landscape, considering it as a logical and positive reflection of a larger social order, and transferring control over its development from the private back to the public sector were all tasks that awaited a new kind of governmental activism in the development process.

"No Crammed Square Mile": Streetmaking Practices from 1850 to 1876

If the men who ran the city government had little clear notion about the proper shape of the urban landscape as of 1850, they nevertheless shared the quite clear assumptions that the continued development of that landscape was both a reasonable thing to expect and a necessary ingredient in the city's growth. New streets, as they surmised, would naturally reflect and contribute to the city's continuing prosperity, just as the completion of streets within the 1841 limits had seemed to symbolize the city's successful expansion thus far. Armed with this faith, the city council blithely imposed a $200,000 annual minimum public expenditure for grading—regardless of whether or not there were people actually ready to move to the new streets created in the process. The effect of that commitment was dramatic. In 1861, city engineer Truman Homer noted, with evident concern, "the tendency of the population to spread out over a large area, and to settle in disconnected additions in the Extended New Limits." For the most part, however, observers of St. Louis's physical growth were convinced of its salutary effect. "Nature has placed no obstacle in the way of its growth in any direction," James Parton wrote of St. Louis in the pages of the *Atlantic Monthly* in 1867, "and therefore there is no crowded thoroughfare, no intense business centre, no crammed square mile." Surveying the new, empty blocks that stretched west toward Grand Avenue, Parton reckoned "that the town could double its population without taking in much more of the prairie."[5] The enthusiastic journalist could not have known that, in the years to come, the task of slowing that unhindered growth would become as vital to the city's interests as the task of encouraging it still seemed in the 1850s and 1860s.

The story of the rapid transformation of the St. Louis landscape during the period of the city's rise to the ranks of America's great metropolitan centers has in its outlines all the elements of high drama; but the actual details of that story—the ill-considered appropriation bills, the malfunctioning rock crushers, the mud-making street sprinkling wagons—are the stuff of low comedy. Much of the script for this bathetic tale is buried in the statistical details and official pronouncements that fill the board minutes and annual reports of the various agencies responsible for street improvements. Yet for an opening scene, one can do no better than to turn to the clumsy rhetorical flourish of Samuel Curtis, newly appointed to the post of city engineer in 1851 and far from the heroic stature that would follow his experience as the Union commander at Pea Ridge, Arkansas, in 1862. "The day is beautiful," Curtis wrote on the 7th of January, "but the streets are very bad. What can be done for them?"[6]

That question would go begging for a satisfactory answer as long as public improvement policy was based on the combination of a *prima facie* belief in the virtues of street development on the one hand, and on the other an essential unwillingness (after a few years of experimentation with the minimum grading allocation) to require citizens to cover its expense. Given that combination, at least three primary impediments to a well-maintained, comprehensive street system were inevitable: a reliance on cheap, substandard materials and paving techniques, an unequal geographic distribution of improvements based on existing conditions in the landscape, and the opening of many more streets than could be improved in a timely way. Each of these shortcomings would make tangible, and then amplify, the growing differences among sections of a city first conceived as looking the same from one end to the other.

Problems with Paving Materials

The self-dramatized frustration with which Curtis embarked on his duties stemmed in part from the city's longstanding reliance on macadamized pavement—a simple, gravel-like surface of crushed limestone laid over a foundation of leveled dirt, which constituted the most frequently used paving material in American cities through most of the nineteenth century. Curtis, like others before him, recognized that the limestone used for the city's streets, most of it taken directly either from the bluffs beside the river or from the subsurface of exhausted clay quarries, was of "miserable" quality; it cracked and turned to dust under the constant stress of city traffic, and a good rain reduced it to a muddy quagmire. Lacking any kind of reliable data on the performance of alternative materials (except for the clearly superior granite block, which was beyond the City's means to afford), Curtis could only recommend that his department begin to experiment in search of materials that presented a more suitable balance of affordability and durability, a potential solution that nevertheless seemed to him "a miserable poor resort in public affairs."[7]

In the face of continuing pressure to pave the greatest number of streets for the lowest possible cost, however, even the miserable poor resort of trial-and-error paving practice failed to gain a foothold in the years that followed. Instead, city paving policy was characterized by a begrudging but unquestioning public commitment to the cheap but short-lived (and high-maintenance) macadam. Under the administration of Curtis's boss, Whig Mayor Luther M. Kennett, the municipal government threw itself wholeheartedly into the task of paving the city's streets by whatever means necessary.[8] Kennett's commitment to quickness and cheapness left a legacy that remained undiminished through three decades of succeeding administrations. From the already extensive figure of 185 miles of macadamized streets recorded by the street commissioner in 1872 (a distance that represented 95 percent of the total mileage of St. Louis's paved streets), the city reached a peak figure of over 300 miles of macadamized thoroughfares by 1881, the year that Mayor Henry Overstoltz desperately pleaded with the house of delegates that "all extensions of our street system in the shape of new streets be avoided."[9]

But year after year, block after block of macadamized roadway was added, even as professional and layman alike futilely reiterated what Samuel Curtis had pointed out in 1851. More than twenty years after Curtis's initial observations, another city engineer still found it necessary to decry "the present system of piling loose macadamizing upon a loose and unsettled clay foundation," although he admitted that macadam's cost made it the only viable option for the foreseeable future. Even the introduction in 1874 of steam-rollers to firm up the foundations of macadamized streets made little effec-tive difference in the long run; paving techniques remained, in Overstoltz's words, "utterly inadequate and defective."[10]

The poor quality of the city's paving methods was no obscure trade secret, much as contractors and nervous municipal officials might have wished it to be. Throughout the period of St. Louis's most rapid growth, the daily remarks of ordinary citizens often spoke more eloquently than did official reports of the problems that macadam streets engendered for city dwellers: their "soft limestone," wrote one, "quickly grinds to powder; ensuring at all times a dis-agreeable dust or an equally disagreeable mud." South Sider Theodore Sand-berg, an inspector at the St. Louis Wheel and Car Company, wondered as late as 1897 "when it will cease and become a thing of the past to see a river of mud in the streets." The question was of more than academic interest to any-one who had shared Sandberg's experience of coming home at the end of the day "with enough Real-Estate on my feet to lay off a town-plat."[11]

Geographic Fragmentation

As poor and temporary a surface as macadam was, it at least represented a first step toward easing the difficulties of travel around the city. But streets could only take a person as far as they led. The historical geography of the city helped ensure that South Side streets almost never led into the faster-developing central corridor. Indeed, the most striking aspect of the scattered street improvements made in the study area prior to 1870 is the near total lack of paved connections between the South Side and downtown (Illustration 6-2). The Pacific Railroad tracks that since 1851 had filled the drained site of the Mill Creek and Chouteau's Pond proved every bit as effective as those ear-lier obstacles in separating the two sides of the city from one another. With the exception of the parallel streetcar routes of Seventh Street and Carondelet Road, both at the neighborhood's eastern edge, no improved street beginning north of Lafayette Avenue continued farther south than Ann Avenue, in the northern half of Allen's additions. Second Carondelet Avenue, which as its name indicated should have offered an alternate route from the city center to the village of Carondelet, was not only unpaved at this time, but its right-of-way was discontinuous and incomplete. With the exception of the Soulard blocks, just south of downtown, the South Side had no complete gridwork of improved streets. Instead, early paving contracts tended to lie on and around a few major streets that ran through the area. These included Lafayette Avenue (the site of an early streetcar route promoted by some of the wealthy men who lived in the area of Lafayette and Grand Avenue) and Gravois Road, which cut a long diagonal through the old Common lands before dead-ending, on its northern end, at the edge of Allen's additions.

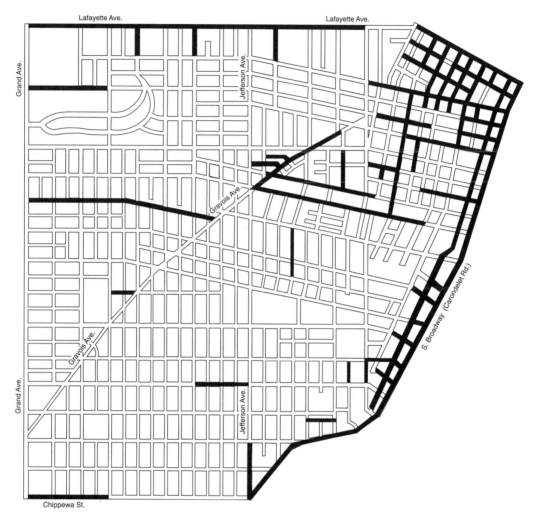

ILLUSTRATION 6-2. *South Side Street-Improvement Ordinances to 1870.* In the early years of its development, South St. Louis grew largely without street connections to the more prosperous and longer-established central corridor of the city. Of those streets that continued north beyond the range of this map, only two—Second Carondelet Avenue and Seventh Street, at the far eastern edge of the study area—continued more than a few blocks into the heart of the South Side. Other north-south streets not only petered out within a few blocks south of Lafayette Avenue but were also cut off at their northern ends by the railroad tracks that extended across the Mill Creek Valley, just south of the central corridor. (Courtesy of the author)

In the early 1870s, the pace of streetmaking in south St. Louis picked up considerably, thanks to the improvement of a few major streets that led, once again, not between the South Side and the rest of the city, but within the area itself (Illustration 6-3). Gravois was macadamized all the way west to Grand Avenue, while the substantial improvement of Russell Avenue and Shenandoah, Lynch, Arsenal, Cherokee, Miami, and Chippewa Streets all improved the flow of traffic west from the Carondelet Road through the Common. Still, to travel north, one had first to go east to Carondelet and Seventh. The partial exception to the rule was Jefferson Avenue, intended as the South Side's primary thoroughfare in DeWard's original, 1836 Common plat, which was finally paved along its entire length north to (but not past) the Mill Creek Valley. The effect of new improvement ordinances, which were passed either by landowners' petitions or at the behest of the city engineer, was to continue to accentuate the traditional geographic distinction between the South Side and the rest of the city. The goal of tying together all of the city's far-flung areas under one street system, evident in the most tentative form in the earlier planning of Grand Avenue, was not in itself strong enough to override the basic impediments to that goal presented by the city's geography. If South St. Louis was beginning to develop a meaningful identity in reference to neighborhoods as disparate as Allen's blocks, Daggett's Barsaloux Addition, and the Third Common Subdivision, that identity was fortified in part by the growing separation of the roads on that side of the city from those that ran elsewhere.

That the newer areas of South St. Louis were developing with even fewer connections than the old to the rest of the city was telling; even more telling was that the streets in those new areas were being paved at a far slower pace than their equivalents elsewhere in town. A good deal of the money allocated for South Side street improvement was spent simply bringing the older parts of the neighborhood up to the standard of improvement typical of the rest of the city. Within the pre-1855 limits, South Side streets had a considerable way to go before they reached that point, the *Benoist* case notwithstanding. Between 1870 and 1873, grading and paving contracts in these "Old Limits" sections of the First and Second Wards (wards that together comprised all of the land from Lafayette south) exceeded the value of contracts issued in Old Limits portions of any of the city's twelve wards.[12] At the same time, however, the South Side wards consistently lagged behind the central and northern wards in money appropriated for the New Limits—that is, for the land that lay between the boundary lines of 1841 and 1855. Since 1870, grading costs for these outlying blocks had been taken from a general New Limits improvement fund. Unlike the previous appropriation system, which had doled New Limits money directly to each ward in proportion to its population, this general fund was distributed at the discretion of City Hall.[13] The centralized discretionary power did little to speed New Limit development on the South Side. The First Ward (from Victor Street south to the city limits)

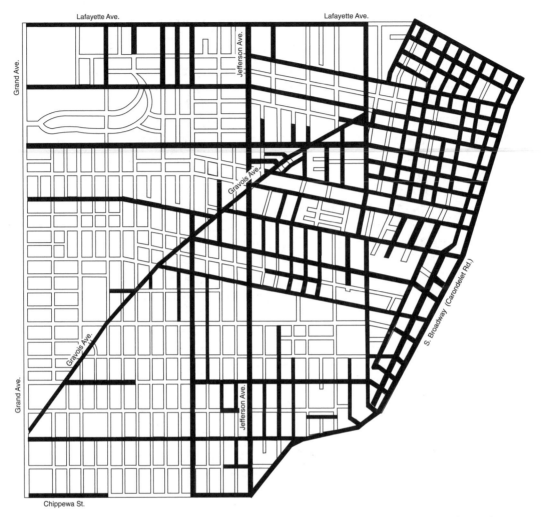

ILLUSTRATION 6-3.   *South Side Street-Improvement Ordinances to 1875.* The early
1870s saw the improvement of many long-opened streets within the old Petite Prairie
property in the eastern half of South St. Louis, as well as of important routes such as Jefferson and Gravois Avenues (for which the cost of improvement was shared by the streetcar companies that had petitioned to lay their tracks there). (Courtesy of the author)

included as much land area as the Eleventh and Twelfth Wards combined,
but only once from 1870 to 1877 did it exceed either of those North Side districts in New Limits improvement expenditures.[14] While the focus of street
improvement in the rest of St. Louis had turned to the newly settled lands
west toward Grand Avenue (and therefore assumed the broader scale predicted by the optimistic boasts of mid-century boosters), South St. Louisans
were still waiting for new gravel to be laid on the streets of their oldest neighborhoods.

The social dimension of the streetmaking process—the interaction occasioned by the actual contracting and carrying out of improvement work—was as effective as the physical dimension in accentuating regional differences within the city. Contracting may have been authorized at a citywide level, but its details unfolded in a highly localized way. The men employed to improve streets were bound by no other requirement than that they be low bidder on the proposed job. Grading and paving work was taken on by dozens of individuals and small firms in this period. Their chief common characteristic seemed to be either an unwillingness to travel far to work, or a productive relationship with their local alderman. Statistics from two particularly active years in the early 1870s bear out this impression. Twenty-three different contractors worked on South St. Louis streets in the fiscal year extending from 1870 to 1871; of these, eighteen are listed with addresses in city directories. All but one of this group lived south of Lafayette (many resided beside their quarries on the blocks just west of the river), and the one exception lived on Park Avenue, still well south of the railroad tracks that separated South St. Louis from the rest of the city. Only four of the twenty-three firms working within the study area had any road contracts north of the railroad tracks; of these, only two worked north of Market Street, on what might justifiably be called "the other side of town." Four years later, work within the study area was divided among a full thirty-six contractors. Of the twenty-six from that group listed in city directories, only two lived north of Lafayette. This time, seven of the firms employed within the study area also worked north of the railroad tracks.[15] In other words, street improvement remained a highly decentralized and, at the same time, a highly localized profession.

The consequences of this fragmentation of labor were augmented by a series of related circumstances. First, the men who improved streets did so without having to file any plans for the City's advance inspection. The techniques on which they relied were determined by tradition (or innovation), not by law. The prominence of a handful of families who remained active in South Side street contracting for several generations (like the Skrainkas or Eyermanns, both of whom built up substantial contracting businesses that extended across several generations into the mid twentieth century) testified to the persistence of these informally taught traditions. Second, the very stone used on streets varied greatly from one end of the city to the other. South Side macadam, which came from South Side quarries, was not as durable as the rock used elsewhere in the city.[16] Finally, once paved, no street was safely protected by what the city engineer dryly termed "restrictions upon the liberty of disturbance of our pavement by private parties."[17] Even when properly carried out, the typical street repair on a busy macadamized thoroughfare lasted for only two or three months; hence, the price of each such "disturbance" (for instance, the excavation of a private sewer, or the laying of streetcar tracks) continued to be paid indefinitely into the future, so long as macadam remained the pavement of choice, or necessity, in St. Louis.[18]

Excessive Street Openings

The combination of a localized outlook and an overriding concern for short-term economizing was responsible for considerable fragmentation and re-duplication of effort in the streetmaking process. In combination with the continued legacy of an earlier faith in the *de facto* virtues of growth, the effects of that wayward quality were amplified and replicated throughout the landscape of the South Side. On paper, the area appeared to be growing quickly and efficiently. The number of streets "opened" there (officially released and dedicated for public use) far outpaced the rate at which they could possibly be improved. A comparison of Illustration 6-2 with contemporaneous city maps reveals the existence of a number of streets that, though they might have existed for the purposes of the mapmaker's product, were likely to have consisted of little more than parallel rows of wooden stakes or rock cairns. The minimal laws drawn up to govern street opening were geared to promoting growth, not control; their methods for apportioning costs ensured that neighborhoods like South St. Louis would never lack for unimproved thoroughfares. Simply to open a street, whether or not it was ready for improvement, cost the treasury little or nothing, while it created at least a slightly higher likelihood that houses and businesses might some-day line the hypothetical roadway created in the process. Government-ordered street openings reflected a continuing faith in the power of landscape improvements to catalyze urban development; they also reflected the City's hope that there were cheaper ways to encourage that development than by earmarking great sums of public money for outlying improvements, as they had done in the 1850s.

By law, streets dedicated to the City as part of a subdivision were surrendered to the public domain without financial compensation to the original owner. In cases where the City exercised its right of eminent domain in appropriating land for streets, the compromise of public and private rights developed earlier in the century had by this time been refined in such a way as to consider more systematically the benefits and damages incurred by both sides in the transaction. Each time the City proposed to take property for street opening, the land commissioner convened a jury of citizens to determine, first, the value of the land appropriated, and second, the offsetting *benefit*, or increased value, that would accrue to adjacent land after the opening of the proposed street. If the owner's losses exceeded his benefit, he was entitled to compensation, but only so much as equaled "the value to the public generally."[19] This highly ambiguous trailer effectively restricted what might otherwise have been construed as a nearly limitless public liability. It contributed to a system that operated through the 1860s with reasonable efficiency. The accounts recorded for the 1856 opening of a stretch of Geyer Avenue offer an example of the assessment practice at work: of thirty-three affected property owners, all received some compensation, and only two (the men with the largest amounts of appropriated land) appealed the jury's decision. The others settled for small sums of between $3.75 and $5.75 for what apparently were 25-foot frontages along the new right-of-way.[20]

In 1867, any fiscal reservations that the city engineer may have had about ordering street openings were considerably lessened by the passage of a revised charter. This act, passed amid a post–Civil War boom in the city's bonded debt (most of it going to such long-needed projects as a new waterworks, sewers, and harbor improvements), pushed improvement expenses farther from general public responsibility and more squarely into the laps of particular property owners. One limited the City's responsibility for payment (that is, "the value to the public generally") to one-tenth of the actual value of the appropriated land. The other extended the definition of who might be assessed for benefits and damages beyond the directly affected abutting residents to include any landholder within one half-block or 150 feet of the opening.[21] These rules essentially ensured that the City would never be forced to slow the street-opening process for want of sufficient funds—a fact that held especially for remote, outlying areas, where land values were low to begin with, and where the benefit of new streets accrued almost entirely to neighboring property owners rather than to the city at large.

Indeed, only rarely did the City pay *any* South Side street-opening costs after the passage of the 1867 10 percent law. In a number of cases, as in the 1871 opening of Allen Avenue from Second Carondelet to Jefferson (a stretch of land owned almost entirely by Thomas Allen), the land jury determined that the owner's benefits and damages were virtually equal, and little or no money actually changed hands. Even in the case of a large and important street like Lafayette Avenue, opened from Jefferson to Grand in 1872, the City was relieved of any financial responsibility. Here, the jury decided on the claims of 113 owners; 70 were determined to owe money for the benefits that they stood to gain over and above the damages incurred by the City's appropriation, while only 40 suffered damages that exceeded the value of their benefits. In all, the City was owed a gross total of $45,767 in benefits for this stretch of land, of which $42,632 was payable back to owners for their damages. The public treasury therefore increased by $3,135 as a result of the transaction. On less crucial routes in the study area, the imbalance of private over public cost shifted in even more lopsided fashion. The sixty-four assessments made on Salena Street, from Lynch Street south to Wyoming Street, totaled $2,475 in private benefits owed to the City, with only $553 in offsetting damages. The path of Second Carondelet Avenue ran through 147 land parcels when that street was extended in the 1870s; the owners of these lots suffered a cumulative total of $2,640 in damages while being assessed $13,642 in benefits: a net total of $11,002 owed by property owners to the City for the "benefit" of having had their land confiscated.[22]

ILLUSTRATION 6-4.
Crittenden Street, bird's-eye view, 1875. One block north of Arsenal Street, Crittenden Street, though legally open, is barely distinguishable as a line of fences passing between yards in Camille Dry's 1875 view. (Reprinted from Camille N. Dry and Richard J. Compton, *Pictorial St. Louis: A Topographical Survey Drawn in Perspective* [St. Louis, 1876], plate 36, courtesy of Missouri Historical Society)

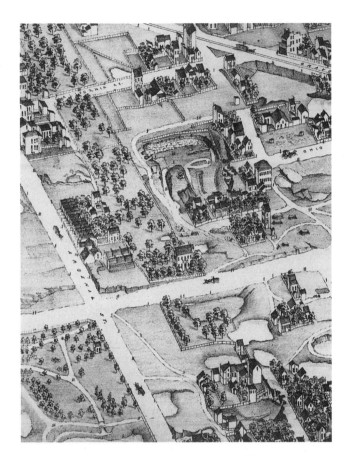

There might have been some justice to such calculations had street opening been a reliable harbinger of the impending physical improvement of a neighborhood. But in the relative absence of planning or order that characterized infrastructural improvements in St. Louis at the time, an "open street" was more often a legal convenience than it was a clear right-of-way awaiting the arrival of the steamroller. Typical of the South Side, in particular, were blocks like Minnesota Street, north of Cherokee Street, a legally opened stretch of road that as of 1878 was reported to be obstructed by the fences of landowners who still considered it a part of their property; or Ann Avenue west of Mississippi Avenue, declared open by the City in 1871 but soon used as the site of a private race track, an inconsistency that escaped official notice for more than two decades.[23] Camille N. Dry's 1875 views offer far more graphic testimony than do written records of the effect of such uneven development on the urban landscape of the South Side. Crittenden Street, open from Second Carondelet west to a point beyond Gravois since 1869, is barely visible as a gap between yards; its route is interrupted by ponds and animal pens (Illustration 6-4).[24] Even in the Second Common Subdivision, developed by the City itself over twenty

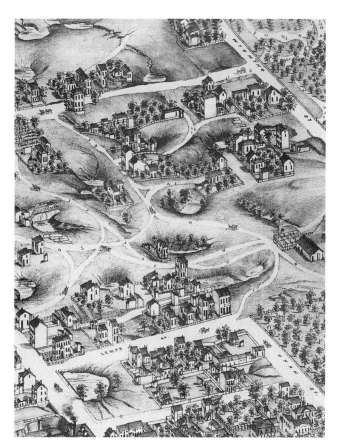

ILLUSTRATION 6-5.
*Utah Street, bird's-eye
view, 1875.* Technically
established in the Second
Common Subdivision of
1854, Utah west of Lemp
Avenue remained little
more than a meandering
path two decades later.
(Reprinted from Camille
N. Dry and Richard J.
Compton, *Pictorial
St. Louis: A Topographical
Survey Drawn in Perspec-
tive* [St. Louis, 1876],
plate 29, courtesy of
Missouri Historical
Society)

years prior to Dry's work, the artist's unblinking look at the land gave the lie
to the neatly mapped, straight lines of the surveyors and mapmakers who preceded him: Utah Street had not actually been opened through the subdivision
until 1875; even then, as Dry showed, it remained little more than a narrow,
curving path skirting the ponds, yards, and quarries that covered what was, on
paper, an orderly grid of 25-foot houselots (Illustration 6-5).

A close look at opening and improvement ordinances in one limited, but
probably not atypical, portion of the South Side—what is today known as the
Benton Park neighborhood, surrounding the McNair area—offers some measure of the unpredictable rate at which streets, once opened, were improved.
The interval between opening and improvement in this area ranged anywhere
from a minimum of one year to the remarkable gap of sixteen years that separated the opening and paving of Second Carondelet Avenue.[25] We can see,
then, that the circumstances under which the public streetscape was developed ensured little relation between growth *per se* and the realization of the
kind of regionally neutral improvements suggested in the Common subdivisions. Instead, the City's continuing reliance on cheap materials, highly

localized improvements, and cost-free street openings ensured that early streetmaking would serve as much to separate the neighborhoods of the South Side from one another (and from the rest of the city) as to pull them together.

The Effects of the 1876 Charter on the South Side Streetscape

There were at least two ways of overcoming the uncoordinated, unpredictable workings of the public improvement process. One was to maintain direct, private control over one's street, to protect it from the vagaries of the City's improvement process by preserving it as the private property of those who owned the land along its route. Instead of paying money to city hall, property owners could then assess themselves the amount they deemed appropriate for the improvement and upkeep of their street. Instead of waiting for municipal officials to authorize such improvement and having no say over the method by which it was carried out, they could hire and oversee the work of whomever they chose. This solution, which led to the creation of what came to be known as "private places" or, more commonly, "private streets," was first employed for Benton Place, a *cul de sac* laid out in 1868 in the exclusive Lafayette Park neighborhood on the near South Side. Benton Place would prove a geographical anomaly; the spate of private street development that followed in subsequent decades was concentrated along the central corridor west of Lucas Place (a restricted but technically public street), just north of the Mill Creek Valley. But the implications of the general model of the private street—of wealthy St. Louisans banding together with the intention of *bypassing* public law, rather than shaping it, as they once might have—resonated far beyond the privileged confines of the central corridor. The private streets became, to many residents of the South Side, a conspicuous reminder of what their own neighborhood lacked: efficient street improvements, for example, or restricted land uses. For this reason if for no other, these streets remained a powerful presence in the minds of those whose only glimpse inside the gates was likely to come as they delivered the coal or carried away the trash.[26]

The other way to improve the flawed streetmaking process was by improving its coordination and supervision at a citywide level—that is, by working within the evolving system of municipal regulation and finance. The idea of establishing a general plan for the layout and improvement of the city's streets was by no means new; it had existed in some form or another since the eighteenth century, and had even been formally ordered across the Common property in the 1855 charter.[27] But a truly comprehensive effort to integrate street planning into an overall plan for improved municipal decision-making awaited the enactment, in 1876, of the country's first home-rule charter, a milestone of municipal legislation that has profoundly affected the city, for good and for ill, to this day.[28] The charter was accompanied by a "Scheme for the Separation of the Governments of St. Louis City and County," which removed county authority from within the city limits and, in exchange for assuming the county's entire debt load, ambitiously extended the city's area threefold, moving its western boundary nearly four miles to a line just beyond the edge of the newly planned Forest Park. Where earlier support for a city-county separation had come from county residents unhappy with the distance required to travel to the seat of government, the new "Scheme" was very much the work of city residents and politicians—among them, the rising newspaper editor Joseph Pulitzer—chafing at the bit of an administrative and judiciary system grown increasingly unsympathetic to the needs of a growing metropolis.

The charter and scheme, authorized by the Missouri constitution of 1875 and drafted in the following year, addressed the problem of updating governmental functions within the newly expanded city. As such, they were packed with a number of features that reflected their framers' disenchantment with past practices of city-building, as well as their concerted effort to encourage efficiency and long-range economy in a city that was conspicuously short on both suits. The members of the board of freeholders that met through the spring and summer months of 1876 were members of a select group; they were elected from a slate of names nominated by a coalition of local business and civic organizations. The board contrived, nevertheless, to prepare a document that would appeal to city residents of all classes, despite the more extreme conservative views of members like Silas Bent, who argued that "municipal government should be a purely business organization, in the success of which each citizen is interested in proportion to the amount of property he has at stake," and who called for votes to be distributed among citizens according to their wealth. The scheme and charter as finally drafted represented a package palatable enough to garner the endorsement of all three of the city's German newspapers, which were traditionally the progressive voice of the South Side's working- and middle-class immigrant population.[29]

Financially, the new system contained much to appeal to the citizen of moderate means: it limited property taxes to 1 percent in the pre-1876 limits and one-quarter of 1 percent within the new bounds; it lifted the 10 percent limit on the city's share of land appropriation costs, while at the same time relieving landowners of any assessment for street improvement that exceeded 25 percent of the value of their property (a provision that, as we will see, was meant to favor residents of the poorer parts of the city).[30]

Administratively, however, the new measures seemed to vest more power in a centralized executive system that was less likely to bend either to the excesses of patronage politics or to the legitimate concerns of neighborhood-based interests. The mayor's term was expanded from two to four years. The old council, which had consisted of two members from each ward, elected for two-year terms, was elevated to a more exclusive upper house of thirteen property-owning men, elected for four-year terms by citywide vote. Beneath it, a newly created house of delegates consisted of twenty-eight members, one from each of the city's wards, each elected for a two-year term.[31] Responsibility for the assessment of street-opening damages and benefits was transferred from the traditional jury of peers to a court-appointed commission of three "disinterested" men who, like council members, had to meet a stiff, five-year minimum residency requirement.[32]

The same spirit of centralization, and the same redistribution of citywide powers among a relatively smaller group of officials, reached into all of the corridors of city hall and the courthouse. In spite of the number of responsibilities taken over by the City from the county and state governments (including authority not only over taxation but over such vital administrative bodies as the police, health, and water boards), the scheme and charter managed to reduce by half the number of boards used to carry out governmental functions.[33] Of those commissions that remained, the mayorally appointed chairmen of five of the most important (the street, sewer, water, harbor-and-wharf, and park commissions) were brought together into one body that was charged with an unprecedented degree of coordination and control over the city landscape: the board of public improvements.

The members of this exclusive board exercised a wider range of duties than had previously been enjoyed by government officials. To these five commissioners was granted the power to make those decisions that had once been scattered about a number of city and county offices: decisions about street openings, the location of sewers, or the advisability of filling ponds or leveling hills. Their deliberations were to be informed at all times by Article 6, Section 1, of the charter, a passage that expressed a broader and more explicit official desire for an ordered landscape than anything seen in St. Louis since the days of the Spanish governor Gálvez. This clause gave to the municipal assembly the task of "establish[ing] a general plan for the location and graduation of streets within the city"; once done, the board would ensure that "in all subdivisions of property hereafter made by the respective owners, they shall conform their streets to said general plan."[34] Here was an opportunity, at last, to impose upon the entire city the kind of preplanned spatial order that, since the American takeover, had been contemplated only for that patch of land that belonged explicitly to the public domain: the Common.

But the promise of order, even had it been kept, was only coincidentally related to the achievement of either an efficient system of inter-neighborhood connections or an equitable distribution of improvements. The scheme and charter were organized primarily around a political vision—one that balanced traditional fiscal conservatism with improved coordination of public functions—rather than a spatial vision.[35] South Side voters might have been less enthusiastic in their support of the new law had they foreseen the ways in which its rationalizing, simplifying intentions would serve primarily to confirm and harden existing inequities in the urban landscape. A generation after the apparent introduction of a more carefully controlled and broadly directed system of land division and distribution (represented in the Second and Third Common Subdivisions), residents of South St. Louis would find that newly strengthened municipal regulation often did little more than apply a public-spirited gloss to decisions that, whether based in self-interest, political favoritism, or geographical necessity, had the cumulative effect of neglecting or delaying the much-needed improvement of their neighborhood. While the fact that *any* system of public improvements should have developed in the city was, in Jon Teaford's phrase, an "unheralded triumph" that deserves its due, it is nevertheless true that for many St. Louisans at the time, the weaknesses of that system were far more obvious than its strengths. Those weaknesses often derived from the implicit presumption (if not the explicit claim) that the city's landscape was still an even playing field, that decisions made for all parts of the city would affect each individual part in the same way, and that citizens rested on roughly the same footing in matters pertaining to their demands for public services and their opportunities to make use of them.

The "general plan" called for in the charter provides a case in point. Its details were left to the discretion of the assembly, with one basic constraint. The document's framers had taken care to provide some measure that might arrest what they considered the needless, excessive proliferation of street openings in the city. To that end, they established a minimum legal distance of 220 feet between parallel east-west streets and 500 feet between north-south streets.[36] This basic regulation effectively mandated the creation of oblong blocks whose short sides fronted on north-south streets—the opposite of the layout already perfected in the Second and Third Common Subdivisions. Such a configuration encouraged the smooth flow of east-west traffic and, indeed, matched the shape of most of the blocks being laid out in the fast-growing central corridor (roughly, from the Pacific Railroad tracks on the south to Morgan Street—today's Delmar Boulevard—on the north). The plan made perfect sense in the context of improving connections from the retail, professional, governmental, and manufacturing facilities clustered around the courthouse and the central waterfront to the residential or secondary commercial areas that spread directly west, unimpeded by major geographical irregularities.

But as we have seen, the South Side was clearly impeded by geographical circumstance from linking neatly to the center of the city; further, even had the central valley and the railroad tracks not blocked this connection, the charter's mandated block-shape, which expedited traffic in an east-west direction, would have been less than ideal for improving traffic flow from either the North or the South Sides toward downtown. Nor did the sole weakness of the charter's vague plan lie in this directional choice. The document also presumed that any new development would take place on undivided land. That presumption offered little help to developers and city officials struggling to rationalize the confounding overlap of extant land divisions that fragmented so much of the city's streetscape. Where the streets of DeWard's Common survey in South St. Louis collided with the dense, angled streetscape that overlay the old common fields, landowners and developers regularly disputed the imposition of one system or the other according to how they had arranged their own property; the charter's simple guidelines offered no system for resolving such disputes.[37]

In those cases where the charter's plan provisions did apply, there was no certainty that they would be followed. In 1878, for instance, the board of public improvements considered opening the streets of the small Compton Hill Addition, which was platted on the property of Richard Graham.[38] The executors of Graham's estate, like previous developers in the immediate vicinity, had laid out this subdivision in keeping with the streets of the nearby Third Common Subdivision. The resultant tall, narrow block was the opposite in its proportions of the block shape mandated by law. After paying lip service to the obvious inconsistency, the board voted to approve the streets as proposed and to ignore the charter.

By the end of the year, the board, charged with introducing and maintaining order on the chaotic, *ad hoc* city landscape, had given up on the very idea of a "general plan." To properly prepare such a plan, they argued, would require years of work. In the meantime, they had been asked to review dozens of new subdivision plats. To postpone approval of these developments in the name of a non-existent plan appeared increasingly ludicrous. By far the most reasonable solution, in the commissioners' minds, was to accept the 220-foot/ 500-foot rule (although we have already seen the depth of their commitment to that clause), then declare each subdivision, after its approval, "a part of the general plan of the city." They asked for and received permission from the city counselor to let this paradigm of cart-before-the-horse planning, essentially a codification of existing practice, substitute for any more positive (and more controversial) action.[39] The idea of the plan was simply too comprehensive, and too far from the prevailing deference to individual initiative, to be successfully implemented.

The charter's "general plan" provision, then, proved at various points either useless or simply dismissable, until at last it was dispensed with. There was as yet no visual image of the city sufficiently compelling, or politically persuasive, to guide a government still only tentatively committed to taking a more active stance toward the shaping of urban space. Other aspects of the charter pertaining to public improvements, equally suggestive of a commitment to imposing a new citywide landscape order, were in the end equally susceptible to a contrary and more immediate commitment to saving money. By centralizing street-improvement decisions under the aegis of the board of public improvements, and by stipulating the manner in which the board should arrive at these decisions, the framers of the charter had given to the paving process a consistency that it had lacked in earlier years. But that consistency, based more on the traditional commitment to expediency than on a specific conception of how the government should control the urban landscape, only worked to arrest the improvement process, not to reform it. Effectively, government control continued to increase the growing distinctiveness of the physical character of areas like the South Side. The hypothetical landscape of equally drawn blocks and equally applied regulations, suggested in the charter, was collapsing under the weight of political, social, and geographic fragmentation.

Citywide, the charter had a dampening effect on the speed with which proposed street improvements could be realized. In 1878, the board reported that it had approved just over a third of the street and alley petitions brought before it; in 1881 that figure had declined to less than 20 percent, and by 1883 the ratio had leveled off at 25 percent.[40] A review, within the board's *Journal*, of street and alley petitions in the heart of South St. Louis reveals that these neighborhoods were, proportionally, even harder-hit by the board's strictness than was the rest of the city. In that period for which records were found (October 1877–February 1880), twenty-six petitions were submitted from this area. Four were approved.[41]

Obstacles to the rapid improvement of the irregular, almost-rural South Side streetscape that Camille Dry had so thoroughly documented just prior to the passage of the charter fell under a handful of general categories. First, the board was required to certify that any petition for sewer or water-pipe extension or for street opening be signed by a majority of the affected property owners. Further, they seem to have applied this standard to paving petitions as well, although not formally required to do so. If an insufficient number of landowners petitioned for improvement, or if those who requested paving represented less than half of the affected frontage, the board denied the request. Rather than reflect an abiding concern with individual rights, the majority-approval clause often served as a legitimization for decisions that the board would have made regardless of neighborhood opinion.[42] If the members of the board decided that opening or improvement was advisable, then resident approval became a moot point. In this manner Ohio Avenue, north of Shenandoah Street, was ordered open on the basis of its value as a drainage route, without the prompting of any petition. In a similar move, the board overrode its own reservations about the legality of opening a sidewalk on a two-block stretch of Second Carondelet Avenue, unbidden by abutting residents. In the latter decision, the ever-frugal commissioners were almost certainly influenced by the fact that sidewalk costs were, in any case, held by the charter to be the responsibility of the owners; the board's decision therefore entailed no commitment of public funds.[43]

Residents' approval was likewise of secondary importance when good-natured political arm-twisting could be substituted in its stead. Such influence peddling generally consisted of little more than the well-timed appearance of one or another elected official at a board meeting. After the board dismissed a petition to open Missouri Avenue north of Utah Street, they heard the combined objections of Councilman Nicholas Berg and Eleventh Ward Delegate A. N. DeMenil, and then proceeded to overturn their own decision.[44] The Ninth Ward's representative in the house of delegates, Ernest H. Vordtriede, was particularly active in lobbying before the board in favor of public improvements in his district. Vordtriede, a developer of property just east of Benton Park, frequently appeared at the board's meetings in the late 1870s, pleading the "urgent public necessity" of various proposed projects.[45] At times, he simply represented the signatories of properly prepared petitions, as when he argued for the filling of the pond that lay just east of Jefferson Avenue, south of Sidney Street (see Illustration 5-11). At other times, Vordtriede arrived before the board fortified only with his convictions and his political influence. He asked for and received authorization for major improvements like the installation of sidewalks on long stretches of Sidney and Victor Streets, although he seems to have been less successful in his efforts to push improvement of the important central stretch of Second Carondelet that lay between Victor and Lynch Streets.[46]

Other impediments to the neighborhood's steady, orderly development were built into the land itself. The board of public improvements proved especially sensitive to the costs of improving uneven, irregular land, something that South St. Louis offered in generous helpings. Time and again, they turned down petitions for street improvement from those residents who most dearly needed it: people whose property was virtually inaccessible, by virtue either of geological accident or of the scars left by earlier quarrying for the stone used to smooth the landscape of the rest of the city. One block near the corner of Jefferson Avenue and Cherokee Street—a block that, as part of the Second Common Subdivision, theoretically had been developed and improved for nearly twenty-five years—was reported by the board to contain a quarry that extended as far as 40 feet below ground level. Residents' petition for an alley through the center of this misshapen land (the construction of which would have necessitated improvement of the entire block) was summarily denied.[47] Certainly, cutting and filling to correct this kind of irregularity, if approved, often created more problems. When a group of landowners in the vicinity of Chippewa Street, for instance, saw that thoroughfare being graded in the autumn of 1879, they asked that their own adjacent blocks of Missouri and Indiana Avenues be improved in order to connect with the newly leveled route. This action, the board discovered, would place the petitioners' house-lots 8 to 10 feet below the new street grade; thus the net effect of the action would have been to worsen, rather than better, their predicament.[48]

However, it was a measure originally designed to win for the charter the support of voters in neighborhoods like the South Side that acted, perversely, to exert the most marked negative impact on the landscape of the area. The roots of Article 6, Section 18, lay in an aspect of city law that had long been a source of bewilderment and irritation to St. Louisans of all walks of life, in every section of town. Like General William Tecumseh Sherman, living out his retirement on a quiet stretch of Garrison Street on the North Side, they wondered why "the city collects 1/2 pc for streets and alleys"—that fraction of municipal taxes reserved for opening and grading costs—"and yet we have to pay separately for their construction and maintenance."[49] The separate paving assessment, which provided a means of bypassing legally mandated property tax limits, was likened by Sherman and others to confiscation of private property. But the general, who feared that the assessor's office had singled him out "as a rich goose to pluck," was less victimized in this respect than were the owners of cheaper lands around the unimproved fringes of the city, for whom a single paving assessment could actually approach the entire value of their property. It was this perceived injustice that the Charter's framers tried to redress by limiting each abutting landowner's share of the cost of street-paving to 25 percent of the assessed value of his property.[50] This clause should have given outlying St. Louis residents an affordable, subsidized means of enjoying the improvements (and the attendant appreciation in property values) that others in the city took for granted. But its motivation, to judge from the board's subsequent interpretation, lay less in a desire to see street improvement spread to poorer neighborhoods (that is, in a positive, visual image of the proper course of urban growth) than in a political conviction that the City had a responsibility to keep its citizens safe from excessive taxation. When combined with the equally strong mandate of public fiscal constraint, this conviction served, once again, to ensure that inefficiencies and inequities in the public landscape were amplified rather than diminished.

Given their *de facto* power to approve or deny street-improvement proposals essentially according to their own criteria, the board opted repeatedly to promote fiscal responsibility over infrastructural investment. Their loss of faith in the once common assumption that the constant expansion of landscape improvements was a necessary catalyst to urban prosperity was summed up bluntly in their annual report of 1880. The board's glum assessment of the state of the city's public improvements that year betrayed a reticence that contrasted sharply with the optimistic expansionism of the 1850s and 1860s: "Until the many, and wide, open spaces that now separate the built up parts of the city are measurably filled up," it concluded, "the construction of new streets is the least important class of public works [to be undertaken]."[51]

The 25 percent clause proved to be the primary means by which the board rationalized its hesitation to promote the improvement of underdeveloped neighborhoods like the South Side. Paving costs were more or less constant throughout the city; land values were not. The improvement of a block on Olive or Pine Street might have resulted in an assessment of each landowner of perhaps 10 percent of the value of his lot; the same work carried out on Rappahannock or Miami Street might require a tax of 50 percent or more of neighboring property values. Under the charter, the City was now compelled to cover that part of such costs in excess of one-quarter of neighboring land values, yet the board proved repeatedly unwilling to make this commitment. Instead, in case after case, "free" paving in the heart of the city was approved summarily, while "expensive" paving on the outskirts was denied.

At the heart of the board's explanations for its decisions in such cases was a specific conception of the priority of public interest, which now lay more in saving money than in promoting unfettered growth, over private interest, which could be loosely defined as getting more from the city than one gave back. In denying the petitioners for the improvement of a two-block stretch of California Street, between Miami and Chippewa Streets, the board first calculated that two-thirds of the cost of the work would have to come from the public treasury; they then reasoned that, because the improvement "will benefit only the few resident property owners," such a civic expenditure was unjustifiable.[52] The case of another California Street petition, this one for the blocks between Cherokee and Rappahannock Streets, provides a more detailed glimpse of the assessment process at work. Of the total $21,992 required for the pavement of this mile-long segment of road, $15,214 (or nearly 70 percent) would have come from City coffers. Suggesting implicitly that some projects might justify that expense, the board asserted in this case: "the street is an unimportant one . . . and is not in any sense of the word a thoroughfare for the public."[53] Decades of haphazard and economically draining growth had proven that expansion, in itself, was no longer key to the city's well-being. The precedent had by this time developed that growth that came at little or no public cost was allowed to occur unquestioned; where public funds were involved, the "public's" benefit had to be far more explicitly justified.

This vaguely defined sense of public utility was the principle on which street-improvement authorization often turned in the years following the passage of the charter. If property owners expected the City's financial assistance, the board reasoned, then they should demonstrate that the City would realize some return on its investment. This return seems to have been defined loosely as the utility of the street either in carrying traffic from one developed neighborhood to another or in improving drainage over a wide surrounding area. If petitioners were unable to prove such utility, then the board considered their benefit to be "private," and expected them to pay their own expenses. The tone that the commissioners employed in explaining their decisions at times verged on the kind of ill-concealed impatience that a parent reserves for a recalcitrant child. Since the use of one South Side street, as they insisted, "would be confined almost entirely to the wants of the few people living on the street," the petitioners clearly had but one alternative: "if the property owners along the street would club together and build a plank sidewalk along the front of their residences, it would relieve them of the greater part of the inconvenience they now suffer."[54] The board, a product of the kind of growing power that municipal government had obtained over factional, private interests since the 1850s, did not hesitate to suggest that the city-building initiative be returned to the private sphere. But the people comprised within that sphere had changed markedly in thirty years; the small-time speculator on Lynch Street or the homeowner on Rappahannock Street had nowhere near the same means as a Thomas Allen to exercise such initiative.

Obviously, the City's assessment of a street's "public necessity" had a prophetic as well as a descriptive aspect. Street paving in unimproved or remote sections of town, where property values were low, was almost certain to require substantial public expense. This locational circumstance was, however, an almost certain guarantor that that expenditure would not be approved by the board of public improvements. By remaining unimproved, such streets acted as impediments to the future improvement of any other streets around them; the board had no reason to pave a street that only led from one unpaved block to another.[55] Thus the mandate given the board, particularly the 25 percent rule, served to slow the rate at which the city's streets were improved and to preserve those inequities in the city's landscape already evident prior to 1876. To this cycle of caution and neglect we can attribute a large degree of the slowness with which the South Side's streets (and, to a lesser extent, those of the far North Side) were graded and paved in the decade following the passage of the charter. The map of improved streets in the study area as of 1886 reads only slightly differently from the map of 1876—in spite of the fact that more than a dozen new subdivisions were dedicated during the same period.[56]

From what we have seen thus far of the rationalization and regulation of street improvement under the aegis of the board of public improvement, it would seem that no outlying or poorly improved area of St. Louis could have fared well in the late 1870s and 1880s. But the board's bottom-line conservatism was belied, here and there, by hints that their definition of the public interest included some surprisingly specific notions about the proper shape of the growing city. Acknowledging the continued isolation of South St. Louis, but denying their own agency in perpetuating it, they reported in 1878 that the railroad tracks in the Mill Creek Valley presented "an almost insurmountable barrier to free communication between the two parts of the city, and have seriously retarded improvement of the southern portion."[57] The board members' treatment of a petition for the improvement of the newly opened Lindell Boulevard two years later suggests that this inequity simply bolstered their own inclinations to concentrate public expenditures in the central corridor. The new road, which led west from the intersection of Grand

Avenue and Olive Street (soon to serve as the site of the new campus of St. Louis University) to the undeveloped expanse of Forest Park at the edge of the city limits, was charted through land as unimproved and as inexpensive as any on the South Side. To improve this sparsely settled thoroughfare would require the same kind of municipal financial commitment that the board had so often abdicated in the case of South Side petitions. But the Lindell application was approved on the first day of its presentation. The board excused its uncharacteristic generosity by explaining that, had they made the more fiscally conservative choice, "we would be justly chargeable with the offense of neglecting an improvement which would greatly tend to the material interest of our city."[58]

The ostensibly objective street-making regulations that attended the 1876 charter had "objectively" tended to encourage the improvement of some neighborhoods (particularly those that could pay for their own improvements, or those that were already well-improved) over others. By 1880, that self-perpetuating cycle was beginning to highlight more clearly than before the differences between one part of the city and another. The result was the emergence of a more subjective sense among those responsible for public improvement as to the specific geographic parameters of the public's "material interest." That interest, in the case of the Lindell petition, apparently lay in promoting the orderly and rapid development of a region whose low density and ample open space already appeared to be less a matter of neglect than of choice. It was the blocks of this burgeoning "West End" of the city that one visiting New Yorker, Walt Whitman, had proclaimed in 1879 "the roomiest by far of any city I have ever seen"; and it was this area that the poet had admired for its "thousands and thousands of fine comfortable 5 or $6000 well built brick or stone houses, with gardens around them."[59] That the favoritism shown toward the West End reflected an apparent class or ethnic bias on the part of the government was perhaps not surprising. Beyond that, however, the board's decision on the Lindell petition suggested a shift away from policies based solely on a desire to curb public expense, toward those that consciously and actively promoted existing differences within the city. In the process, a new and more specific notion of the proper shape of the city was coming into sharper focus.

The City Takes the Initiative: Reconstruction and Boulevards

The decision to pave Lindell was not acted upon for several years more; once realized, it helped to speed the migration of wealthier St. Louisans out along the blocks of the central corridor to the West End. Just as important, it signaled the onset in the early 1880s of a new and more aggressive municipal approach to the selective improvement of the streetscape. This new direction was in large part an attempt to deal with the contradictions contained within the existing system of street improvement. On the one hand, the obvious deterioration of the city's macadamized streets made driving conditions almost impossible (or, at best, unpredictable) and necessitated constant repair, as well as the sprinkling of some heavily traveled blocks up to five times daily.[60] By any standard, and particularly in comparison with the well-maintained, limited-access private streets whose concurrent development dramatically punctuated parts of the city, the soft, uneven gravel roadbeds that crisscrossed old and new neighborhoods alike were untenable. To improve and maintain them in more durable fashion, on the other hand, required money that simply did not exist—especially given the 25 percent clause, as well as the even deeper problem of a 1 percent general tax that had somehow to be stretched to include all those services once assessed and provided separately by the county.[61] The City's power to exercise its discretion regarding street improvement in the late 1870s, strengthened as it was by the charter, was in large part limited to the ability to say no—to use frugality, rather than largesse, as a tool for shaping the landscape in desired ways.

This conflict of growing needs and limited resources found its resolution in two primary innovations in the street laws of the 1880s, both of which furthered the post-charter trend of using public authority to mandate private responsibility for the landscape, but each of which displayed a new geographical specificity to street policies. The first was a system for ordering the reconstruction of selected streets at the full expense of abutting property owners, the second a "Boulevard Law" that allowed the City to levy special assessments for the improvement of streets that would be restricted from undesirable development or commercial traffic. Both innovations shifted the expense of street improvement further toward individual assessments, even where such improvement was demonstrably of citywide value. Both served, like the Lindell Boulevard allocation, to increase the lopsided, sectional character of the quality of city streets. An implicit promise had been made in the Second and Third Common Subdivisions, and later encouraged in Article 6 of the charter, that strengthened public powers would be used to expedite to areas like South St. Louis the kinds of public works they badly needed. However, boulevards and reconstructed streets rested on the frank admission that the government, as it usually had in the past, would give the most to those of its citizens able to pay the most. The longstanding tradition of special assessments ensured that, when the government did exercise its new willingness to tax, it was obliged to assure the affected parties that their money was earmarked specifically for the blocks where they themselves lived and worked.

Much of the City's newfound power to order private contributions came about through its unending and long-unsuccessful effort to reconstruct worn-out macadam streets. The search for alternative paving materials had been conducted on a serious basis since the late 1860s, though always at a highly circumscribed, cautious scale. The closest thing to a "contending" material in those years was Nicolson pavement, a system of closely laid wooden blocks, sealed with tar, that was one of a number of wooden pavements gaining favor in American cities at the same time.[62] By 1872, there were 10 miles of Nicolson pavement in St. Louis; at around the same time, the unsuitability of these wood streets became unavoidably apparent.[63] The city engineer, citing in various reports inadequate sealing techniques and the inevitable weakening of lumber that resulted from its long river trip south from the forests of Wisconsin and Minnesota, estimated an average useful life of only five to six years for Nicolson streets.[64] Still, the budgetary constraints on street improvements militated against regular maintenance, and many of the wood-paved streets of the 1860s were simply left to deteriorate until well into the 1880s, by which time the street commissioner reported finding "nothing left of them but broken fragments and shreds of wood."[65]

The 1860s had seen the tentative introduction of a number of other experimental paving materials—including porphyry, concrete, even iron shavings—all of which had proven even more uniformly inadequate than Nicolson blocks.[66] By the following decade, this grab-bag of potential materials had been narrowed to a less exotic and more reliable list. Asphalt, which later dominated the city's street system, appeared as early as 1872, although various problems of greater or lesser gravity kept it from gaining popularity until a much later date.[67] An improved system of macadamizing, patented by the Telford Pavement Company of Orange, New Jersey, received its first tryout in 1873–1874. Although Telford paving methods eventually supplanted original macadam techniques as the city's most common form of inexpensive paving, they were initially almost as slow to gain favor as asphalt.[68]

The most promising and immediately usable paving material was also, unfortunately, the most expensive: granite block. Granite was only slightly less "homegrown" than limestone. It was quarried from the ample outcroppings of the St. Francis Mountains in southeastern Missouri, an area linked directly to St. Louis by way of the Iron Mountain Railroad. Still, a number of problems slowed granite's widespread acceptance. While its volcanic hardness ensured it a longer life than that of any other paving material, that quality also made it difficult to quarry and cut. Owing to the extra time necessary for its preparation, together with the added expense of rail transport to bring it into the city, granite had a basic cost approximately six times greater than macadam.[69] No engineering consideration could weigh more heavily than this simple fiscal fact when it came time to consider paving materials.

In 1869, the city engineer's office cautiously authorized a tiny amount of granite-block repaving (less than one-twentieth of a mile in total length) at City expense. Four years later, a similarly parsimonious amount was approved. A year after that, a relatively ambitious quarter-mile length of paving was laid.

By 1875, St. Louis could boast just one-third of a mile of granite-paved streets, an amenity that the City had acquired at a cost to the public treasury of more than $50,000. After city voters refused to pass an 1874 bond issue that would have raised an additional $2.5 million for street reconstruction, the municipal assembly resolved at last to relieve the public coffers by reclassifying street reconstruction not as "repair" (which was by law carried out at City cost) but as paving, fully chargeable to abutting landowners. The provision was retained in the new charter, where it was intentionally protected from the 25 percent limit that governed ordinary street improvement.[70]

What made sense to the guardians of the city budget, however, did not necessarily accord with the wishes of the citizens in whose names they served. Street reconstruction was seen, by those who suffered most from its glacial pace, as a fundamental right to which they were entitled, and for which they had already paid. When property owners on heavily traveled Second Street petitioned the board of public improvements for new granite paving, they were reminded that they themselves would pay for the project; the petition was promptly withdrawn. The same impasse was reached a year later, when four hundred downtown landowners requested, then rejected, the reconstruction of Main Street, again on the grounds of expense. In its explanation of the latter episode, the board saw fit to question the legislated frugality that it had always accepted as a given in its review of South Side petitions. The commissioners in this case asked legislators for more funding, warning that "there will, for the present be [no] street reconstruction in St. Louis, until the burden of it is shifted onto the city at large."[71] Their own practical task, then, led the board to endorse a method of financing that conflicted with the method endorsed by elected officials. This emerging gap between efficiency and political expediency would suggest to some that public improvements be further removed from the vagaries of the political process, and that decision-making in regard to the shape of the landscape be placed still more firmly in the hands of professionals.

That the board and its earlier counterpart, the city engineer's office, had by this time developed a clear, geographically based idea of which streets served a public rather than purely local function has been demonstrated. In the matter of street reconstruction, their biases were no less evident. Calling in his 1877 report for an additional $50,000 appropriation for the repaving of downtown streets, the city engineer argued that such work benefited the entire city and should be financed accordingly. Where the owner of property in a distant residential district stood to reap personal benefits in the value of his land after street reconstruction, the owner of already valuable downtown land would see, in contrast, only "a trifling increase of the value of his property" after such work, hence the engineer's justification for asking the entire city to foot the bill for downtown improvements.[72] By 1881, Mayor William L. Ewing, remarking on the "harshness" of the reconstruction assessment law, complained that no extended scheme of reconstruction was feasible until the City agreed to lift the financial burden from individual owners. Since reconstruction had never been seriously proposed beyond the limits of the heavily traveled streets of downtown, the specific identity of the constituency that the mayor proposed to relieve was clear to anyone who read his plea.[73]

A portion of that relief was forthcoming later in the same year, when the assembly belatedly agreed to city officials' request for the $50,000 reconstruction appropriation. This money was stretched, in the following months, to cover the cost of another mile of granite paving downtown.[74] The prospect of this dramatic and hopefully permanent improvement to the tired streets of the waterfront inspired one optimistic reporter for the *Globe-Democrat* to enthuse that "the avenues of trade and travel will be made new wherever necessary, because property owners have so willed, and large numbers have expressed their determination to put their hands down deep into their pockets to see it done."[75] This confident prediction of willing private sacrifice for the public good proved to be less prescient than it was wishful. In the end, it was the members of the municipal assembly, at last risking the inevitable political fallout, who reached deep into the pockets of downtown property owners, authorizing extensive assessment for granite repavement against their wishes.[76] Once begun, such mandated improvements accelerated at a steady pace. The annual assessments collected by the City increased nearly sevenfold in the five years that followed the first large repavement mandate. By 1887, nearly 30 miles of additional granite paving covered the streets of downtown.[77]

Once it was known that landowners could be expected to shoulder the burden of financing street improvement, the focus of the board's efforts shifted demonstrably. The natural corollary to repaved downtown streets was, in the minds of public officials, a series of improved thoroughfares leading from the city center to selected residential neighborhoods. In the case of these newer, outlying streets, "improvement" was defined primarily not by the substitution of one stone for another, but by something less tangible: the regulation of permissible uses to conform to and encourage a specific, desirable neighborhood character. Although *de facto* zoning, in the form of subdivision land-use restrictions, was an increasingly accepted practice in St. Louis, the idea of actually dictating the use of the streets had hitherto been confined to the private places, where it presented no legal difficulty.[78] In August 1883, the board succeeded in pushing through the assembly an ordinance for the improvement of Lindell, Locust, Lucas, and Pine Streets. The law restricted each roadway to "light driving": a term that excluded streetcars, wagons and trucks, cattle, and delivery vehicles.[79] In exchange for the protection offered by these restrictions (protection not only of simple peace and quiet but of property values as well), the City assessed affected property owners both for paving and, in a charter-defying move, for grading. In effect, the government had created private streets without surrendering control of their use. The process of expanding the public role in shaping space, in a manner that resembled more closely the role hitherto played by private developers, had begun.

The act of placing limits on the free use of streets seemed to some observers a highly suspect operation, even without the questionable practice of unilaterally charging owners for grading costs.[80] Supporters sought to justify their stand with a new and more compelling articulation of the greater public good. Their awareness of the City's shaky legal grounds for enforcing these kinds of restrictions therefore coincided with a growing ambition, on the part of government and business leaders, to develop not simply a few isolated streets but "an imperial system of broad and spacious highways" that might span the breadth of the city and establish more firmly the government's role in shaping the city's growth.[81] Bolstering their customary practical arguments with an increasingly aesthetic rationale, the board of public improvements was joined by influential citizens like the merchant and industrial developer Samuel Cupples in calling for, and in 1891 securing, the passage of a Boulevard Law for the City of St. Louis.[82]

The Boulevard Law continued the precedent of the Lindell improvement ordinance in establishing public powers similar to, but ultimately greater than, the powers that private developers had begun to exercise. The law gave to the City the right to restrict development along selected streets to residential use only, to establish traffic limitations and uniform building setbacks, and to assess the owners of property along such streets for the entire expense of their construction. While Street Commissioner M. J. Murphy promised "a system that will equitably include all [of the city's] interests," the thoroughfares chosen as boulevards continued to reflect the geographical biases of earlier street-reconstruction efforts. Initial speculation about the application of the pending law had centered on Grand Avenue—the original north-south ring road that had traversed the city along its 1855 boundary—and Kingshighway, which served the same function as Grand but ran a mile to the west, through land included within the 1876 limits.[83] While Kingshighway (which connected the exclusive West End to points north and south) was among those streets advocated by the board for boulevard status after passage of the law, Grand was not. In fact, the other proposed boulevards constituted an "imperial system" within only the narrowest of empires: they all ran within the central corridor (Illustration 6-6).[84] Collectively, they offered further evidence that the decision-makers in city hall had continued to hold to a blind-sided view of the city. This view focused their attention on infrastructural improvement within a mile-wide strip that included most of the residences and workplaces of St. Louis's wealthiest citizens.

The Boulevard Law did have a lasting impact on the city's landscape, but it would be years before that impact became clear. Plagued from its inception by lawsuits from reluctant property owners, the law was struck down by the

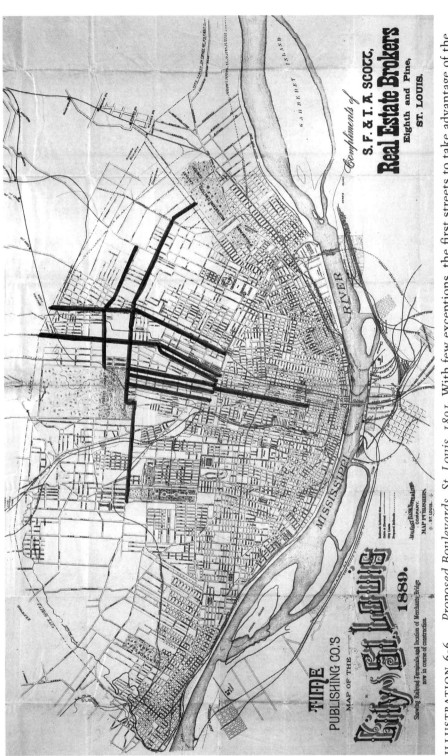

ILLUSTRATION 6-6. *Proposed Boulevards, St. Louis, 1891.* With few exceptions, the first streets to take advantage of the Boulevard Law were confined to the affluent central corridor, particularly in the newer neighborhoods of the West End. Only Kingshighway, which strategically linked Forest Park with Tower Grove Park, on the South Side, and O'Fallon Park, on the north, extended far into working-class neighborhoods. (Courtesy of the author; original map courtesy of the Missouri Historical Society)

state supreme court in 1897. In its six-year life, only a limited amount of boulevard improvement had actually been carried out, and only a limited amount of the costs of such improvements had actually been collected in keeping with the procedures allowed by the law.[85]

In terms of the "system" that boulevard advocates hoped to initiate across the city, the few improvements realized by the mid-1890s, all of them based on existing rights-of-way, hardly represented so much as a beginning. The board admitted in 1896 that the long-hoped-for development of a street plan "has remained a dead letter" and suggested that in the future the City consider planning main thoroughfares that, unlike the boulevards, "need not be straight nor parallel, nor laid with regard to property lines."[86] At the end of the century, local residents continued, as they had in decades past, to decry what local attorney Edward Schneiderhahn called the City's "shiftless, systemless handling of the streets," and continued to ask in vain for a "plan beforehand strictly adhered to."[87] Even the barest pretense of such a plan was officially dropped in the amended city charter, first proposed in 1898 and finally approved in 1901, which at last dropped the 220-foot/500-foot block-size requirement and suggested, rather feebly, that the municipal assembly "establish from time to time such streets as may be necessary to provide public thoroughfares for free and convenient traffic and communication" through the city.[88]

One effect of the law was clear from the outset: it signaled the beginning of a trend toward ever greater private assessments for public works. Even as residents of Lindell, West Pine, and the other boulevards received their first tax bills, the street commissioner was complaining about the financial constraints that continued to hamper improvement of the rest of the city's streets.[89] Hard pressed even in the best of times, the City's public-works budget felt the additional strain of the depression of 1893, which had unfortunately coincided with major public expenditures for the construction of a new city hall, as well as an unsuccessful effort to realize a fair sale price on the site of the structure that it replaced.[90] In June 1893, the state legislature relieved the City of any remaining fiscal burden associated with streetmaking; their law made the grading, paving, and reconstruction of streets, as well as the repair of alleys and sidewalks, the financial responsibility of abutting property owners.

Beyond adding these functions to the list of taxable services, the new law also removed the 25 percent clause of the 1876 charter. This alteration proved to be the law's most conspicuous and controversial feature. Reactions to it depended on whether one viewed the salient importance of the old limit as its theoretical guarantee of justice for poorer landowners, or as its practical effect of stalling the improvement process. Street Commissioner Murphy, steeped in the old faith in the *ipso facto* value of new streets, exclaimed that the removal of the 25 percent limit would "advance the interests of this city a great many years and ... remove the barrier to its prosperity that was becoming more and more apparent." Others, like Board President George Burnet, warned that the new system would "result in virtually confiscating many poor people's property in the north and south ends of the city."[91]

While the 1893 law, like the Boulevard Law before it, came under legal scrutiny (in this case, because the State-ordered legislation overrode aspects of a home-rule charter), it was supplanted by a similar, uncontested provision in the 1901 city charter. During the period in which the question of street-improvement assessment remained in limbo, the board of public improvements managed to slow the pace of South Side streetmaking to a crawl; the map of the study area as of 1903 (Illustration 6-7) differs from that of a decade earlier in the addition of a few improved streets through the southwest portion of the neighborhood, but little else. Self-initiated, self-financed improvements like those undertaken by the Connecticut Realty Company proved to be not just a good idea but a necessary one. Major gaps between streets remained; residents complained that even "what our City Fathers call streets or imitations thereof" were regularly reduced to the appearance of "a general hog wallowing pond," and indeed, the city health commissioner reported finding seventeen ponds—a polite term for garbage-strewn sinkholes—that covered public property within the study area alone (Illustration 6-8).[92] The board's attitude toward improvement petitions continued to be, by its own admission, that "in most cases, the improvement is of no general utility"; but its own inability to create new streets that would possess such general utility guaranteed that little change was likely.[93] Citywide, additional assessments levied against residents constituted an ever greater share of the cost of making roadways: where the City had paid, on average, 64 percent of the amount assessed to individuals for street costs through the 1870s, that figure sank to 21 percent in the 1890s, then declined to zero after the 1901 charter.[94]

The 1900 federal census revealed that St. Louis had climbed to the rank of America's fourth-largest city. By this time, the city's landscape was far more developed, and yet in a way far less finished, than it had been fifty years earlier. Streetmaking practices reflected and promoted that state of affairs. After the 1890s, the costs of providing for that nebulous concept known as the "public interest" were entirely assumed by private landowners, working without even the pretense of a larger plan dictated by the City; five decades of strengthened governmental responsibility had been put to the service of lessening whatever minimal vision the government had once had of its own positive power to shape the city toward desired ends. Boulevards and reconstructed streets represented the tentative manner in which that abdication of responsibility could begin to be turned into a more positive sense of a publicly instigated landscape order. They also laid the groundwork for a more regionally specific translation of public interest.

ILLUSTRATION 6-7. *South Side Street-Improvement Ordinances to 1903.* By the turn of the twentieth century, street improvement in South St. Louis neighborhoods was enmired in the deliberative process of city government. The pace of new paving ordinances had slowed to a virtual standstill. (Courtesy of the author)

The resistance that central-corridor businesses and residents offered to each of those measures, however, suggested that the government's newly evolving notions of its proper role in landscape improvement did not yet accord with the self-interested viewpoint of affected citizens. The public interest would have to be articulated more compellingly than in the rhetoric of simple fiscal efficiency before those two opposing views could be fused in one shared vision of the city's appropriate future growth. The vision of certain neighborhoods as integral pieces of a "wider setting," when at last it developed,

ILLUSTRATION 6-8.   *Unidentified Sinkhole, c. 1910.* Whether small or large, South St. Louis's sinkholes posed a major problem to property owners, residents, and city officials seeking to improve the urban landscape. (Courtesy of School Sisters of Notre Dame, St. Louis)

would prove compelling not only within its own terms but in terms of what it was *not:* its power would derive from a new sense of opposition to the "fenced-off corners" on the other side of town. That opposition, in turn, was itself a partial (and inadvertent) product of the streetmaking process as it had developed through the nineteenth century.

The overall neglect of the city's outlying streets—an undeniable fact as of 1900—could be interpreted in several ways, and could suggest several courses of action. For government officials, steeped in the tradition of fiscal conservatism, it simply provided further evidence of the continued good sense of tending to the better-heeled, more easily serviced central corridor. On the other hand, the obvious specificity of the location of "good" streets and "bad" streets began to kindle a broader sense of common interest among the residents of the fenced-off corners themselves. South Siders whose previous sense of community had been far more strongly defined by domestic space than by their identification with any public, exterior landscape began to articulate a new sense of community that in a sense leaned on the undelivered promises of the Common subdivisions and the 1876 charter: promises of the municipal government's responsibility to take an active role in evening out the urban landscape. Because those promises, and the kind of landscape order that they might have represented, had never been more powerful than the overriding desire for frugality and expediency, they had been largely dismissed by shapers of urban policy. Instead, those shapers' conception of the "whole" city, of the landscape as it was meant to be, was molded by the image of the landscape as it had happened to develop under the considerable private activity and minimal public guidance typical of the late nineteenth century.

Armed with this growing sense of a proper (rather than merely inadvertent) order, the supporters of central-corridor improvements framed their position just as their predecessors had in regard to the first sale of the Common: they characterized their opposition's argument as the argument of special interests, of "individuals"; while their own concerns, in contrast, spoke for the "inhabitants" of the entire city. By 1900, battle lines were being drawn in the fight for control over the shaping and improvement of urban space. Not surprisingly, troops were massed on either side of the railroad tracks that divided the central corridor from the South Side.

Part III

Conceiving the
Wider Setting

CHAPTER 7

The Evolution of Civic Improvement and City Planning Ideals from 1890 to 1950

South St. Louis, 21 March 1910

Two quite different public gatherings took place in South St. Louis on the first day of spring in 1910. Tolling church bells and half-lowered flags on neighborhood buildings set the tone for the first. In front of the home at 3321 South Thirteenth Street, a line of men and women stood waiting to pay their final respects to the former mayor of the City of St. Louis, Henry Ziegenhein. Just a few blocks north, the sound of ringing bells was supplanted by the strains of a heavily accented rendition of "My Country 'tis of Thee." On the steps of a distinguished-looking brick-and-granite building stood a children's choir; a crowd gathered on the cleared plot of land that separated the children from the open-air market across the street. The choir's performance was followed by a series of hortatory addresses, one of them delivered in an unfamiliar, Slavic-sounding tongue, and at last by the announcement that the Soulard Branch of the St. Louis Public Library was now officially open (Illustration 7-1).[1]

More than a few minutes' streetcar ride lay between Ziegenhein's funeral and the Soulard Library dedication. The two events encapsulated diverging paths in the organization of the city's social and physical landscape—paths that led directly to the contradictions of the city of fenced-off corners and wider settings. I have attempted to trace those paths, in this book, from their

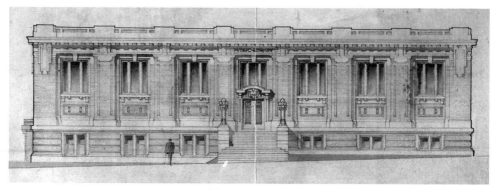

ILLUSTRATION 7-1.   *St. Louis Public Library, Soulard Branch, c. 1909.* The Soulard Branch Library, commissioned by city officials as part of a larger neighborhood "civic center," exemplified the kinds of dispersed public institutions through which St. Louis planners hoped to bring working-class, immigrant neighborhoods into the "wider setting" of the city as a whole. (Courtesy of Missouri Historical Society)

common origin in the ideally conceived landscape of the colonial village, where a mesh of mutual benefits and obligations was meant to tie the interests of each of the city's parts to a stable physical and political whole. We saw their early divergence in the efforts of antebellum St. Louisans to translate colonial ideal into republican reality—either by developing the means for assembling many coordinated parts to make an urban whole, or by conceiving of a whole that defined and coordinated its constituent parts. For a time, it seemed as though either route might converge upon the same desired end. But as we followed the intertwined acts of shaping, consuming, and regulating late-nineteenth-century urban space, we saw that neither approach was capable of delivering both liberty and justice in an increasingly diversified St. Louis—of molding a coherent landscape that truly accommodated the interests of the city's now diverse "inhabitants."

The diverging historical paths that we have followed to this point crossed again in South St. Louis on that March morning in 1910. Notwithstanding the common neighborhood in which the two episodes unfolded, it would still be accurate to say that the paths had begun to converge once again by the turn of the twentieth century. Each threaded a particular track through that thicket of ideals and exigencies that marked life in the American city. Each charted a way through the complicated realities of existing forms and geographic limitations, and each did so within its own republican-derived vision of a just balance between public and private, shared and separated domains in the city. The question that remained for St. Louisans in 1910 was not unlike that which they had faced in the 1790s or the 1850s: on whose terms would those paths be brought together?

St. Louis in 1910 was a politically and spatially divided place. A changing population and a changing city-building process, along with a public policy that followed and amplified the effects of that process, had helped to make more visible than before the social contrasts between one part of town and another. The old ideal of a simply delineated, encompassing landscape that accommodated equally the "inhabitants" of the city may have originated in the comforting notion that those inhabitants were more or less the same. If that perception was mistaken in the 1830s, then it was all the more so in 1910, when the ethnic, social, and economic makeup of the city reflected all of the diversity of urban America. Inevitably, by that time, widening social differences within the growing metropolis were seen and expressed in terms of their reflection in the landscape. Class inequities were tied more than ever in the public mind to spatial inequities: to note social differences was to note spatial differences. When the Socialist Labor Party formed a St. Louis branch in 1893, it included within its party platform a demand that "in the matter of public services and improvements, the municipal government shall give the same attention to the districts inhabited by working men and small businessmen as to the grand west end boulevard districts inhabited by the 'better class.'"[2] The districts in need of attention were, it went without saying, on the north and south sides of the city, particularly near the river.

The career of ward boss, neighborhood banker, and populist leader Henry Ziegenhein had unfolded amidst this period of increased social and sectional identity, and Ziegenhein had used it to his own advantage. His success depended on his ability to turn toward positive ends the sense of local distinctiveness that had arisen more as a matter of fact than of choice in South St. Louis. With his removal from power, and then his death nine years later, came advance warning of the passing of the paradoxical opportunity that his success had represented: an opportunity for neighborhood residents to use their strengthened sense of neighborhood identity in order to expedite the kinds of improvements needed to diminish that very distinctiveness. Behind the opportunity to obtain improved public services in the landscape lay the long-deferred promise represented by the Common subdivisions and the 1876 charter: a promise that government would work to maintain one continuous landscape that functioned equally well for everyone in the city.

The library opening, and the creation of the Soulard Civic Center, of which that building formed a part, corresponded to a complex of practical and conceptual changes in the city-building process, the outlines of which had become clear by around 1890. On the far fringes of the south and north sides of the city, in neighborhoods like the Halliday area, the developments of diversified corporations like the Connecticut Mutual Life Insurance Company signaled the beginning of a large-scale, highly organized approach to subdivision and housing construction, the investors in which were as likely to be out-of-town capitalists as they were local landowners. The level of coordination and capitalization at which those investors and builders operated allowed them to develop the public landscape of streets and utilities at their own expense, and to build a neighborhood whose appearance was predictable from the start. Such neighborhoods attracted a community that was defined as much by class as by the ethnic distinctiveness or geographic conservatism that characterized other parts of the South Side.

This new kind of land development coincided with the emergence of an increasingly well-defined "downtown community" in St. Louis. Early downtown-based trade groups, like the Merchants' and Real Estate Exchanges, were now joined by organizations formed not specifically to transact business, but to look after the general concerns of their members and of the business community; such was the purpose of groups like the Business Men's League, formed in 1893, and the Civic Federation, founded in 1895. Historian Scot McConachie has shown how such groups reflected and promoted a "growing awareness of a common interest within the downtown community" and further how their formation accompanied the increasing consolidation of the city's industry and finance into the hands of a small, powerful group of men.[3] Downtown commerce in St. Louis in the 1890s was typified by new, centralized corporations like Ellis Wainwright's Brewing Association, which merged eighteen of the city's twenty-one breweries in 1889; or, more infamously, by the United Railways Company, which joined all of the city's streetcar franchises in one private enterprise in 1898 and later suffered the zealous glare of Lincoln Steffens, in his *McClure's* magazine series on "The Shame of the Cities."

Despite its location, the Soulard Civic Center was a product of the downtown community, and in its development lay evidence that civic reformers had seized on the implications of the trend toward large-scale consolidation (in commerce in general, and in land development in particular) to articulate a new and compelling picture of urban order: the city of fenced-off corners and wider settings. More specifically, the civic center signaled the beginning of an effort, led principally by residents of the central-corridor neighborhoods, to turn the diverse, turn-of-the-century urban landscape—a landscape of discrete and distinctive pieces—from an inadvertent fact into a positive ideal. The downtown community, through the work of a series of civic improvement groups, would work to bring areas like the Soulard neighborhood into the civic fold, to make them satellite neighborhoods that orbited closely around city hall and fit neatly into an integrated, citywide system of streets, open spaces, and not least, common values. The example of well-organized private development efforts, like those taking place in and around the Halliday area, provided a compelling model for reformers who sought to justify and promote an ideal of urban space built on existing conditions and immediately feasible solutions.

This chapter examines the origins of that way of thinking about the urban landscape, and its subsequent development into a well-defined city planning movement in St. Louis. Planning offered both a practical program and an ideological framework for the establishment of a level of order and control over urban space that exceeded anything seen in St. Louis since the earliest days of the colonial village. That program and that ideology held stationary for a period the constant, shifting dynamic of people and place that had for so long characterized the city's growth. Inevitably, the balance would tilt once again, in spite of the relative success of planning reform. When it did, St. Louis's fenced-off corners were likelier to be found among the two-acre lots and golf courses of west St. Louis County than they were beside the narrow rowhouses of South Thirteenth Street.

Choosing Sides: The Sectional Politics of Turn-of-the-Century Reform

The polarization of downtown and neighborhood interests, long building in late-nineteenth-century St. Louis, was brought into sharp relief by the 1897 mayoral election, which pitted former South Side councilman Henry Ziegenhein, a Republican, against Democrat Edwin Harrison, a wealthy industrialist who enjoyed the support of the city's business community and of the major newspapers.[4] Ziegenhein tapped a wellspring of distrust against downtown and the central corridor, campaigning successfully as a candidate for the working people of the city's poorer quarters. Even after he took office, "Uncle Henry," as the mayor's detractors took to calling him, continued to exploit sectional resentment. "My friends," he told the audience at a Republican Party rally on the eve of the 1898 presidential election, "if you travel over that portion of the city where I hail from, South St. Louis, you would think it is the healthiest place on God's earth. North St. Louis needn't take a back seat either," he continued, "and we can make up for the West End."[5]

Ziegenhein's first opportunity to deliver on his promises of neighborhood improvement came with his endorsement of a series of proposed charter amendments scheduled for public referendum in July 1898. Central to the amendments was a handful of measures designed to remove many of the obstacles to efficient, organized street improvement that had hitherto hampered the city's development. While passage of these new measures promised to assist Ziegenhein in his goal of improved public services for working-class neighborhoods, they exacted a high cost in return. One removed the right of property owners to petition for street improvements and further lessened public say in land issues by requiring that only a majority (rather than all) of the members of the board of public improvements be required to veto neighbors' objections to proposed paving projects. Other sections of the bill would have ensured more money for improvements, adding grading costs (hitherto covered by the City) to the list of expenses covered by special assessment, removing the 25 percent limit on owners' liability, and assessing an entire benefit district around proposed street improvements. These changes, combined with a reassertion of the Boulevard Law and a renunciation of the old 220-foot/ 500-foot minimum street-distance rule, actually grew out of the reform agenda long urged by the board of public improvements. To Ziegenhein, they also seemed to offer the only hope for lifting the mantle of neglect that previous street-making customs, particularly the 25 percent rule, had spread over areas like South St. Louis. The mayor, then, chose to back increased City initiative and special assessment privileges in exchange for the improvements that they would encourage, particularly in those parts of the city that continued to lag behind in the quality of their streets. Given the relative failure of the supposedly neighborhood-oriented provisions of the 1876 charter to bring major improvement to the South Side, this seemingly Faustian bargain was less surprising than it might at first glance have appeared.[6]

Equally unsurprising, perhaps, was the reaction of the mayor's downtown opponents against the bill, which they decried as an opportunity for graft and plunder, masquerading in the guise of a plea for "good streets." The members of the Real Estate Exchange declared the amendments "grossly unfair to the property interests of the city." The editors of the *Post-Dispatch* dismissed the amendments as "an undigested mass of loosely drawn provisions" and confidently predicted that "the good citizens of St. Louis who have acquired property will not grant to politicians and crooked contractors the right to confiscate it."[7] Whether such groups would have reacted with equal vigor had the bill happened to come before the public during the previous administration of the West End resident Cyrus Walbridge is a matter for speculation.[8] Their resistance to Ziegenhein prevailed, however, and the amendments were defeated in every ward but the Fifth (which roughly covered the area of the Soulard Additions, just north of the Mayor's home). The editors of the *Republican* set the rhetorical tone for the post-election victors, declaring that "the home-owner [had] stood up manfully for his home."[9] The newspaper neglected to mention that in some city neighborhoods the ground on which that homeowner stood was likely a pool of mud, slowly sinking beneath him.

Several other political crises that unfolded during Ziegenhein's term served, like the charter election, to increase public awareness of sectional differences in the city and to encourage some St. Louisans to link civic problems, not always accurately, to the man on whose watch they occurred. The granting of public franchises was, in St. Louis as in other cities, fraught with the potential for graft and favoritism. The Central Traction bill, which joined more than 280 miles of streetcar track under the aegis of a single corporate structure (the United Railways Company, later the St. Louis Transit Company) became a national symbol for the abuses of municipal power that proliferated at the turn of the century. The unscrupulous means by which this monopolistic charter was granted were soon exposed by a grand jury investigation led by crusading attorney Joseph W. Folk. Folk's efforts, in turn, gained nationwide notice through the writings of Lincoln Steffens, who singled out St. Louis as one of the nation's most notorious centers of municipal corruption.[10]

Like other advocates of progressive reform, Steffens saw such corruption not as the result of the intrusion of commercial interests into the business of governance, but as the debasement of those interests from the beneficent ends that they were capable of serving. "The best citizens," Steffens recalled of St. Louis, were "the merchants and big financiers . . . [who] used to rule the town, and they ruled it well. . . . But a change occurred. Public spirit became private spirit, public enterprise became private greed." While Folk discovered evidence of that greed throughout the many branches of city government and finance, Steffens singled out Uncle Henry, who had in fact vetoed the Central Traction bill only to be overridden by the city council, as being particularly culpable for its excesses.[11] Steffens, like others who followed in the reformist paradigm that he had helped to articulate, sensed the breakdown of the old identification of a narrow class of private citizens with the management of municipal affairs. But he remained warier of the abuses that might result from the disintegration of the old unity of public and private interest than of the abuses that might attend their reunification. The people who best represented the fragmentation of political power from its earlier concentration within narrow class and ethnic lines were the "ward-heelers" and "bosses" of the newly influential political machines, who derived their power by appealing to working-class voters in ethnic neighborhoods. Henry Ziegenhein fit that profile perfectly; it is not surprising that Steffens reserved particular opprobrium for the mayor.

Regional and social divisions within the city were further amplified by the city's most violent labor unrest since the general strike of 1877. In May 1900, the employees of the new St. Louis Transit Company demanded a ten-hour workday and a minimum 25-cent hourly wage. When the company refused, workers walked out on their jobs. In the ensuing strike, streetcar service came to a complete halt throughout the city and violence spread through a number of neighborhoods, including the South Side. In June, with no end to the strike in sight, a *posse comitatus*, formed largely of well-off West End businessmen, was formed to enforce order. The *posse* opened fire on strikers during a particularly tense demonstration on June 10, killing two. Strong South Side support for the strike, both before and after the shootings, did not go unnoticed by members and sympathizers of the *posse*, who were disposed to blame the unrest on the "lower class of Germans at the South End."[12] By the time the strike was settled in July, it had further solidified a citywide sense of division—far stronger than that which had followed the 1877 strike—between the central corridor and the neighborhoods on either side of it. How that division was explained depended on which side one stood on.

In 1901, Ziegenhein was succeeded by Democrat Rolla Wells, whose campaign pitted the presumed interests of the city at large against the corruption and sectionalism that Ziegenhein's administration was made to represent. One of Wells's first decisions in office, ironically, was to support a package of charter amendments virtually identical to the Ziegenhein-endorsed bill that had been defeated three years earlier.[13] Under the Democrats and their ready defenders at the *Post-Dispatch*, the amendments came to mean something quite different from the pork-barrel politics that they supposedly had represented in 1898. The charter election was framed as an opportunity to realize the dream of the "City Beautiful," a chance to clean up the city in time for the Louisiana Purchase Exposition (originally planned for 1903, held in 1904), when the eyes of the world would be fixed upon St. Louis. The issue at hand was simple: would St. Louis take a bold step forward or, by neglecting to act, would it slide backward? The *Post* put the question in even simpler terms: "Are you for or against New St. Louis—a healthy, attractive and progressive city?"[14]

Enough people found it difficult to say no to such a question that, on 22 October 1901, the charter amendments were passed by a convincing margin. The distribution of the vote, which contrasted sharply with the pattern of the 1898 election, showed the extent to which regional and political loyalties superseded debate over the substance of the nearly identical amendments. As predicted, central and West End wards lent stronger support than did those of the North Side and South St. Louis; only three precincts—two in the South Side, one in the North Side—voted against the changes. The editors of the *Post* intoned that the vote had ensured "the reputation of St. Louis as a progressive city, inhabited by enlightened and progressive people." The measures that, three years earlier, were proof of a scheme to pad the pockets of "crooked contractors" now demonstrated "what can be done when the better elements, the forces that make for progress, get together and work for public welfare."[15]

The supporters of the amendments were not unaware of the political irony of the situation, but they nevertheless saw their turnabout between the two elections as perfectly justifiable in light of the intervening changes in city hall. With the voices of sectionalism (specifically, the Ziegenhein administration) replaced by the "better elements" of the city, the new charter measures could be considered safe from exploitation by divisive private interests. The *Post* lampooned Ziegenhein's failure to pass the amendments during his own term, printing a fictitious conversation between the former mayor's "factotum," Julius Wurzburger, and an unnamed bystander. "'Dese charter amendments,'" complained the baffled Wurzburger, "iss the same t'ing we offered te puplic t'ree years ago. . . . If te people are votin' fe-er 'em t'-tay, vy titn't tey vote fe-e-r 'em ten?" The other man responded with what the newspaper's editors must have felt was entirely justifiable smugness: "I think you know the answer to that, Julius."[16] Ziegenhein had supported a series of measures, originally developed in the name of the general public interest, with the frank intention of speeding improvements for one segment of the public. Under Wells's authority, the effect of those measures was equally localized, as street improvement had been for decades. But because the principal affected area—the central corridor—had for years been identified with the general interests of the city, Wells appeared to be the more selfless guardian of the public welfare.

Shortly after the amendment victory, Wells's administration began to plan for a completely new city charter, one whose features went far beyond the practical aspects of the 1901 amendments. This charter, finally brought before the electorate a year after Ziegenhein's death, grew directly out of the reactions of the downtown business community to the crises of the turn of the century. Its most sweeping and controversial aspect was a provision to further the centralization of government begun in 1876, by eliminating the ward-based House of Delegates and leaving the board of aldermen (the members of which were elected on a citywide basis) as the city's only elected legislative body.

The abolition of ward-by-ward representation was defended by the framers of the charter, and by their allies at major papers like the *Republican* and the *Post-Dispatch*, as the triumph of a single, streamlined system for representing and furthering the interests of the entire city, free from the interference of those who would place their own welfare above that of the body politic. As we saw in the previous chapter, ward delegates were at times the only people who could bring to South Side neighborhoods the necessary improvements that they were otherwise likely to be denied. But to men like Dwight Davis— businessman, public-parks advocate, and one of the men who drafted the new charter—city government had become "a machine of infinite complexity, which in a modern business corporation would soon be thrown on the scrap heap as antiquated and incapable of properly performing its work."[17] They proposed instead to replace it with a modern, corporate structure, headed by an enlightened executive whose decisions were untainted by special-interest compromise or deal-making. The editors of the *Republican* characterized charter opponents as unionists, Socialists, machine politicians, and political naifs, never mind the often mutually exclusive membership of these varied groups.[18] Newspaper editorials prior to the election echoed the republican ideology that had served to justify government initiative since the days of the original Common subdivision: they stressed the new charter as the triumph of the whole over the part, explaining that under the present system the "people as a whole have no recourse against boss domination in local districts," and promising that the day would soon come when "no fenced-off corner of the city . . . can force an unworthy man upon the community."[19]

The rhetoric that equated the "whole" with "the community," and opposed both terms to the narrow interests of the fenced-off corner, had itself a localized bias; this became apparent on the day of the election, when the charter was defeated by a margin of more than two to one. The ward-by-ward breakdown of the vote was telling. Only three wards had voted in favor of change:

the Twenty-third, Twenty-fifth, and Twenty-eighth, which together constituted the West End. On the South Side, in contrast, the charter was defeated
by larger margins than in any other single area—up to ten to one in certain
wards.[20] As had been clear from the early days of the Boulevard Law, the residents of the central corridor had captured the prerogative of identifying their
own interests with those of the city as a whole. Evidently, however, that conviction only helped to solidify regionally based resistance elsewhere in the city.

The residents of the city's fenced-off corners did not feel that their interests were adequately represented by those downtown and West End voices that
claimed to represent "the people as a whole." Their collective voice spoke
loudly enough to forestall the changes in city government that Mayor Wells
and his supporters backed. But the 1911 charter fight ultimately proved valuable field training for the advocates of comprehensive civic reform. It was a
temporary setback, rather than a crushing defeat, in a larger drive to central-
ize the management of the increasingly diverse and heterogeneous city in the
hands of a more select, but more powerful group of civic leaders. That drive
would be most pronounced not in the realm of the political process *per se*,
but in the efforts of reformers to improve the landscape of the city.

Planning for Municipal Beauty: Kingshighway, the Public Buildings Group, and the Early Years of the Civic Improvement League

A survey of St. Louis's role in that chapter of Progressive Era history known
loosely as the "City Beautiful movement" shows the extent to which the
urban landscape continued to serve simultaneously as both a metaphor and
an actual proving ground for conflicting ideas about urban order. It also reveals
the enduring influence of earlier spatial divisions, not only on the subsequent
shape of the land, but on the terms of that larger debate about the nature of
the city.[21] While early city planning efforts paid conspicuously little attention
to areas like South St. Louis, we can read into their image of a new physical
order a conscious development of the differentiated landscape that was already
beginning to separate the South Side from the central corridor.

In its broadest sense, City Beautiful planning in St. Louis did not begin at
any particular date; its arrival was not heralded by the publication of any
manifesto or the laying of any cornerstone. It reached back, instead, as far as
the history of the city itself. Its roots can be traced to events as diverse as the
early subdivision of the Common and the simultaneous creation of an
improvement district around Lafayette Park (1836), the initial plan for Grand
Avenue (1851), the purchase and subsequent layout of Forest Park (1874), and

the Boulevard Law (1891). In each instance, the City set out to order and improve a particular, delimited extent of public land for the purpose of promoting real estate values, improving traffic circulation, or simply beautifying the landscape.

It was in this same spirit that two city-appointed planning groups, the Kingshighway Commission and the Public Buildings Commission, were chartered in 1902 and 1904.[22] In the case of the former, Mayor Wells had asked for the creation of an "attractive boulevard and pleasure drive" that would stretch the entire length of the city, linking Forest Park with O'Fallon Park on the north, and Tower Grove and Carondelet Parks on the south. With the prize of a World's Fair (originally solicited for 1892, only to be handed instead to arch rival Chicago) now in hand, Wells sensed correctly that the time was ripe for massive urban improvements. It was perhaps the Kingshighway Commission's secretary, Julius Pitzman, who suggested that prominent Kansas City–based landscape architect George Kessler be hired in the fall of 1902 to supervise the detailed preparation of the plan.[23] Kessler had already begun to consult with the City on the landscape planning for the Louisiana Purchase Exposition in Forest Park, and his experience creating Kansas City's renowned parkway system made him an ideal choice for the Kingshighway project.

Using for their base the existing street that marked the former western border of the Grand Prairie common fields on the South Side and then continued north along the eastern edge of Forest Park, Kessler and the commission designed a multi-laned, landscaped boulevard conceived principally in keeping with Wells's mandate for "pleasure driving."[24] They explained its importance not in purely practical terms but in terms of its recreational and symbolic value. Citing the precedents of Kansas City and Boston, their report promised St. Louis not only a similar link between its major parks but a picturesque embellishment that might keep within the city a population that appeared increasingly intent on migrating ever farther westward. "How are we to retain them," the commissioners argued, "unless the City offers something in which they feel a civic pride?"[25] An extended and beautified Kingshighway, linking together disparate sections of St. Louis along a single, continuous route, would be one improvement to which the entire city could lay claim. It represented an opportunity to take advantage of the sentiment and the legal means that seemed at last to exist for dressing up the city on a grand scale.

The other specially appointed group concerned with the public landscape during the early years of Rolla Wells's mayoralty was the Public Buildings Commission, which consisted of three prominent St. Louis architects, John Mauran, William Eames, and Albert Groves. Their appointment was occasioned by the decision to build a new municipal courthouse near the city hall, and an apparent commitment on the mayor's part to create some kind of coherent civic center in the area west of Twelfth Street, between Clark Street and Washington Avenue. This district had shown signs of becoming a second municipal hub since the mid-1800s, when development had first begun moving westward from the riverfront. From an initial period when it attracted a number of the city's most prominent religious and educational institutions, the area eventually housed most of St. Louis's public buildings, including the exposition hall, art museum, municipal courthouse, train station, and most importantly, city hall. These buildings were scattered about a neighborhood of aging tenements, newer apartment hotels, and small-scale wholesale and retail facilities, as well as the deteriorating homes of once fashionable Lucas Place.

Mauran, Eames, and Groves developed their "Municipal Court and Public Parkway" scheme as a way of bringing some monumental order to this architectural melange (Illustration 7-2). The architects proposed to create a block-wide landscaped parkway running between city hall and the new courthouse that would flank it symmetrically, one block to the west. The parkway extended south to a domed "Executive Building" (a fitting symbol of the added power with which progressive reformers proposed to vest the mayor's office) and north to a new public library on the site of the existing Exposition Building. The court-and-parkway plan, while it shared with the Kingshighway improvement a focus on one succinct piece of urban design, went beyond that project in the manner in which it was rationalized. This was not only a beautification project; it was also an effort to redirect the existing social geography of the city. The commissioners' report pointed with special pride to the three crowded city blocks that would be leveled to carry their second plan through, calling "particular attention . . . to the class of building and the tenantry which would be removed by such a healthy cleaning out."[26] Their willingness to preserve certain existing uses (the business blocks along Twelfth Street, which were considered but then rejected as the site for the parkway) and to destroy others (the crowded, mixed-use district west of Twelfth, between Market and Olive Streets) reflected a social agenda that exceeded that of the Kingshighway Commission in its scope, and also went beyond the simple architectural mandate with which they had begun their work. In a manner not entirely different from that of contemporary private developers like Connecticut Realty, they employed their centralized city-building powers to lay out an easily readable landscape, the edges of which were tightly bounded by their architectural distinctiveness from surrounding neighborhoods. In contrast to private developers, however, the City's powers of eminent domain, and the vast potential sources of financing available to it in the form of taxation or bonded indebtedness, made it possible to plan sweeping architectural changes across land that was already developed and inhabited.

The ambitions suggested in the Public Buildings study corresponded to similar stirrings elsewhere in the city for a plan of urban improvement that would go beyond the simple concern for beautification and the custom of *ad hoc* responses to particular problems in the landscape. The Civic Federation in the 1890s had represented one venue for such an inclusive approach to reform,

ILLUSTRATION 7-2. *Proposed Public-Buildings Group, 1902.* The new public-buildings group, as envisioned by the Civic League, would over-shadow in political and architectural terms the shadowy corridors of the Ziegenhein-era city hall, seen in this view at the top left. This 1902 scheme was revived as a major priority of the 1907 City Plan. The public-buildings group as it actually developed in the following decades was marked by considerably less architectural unity, and lacked the central focus of the originally envisioned administration building, seen here at the top center. (Reprinted from Civic League of St. Louis, *A City Plan for St. Louis* [St. Louis, 1907], courtesy of Missouri Historical Society)

but its life had been short, and its goals primarily political.[27] The board of public improvements had long since given up making plans that reached beyond the day-to-day business of maintaining the city's infrastructure. Comprehensive planning ideals still lacked a suitably powerful sponsor. On 14 November 1901, just weeks after passage of the new charter amendments had signaled the City's official abandonment of its earlier commitment to creating a general plan, a group of downtown businessmen stepped in to fill the void. On that night, and through the winter, they met to discuss the prospects for an organization that might be dedicated to the systematic beautification of the city. Three months after their first meeting, the Civic Improvement League of St. Louis was officially chartered. By the end of 1902, the League boasted more than nine hundred members.[28]

Part of the extraordinary success of the Civic Improvement League in attracting members so quickly may have been due to its efforts to draw mainly from the ranks of those downtown business and professional classes that were, as we saw, already aligned into a kind of informal community. As such, it functioned as a kind of civic-minded social club, an uncontroversial cause to which successful St. Louisans would gladly lend their names. In keeping with this image, the league's executive board vowed explicitly to stay away from political issues, and to adhere to set of goals which were "not chiefly aesthetic, though they all be in the direction of cultivating a taste for municipal beauty." This simple emphasis on beautification, together with a self-appointed responsibility to "work up steadily a sentiment among the people" of the city, characterized the league's first several years, giving members an uncomplicated common goal that flattered their own sense of importance as it aided their city.[29]

The league's commitment to exercising its powers of persuasion rather than entering into the political fray reflected, in part, the low esteem in which municipal politics was held as of 1902: Folk's grand jury report was issued two months after the Civic Improvement League was chartered. In part, too, the influential character of the league's members seems often to have obviated the need for formal political activity. When the executive board wanted to meet with the board of public improvements, or with members of the city council, they simply set up the meeting and government officials came as invited. When they worried over how to respond to the growing menace of air pollution, they resolved to send offending factory owners "a friendly letter appealing to their civic pride."[30] In this spirit of consensus and voluntarism, the Kingshighway Commission was actually appointed at the league's behest; three of the commission's members were league members.[31]

Just as important in these early years were attempts to reach out beyond the corridors of power in order to persuade the general public of the desirability of the league's goals. Here, success proved somewhat harder to measure, if not more elusive. Early efforts seem to have focused primarily on promoting simple public-minded causes, such as a 1902 campaign to "stir up the citizens to the necessity of maintaining a clean condition of streets and alleys."[32]

By 1905, St. Louisans had successfully weathered the challenge of hosting 20 million visitors to the Louisiana Purchase Exposition in Forest Park. In addition to its importance as an icon of the city's "arrival" on the international scene, the 1904 World's Fair had demonstrated to all St. Louisans what a well-organized, well-financed, politically astute organization could achieve. Fair organizers under the leadership of Governor David R. Francis had raised the millions of dollars necessary to bring the event to St. Louis—but, more broadly, they had also helped to push across a variety of public improvements—including the substantial reconstruction of the city's waterworks—in time for its opening.

In the wake of the fair, Civic Improvement League members (many of them instrumental in the success of the event) had ceased to place their collective faith so heavily in the power of either casual interchange with government officials or whipped-up public opinion as a means of effecting change. A revised constitution prepared in March 1905 continued to emphasize the organization's interest in "stimulat[ing] public sentiment in favor of making St. Louis a better place to live," but listed that goal after an altogether new commitment "to secure better civic conditions; to promote local municipal improvements; [and] to further wholesome legislation."[33] A municipal committee charged with monitoring events in city hall had been in place for a year; by the time of the new constitution, the league also included committees on parks and boulevards, tenement houses, and charter reform.[34] By 1907, the group could proclaim that it was no longer a general gathering-place for miscellaneous charitable causes but that it now concentrated solely on "civic endeavors." In keeping with this new, sharpened focus, its members elected to adopt a simpler moniker: the Civic League.[35] Implicit in the name change was a level of ambition and confidence. In a manner that recalled the simultaneous transformation of the private city-building industry, league members sought to enhance their effectiveness not by reversing the complex series of operations now involved in shaping the landscape, but by taking responsibility for the full range of those operations.

The principal evidence of the Civic League's new sense of purpose first appeared in a meeting of September 1905. It was then that members first called for "the leading architects, engineers, business and professional men of the city" to form a city plan committee, in order to consider comprehensively the range of related problems affecting the landscape of the metropolitan area.[36] Two months later, the executive board determined the specific composition of this new committee, dividing it into subcommittees concerned with street improvement, inner and outer parks, municipal art, civic centers, and legislation. Among the committee's members were most of those men who had already been active in planning, either with the league or with the

City, including Julius Pitzman, Dwight Davis, Mauran, and Kessler, as well as a young architect named Henry Wright, who had assisted Kessler on his Kingshighway plans. A year later, they and their colleagues had completed a draft of the plan; on 2 February 1907, they revealed its contents to the public.

The crowd that gathered for dinner that night in the Jefferson Hotel on Twelfth Street heard a forecast for the future of their city that was new less in its basic details than in their combination in a single document. Like the ongoing improvement of Washington, D.C., described by Daniel Burnham in the evening's keynote address, the Civic League's *City Plan for St. Louis* rested on a shared faith in the combined symbolic and economic value of orderly planning—a faith that would have required little justification among an audience of Progressive Era civic and business leaders. Arguing that "[the] city, after all, is a great business establishment," the plan's authors reasoned that the "riot of conflicting and selfish interests" that characterized earlier, scattered land development practices could only harm the productive capacity of this money-making enterprise. The importance of the plan was justified in language that could not have been clearer or more compelling to its intended readers: "The industrial future of the city demands it."[37] By equating the fate of the city with the fate of its economy (an economy defined, in the tradition of Lincoln Steffens, as the proper domain of a limited group of "the best citizens," rather than the sum total of a "riot of conflicting interests"), the league was beginning to reestablish the public-private link that had proved so evasive in the city's colonial past and in the brief mid-century ascendance of politician-developers like Thomas Allen. The rhetoric of the new plan continued to suggest that the kind of structure that now increasingly characterized the city's economy generally and the city-building industry in particular—that of a tighter group of agents controlling and coordinating a diverse range of once scattered activities—be extended to the making of urban policy. This combination of expanding means and a tightened source of control and oversight, as suggested in the plan, would in turn make possible fundamental changes in the shape of the city that went beyond the specificity of the boulevards or the early beautification projects.

Despite the potentially radical implications of this political shift, the overall tone of the plan remained relatively conservative. While the league lamented "the absence throughout [St. Louis's] history of a well-considered plan to guide the city," they nevertheless considered "any attempt to alter the general street plan as it exists today [to be] out of the question."[38] While they bemoaned the encroachment of industry and apartment dwellings on the city's "beautiful residential sections" (i.e., the once prosperous portions of the central corridor), they offered no program for limiting such objectionable uses to restricted areas.

Instead, the plan continued to treat the city as a series of distinct parts. It accepted the unevenly developed landscape of the late 1800s and worked more to officialize than to reorder it. Recommendations that entailed the appropriation or restriction of private property were confined, as they had been in the Kingshighway and Public Buildings reports, to particular, geographically limited projects. Political changes, too, continued to reflect the existing paradigm of the city as a collection of separate interests awaiting central coordination. The legislation committee recommended several measures that would have strengthened the City's powers to collect special assessments, but the idea of encouraging additional payments from taxpayers as a whole for municipal improvements—through, for instance, increasing the city's low, 5 percent bonded debt limit—was dismissed outright.[39] Public improvement was still considered the financial responsibility of those particular people who were directly affected by it. As such, it continued to be earmarked primarily for those areas where people might be expected to afford it. The continued reliance on special assessment effectively ensured that public improvements would continue to develop much as they had before the days of the Civic League and the plan.

One of the plan's few genuinely new recommendations for the city focused not on downtown or the boulevard areas, but on a few neighborhoods that had as yet seen little in the way of civic improvement. The civic centers committee, which included Dwight Davis and Henry Wright, had calculated that the land east of Jefferson Avenue, where nearly half of the city's population lived, included barely 7 percent of the city's park area. This inequity looked even more dramatic when framed within a related set of statistics: where an examination of the area west of Grand Avenue revealed one acre of parkland for every ninety-six residents, the same calculations applied to the city east of Grand produced a figure of one acre for every 1,871 people.[40] The committee seized on these striking figures to support its call for additional recreational space in inner-city neighborhoods, space that they proposed to surround with public and semi-public buildings. But the entire ensemble, labeled a "civic center," was more than a device for providing crowded neighborhoods with extra open space. It was intended to reproduce in miniature the effect that the public buildings group would exercise on the city at large. Object lessons in progressive city planning, the civic centers were directed at those people most in need of instruction. They would, as the committee wrote, "give to the immigrant—ignorant of our customs and institutions—a personal contact with the higher forms which the government exercises toward him."[41]

The immigrant neighborhoods chosen as the focus for this experiment in civic education included two in the near North Side, the section of town that housed most of St. Louis's poor Eastern and Southern European immigrant population and was generally described as the city's worst slum, and one in the South Side, in the blocks beside the Soulard Market. This third area, in the northern portion of the Soulard Additions, was socially and physically not far removed from the Menard area; it was crowded with two- and three-story urbanized-Creole houses, which the commission reported were full of "poor, self-respecting, law-abiding [and] ambitious" men and women, many of them Bohemians, who were eager to receive instruction in the ways of American life.[42] The civic center plan provided them with a school, library, bath house, model tenement, settlement house, and police and fire stations on newly cleared land surrounding a park (Illustration 7-3). Further land would be cleared from the park west to the neighborhood parish church, St. John Nepomuk, which would then join the civic center in a symbolic union of sacred and secular, local and municipal functions.

The Soulard Civic Center represented a break, literally and figuratively, from the traditional form of community in areas like the Soulard and Allen Additions. It created shared spaces—common areas that defined shared ties among the people who used them—in a publicly administered open space, rather than within the sheltered, domestic world. The cordon of public buildings that ringed this space represented a boundary between neighborhood and city that resembled neither the careful separation characteristic of contemporary, privately developed neighborhoods like Halliday, nor the fluid, undifferentiated connection typical of the Soulard area's initial development. Here, instead, was a new type of link between the part and the whole in the urban landscape. While the civic center's public structures gave a new level of visual distinctiveness to a neighborhood whose earlier social and spatial foci had been more scattered and specific, they also established that distinctiveness as an intentional, publicly created phenomenon. Their presence brought the neighborhood into the surrounding urban system by establishing it as a symbolic outpost of the order and authority that would emanate from the new public buildings group, downtown. The neighborhood would, for the first time, be made physically distinct from the city at large, but that distinctiveness was itself controlled from the center. The ideal landscape of which the civic centers formed a part was a visual analogue of the new centralized complexity of the Civic League: in each instance, many pieces (distinct scattered neighborhoods in the former case, or distinct aspects of the city planning process in the latter) were encompassed within the structure of a single organization.

As I have noted on a number of occasions, the relation between the part and the whole, between neighborhood and city, had been subject to differing interpretations through time. The civic center idea brought those differences into particularly sharp focus. In its emphasis on promoting "personal contact" between the government and residents of areas like the Soulard Market district, and in its concern for "develop[ing] a neighborhood feeling" within outlying or working-class areas, the civic center plan rested on the same belief in the constructive value of marshalling public opinion, and the same fear of fenced-off corners in the city, that characterized other civic reform efforts occurring in St. Louis around the same time.[43] But "neighborhood feeling" and "personal contact," which seemed incontestable enough in principle, could

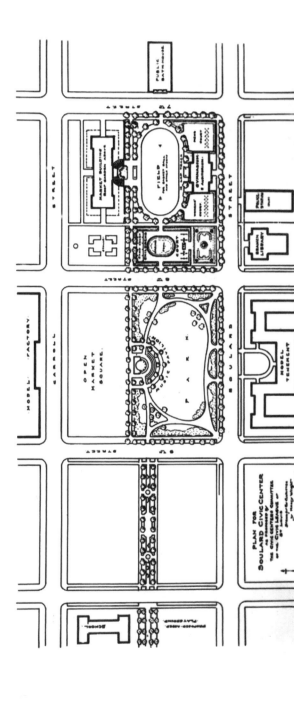

ILLUSTRATION 7-3. *Soulard Civic Center, site plan, 1907.* In neighborhood civic centers scattered across the city's poorest neighborhoods, Civic League planners proposed to improve slum conditions while making manifest the benefits of citizenship. Architect Henry Wright's role on the civic centers committee was an important precursor to his later and better-recognized work as a socially progressive city planner in the 1920s and 1930s. (Reprinted from Civic League of St. Louis, *A City Plan for St. Louis* [St. Louis, 1907], courtesy of Missouri Historical Society)

actually be construed in quite different ways. The difference depended on whether one took the whole, or its constituent pieces, as the essential units of the city's physical and social landscape. Surprisingly, the appeal of Henry Ziegenhein actually rested on the enduring attraction, within the city's fenced-off corners, of the vision of a preexisting whole—an accommodative landscape within which change and improvement were easily made. The unified city of planning reformers, on the other hand, was tightly controlled; it began with pieces and assembled them into a new whole.

To a politician like Henry Ziegenhein, neighborhood feeling described a sense of pride derived from the same geographical distinctiveness that had originally reflected the relative powerlessness of South St. Louis. That pride was provoked and in part defined by an accompanying resentment of the "non-neighborhood" or downtown-based feeling that had grown more pronounced in St. Louis toward the close of the nineteenth century. In areas like the Soulard Additions, the sense of community as a "neighborhood" phenomenon, rather than as an outgrowth of domestic relations on the one hand, or of integral ties to the rest of the city on the other, had actually grown, rather than diminished, before the appearance of the *City Plan*. That growing sense was, as I posited in the previous chapter, largely attributable to the inadvertent results of bottom-line public improvement policies. The South Side had come to seem a "piece," distinct from the "whole," thanks in part to decisions made in the name of that whole. The civic center plan, by giving to its surrounding neighborhood a new level of visual distinctiveness, actually served to further that trend. Ziegenhein and his ilk did not invent sectional loyalties; they simply recognized that the conditions for such feelings had been created and went on to use them for their own political ends.

The reason that the embryonic "neighborhood feeling" seized upon by Ziegenhein represented a threat to plan sympathizers was embedded within the historical circumstances that surrounded the formation of social space in such older areas of the city's North and South Sides. Beneath Ziegenhein's appeal was a sense of entitlement, a desire not to be left alone by the City (which was all well and good for those neighborhoods whose residents could afford to pay for their own improvements), but to have the city government make good on the promise of truly representational public services. Historically, residents of the older South Side neighborhoods had only a weak spatial identification with a definable, delimited area. Their blocks resembled those of the entire streetscape of early St. Louis. This basic formal sameness had accorded with the spirit of the Common subdivisions and the 1876 charter, which were themselves rooted in the conception of the city as a preexisting whole unit, divisible in equal parts. Given that earlier conception, to live on one block was the same as living on any other, in terms of the likelihood of public improvement. The task that faced even the most radically minded residents, as the Socialist Labor Party platform suggested, was simply to catch up, to see that their portion of the public landscape looked roughly the same as others.

The post-charter structure of the improvements process seemed to provide a formal means for organizing the "contact" of citizens and government toward realizing that apparently benign ideal. But to go through proper channels—to gather signatures from neighboring landowners, to petition the board of public improvements, and to expect relief through the 25 percent law—had proven far less effective than having one's alderman use his influence on the board. "Personal contact" with government, therefore, came to mean familiarity with the workings of a ward-based political machine, and the expectation that the goal of an even footing in the improvements process could be met through sufficient influence in the corridors of city hall. Ziegenhein had offered South St. Louisans this opportunity, even though he had advocated some surprising political stances in order to make it happen. In spite of his support for the 1898 charter amendments, which anticipated key features of the Democratic-supported 1901 changes, as well as of the 1911 charter proposal, he was dismissed by the eventual advocates of that later legislation as a corrupt tool of special interest groups. Supporting the "equal-opportunity" landscape of the mid-nineteenth century, a landscape that began from the level of the whole and worked downward in more or less democratic fashion to include each of its constituent pieces, had come to be a subversive, or oppositional political program in a city that had increasingly come to accept fragmentation and differentiation as inevitable and, eventually, proper.[44]

To civic reformers, and particularly to Dwight Davis, who had a direct hand in the civic center plans and the proposed 1911 charter, neighborhood feeling meant an identification with a particular, well-marked space, the bounds of which were readily identifiable and controllable from a citywide level. Personal contact with the government implied an immediate identification with institutions and social standards that were administered by a tightly defined group—institutions and standards that originated downtown and were disseminated in uniform fashion throughout the city. Reformers also presumed the necessity of a firm connection between individual citizens and the larger public interest. They differed from their opponents in believing that that connection was impeded, rather than aided, by the intervention of neighborhood-based delegates and their self-interested cronies. In the place of an accommodative landscape, administered by ward-based politicians looking after the interests of particular sections of the city, reformers looked to the precedent already clearly established within the private city-building industry: they envisioned a preset landscape, administered by city-based politicians looking after the interest of the entire city. In place of the city of fenced-off corners that they feared, reformers proposed to place a fence around the entire city, one that held in check the social and physical forms of the landscape as they had developed up to that point. When the principal realized element of the

Soulard Civic Center plan—the branch library—was finally opened on 21 March 1910, Henry Ziegenhein was no longer in any condition to fight their pending victory. The Civic League and its allies, on the other hand, had just begun to test their strength. The presentation of the city plan signaled their increasing ability to speak with one voice, and to offer clear, practical direction and compelling rhetoric for a new vision of the city.

Selling Civic Improvement: 1911–1915

The success of civic improvement did not, however, follow an entirely smooth, upward curve. It came at the cost of a period of frustration and confused self-definition that followed in the wake of the initial excitement over the 1907 plan and the subsequent failure of the 1911 charter. Despite the pride with which the Civic League's own publications customarily pointed to the group's successes in the years after the plan, individual members did not hesitate to express their frustration with what Wright termed the "lamentable lack of tangible results" arising from the plan.[45] Chief among the perceived symptoms of civic improvement's slow progress was the persistence of a sectionalism that went beyond the kind of coordinated-parts-within-the-whole approach that reformers had advocated. Executive board member George Markham admitted that the league's efforts to enlist grassroots support from the city's neighborhoods had largely failed. Existing neighborhood groups, he wrote, "are not united and most of them know little of the efforts of the Civic League." Kessler, now officially employed as the City's consulting landscape architect, seconded the lament, complaining that St. Louis remained no more than "a group of segregated villages." In 1911, in a rare show of public candor, the Civic League's president suggested that part of the responsibility for these shortcomings lay with the reformers themselves. "The fact must be admitted," he wrote, "that the Civic League has always been an organization of the well-to-do and well-educated men and women of the community and has not enlisted the interest and cooperation of all sectors of the city and men and women in all walks of life."[46]

Perhaps because of its continued public affiliation with the narrow class interests that had proven vulnerable in the 1911 charter election, the Civic League began to lose its status as the leading voice of civic improvement. Already, in March 1910, some of its members had united to form a new organization—the City Plan Association—which they hoped would begin to bridge the still-wide gap between advocacy and public policy. Dissatisfied with an approach to planning that created "temporary commissions ... for special problems," the association's founders set themselves to the task of overseeing the progress of the 1907 plan and ensuring the establishment of the necessary means for its adoption.[47]

In their recommendations, Secretary Henry Wright and his colleagues did indeed go beyond the "special problems" approach that had characterized the Civic League and the early city-sponsored planning reports. In some cases, they recast existing recommendations on a larger scale: previously planned plazas in front of city hall and Union Station, for example, were now linked as parts of a projected "central parkway" that would extend all the way from Twelfth Street west through densely settled, largely African American neighborhoods to "the logical heart of the city" at Olive Street and Grand Avenue. At other points, the association raised altogether new possibilities for improvement, as in its bold suggestion that the city be zoned into residential and business districts, "to the end that the haphazard location of these districts . . . may be, so far as possible, avoided."[48] Their solution to the problem of implementing and overseeing such changes was to recommend a successor organization to their own, a City Plan Commission, that would include citizens and public officials and would exercise legislated control over city planning decisions.

The City Plan Commission ordinance was passed in the assembly on 27 March 1911.[49] The new government body consisted of nine citizens, together with the members of the board of public service (which had replaced the old board of public improvements), the commissioners of parks, buildings, and streets, the speaker of the house of delegates, and the president of the city council. The ordinance that created the commission gave the group purview over a variety of planning-related issues, from the design of specific areas like the environs of Union Station and the public buildings group, to the planning of citywide improvements such as a park-and-boulevard system, to the implementation of legislative controls over subdivision and land use practices.[50]

In spite of its formalized powers and its broadly drawn mandate, the City Plan Commission was still an untried experiment in city management, the success of which depended, in its early years, as much on persuasive rhetoric as on actual, substantive proposals. Part of that rhetorical presentation involved the establishment and dissemination of a clearer sense of the "proper" spatial order of the city; commission members understood the continued value of linking the city's neighborhoods together into a clearly seen, larger whole, controlled from the center. Some sense of their idealized view of the shape of the city emerges from their *Municipal Institutions of St. Louis: Where to Go, What to See*, published in 1914. The booklet, prepared in order to make "the city's assets . . . better known and appreciated," essentially catalogued the achievements of the planning movement, paying particular attention, as its title indicated, to the evidence of public institutions in the landscape. In a series of suggested itineraries through the city, the commission revealed more about the outlines of the consolidated public/private landscape that planners had striven to achieve since the preparation of the 1907 plan. These tours were meant not merely to show off the "institutions of St. Louis," but to introduce the neighborhoods of St. Louis in a way that made them seem integrally related to those institutions. The commission provided its readers with highly selective maps that derived their visual or rhetorical power not, as J. H. Fisher's had sixty years earlier, from highlighting the shifting, spreading traces of the city's complex growth, but from turning the streetscape into a readable, simple series of circuits radiating outward from the center.

The recommended trip through South St. Louis described a perimeter around the most populous portions of the South Side, along a route that included a number of the area's public and religious institutions and, not incidentally, its nicest residential neighborhoods. The tour began, tellingly, at city hall, whence it continued south to Lafayette Avenue. Out Lafayette, long the South Side's best-developed and toniest major street, it passed Lafayette Park and, after a detour to include the new neighborhood park of Buder Place, continued to the reservoir at the corner of Grand Avenue. Once arrived at the recently improved reservoir park, the route showed off the mansions of Compton Heights along Russell Avenue and Hawthorne Boulevard. Hawthorne, like Flora Boulevard on the opposite side of Grand, was more than a pleasant residential street; it was also testament to the City's successful imposition of land-use controls over a publicly maintained right-of-way. The boulevards were municipal institutions as well.

From the boulevards, the tour led past two other examples of civic beautification that owed their existence to the union of public and private interests, the Missouri Botanical Garden and Tower Grove Park. Both were bequests from the industrialist Henry Shaw, who had lived on the lands that they occupied. The Botanical Garden was privately maintained but open to the public, while the park belonged to the city.[51] As the route headed south from Tower Grove, it ran along Grand once again—this time through the Connecticut Realty Company's Tower Grove Park and Grand Avenue Addition—then jogged eastward to pass Gravois Park, another small public recreational facility. Farther south, along Meramec Street, it passed a handful of Catholic institutions and a public school, then turned back north.

The trip north through the older blocks of South St. Louis seemed, once again, designed more to expose visitors to the rare spots of publicly administered landscape than to highlight the full physical and social variety of the South Side's neighborhoods. Passing two more public parks, Benton and Lyon, the route intentionally jogged past the towering buildings of the Anheuser-Busch brewery at Broadway and Pestalozzi (which offered impressive testimony to the kind of business interests whose support reformers had long enlisted), then made a beeline for two of the improvements adopted after the recommendations in the 1907 plan: Pontiac Square, a block-square park designed by Henry Wright in the middle of the Allen Additions, and finally, the Soulard Civic Center. In effect, the fifteen-mile tour made of the entire South Side one distinct but accessible neighborhood, the parts of which were connected to one another in a transparent manner, and the unity of which was due to the guiding hand of a tightly controlled, forward-thinking city government.

The plan commission's concern for developing a simplified, hierarchical sense of space in the contemporary city represented one aspect of its rhetorical presentation to the public. Just as important was the accompanying, larger goal of sealing more firmly the bonds between big business, "progressive" civic ideals, and public policy. As Ziegenhein's example had shown, a tightened urban landscape did not serve the progressive cause unless it was administered and controlled by a tightened coalition of public and private interests. George Kessler, who understood well from his long experience in both Kansas City and St. Louis the necessity of enlisting meaningful government support at each step of the way, urged city council president and longtime Civic League activist John Gundlach not to let the new group degenerate into yet another "citizens' commission"; it was only through an effective combination of legal authority and far-seeing recommendations, Kessler warned, that a plan could ever be realized.[52]

Gundlach, a real estate agent from North St. Louis, was the city's most tireless spokesman for planning in the 1910s, eventually emerging onto the national scene as a board member of the American Civic Association. He worked to convince St. Louisans that planning, and the attendant restriction on private property that it entailed, was in their interests; in doing so, he hoped to cultivate that balance of private and governmental support that Kessler had warned would be necessary to the commission's success. At the same time, Gundlach cast the issue of planning more firmly than ever before in terms of its value as a business proposition. He directed his powers of persuasion primarily at the business community, confident that once the city's most powerful interests supported planning, others would fall into place behind them.

Gundlach continually stressed, in his numerous statements and public appearances, the city-as-business analogy that had underlain the philosophy of the 1907 plan. "Modern municipal government," he noted, "is nothing less than the application of business principles to a corporation in which . . . every human being whose home and interest is in the City share in the benefits and losses." It followed implicitly from such an explanation that some human beings held more shares in the municipal corporation than others; it was to these major shareholders that Gundlach directed his plea for an enlightened "paternalism" in civic affairs.[53] His theory rested on the presumption that the management of the modern city was better left in the hands of an enlightened few than in the inertial quagmire sure to attend a fully democratic decision-making process; paternalism, properly exercised, would benefit everyone. Gundlach evidently perceived little contradiction in describing such an approach to planning as "the great lever by which the masses can lift themselves up to the level heretofore appropriated by the privileged few" yet assuring his audience in the same speech that "no class of our citizens will be benefited more than the real estate owners."[54]

To some extent, Gundlach's role as a business advocate was calculated. He kept among his papers a letter from Mayo Fesler, a Civic League colleague who had since gone on to head the successful Civic League of Cleveland, advising him how to deal with local political and financial leaders. "You must avoid going too fast with them," Fesler counseled. "You ought to have a conservative such as myself in the saddle; then the highbrows would not become suspicious."[55] But the greater part of Gundlach's rhetoric came naturally. A real estate man himself, he understood well the bottom-line arguments for encouraging predictable land use, and his appeals to commercial and industrial interests were more frequent and more canny than his occasional professions of a desire to "lift up the masses." Planning became, in his writing, the necessary correlate of commercial progress: "Industrial St. Louis and Beautiful St. Louis," he announced, "must advance hand in hand." Gundlach reminded his skeptical colleagues that planning involved more "than calling in the architect and engineer"; that it was nothing less than "the economics of community." In personal correspondence, he made a point of soliciting the support of local business leaders like August Busch in the hopes that broader-based community support would follow.[56]

The history of local civic reform in the early 1910s suggests that Gundlach was, for the most part, preaching to the converted. Whatever road blocks the City Plan Commission faced in its first years, few seem to have been erected by the business community that he devoted so much of his effort to winning over. The kind of resistance faced in the early days of boulevard and street reconstruction ordinances had all but disappeared. Instead, the interests of a downtown and West End–based group continued to coalesce, as in previous decades, around a variety of civic issues. In 1914, another new charter was placed before city voters. This one resembled the 1911 proposal but included calls for the municipalization of all utilities, the introduction of a civil service board, districtwide assessment of boulevard improvements, and in a significant compromise, a single legislative body elected by ward rather than at-large. The new charter was supported by the Civic League and other reform groups. While Mayor Henry Kiel promised that it was "more in the interests of the poor man, the man of small means, than any other," backers of the new law predicted that its principal support would come from the West End.[57] To add to the push for wider public acceptance, Civic League alumni organized a grand "Pageant and Masque" in Forest Park. This several-day production, which featured a cast of seven thousand St. Louisans, set the upcoming charter election in the context of a dramatic reiteration of the city's grand history. Once again, St. Louis civic leaders found themselves drawing from the trough of their city's deep, if little understood, history in order to feed an idealized image of historic unity and paternalistic well-being. The success of the Pageant and Masque as a summertime diversion, however, nearly eclipsed its intended accompanying function as a motivator of a reluctant electorate. Overall, only thirteen of the city's twenty-eight wards—concentrated, predictably in the center and western neighborhoods of the city—voted in favor of the new charter. Nevertheless, the higher turnout in these wards pushed it to a bare victory. The charter passed with just 51 percent of the total votes cast.[58] The cause of progressive planning, in spite of this nominal step forward, continued to divide rather than to unite the city along regional lines.

With the charter passed, the City Plan Commission pressed ahead with its chief improvement plan: the central traffic parkway. Here again, the problem that reformers faced lay not in garnering the support of the wealthier downtown and West End axis, but in convincing *others*—poorer citizens, residents of outlying areas—that the planning agenda was necessary and good. The parkway plan entailed clearing a long swath of land whose width extended from Chestnut Street south to Market Street (Illustration 7-4). This selective clearance would have created a continuous, landscaped vista from the evolving public-buildings group at Twelfth Street, past the train station, and west to a projected plaza at Grand Avenue. Although it was a highly localized improvement, set entirely within the central corridor, the parkway's supporters tried to justify the road's value in citywide terms. But those terms changed, depending on their intended audience. To residents of the older neighborhoods on the North and South Sides, Commission Secretary Walter B. Stevens suggested to his colleagues that they promote the idea of the parkway as a central recreational space, easily accessible to citizens who lived far from Forest Park. Like the public-buildings group, it would therefore serve as a central gathering place, a spatial focus for the previously scattered or atomized neighborhoods of pre-planning days. Nevertheless, the road was a "traffic" parkway; its main function was ultimately more centrifugal than centripetal. The commission's report explained the parkway not as a gathering place, but as an efficient transportation corridor, a realization of the group's simple (and prescient) maxim that "the best city planning is that which permits traffic to pass from any point to any other point in a city by the most direct and expeditious routes."

Between Stevens's off-the-record remarks and the commission's published explanation lay a curious divergence of opinion as to the value of the consolidated landscape of the planned city. If the city's poorer citizens were considered to be better served (or at any rate to consider *themselves* to be better served, since Stevens's remark was aimed at garnering political support) by having a central place in which to gather away from their homes, then the wealthier residents of the West End were deemed to benefit from an improvement that allowed them to *escape* the center and return to their homes more quickly than before.[59] The central parkway would somehow draw in those

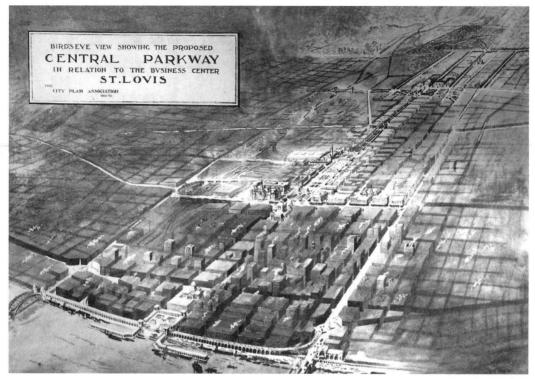

BIRDSEYE VIEW SHOWING THE PROPOSED
CENTRAL   PARKWAY
IN RELATION TO THE BVSINESS CENTER
ST.LOVIS
THE
CITY PLAN ASSOCIATION

ILLUSTRATION 7-4.   *Proposed Central Traffic-Parkway, bird's-eye view, 1912.* Although decades passed before its realization, the Central Traffic-Parkway as envisioned in 1911–12 stood as a symbol of Progressive Era clearance plans and of the neighborhood-based opposition they garnered in the early 1900s. This thoroughfare extending along Market Street from a proposed public building at Twelfth Street (the eventual site of the monumental Civil Courts Building), past Union Station and west toward Grand Avenue, cut through some of the most densely populated blocks in the city. (Reprinted from St. Louis City Plan Association, *St. Louis Central Traffic-Parkway* [St. Louis, 1912], courtesy of Missouri Historical Society)

citizens whose neighborhoods were insufficiently tied to the center and at the same time let out those who presumably needed no such demonstrative tie.

The parkway was supported by a variety of people, including those who stood to benefit directly from its effect on neighboring land values, those who looked forward to improved access between downtown and the West End, and those who, like Mayor Kiel, continued simply to believe in the inherent virtue of projects that would "connect the various sections of the city."[60] Among the organizations that joined the City Plan Commission and the Civic League in backing the plan were such business-based groups as the Real Estate Exchange and the Business Men's League. Like the commission, the Business Men's League (which included Walter Stevens on its city planning committee) was concerned primarily with the commercial efficacy of the new road; like the commission, too, the Business Men's League nevertheless felt compelled to anticipate the inevitable reservations of the North and South Sides, arguing that to contend "that stately drives and parkways are for the rich alone is an utter fallacy." A less likely base of support appeared among such representatives of the city's African American population as the Rev. B. F. Abbott, who despite remarking dryly that "if the [parkway] committee had carefully planned to disturb the negro business life of the city and to handicap his church life he could not arrange a more perfect program to accomplish it," nevertheless worried about the political consequences of being perceived as opposing civic betterment.[61]

But as the parkway referendum drew nearer, the rhetoric on both sides of the issue grew more heated and less conciliatory. South St. Louisans wondered why they should be made to pay, by means of a public bond issue, for an improvement that held no apparent benefit for their own neighborhood. Disinclined to accept Stevens's argument that the parkway provided them with much-needed, accessible recreational space, they focused instead on the more direct benefits that it offered to residents and property owners within the central corridor. In local citizens' meetings, they directed particular vitriol against wealthy West End attorney Isaac Lionberger, who owned substantial tracts of land beside the proposed parkway route and had lobbied to have the road financed through a citywide bond issue rather than through the district assessment provided for in the recent charter. Meanwhile, a group of pro-segregation organizations operating under the collective title of the United Welfare Association (and working, even at this point, toward the referendum that would in 1916 enact the nation's first popularly voted racial segregation ordinance) warned St. Louisans that "some 15,000 negroes who now live in [the parkway] district will be forced to find other quarters, and some of them may move next to you."[62]

The parkway issue ultimately served, like other planning controversies before it, to emphasize continued regional divisions in the city that were far more deeply etched in the landscape than supporters of the planning agenda might have wished. The voices of opposition, collectively characterized by the editors of the *Republican* as the same "forces of civic reaction and political grab" that had resisted the 1914 charter, united to send it to defeat in June 1915. Predictably, the bill was easily approved in West End wards and crushed on the South Side.[63] Frustrated by the failure of this key first planning initiative, and angered by a nervous Henry Kiel's subsequent withdrawal of support for the City Plan Commission, commission members collectively resigned their posts in protest.[64] The parkway's defeat thus triggered a more general crisis in the progress of civic improvement in St. Louis. As ambitious plans were put to the test of implementation, the bright vision of 1907 seemed ready to fade into the smoky haze that each day hung more heavily over downtown streets.

Shortly after the parkway debacle, curtains began to fall on the city's other primary boulevard improvement: Kingshighway. By 1916, the initial $500,000 appropriation for the street was spent. Little evidence remained of the grand, landscaped thoroughfare first planned over a decade earlier. North of Easton Avenue (today's Martin Luther King Jr. Drive), the roadway had been stopped cold since 1909 by a series of lawsuits brought against the city by neighboring landowners. Farther south, where the street had in fact been improved, it was overrun by business traffic, causing a bitter Kessler to complain to City Park Commissioner Nelson Cunliff that his envisioned promenade was now "nothing ... but a trafficway," and prompting him to pronounce himself "thoroughly discouraged as to conditions in the attempt to establish worthy things" in St. Louis.[65]

The slow progress of physical improvements reflected the equally slow pace of that general attitudinal change that reformers had hoped to catalyze around the city. Almost ten years after the Civic League had announced its campaign to promote "neighborhood feeling" on the South Side, John Gundlach bemoaned "the present feeling of sectionalism" that continued to hold the area apart from the systematically integrated urban landscape envisioned by civic improvement advocates. Kessler's own aspirations to create a crosstown network of "wide pleasure highways" that would somehow convey not only carriages and automobiles but a shared sense of civic destiny—in the process "entirely eliminating the terms North and South St. Louis"—remained a dream.[66] The city was still a physically and socially fragmented place.

Plan Becomes Reality: Harland Bartholomew's Early Years in St. Louis

Henry Wright was not in St. Louis when the parkway referendum went down to defeat. Instead, June 1915 found him in Detroit, attending the Seventh National Conference on City Planning. Wright was informed of the election results by telegram, and he happened to share his bad news with a twenty-five-year-old engineer from New Jersey. The young man, Harland Bartholomew, listened with more than passing interest to Wright's account of the difficulty of implementing major planning decisions in a city as large and as fragmented as St. Louis. Bartholomew, too, was engaged in developing a city plan, although he enjoyed the benefits of working in a much smaller city—Newark—and of receiving the full support there of a cooperative local government.

A civil engineer by training, Bartholomew had in 1912 gone to work in the New York office of E. P. Goodrich, where he assisted in the design of port facilities for Los Angeles, Portland, Oregon, and finally Newark. Goodrich's work in Newark was carried out in conjunction with the firm of planning pioneer

George Ford; together, the two offices had worked to prepare a comprehensive study of existing conditions and recommended improvements for the city. The first result of that effort was the 1913 report *City Planning for Newark*, to which Bartholomew contributed. The engineer was then hired directly by the city in what at the time was an unprecedented capacity: director of city planning. He oversaw preparation of a comprehensive city plan based on the 1913 study; that plan was completed around the same time that Wright and Bartholomew met in Detroit.[67] Exactly who initiated the idea of bringing Bartholomew to work in the same position in St. Louis is uncertain, although it seems to have been discussed with Wright at the conference. Before the end of the year, he left Newark to accept an unofficial post as planning advisor to St. Louis. The City Plan Commission was reconstituted in April 1916, and one year later Bartholomew became an official city employee, with the title of Engineer of the City Plan Commission.

Bartholomew's first major report for the commission, *Problems of St. Louis*, was completed in fall 1916 and issued in published form early the following year. The report, like *City Planning for Newark*, enumerated existing problems in the city's landscape and outlined a series of potential solutions, not in great detail but simply, as the commission wrote in its summary letter to the City, "to serve as a basis for future work."[68] As such, *Problems of St. Louis* presaged many of the planning efforts undertaken in the city prior to the onset of the Depression, both in its agenda of particular tasks and in the general rationale it provided of the importance of planning in St. Louis.

In 1914, Kessler had called for a city plan that would be organized in much the same manner as the complex, centrally controlled landscape that he and his colleagues envisioned for the city. The plan would consist not of a single, encompassing report but of discrete, focused studies devoted to various aspects of the city, such as its streets, transportation systems, and utilities.[69] *Problems of St. Louis* preserved Kessler's approach, promising separate reports on streets, transit, markets, recreation areas, a public-buildings group, housing, and "districting" or, as it soon came to be known, zoning. Each of these areas (with the exception of markets) was briefly analyzed in one chapter of the report. Taken together, they represented the range of topics deemed appropriate to the purview of the newly strengthened machinery of city planning.

The variety of concerns to be addressed in the new city plan, which encompassed legal, economic, and aesthetic issues, was subsumed within the overall unity of approach that Bartholomew, like Gundlach and others before his arrival, strove to articulate. This unity was quite different from nineteenth-century attempts to put the city's growth under clear, controlling guidelines. Gone was the simple mandate for uniform physical order represented in the Common subdivisions and the earlier calls for a new city plan. In those cases, the relation between physical order and social order, between equality of spatial division and equality of social opportunity, had been implicit. Twentieth-century planning, like the twentieth-century urban landscape, was a complex affair. Acknowledging that complexity had become key to controlling it. Like the patchwork of distinct neighborhoods that reformers hoped to bring under the moral and political aegis of a single civic ideal, the subjects covered in the new city plan constituted a complex range of issues. That complexity could not be denied, but it could be explained as evidence of a larger pattern of order. To do so required a convincing restatement of the progressive paradigm that united public to private, part to whole. By finding the words with which to make that paradigm a persuasive one, and by backing them up with an authority that decisively circumvented the kind of bottom-up decision-making advocated by Ziegenhein and others of his kind, Bartholomew made the ideals of the old Civic League seem relatively timid in their scope. *Problems* picked up where the 1907 plan left off, but the long series of reports and recommendations that followed from it introduced a scale of physical change in the urban landscape never before seen in St. Louis.

Beginning with the now-familiar proposition that "cities are nothing more than great business institutions," Bartholomew reasoned that, within such complex institutions, the *"welfare of the group"* necessarily took precedence over the *"rights of the individual."*[70] Capitalist investment practices were, paradoxically, both the principal threat to, and the principal potential beneficiary of, this common welfare. While the excesses of "private land development" and the "onward march of progress" were responsible for the blighted condition of so many of the city's neighborhoods, nervous St. Louisans were assured that one of the primary goals of the city plan was to restore property values. Such relief would not come automatically. Like the incorporation of a large business, the making of a city was "an artificial, not a natural process." It therefore required artificial controls (i.e., planning) in order to function smoothly.[71] Bartholomew's appeal, therefore, was in essence a reassurance that there was enough to go around, if everyone would submit to the organizing hand of the planners. He implied that, with patience and perseverance, the city could be made into a highly productive institution, one that yielded much higher dividends (and at a much more reliable rate) than it did at present. By explaining the planner's role as that of maintaining the free flow of capital and insuring the continued pursuit of wealth, he managed to make a potentially radical proposal—the imposition of governmental control over not only public, but private spaces—seem like the logical consequence of a faith in free enterprise. As if to anticipate the reservations that conservative St. Louisans might still harbor toward his proposals, he stressed, finally, that none of his proposals "substantially digress[ed] from views already generally accepted throughout the city."[72]

In the years that followed, Bartholomew and the commission continued this political balancing act through the thirteen additional volumes that together described the city plan.[73] A look at a few of the most comprehensive of these reports reveals that, just as he tried to strike a balance between conservation and change, Bartholomew divided his attention between treating the landscape as the sum of disparate pieces and formulating a new picture of an encompassing whole. He attempted to combine and rectify the two views of landscape order that had, up to the time of his arrival, divided St. Louisans. Although his direct concern with areas like South St. Louis was fairly minimal, the relation of such neighborhoods to the central corridor was nevertheless profoundly affected by Bartholomew's evolving program. His emphasis on comprehensive, regionwide planning may not have resulted in precisely the regionwide landscape that he had anticipated, but it sealed even more firmly than before the intermeshed nature of the fate of each of the city's separate neighborhoods.

The most striking and fundamental example of the first view was *The Zone Plan*, issued in 1919. Districting, or zoning, had been integral to the local planning agenda at least since the formation of the City Plan Association in 1911. It received its first official encouragement in 1916, with the appropriation of $10,000 for an initial study of land use, building height, and lot coverage in the city.[74] In addition to data collection, the commission devoted a good proportion of its early efforts to soliciting the opinions of the public, first by polling several hundred "representative business and professional men" and then, after developing an initial level of consensus based on their responses, through a series of open public hearings.[75] Their zoning ordinance was completed in the fall of 1917, in time to show off to the National Conference on City Planning held in St. Louis the following May, and passed into law on 28 June 1918.[76]

Like earlier planning documents, *The Zone Plan* was based on the recognition and acceptance of the tightened urban landscape. Like other documents, too, it was written in such a way as to excuse and justify its provisions to precisely that group that actually stood to benefit the most, the city's better-off residents. As we saw in the earlier history of the local planning movement, appeals aimed at poorer citizens had tended to emphasize the benefits of open space, of improved recreational facilities, of closer contact with civic ideals. The tone of Bartholomew's writing in *The Zone Plan* made it clear that his intended audience lay elsewhere. Early in the text, he reminded his readers that the general goal of city planning was not "to make cities merely beautiful" but to make them profitable as well. Gundlach contributed an essay, appended to the report, testifying pointedly to the "economic advantages of use segregation."[77]

There was little question, in the structure of the report, as to whose "economic advantage" was most carefully attended to. Bartholomew began by justifying zoning as a solution not simply to problems such as overcrowding and poor sanitation, which afflicted poor districts, but as an antidote to the "wholesale shifting of neighborhoods with consequent deterioration and depreciation of property value." This general statement was developed, later in the report, into the more specific assertion that "no city has suffered more through decline of property values *in the former good residential districts* . . . than has St. Louis."[78] Finally, another appended testimonial, by Isaac Lionberger, brought this tale of shifting property values into sharp focus. Lionberger's list of the places he had lived read like a diagram of wealthy St. Louis's flight along the central corridor: the attorney had moved from the 600 block of Chestnut Street, to the 900 block of Chestnut, to the 1600 block of Olive Street, thence west to the 3200 block of Washington Avenue, the 3600 block of Delmar, and finally to the protected enclave of Westmoreland Place in the West End. "The result of each move," he wrote, "was the loss of money invested in the abandoned home."[79] The property value question, which was key to the drafting of the zoning law, was then largely a question of property values within the rapidly changing central corridor, where initially higher land values had created the greatest pressure for speculative investment and for more intensive land uses. Those tendencies had led, in turn, to blight, desertion, and the eventual collapse of property investments. Restrictive zoning was meant to lock in land values through time, by alleviating the kind of rapid succession of land uses that had come as a result of the very success enjoyed by the central corridor. It gave legal status to the kind of neighborhood-level distinctiveness being developed by private builders at the same time.

Philosophically, *The Zone Plan* reflected a quiet but telling shift from *Problems of St. Louis*. Although Bartholomew had spoken frankly in the earlier study of city-building and city planning as "artificial" processes, he described the zoning ordinance in quite different terms. The new use-districts, as he explained them, represented "merely the perpetuation and regulation of the majority of present tendencies"; they were designed to "let present growth adjust itself to its most natural functions."[80] In fact, "first residential" districts, the most restrictive category, were confined to streets already limited by private deed restriction to single-family homes. (Such restrictions could hardly be considered natural, but they did constitute one aspect of "present growth.") "Second residential," commercial, industrial, and unrestricted zones all corresponded to areas within the city already characterized by the mixture of uses encouraged in each category. The planner's job, then, was not to impose any new order on the structure of the city but rather to shepherd the "natural" process by which one part of town developed differently from another, and to "promote the natural processes and so to curb the artificial processes of growth that the city may become a place of safety . . . where healthy living conditions obtain."[81] By emphasizing and praising the natural or organic aspects of urban growth, Bartholomew stressed the role of the city planner as conservator, rather than innovator, and positioned himself firmly in favor of the *status quo* of extant growth patterns and social divisions within St. Louis.[82] While those patterns and divisions had originally evolved apart from the guiding hand of public regulation, they were now redefined and conserved in terms that sprang from the government alone. Zoning districts, which made a second residential area on the South Side the effective equivalent of another in Carondelet or North St. Louis, developed a new citywide uniformity out of the existing unevenness of the landscape. The city was tightly bound together within a new, loose package of regulations and civic ideals.[83]

In 1917, while the zoning ordinance was being prepared, the City Plan Commission released what Bartholomew later recalled as his proudest accomplishment: his *Major Street Plan for St. Louis.*[84] The street plan, much of which had been revealed in *Problems of St. Louis,* was premised on much the same concern for unexpected change and unpredictable land values that motivated Bartholomew's *Zone Plan.*[85] As in the *Zone Plan,* the engineer posited the existence of a natural pattern of urban growth that, if understood and adhered to, would rationalize traffic circulation and protect property values. But instead of focusing on ways of clearly setting off the component parts of the city, the street plan began the accompanying task of tying them together. In developing the systematic, citywide approach that characterized the major street plan, Bartholomew attempted to transcend the old case-by-case, bottom-line approach to street improvement. Nevertheless, the traces of that earlier process cast sharp shadows across the supposedly comprehensive and forward-thinking plan.

Bartholomew began by abstracting the city's complex street plan into a relatively simple, weblike diagram (Illustration 7-5). A series of roads originating at the central waterfront extended radially to the southwest, northwest, or due west through the central corridor, while major north-south streets either paralleled the gentle curve of the river or, like Grand Avenue and Kingshighway Boulevard, formed concentric rings around the city. This diagrammatic configuration gave Bartholomew a basic foundation on which to build his plan. He characterized the two major street types as "radial" and "crosstown" thoroughfares, respectively, then interposed a third essential type, residential streets, which made up the fine-meshed webbing that stretched between the major roads. As Bartholomew explained it, the problem faced in developing the street plan was not one of redirecting or reshaping the city's circulation patterns, but of better articulating the three-part circulation system that already existed. Toward that end, he proposed narrowing the width of residential streets, widening the principal crosstowns and radials, and establishing the connections necessary to complete a few important gaps in the system.[86] The abstract, weblike system appeared, on paper,

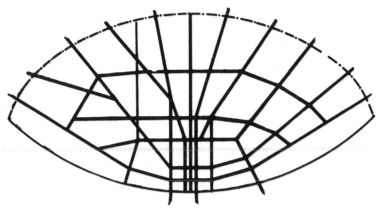

ILLUSTRATION 7-5.   *Diagrammatic View of Major Streets in St. Louis, 1917.* Using quantitative analysis and extensive mapping techniques, Harland Bartholomew proposed to discern, and then build upon, the underlying order represented by St. Louis's longstanding system of streets radiating outward from the city center. (Reprinted from St. Louis City Plan Commission, Harland Bartholomew, engineer, *A Major Street Plan for St. Louis* [St. Louis, 1917], courtesy of Missouri Historical Society)

to represent a major step toward Kessler's goal of using street improvements to "eliminate the terms North St. Louis and South St. Louis": it seemed not to favor any section of the city over another, and to offer a seamless, undifferentiated network of connections emanating from the downtown waterfront.

In practice, however, the street plan displayed familiar, localized biases. These leanings were at once more entrenched and less obvious than they had been in the past, thanks to Bartholomew's evolutionary faith, that that which existed was that which was meant to be. As in the zoning study, the empirical grounding of the *Major Street Plan* carried with it an implicit assumption that most existing conditions in the city had come about for good reason and, further, that they should be encouraged to continue after their "natural" inclination. Such was the reasoning, for instance, behind Bartholomew's response to the data he generated from a study of vehicular traffic into and out of downtown. The study showed that 51 percent of automobiles arriving downtown came from the central corridor—defined as the area between the railroad tracks and Easton Avenue. Another 30 percent originated north of Easton, while only 19 percent came from the South Side. Streetcar traffic showed a similar distribution: 47, 35, and 18 percent, respectively. Yet South St. Louis housed a full 38 percent of the city's population, as compared to 30 percent on the North Side and 32 percent in the central corridor.[87] Taken together, these statistics might have indicated any of several things, including perhaps the poor street connections that continued to limit traffic between downtown and South St. Louis. Whether inadequate improvements were a cause or effect of the minimal traffic arriving downtown from the south, the numbers in any case suggested the persistent, long-lasting effects of South St. Louis's historical isolation from downtown. But to the commission, they seemed more than anything else irrefutable evidence of the continued priority of traffic improvements through the heavily traveled central corridor. If those streets saw more traffic, the commissioners reasoned, then that was where heavier traffic must be anticipated.

A year later, when the commission printed a map showing the updated status of its original recommendations, the practical effects of this interpretation became clear. Of nineteen improvements either completed or under ordinance, eleven were located between Easton and the railroad tracks, including such massive street-widening projects as Market Street from Third Street to Vandeventer Avenue, and Washington Boulevard from Jefferson to Grand Avenues. Only two projects were underway in the older areas of the South Side, east of Grand; both of them were related to the extension of Twelfth Street south from downtown. The other South Side improvements suggested in the *Major Street Plan*, including the widening of Jefferson Avenue and Nebraska, Eighteenth, Compton, Chippewa, Utah, and Arsenal Streets, were omitted from the list of originally proposed changes.[88] In spite of their express desire to "benefit every section of the city rather than to provide for a few pretentious thoroughfares," in spite of their stated intention to pay particularly close attention to circulation "north and south from the business district," Bartholomew and the commission chose to focus their early efforts almost exclusively on the same area that had seen the original boulevard ordinances thirty years earlier, the east-west streets of the central corridor.[89]

The care and attention devoted to improving traffic arteries in the center of the city was part and parcel of a larger, centralizing focus to the concerns and methods of planning that was obvious by 1920. In the relative prosperity of the postwar years, massive schemes for land clearance, public works improvements, and public buildings construction would begin to seem feasible and reasonable investments of public wealth.[90] Increasingly, the planning agenda concentrated on downtown improvements, and increasingly, the City Plan Commission called for projects whose scale and expense dwarfed those of the neighborhood civic center plans, or even of such ambitious earlier schemes as the public buildings group. This change of scale and location corresponded to a conceptual change in the manner in which planners treated the urban landscape. With the legal division of the city, not into dozens of neighborhoods but into a handful of land-use districts, with projected roads slicing through all sections of town with equanimity, and with downtown anchored by major public building improvements, the public landscape began once again to acquire that quality of a whole, superseding its component pieces, that it had momentarily attained at those times in the city's history when control of urban space was at its most centralized.

Another aspect of the growing power of city planners during the 1920s was their increasing flexibility with financing mechanisms. Funding for improvement activities was provided at a far broader scale than had been previously possible, through the relatively untested means of municipal bond issues. One of the first was brought before city voters in 1920. Bartholomew had proposed $24 million in improvements, including a reworked version of the public-buildings group (which he labeled the "climax of the physical structure of the city"), as well as considerable downtown street improvement.[91] In spite of the predictable overwhelming support of the West End wards, only five of the eighteen items on the ballot, representing a collective total value of less than $4 million, were approved by city voters.[92]

Bartholomew's next attempt, the St. Louis General Improvement Bond Issue of 9 February 1923, was unlike any that had come before it. The effectiveness of earlier efforts, like the 1920 election, had been necessarily limited by the 5 percent debt ceiling, a restriction that even the authors of the 1907 plan had vowed to enforce. In 1919, Bartholomew and W. W. Harmon, an engineer for the board of public service, had begun to consider ways to implement the new city plan. In the three years since its initial formulation, the plan was still hamstrung by a lack of money; in Bartholomew's later recollection, "there was nothing going on and nothing could be done."[93] With Harmon's assistance, he solicited estimates from every City department as to their monetary needs over the following decade. The resulting total, $96 million, they winnowed down to $76 million, or 10 percent of the City's total assessed valuation. Over the next few years, they lobbied state representatives for an amendment to the constitution that would raise the allowable debt limit in major cities from 5 to 10 percent; when this at last was granted, they began to draft the City's largest-ever bond issue, one that would keep money flowing in regular increments for ten years and would be fully repaid after thirty. To the $76 million was added a separate allocation of $12 million, payable from local water revenues, for a new water works along the Missouri River, bringing the total bond sale to $88 million.[94] Support for most of the massive improvement measure was citywide: every one of the twenty-one separate issues was passed by the necessary two-thirds plurality.

The 1923 bond issue signaled the advent of a new period in the shaping of St. Louis's landscape. Since the election came in the midst of the long series of reports that made up Bartholomew's city plan, it did not specifically inaugurate a new direction in the City Plan Commission's work; nevertheless, the money that it made available allowed for the widespread realization of dozens of projects that might never have been realized under earlier, piece-meal funding programs, and it familiarized St. Louisans with a scale of gov-ernment-sponsored change that would eventually become commonplace in the city.

With the new financial and political security that underlay the City Plan Commission's efforts, Bartholomew and his colleagues continued to focus less on scattered neighborhood improvements and more on the major over-haul of the downtown area. In their quest to provide a fitting "climax" to the unified landscape of the fully planned city, they inevitably faced the problem of having to change what already existed in this, the historic and symbolic heart of the city. Downtown was not a *tabula rasa* on which to build anew; it was a dense, problematic but commercially vital center of a major metro-politan region. In planning to reshape the public landscape of downtown, the commission effectively did more than instill the kind of "neighborhood feel-ing" that planners had previously targeted at the denizens of the fenced-off corners of the North and South Sides. Now, a new "city feeling" was being disseminated, one that was directed across the city—even at the most entrenched members of that public-private fusion that had pushed planning reform since the 1890s.

Nowhere was the friction produced by this new effort more evident than in the controversy surrounding the bond issue item that called for a new courthouse facing the proposed plaza of the public-buildings group on Twelfth Street. This new building (eventually known as the Civil Courts Building) would house the services that up to that time had been contained in the his-toric old courthouse on Fourth and Market Streets. With his decision to place the courthouse on the plaza, Bartholomew at last ran afoul of a large segment of that business community he had worked to cultivate since 1916. Chief among his opponents was John Gundlach, who in the months that followed lobbied hard against the public-buildings plan. This struggle against the group that he had helped to found was the last planning battle of Gundlach's life; his defection from their ranks indicated the extent to which the courthouse question had forced to the fore larger questions about the efficacy of planning and civic improvement.

Opponents of a Twelfth Street courthouse site demanded that the building instead be located downtown, beside the old courthouse on Fourth Street. To remove the courts from that location, they argued, would do incalculable damage to downtown property values. The threat of seeing in the historic core of the city the kind of turnover, blight, and decay that typified the blocks far-ther west in the central corridor was enough to lend to the City Plan Com-mission's work a suddenly threatening complexion. City planning, for so long justified as the logical encouragement of natural, mutually beneficial patterns of urban growth, suddenly appeared to be a means for building up one neighborhood at the expense of another. Beautification, for so long sold as the necessary accompaniment of stabilized property values, suddenly seemed an excuse for sabotaging private investment.

Gundlach, among other irate downtown landowners, phrased his objections in terms that echoed the persuasive rhetoric of the planning movement: they felt entitled to their own interpretation of "city feeling." Since 1904, the public-buildings group had been explained by its advocates as the symbol of a new era of citywide devotion to high civic ideals. Gundlach now described it as evidence of the corruption of those very ideals. Supporters of the new plan, he maintained, were "so absorbed by the bewitching glamour of this new found jewel of civic improvement that they fail to note the wider setting of which the plaza is but a part." He likewise turned around the longstanding assumption that a grand ensemble of public buildings was a necessary accoutrement of civic greatness. Any city as big and as ambitious as St. Louis was "large enough to have more than one group of public buildings"; if anything, he countered, "cluttering all public buildings in one center would stamp St. Louis as an overgrown county-seat town."[95]

The courthouse argument did not signal the disintegration of the city planning movement in St. Louis, but it did show some of the weak links in the hitherto solid chain that had held together planning and business interests. Furthermore, it engendered some odd political realignments, as an east–west split formed in place of earlier upper-lower class or center–North and South divisions. The committee formed to save the downtown site was heavy with corporate and banking executives, and plaza proponents like the Reverend W. C. Bitting (of the Second Baptist Church) were quick to decry the prospect of "having public policies dictated by financial interests." But in the final vote, opposition to the new site came from the riverfront wards, north and south alike, which included some of the city's poorest neighborhoods.[96] The politics of civic progress had in a sense forced men like John Gundlach into the fenced-off corners of the city. A common opposition to the planning agenda had tied together distant ends of the city more effectively than any reformer could have hoped.

Bartholomew's decision, in the final volumes of the city plan, to return to the heart of the old city provided a fitting cap to his efforts to reconceptualize the historic and symbolic order of the landscape at a scale far beyond that of the 1907 plan. It also demonstrated once again that the most ambitious unifying schemes were also the most potentially divisive. *A Plan for the Central River Front* returned to the blocks that Auguste Chouteau had surveyed in 1764; the document proposed to stamp the land beside the levee with a scheme as emblematic of its own time as Chouteau's grid plan had been of his. The increasing obsolescence of the city's crowded waterfront had been a sore point for planning advocates from the start; the 1907 plan had featured among its illustrations a photograph of the area "As It Is" and a contrasting rendering, drawn by Henry Wright from a design by Wilbur Trueblood, that showed the sloping blocks from the levee up to Fourth Street replaced by a grand terraced plaza, lined along its western edge by a uniform row of commercial buildings, each a block-square in size. These structures gave way, between Chestnut and Market Streets, to an open mall that extended from the courthouse, on the west, to a monumental ramp that descended from the elevated plaza level to the levee. Inspirational as it may have been, this riverfront ensemble never received the kind of detailed planning that accompanied the public-buildings group, a mile to the west. Through the 1910s, riverfront planning centered more on the practical exigencies of clearing land titles, establishing a beltline railroad, and updating the city's docking facilities.[97]

In the mid-1920s, Bartholomew returned to the idea of creating a grand entryway along the central waterfront. While the basic design of his solution owed a direct debt to Trueblood's earlier scheme, it rested on an altogether new faith in the automobile as the arbiter of urban design. Bartholomew intended for his design to generate "the large volume of traffic necessary to rehabilitate and enliven the eastern end of the business district."[98] Indeed, the real *raison d'être* of the $50 million proposal seems to have had more to do with accommodating automotive traffic, in and for itself, than enlivening the waterfront. In a manner that had developed logically from the ambitious scale of the *Major Street Plan* a decade earlier, roadways now constituted the essence of an improved space, rather than the means of traveling to and from it. The central waterfront, once vital to the city because of the capital generated by the trade that was based there, would now be restored to its original importance: this time, however, its key role lay in its suitability as a place from which to expedite traffic through the rest of the region. Key to the entire plan was a 140-foot-wide, "elevated traffic way" built over the existing path of Third Street; the original street was then converted into a service and delivery road for the massive new warehouses that lined its east side. The elevated throughway allowed traffic to pass from north to south in the city without stopping downtown. Traffic headed south was funneled from the main road to a 100-foot-wide diagonal boulevard that would cut through the near South Side, directly onto a widened Gravois Avenue. For the driver who chose to stop to see the rehabilitated business district, ramps from Third Street led down to two levels of parking, stretching from Poplar Street eleven blocks north to Morgan Street: eight thousand spaces in all (Illustration 7-6). To cross from the west end of the lot to the east end, he would have left his car, walked down a row seventy parking spaces in length, then confronted a 30-foot-high concrete arcade within which trains coursed back and forth. After making his way to the plaza atop this arcade, he would then have walked across some

ILLUSTRATION 7-6. *Proposed Central Riverfront Improvements, 1928.* Well before the conception of the Jefferson National Expansion Memorial (eventually realized as the Gateway Arch), St. Louis investors and planners conceived of the clearance of the city's oldest and most historic blocks as a solution to the growing traffic congestion and unstable property values that threatened downtown. A comparison of artist Fred Graf's aerial view of the plan commission's proposal for waterfront parking and warehousing with early St. Louis maps (see Ills. 2-1 and 2-3) reveals how closely the redevelopment area matched the original extent of the colonial village. (Reprinted from St. Louis City Plan Commission, Harland Bartholomew, engineer, *A Plan for the Central River Front, St. Louis, Missouri* [St. Louis, 1928], courtesy of Missouri Historical Society)

250 feet of pavement to a precipice 60 feet above the levee, to which he could then descend by either of two side-facing staircases. Once he reached the water, he might have pulled out his copy of the *Plan for the Central River Front* and read the passage in which Bartholomew explained what was wrong with downtown. "St. Louis," wrote the engineer without a shade of irony, "has turned its back upon the river."[99]

The justification of a 600-foot-wide concrete tourniquet beside the waterfront as a return to the neglected center of town seems tenuous in retrospect, but it developed logically from the circumstances of the time, and it had a specific bearing on the relation between the whole city and its constituent neighborhoods in the twentieth century. The redefinition of the center depended on a developing definition both of the purpose of city planning and of the economic and symbolic value of the heart of the city. It was Bartholomew's insistence on planning as the conservation of natural conditions that had helped him succeed in his early years in St. Louis. This same conservatism had led him, in the *Major Street Plan*, to see the expansion of trafficways in and out of downtown as a current need and therefore a future imperative. That imperative led, in turn, to the idea of modifying the original, vague waterfront improvement scheme by transforming Third Street into an expressway and the adjoining waterfront blocks into a colossal parking lot. In a fulfillment of its earlier avowed belief that "the best city planning is that which permits traffic to pass from any point to any other point in the city," the plan commission had begun to reconfigure the city from a static collection of neighborhoods into a dynamic network of transit routes, an organism whose survival depended not on its bodily structure *per se*, but on the constant, free circulation of vital functions within that structure. Traffic improvements introduced a loose network of connecting tissues through the highly articulated mid-twentieth–century landscape. Eventually, those tissues defined a landscape in their own right: a landscape characterized by easy movement and rapid access between distant points, and by roads defining discrete spaces, rather than by discrete spaces connected by roads.

When the central waterfront was given over in the 1930s to the federal government for the making of the Jefferson National Expansion Memorial, it lost the automotive and wholesaling orientation of the 1928 plan but retained the ambitiousness of scale that had marked that earlier scheme. The *Comprehensive City Plan* of 1947, which incorporated the memorial in its recommendations, carried the trends of the late 1920s one step farther still. The essence of Bartholomew's new, single-volume report was, by his own estimation, "surprisingly simple in nature," but that simplicity disguised a sweeping ambition to transform what remained of the complex, differentiated landscape of the nineteenth-century city into the image of a unified, modern urban landscape.[100]

In the interstices between the busy roads that crisscrossed the city, Bartholomew proposed "a comprehensive system of homogeneous neighborhoods" to replace the massive "blighted" and "obsolete" districts that he identified as covering so much of the city at the time.[101] His plan for the Soulard area, covering the vast stretch of land from Russell Avenue (in the old Allen Additions) north to Park Avenue, and from South Broadway (formerly Carondelet Road) west to Eighteenth Street, reached far beyond the kind of symbolic infill represented in the old civic center plan (Illustration 7-7). Instead, he asked for "the complete reconstruction of the neighborhood into super residential blocks," cut off almost entirely from the surrounding city grid. All that would have remained in the district was the still-incomplete civic center. Gone was either the inward, domestic focus or the easy connection between neighborhood and city that had characterized the old Allen and Soulard areas. Low-rise garden apartments, arrayed around the perimeters of unevenly shaped blocks, focused home life outward, even as they kept neighborhood life turned inward, away from the rest of the city. The experience of urban space available to residents of Soulard and other allegedly blighted neighborhoods would, in the reconstructed city, be at once opened up and definitively shut off—in either case, it was held firmly in place by architectural form. For all of the freedom of movement through space that the new plan strove to achieve, it also sought to freeze in time, more strongly than ever before, the character of each quarter of the city. That character, in turn, was the product of deliberate decisions made far from the level of the yard, the home, or the block.

If there is one enduring image that best reflects the spirit of the 1947 plan and its treatment of the existing city landscape, it is not the picture showing the drastic effects of modernist planning techniques on a particular neighborhood like Soulard. Those techniques were, in any case, never actually applied to the area. Instead, we might turn to a simple map of the city's "obsolete" and "blighted" districts, prepared earlier under the auspices of the Federal Emergency Relief Administration and included by Bartholomew in order to justify the scope of his rebuilding recommendations (Illustration 7-8). The map does more than simply inform readers of the extent of the city's decaying housing stock. It also suggests the degree to which the multi-centered, shifting, growing landscape of the city could be subsumed under a single, encompassing vision of a whole and complete city. Unlike earlier visions of that urban whole, Bartholomew's simple visual device was laid out over a city that already existed, not one that was waiting to be made. Beneath the broad swaths of cross-hatching that joined North Side to South, and obscured divisions from one block to another, were the crowded blocks of Menard, the rowhouses of McNair, the flats and neat yards of Pennsylvania. Now, two words—"blighted" and "obsolete"—comprehended all that one needed to know about their character and their history.[102]

ILLUSTRATION 7-7. *Soulard Neighborhood, Proposed Redevelopment, 1947.*
Bartholomew's superblock plan for the redevelopment of the Soulard neighborhood
reflected the pre-war progressive planning ideals in which he was well immersed;
it also anticipated the scale of rebuilding made possible in St. Louis and other cities
with the infusion of federal urban renewal money after World War II. The 1947 proposal covered much of the Soulard and Thomas Allen Additions, including the Soulard Civic Center area (*centered at Lafayette and Seventh Streets, near the bottom
of the image*) and a completely redesigned Lafayette Park (*at the top right corner*).
(Reprinted from St. Louis City Plan Commission, Harland Bartholomew, engineer,
Comprehensive City Plan: St. Louis, Missouri [St. Louis, 1947], courtesy of Missouri Historical Society)

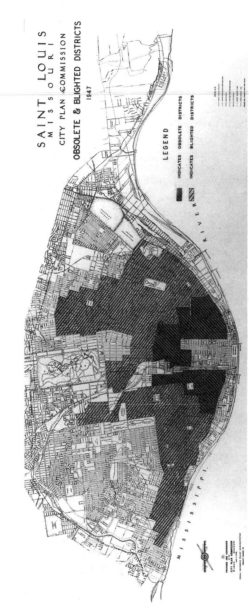

ILLUSTRATION 7-8.   *Obsolete or Blighted Neighborhoods, 1947.* By the City Plan Commission's definition, St. Louis in the 1940s comprised vast tracts of functionally equivalent neighborhoods. At the city's edges, as in the affluent West End, the city thrived; closer to the center, "blighted" or "obsolete" neighborhoods demanded immediate repair or wholesale reconstruction, respectively. In addition to the oldest portions of the South Side—at the northern end of the Soulard neighborhood—the "obsolete" banner included primarily the working-class African American neighborhoods clustered on either side of the railroad tracks (in the Mill Creek Valley) and on the city's near North Side. (Reprinted from St. Louis City Plan Commission, Harland Bartholomew, engineer, *Comprehensive City Plan: St. Louis, Missouri* [St. Louis, 1947], courtesy Missouri Historical Society)

Nearly one hundred years earlier, J. H. Fisher had managed to suggest the diverging, even exploding paths of publicly and privately maintained land divisions as they spread across the young city. Fisher's map had suggested that, as simple and relatively small as St. Louis yet was, the city was capable of growing in a dozen directions at once; that only the imagination might predict the physical form that would accompany its inevitable emergence as a great metropolis. Maps like Bartholomew's served, on the contrary, to limit and downplay the complexity that had in fact developed in the ensuing century. In the barely conscious, persuasive function that accompanied their more evident, descriptive function, those maps suggested to readers of the new city plan that St. Louis was, at long last, a whole that surpassed the sum of its pieces.

CHAPTER 8

Epilogue

Rethinking the Contours of Community in the Declining City, 1950 to the Present

In 1920, civic leader, planning advocate, and amateur historian Isaac Lionberger began to write about his life. Beyond the drawn blinds of his Westmoreland Place mansion, down the street and past the gatehouse that stood sentinel at the corner, past the still fashionable shops of Euclid Avenue, two blocks to the east, there stretched block after block of large brick houses, their facades blackened by coal soot, their wooden trim cracked and peeling, the faded "Room to Let" signs hanging permanently in their parlor windows. Their former residents had moved, or would shortly, to fast-growing, leafy suburban towns like University City, Clayton, and Ladue. Here and there, between the houses that they left behind, a machine shop or an untended vacant lot interrupted the shabby domestic procession.

"Formerly the world was sociable!" Lionberger exclaimed. The evidence that such was no longer the case was most obvious, as he noted, in the urban landscape around him. "The old families of the town are scattered and submerged," he wrote. "He who has built for another's use has had to contend with the shifting propensities of growth. . . . Whole districts are deserted, and a city full of empty dwellings is ever building new ones. . . . Those who have the means move continually. . . . The result of all these propensities"—and here he must have paused in search of the properly critical but judicious phrase—"is a broken and uneven city."[1]

For Isaac Lionberger, the "broken and uneven city" referred both to the reality of the world that lay beyond Westmoreland Place, and to a larger, more ephemeral idea: that of the break between "sociability," or a sense of shared identity, and the specific urban spaces to which it had once been anchored. The "shifting propensities of growth" that accompanied the transformation of land from its status as an active element of community to an indifferent form of commodity signaled to Lionberger and others of his class not just the visible, physical decline of buildings, streets, and neighborhoods they had once called home, but the end of a long-assumed ability to control the form of their city.

Had he begun his jeremiad thirty years later, Lionberger might have done well to consider the work of his colleagues in the city planning effort alongside that of the irresponsible, shortsighted private speculators who served as his primary target. Like the real estate developers that they devoted such effort to winning over, civic reformers in St. Louis had always been motivated by a desire to ensure the profitability of land investment; they were innovative chiefly in justifying and expanding this simple concern in terms of a faith in the value of civic beauty and a larger (and honestly believed) ideal of the city as a unified community. In the years to come, that ideal would help to justify a plan of action that differed in scale, far more than in kind, from the activities of self-interested developers.

The practical ramifications of the planning ideal had for years come up against resistance or indifference outside of the central corridor (as evidenced in South St. Louis's response to the 1911 charter or the central parkway), but they had never created serious dissension within the ranks of those who identified with the planning movement itself until the courthouse controversy of 1923–24. It was at that point that a Civic League veteran like John Gundlach could find himself using the rhetoric of the progressive urban vision to dispute an agenda that other adherents of that vision had set forth; and it was then that a Gundlach could perceive that some planning decisions might actually divide, rather than unite, the interests of different sections of the city— indeed, he found himself politically allied to some of those same neighborhoods whose divisive outlook he had once worked to overcome. Where earlier beautification and improvement schemes like Kingshighway had been projected across largely undeveloped areas, they had encountered little initial resistance. Where they had entailed the "healthy cleaning out" of existing buildings, as in the blocks reserved for the public-buildings group, the objections of affected property owners were not—or were not considered to be— significant. But when the City Plan Commission's decisions jeopardized downtown property values, the potential adverse side effects of improvement finally came home to roost. These side effects would become increasingly clear in the decades to come. Fuelled by the fiscal power that followed the 1923 bond issue, as well as by a continued faith in the redemptive power of the automobile, the commission's efforts would acquire the same kind of inexorable,

steamrolling effectiveness—and show the same knack for breaking up neighborhoods—that had once been the province of precisely those opportunistic
developers whom Bartholomew and his colleagues tried to curb. The new
wider setting only created new fenced-off corners.

Ironically, the greatest amount of government-sponsored clearance and
rebuilding in the coming years took place in and around the area that once
had been conceived as the emblem of the wider setting: the central corridor,
where wealth and poverty—and black and white—came most closely, and
uncomfortably, together. The Jefferson National Expansion Memorial (eventually better known as the Gateway Arch), first authorized in the 1930s and
not finally realized for more than three decades, was the first and most graphic
example of St. Louisans' effort to begin their housecleaning at the center.
Here, thanks in large part to the combined political shrewdness of Democratic Mayor Bernard Dickman and Republican attorney Luther Ely Smith, the
long-simmering waterfront redevelopment scheme was transformed into a
New Deal–supported federal park project; the price for that transformation—
removal of the city's key central warehousing district—seemed relatively
small, given the long and evidently irreversible economic decline of these
once key blocks.

Waterfront clearance, which commenced shortly after the arrival of federal
funds in 1934 and continued into the early 1940s, never met with the kind of
well-heeled opposition that attended the earlier courthouse project. Yet it
spurred a series of wholesale clearance projects—most of them far more controversial—in the central blocks through which families like Isaac Lionberger's
moved in decades past. Due west of the Arch grounds, planners in the 1950s
and 1960s began to conceive of a way to turn the increasing dereliction of
many of downtown's early-twentieth-century office buildings (some of which
were already being torn down by owners who preferred to use their property
as parking lots while they awaited a higher and better use) into an opportunity to provide a visual uniformity that, amid a more promising real estate
market, would have been unattainable. The Gateway Mall, in the making
through the mid-1980s, cut a block-wide swath through the heart of downtown from the Old Courthouse to the Civil Courts Building on Eleventh
Street, mirroring on a smaller scale the earlier-completed central parkway
that stretched west from Twelfth Street to Union Station. South of the Mall,
Missouri's generous redevelopment laws (passed prior to the introduction of
similar federal legislation in the late 1940s and early 1950s) allowed the blight-
ing and acquisition of a roughly thirty-block area, including St. Louis's small
Chinatown, by the Civic Center Redevelopment Corporation (CCRC), a group
of prominent local investors who developed new office buildings, parking
garages, and most conspicuously, Busch Memorial Stadium on the site.

Farther west in the central corridor, the Mill Creek slum clearance of 1960
continued the wholesale clearance model set by the adjacent central traffic

parkway project (first conceived in the 1910s, finally completed in 1953), replacing more than four hundred acres of housing and small businesses—most of it poor, virtually all of it African American—with light industrial development and an extension of the Daniel Boone Expressway (U.S. 40, now I-64). On either side of this "Hiroshima Flats" area—in the "obsolete" districts immediately to the north and south—rose the city's huge postwar housing projects: Darst-Webbe, Cochran Gardens, Vaughan, Pruitt-Igoe.

In a story familiar to most American cities, these public initiatives did as much to catalyze private disinvestment as they did to arrest it. While limited areas of downtown were preserved for the use of corporate tenants and professional sports organizations, the CCRC effort did little to stem the ongoing exodus of street-level business and smaller office tenants—insurance agents, attorneys, and the like—to suburban business districts such as Clayton (which presciently loosened its commercial zoning restrictions in 1959, just as the downtown exodus was gaining steam); nor did it slow the resultant decline—in absolute and relative terms—in the size of downtown as a regional employment center.

In the neighborhoods of central and North St. Louis, enforced housing desegregation (thanks in part to the St. Louis–based, 1948 Supreme Court case of *Shelley v. Kraemer*) at last allowed the city's fast-growing number of African American families to seek housing outside of Mill Creek and the near North Side, the areas to which they had previously been confined (first by the 1916 segregation ordinance and then, after that law was declared unenforceable in 1918, by the efforts of the St. Louis Real Estate Exchange)—but only as racial fears and government disincentives combined to drive away middle-class white families and depress property values within those same neighborhoods.[2] While the private places of the West End remained successfully protected enclaves of privilege, the blocks around them had by the late 1960s decayed to a state far beyond anything that Isaac Lionberger was likely to have imagined.

In postwar St. Louis, then, "civic improvement" and civic decline came so close to one another in time and space that it was hard, at times, to tell which had come first. The "broken and uneven" landscape of the central corridor eventually seemed due at least in part to the effects (direct and indirect) of the very attention that the City had always lavished on that area. Instead of tying together a city, the cumulative effects of years of planning had helped, in this case, to tear asunder neighborhoods.

In South St. Louis, where Thomas Allen and his survey party had walked, where crowds of German immigrants had stood to bid on the lots of the Second Common Subdivision, the direct effects of civic improvement were relatively few; so too were the signs of decline and wholesale exodus that Isaac Lionberger had seen around the West End. In 1932, local geographer Lewis F. Thomas summarized the state of affairs in the area with laconic brevity: "The personnel of this neighborhood," he wrote, "has changed slowly, if at all. . . . The typical attitude is to let well enough alone."[3]

Through the period of St. Louis's much-noted decline in the postwar years, the South Side remained a fenced-off corner of the city. During that time, however, the unseen fences that separated it from the land north of the railroad tracks also served to shelter it from the rapid change that men like Lionberger found so alarming. The neighborhood's relative immunity to that change did not come through the fulfillment of Henry Ziegenhein's populist promise to "make up for the West End." Had Ziegenhein and his supporters succeeded in evening out the urban landscape in a manner that fulfilled the vague promises of mid-nineteenth-century republican-derived development policies, they would have set up their home turf to suffer the same shock waves that were felt in faster-changing sections of the city. Ironically, the preservation of a cohesive neighborhood came instead from many of the same fundamental geographic and social divisions that had kept South St. Louisans from having well-paved streets or easy-to-obtain mortgages—divisions that, in spite of the partial inroads made by outside real estate developers after the 1890s, continued to buffer their area from the more rapid pace of development elsewhere in the city. Just as surprising, the South Side's isolation was helped along by the unexpected consequences of a carefully reasoned "paternalism" that had tried, in the creation of the Soulard Civic Center, to make the fortunes of the South Side and the fortunes of the central corridor one and the same. That paternalism, too, had found its justification in a deeply resonant republican rhetoric that balanced individual rights with the good of the community. But the controlled urban landscape of Progressive Era planning had proved as fleeting, and as susceptible to change, as all of the other momentary balances of social and spatial form that had preceded it. Even the powerful ideological formulations and fiscal innovations of the city planning movement were insufficient to contain the active and inherently dynamic qualities of urban space that had propelled the city's growth since the eighteenth century.

In recent decades, Lewis Thomas's appraisal of the South Side has grown somewhat less apt, as former residents of rural Missouri, the North Side, and even (to a lesser extent) of the wealthier suburbs of the central corridor have all found a home in parts of South St. Louis. They are joined by significant populations of Southeast Asian, African, and especially Bosnian immigrants, while most of the descendants of the area's older German and Central European population have continued to move in a general vector to the southwest.[4] Nevertheless, the original physical fabric of the South Side remains more intact and better maintained than that of most other parts of the city. The continuing particularity and distinctiveness of its neighborhoods in the face of suburban flight, crime, and the attendant ills of the late-twentieth-century city have become positive points, especially in the eyes of city administrators looking for a way out of the downward cycles of neglectful governance and civic lassitude that marred the city's recent history. As the city of St. Louis's population has spiraled downward—from a peak of over 800,000 in the 1950s to less than 350,000 at the time of this writing—planners, property owners, and neighborhood activists alike seek to market the physical attractions that remain in older areas like South St. Louis. In a trend that grows both out of the realities of community development, and out of the critical revaluation of neighborhood life spurred in the last several generations by a familiar litany of factors ranging from the writings of Jane Jacobs to the Historic Preservation Act of 1966 to the oil crisis of the 1970s, the fenced-off corner has become a selling point, rather than an impediment, of urban development.

What separates this return to a parts-define-the-whole model from its articulation in Henry Ziegenhein's day is a difference in scale that obscures the "whole." Small, physically focused communities seem to some to provide the only wayfinders through the so-called geography of nowhere; rather than representing an alternative spatial and political model, they seem to offer the *only* model that can be easily comprehended. It is the wider setting, rather than the fenced-off corner, that has come to seem "broken and uneven" to St. Louisans.

The city's growing interconnection with a much vaster metropolitan landscape is key to this change. St. Louis neighborhoods struggle to attract a market—of tenants, investors, builders, home-buyers, businesses—that is spread wide, and that already enjoys a multitude of choices. In a process that began with the city-county split of 1876, St. Louis County (not to mention the nine other Illinois and Missouri counties comprised within St. Louis's Metropolitan Statistical Area) holds an ever-greater proportion of the region's residents. They are housed within ever greater numbers of separate municipalities (including more than ninety in St. Louis County alone), covering ever more acres of developed land. The city's population has declined not only in absolute but in relative terms—from more than 60 percent of the region's total in 1950 to less than 15 percent today. Geographically, too, it constitutes an ever diminishing part of the region: while metropolitan population has grown by 45 percent over the same fifty-year period, the amount of developed land occupied by that population has grown by an astounding 223 percent. The boundaries of the city, in contrast, remained locked in place, as they have been for more than a century.[5]

In St. Louis County, separate municipal governments, enforcing pre-established zoning codes, have codified distinct community identities that tend to supercede county residents' common sense of citizenship within a single political entity. This balkanized pattern of growth, which accelerated just as the city planning agenda came to the fore in the 1920s, is an apt expression—and in many ways a direct outgrowth—of the lessons of the city of fenced-off corners and wider settings. The municipalities of St. Louis County offered, like the idealized neighborhoods of Harland Bartholomew (who himself authored a number of their initial planning codes), a variety of distinct and carefully controlled environments that worked together within a common whole. Yet that balance, if ever taken seriously, has not held. More and more county citizens live in separate municipalities; fewer and fewer live in unincorporated zones. The heated rhetoric attending the incorporation of a new suburban community like Wildwood is just one indication that the common whole—the wider setting—is the target of increasing mistrust from at least some of the St. Louisans whose wealth and political willpower most resemble those of the early West End civic reformers. Instead, these St. Louisans advocate for themselves a place where, as Wildwood's residents put it, they can "protect their interests and not that of others." The fenced-off corner is back in style, the wider setting out of sight.

Within the city of St. Louis, too, the appeal to separate interests enjoys political fashion, if only for want of a clearly defined alternative. In place of the simplifying, centralizing image of urban order represented in the 1947 housing map, today's policy strategies are best captured by another map, in common use at a variety of city agencies, that shows the city broken into no less than seventy-nine distinct neighborhood areas—seven within the South Side study area alone.[6] These neighborhoods, first defined by the city's Community Development Agency (C.D.A; the successor to the old City Plan Commission) in 1989, and characterized by neologistic titles like "Grand-Oak Hill," correspond less to St. Louisans' actual sense of where their neighborhoods begin and end than they do to the city's renewed zeal in "promoting neighborhood feeling"—less as an outgrowth of a clear, centralized authority, this time, than as the framework from which a more workable but still uncertain whole might someday be refashioned. Like J. H. Fisher's map of the 1850s, the C.D.A. map presents its audience with an urban landscape that has broken out of its former confining uniformity and fragmented dynamically into many smaller pieces. Like that earlier document, too, it captures in spatial terms a larger tension inherent in American culture between individual and community, between separate liberties and shared justice.

Now, as throughout the history of St. Louis, that tension finds its clearest expression in the urban landscape. The difficulties that Americans face in comprehending the order of such landscapes today need not suggest that we have failed as a society. In fact, we find ourselves, as ever, riding along the edge of a continually unstable dynamic between the urban whole and its constituent parts, between a definition of community that springs from distinct, intimate spaces and one that comprehends a larger, shared political entity. What our current befuddlement suggests is the long reach of an image that was developed to explain one moment in that dynamic: the image of the city of fenced-off corners and wider settings. An *ad hoc* but particularly compelling response to a particular moment of crisis, the ideal of the wider setting has come to seem as concrete as the civic monuments that were erected in its wake. Imagining with colonial overseers or with Progressive Era civic leaders that the contours of a shared community might be set in stone and preserved for the ages, we have lost sight of the unending capacity for change that is built not only into our cities but into our society. The intersections that connect the rooms, buildings, and streets of the city to the people whose lives are joined or separated within them will continue to shift and to re-form themselves. As they do, those shifts will reflect and impel our continued struggle to resolve the question of what it means to be Americans.

Our metropolitan regions, fragmented and sprawling as they are, remain the most fertile ground we have on which to develop new resolutions to the tensions that inhere in a pluralistic, democratic culture. Neither propping up an anachronistic vision of the wider setting nor hiding within the safety of newly valued fenced-off corners, reassuring as these images might be, will help us to understand the city of the new century. Instead, we will have to rededicate ourselves to accepting and refining the continuous process of change that governs relations between people and place, part and whole in the city—a process that remains in itself, more than for any particular outcome it has produced, our most valuable inheritance from two centuries of contested urban growth.

Notes

Chapter One

1. Lewis Mumford, *The City in History: Its Origins, Its Transformations, and Its Prospects* (New York: Harcourt, Brace, 1961), 113. For a concise statement of this principle from the geographer's perspective, see James Vance, "Geography and the Study of Cities," *American Behavioral Scientist* 22 (1) (1978): 134.

2. *St. Louis Post-Dispatch*, 5 February 1995. While this particular project was ultimately approved under St. Louis County zoning review and therefore not subject to later Wildwood standards, it subsequently failed to gain the approval of all of the existing landowners on the site and has, therefore, remained unrealized as the new municipality has developed around it.

3. "Plan of Intent for Wildwood, a Proposed City in St. Louis County, Mo." (Chesterfield, Mo., 1992), i.

4. Andres Duany and Elizabeth Plater-Zyberk, "Draft Master Plan and Codes for Wildwood Town Center, Wildwood, Missouri" (rev. 7 May 1996), n.p.

5. For a critique of the contemporary American landscape from the point of view of the most prominent practitioners of the so-called "New Urbanism," see Andres Duany, Elizabeth Plater-Zyberk, and Jeff Speck, *Suburban Nation: The Rise of Sprawl and the Decline of the American Dream* (San Francisco: North Point Books, 2000).

6. James Howard Kunstler, *The Geography of Nowhere: The Rise and Decline of America's Man-Made Landscape* (New York: Touchstone, 1993); Robert D. Kaplan, *An Empire Wilderness: Reflections into America's Future* (New York: Random House, 1998). For a defining application of the biological metaphor to city life, see Patrick Geddes, *The City in Evolution: An Introduction to the Town Planning Movement and to the Study of Civics* (London: Williams and Norgate, 1915). The neo-Marxist critique of city planning is exemplified, among other places, in M. Christine Boyer, *Dreaming the Rational City: The Myth of American City Planning* (Cambridge, Mass.: MIT Press, 1983).

7. The roots of environmental determinism lie deep within western intellectual and cultural history. For a good account of the history of such suppositions as they underlay the practice of architecture, see David Watkin, *Morality and Architecture: The*

Development of a Theme in Architectural History and Theory from the Gothic Revival to the Modern Movement (Oxford: Clarendon Press, 1977). The amount of work questioning the necessary links between particular forms and given behaviors has grown vastly in recent decades, thanks in part to the influential perspective of Henri Lefebvre. See his *The Production of Space* (trans. Donald Nicholson-Smith; Oxford: Blackwell, 1991), as well as another useful theoretical work, J. Nicholas Entrikin, *The Betweenness of Place: Towards a Geography of Modernity* (Baltimore: Johns Hopkins University Press, 1991). Particular case studies demonstrating the malleability and multivalent quality of architectural and urban form in the context of contemporary American urbanism include Barbara M. Kelly, *Expanding the American Dream: Building and Rebuilding Levittown* (Albany: State University of New York Press, 1993) and Anne Vernez Moudon, *Built for Change: Neighborhood Architecture in San Francisco* (Cambridge, Mass.: MIT Press, 1986).

8. Robin L. Einhorn, *Property Rules: Political Economy in Chicago, 1833–1872* (Chicago: University of Chicago Press, 1991).

9. Sam Bass Warner, *Streetcar Suburbs: The Process of Growth in Boston (1870–1900)*, 2d ed. (Cambridge, Mass.: Harvard University Press, 1978), 2.

Chapter Two

1. *Missouri Republican,* 27 November 1822 (2:4).

2. An overview of the legal basis of the American city is contained in Gerald Frug, "The City as a Legal Concept," *Harvard Law Review* 93 (1980): 1057–54. For an admirable assessment of how that legal identity relates to broader historical conceptions of the city, see Hendrik Hartog, *Public Property and Private Power: The Corporation of the City of New York in American Law, 1730–1870* (Chapel Hill: University of North Carolina Press, 1983), which provides a valuable perspective on a number of the recurring issues in this study. While Hartog's analysis of the implicit "dichotomous relationship" between public and private spheres in the city is essential to the arguments presented here, one of his central theses—that a socially based notion of public functions preceded the actual, legal incorporation of the city—seems to hold truer of the older, larger city of New York than it does of St. Louis, where incorporation spurred both a public agenda and a way of articulating the public interest that had been absent before. In the pages that follow, "the City," with a capital "C," will identify what Hartog refers to as "the corporation": that is, the legal and administrative apparatus of municipal government, rather than simply the land within the boundaries of St. Louis.

3. Auguste Chouteau, in "Testimony of Theodore Hunt, Recorder of Land Titles . . . ," vol. 1, 125, Hunt Papers, Missouri Historical Society (hereafter cited as MHS) Archives.

4. John Paxton, "Notes on St. Louis," in John F. McDermott, ed., *The Early Histories of St. Louis* (St. Louis: St. Louis Historical Documents Foundation, 1952), 4.

5. William Carr Lane to the St. Louis Board of Aldermen, 14 April 1823, in "Minutes of the Board of Aldermen, City of St. Louis," vol. 1 (n.p.), unpublished, typewritten transcript held in the MHS library; unnumbered ordinance, 17 May 1823, in *The Acts of the Assembly Incorporating the City of St. Louis and the Ordinances of the City*

Which Are Now in Force (St. Louis: Orr and Keemle, 1828), 85. (Wherever possible, early unnumbered ordinances will be given bibliographic citations for easier references. Numbered ordinances, which have been reprinted in a number of sources, will be listed simply by number and date.)

6. *Missouri Republican*, 16 July 1823 (2:4). This rather remarkable admission of futility contrasts with Hartog (see above, n. 2), as well as with the activist picture provided of early American cities in Jon Teaford, *The Municipal Revolution in America: Origins of Modern Urban Government, 1650–1825* (Chicago: University of Chicago Press, 1975).

7. Perhaps the best statement of the larger importance of reconceiving the North American city in terms of successive stages of political control comes in a case study, not of American but of colonial succession: Donna Merwick's *Possessing Albany, 1630–1710: The Dutch and English Experience* (Cambridge: Cambridge University Press, 1990). More broadly, on the importance of historical documentation as a vital means by which "abstract transformations in the city were translated into private memory … and … reverberat[ed] back into the public sphere," see Max Page's discussion of I. N. Phelps Stokes's *Iconography of Manhattan Island* in Page's *The Creative Destruction of Manhattan, 1900–1940* (Chicago: University of Chicago Press, 1999).

8. The conflicting accounts of St. Louis's foundation have been frequently acknowledged—and even published in a common volume (McDermott, ed., *The Early Histories*)—but, curiously, never carefully evaluated against one another. Paxton writes in his 1821 essay, "Notes on St. Louis," that Laclède led Chouteau and the rest of their party upriver from their base at Fort de Chartres in December, at which time the older man determined the final site of his settlement, laid the outlines of the town plan, and pronounced his certainty of its glorious future. Chouteau, recalling the events before Theodore Hunt's land commission in 1825, claimed that he, not Laclède, first determined the site and "drew the lines of a Town"—and then, not until February. The next printed account of the town's history, written by Wilson Primm in 1832 (three years after Chouteau's death) reflected Primm's conviction that no one as young as Chouteau—who was just thirteen at the time of the expedition—could have handled the responsibilities that he claimed to have taken on. Primm claimed not only that Laclède had led the advance party in December, but that he was present in February as well to supervise the commencement of construction. Finally, the "Narrative of the Founding of St. Louis," undated and allegedly written in Chouteau's hand but not found until his son, Gabriel, revealed it in 1855, contradicts Chouteau's sworn testimony. This document, which has since become the most often accepted account available, restores to Laclède the responsibility for choosing the site and determining the layout of the town. For more on the significance of these conflicting stories in the context of nineteenth-century St. Louis, see Chapter 3.

9. James Neal Primm, *Lion of the Valley: St. Louis, Missouri, 1764–1980*, 3d ed. (St. Louis: Missouri Historical Society Press, 1998), 22. The most comprehensive account of French colonial land practices in the area is Carl J. Ekberg, *French Roots in the Illinois Country: The Mississippi Frontier in Colonial Times* (Urbana and Chicago: University of Illinois Press, 1998). See also Michael Roark, ed., *French and Germans in the Mississippi Valley: Landscape and Cultural Traditions* (Cape Girardeau, Mo.: Center for Regional History and Cultural Heritage, 1988); for a comparison with French practices elsewhere in North America, see Richard C. Harris, *The Seigneurial*

System in Early Canada (Quebec: Laval, 1968). The problem of the relation between French and Spanish traditions receives explicit attention in C. Richard Arena, "Land Settlement Practices in Spanish Louisiana," in John F. McDermott, ed., *The Spanish in the Mississippi Valley, 1762–1804* (Urbana: University of Illinois Press, 1974), 52ff. An attempt to attribute the plan of St. Louis to the Spanish Laws of the Indies can be found in Dora P. Crouch, Daniel J. Garr, and Axel Mundigo, *Spanish City Planning in America* (Cambridge, Mass., MIT Press, 1982), 116–49. This account includes a useful translation of those portions of the Laws of the Indies relevant to town planning. Certain sections, particularly 129 and 130 (16), highlight the essential similarity between French and Spanish planning practices.

10. Auguste Chouteau, in "Testimony of Theodore Hunt," vol. 1, 125. All references to "feet" in the colonial period refer to French feet—the equivalent of 12.7893 English inches. Charles Peterson, *Colonial St. Louis: Building a Creole Capital* (Tucson: Patrice Press, 1993), 7.

11. Peterson, ibid., notes the prevalence of the 300-foot-square block, not only in New Orleans, but in the other colonial settlements of Missouri.

12. Clarence Walworth Alvord, *The Illinois Country, 1673–1818*, vol. 1 of *The Centennial History of Illinois* (Springfield: Illinois Centennial Commission, 1920), 266.

13. Louis Houck, *The Spanish Regime in Missouri*, 2 vols. (Chicago: R. R. Donnelley, 1909), 1: 156. Gálvez's insistence that settlers make use of their land grants is consistent with the longstanding Spanish requirement of improvement of one's lot within the period of a year and a day.

14. Charles Larpenteur, *Forty Years a Fur Trader on the Upper Missouri: The Personal Narrative of Charles Larpenteur, 1833–1872* (Chicago: Lakeside Press, 1933; reprint, Lincoln: University of Nebraska Press, 1989), 10.

15. Amos Stoddard, *Sketches, Historical and Descriptive, of Louisiana* (Philadelphia: Matthew Carey, 1812), 254.

16. Peterson, *Colonial St. Louis*, 11–12.

17. Michael Marli, 1847 testimony, reprinted in Henry W. Williams, *History, Abstracts of Title, Evidences of Location, &c. Relating to the Common Field Lots of the South Grand Prairie and Cul de Sac of the Grand Prairie, and an Argument in Support of Cozens' Surveys* (St. Louis: Missouri Republican, 1854), appen., 5.

18. Houck, *The Spanish Regime*, 2: 198–99, 202. The Spanish official's gibes referred obliquely to St. Louis's common French nickname during this period—Pain Court—"short of bread."

19. Lemont K. Richardson, "Private Land Claims in Missouri," *Missouri Historical Review* (hereafter cited as *MHR*) 50 (1956): 279.

20. Alvord, *Illinois Country*, 220; Peterson, *Colonial St. Louis*, 7.

21. Wilson Primm, "History of St. Louis" (1832), in McDermott, *Early Histories*, 115.

22. Glen Holt, "The Shaping of St. Louis, 1763–1860" (Ph.D. diss., University of Chicago, 1975), 43. The "district" for which Holt calculated his population figures included an area roughly the same as today's City and County of St. Louis.

The breakdown of a fixed, hierarchical social order, and its bearing upon the question of land distribution and ownership, are familiar themes in colonial American scholarship. Unfortunately for our purposes, they have been far better documented in the case of North America's British settlements than they have for other parts of the continent. One survey of British American towns that delves deeply into the breakdown of their original ideological underpinnings is Sylvia Dougherty Fries, *The Urban Idea in Colonial America* (Philadelphia: Temple University Press, 1977). The question is treated in greater detail in the series of loosely related New England town studies of the 1960s and 1970s that followed in the wake of Sumner Chilton Powell's *Puritan Village: The Formation of a New England Town* (Middletown: Wesleyan University Press, 1963). Among the others, see also Kenneth A. Lockridge, *A New England Town, The First Hundred Years: Dedham, Massachusetts, 1636–1736* (New York: Norton, 1970); and Michael Zuckerman, *Peaceable Kingdoms: New England Towns in the Eighteenth Century* (New York: Vintage, 1970), both of which emphasize the relatively conservative and accommodating manner in which change took place in the late-colonial period. Richard L. Bushman, in *From Puritan to Yankee: Character and the Social Order in Connecticut, 1690–1765* (New York: Norton, 1970), provides an analysis of the rise of "self-interest" as a motivating rationale behind the justification for new forms of authority that is more relevant in terms of a model to be extended to the case of St. Louis (see especially, 276–82).

23. Alvord, *The Illinois Country*, 419. For background on the congressional grid, see Hildegard Binder Johnson, *Order Upon the Land: The United States Rectangular Land Survey and the Upper Mississippi Country* (New York: Oxford University Press, 1976); William D. Pattison, *The Beginnings of the American Rectangular Land Survey System, 1784–1800* (Chicago: University of Chicago Department of Geography, Research Paper no. 50, 1957); and Malcolm T. Rohrbaugh, *The Land Office Business: The Settlement and Administration of American Public Lands, 1789–1837* (New York: Oxford University Press, 1968). Two succinct cultural interpretations of the grid, both of which focus on its suitability to the republican ideals of late-eighteenth-century America, can be found in John R. Stilgoe, *Common Landscape of America, 1580 to 1845* (New Haven: Yale University Press, 1982), 99–107; and Daniel J. Boorstin, *The Americans: The National Experience* (New York: Vintage, 1967), 243–48.

24. Stoddard, *Sketches*, 254; Richardson, "Private Land Claims," 136.

25. Stoddard, *Sketches*, 245, 247; Richardson, "Private Land Claims," 279.

26. The general history of this period is well recounted in Richardson, "Private Land Claims." For a more compact account, see J. Primm, *Lion of the Valley*, 79–81, 111–12.

27. Richardson, "Private Land Claims," 286.

28. *St. Louis Enquirer*, 14 December 1822 (1:4). The assessment of fraudulent claims comes from Henry W. Williams, *History, Abstracts of Title, Evidences of Location, &c. Relating to the Common Field Lots of the South Grand Prairie and Cul de Sac of the Grand Prairie, and an Argument in Support of Cozens' Surveys* (St. Louis: Missouri Republican, 1854), 70.

29. J. Primm, *Lion of the Valley*, 105–8, 119–20; Hattie M. Anderson, "Frontier Economic Problems in Missouri, 1815–1828," *MHR* 34 (1939): 54–64.

Chapter Three

1. "Minutes of the Board of Aldermen, City of St. Louis," vol. 1, 3 July 1826, 205; unnumbered ordinance, 3 July 1826, in *The Acts of the Assembly Incorporating the City of St. Louis and the Ordinances of the City Which are Now in Force* (St. Louis: Orr and Keemle, 1828), 97.

2. John Paxton, "Notes on St. Louis," in John F. McDermott, ed., *The Early Histories of St. Louis* (St. Louis: St. Louis Historical Documents Foundation), 1952, 71. Such comments were relatively common among travelers during this period; among other examples cited in the historical literature are Timothy Flint (1828), quoted in James Neal Primm, *Lion of the Valley: St. Louis, Missouri, 1764–1980*, 3d ed. (St. Louis: Missouri Historical Society Press, 1998), 133, and Caleb Atwater (1829), quoted in Hattie M. Anderson, "Missouri, 1804–1828: Peopling a Frontier State," *MHR* 31 (1937): 180.

3. "An Act to Incorporate the Inhabitants of the Town of St. Louis," 9 December 1822, in *The Ordinances of the City of St. Louis* (St. Louis: George Knapp and Co., 1856), 54.

4. Ibid. Cf. Robin L. Einhorn, *Property Rules: Political Economy in Chicago, 1833–1872* (Chicago: University of Chicago Press, 1991), esp. pp. 108ff., and Hendrik Hartog, *Public Property and Private Power: The Corporation of the City of New York in American Law, 1730–1870* (Chapel Hill: University of North Carolina Press, 1983) 167ff., for a comparison of similar rules in Chicago and New York, as well as for a broader evaluation of the place of special assessments in the evolution of American political culture.

5. Paxton, in McDermott, *Early Histories*, 69. As we will see in Chapter 4, Paxton was but one of many St. Louisans throughout the century who applied their literary talents to the challenge of describing the wretched condition of the city's streets.

6. "Minutes of the Board of Aldermen," vol. 1, 23 August, 1823; unnumbered ordinance, 13 August 1823, in *Acts of the Assembly*, 86–88.

7. Ibid.

8. Unnumbered ordinance, 22 June 1826, in ibid., 96.

9. *Eleventh Census of the United States*, vol. 1, *Population* (Washington: Government Printing Office, 1890), 370–71.

10. "Memorial of the Citizens of St. Louis, Missouri, Praying That the Cumberland Road Be Located to Pass Through That Place, in the Route to Jefferson City," 23 February 1836 (collection Bancroft Library, University of California, Berkeley). The Cumberland Road Memorial was but one early example of a long (and long-winded) tradition of colorful local promotion, at the apex of which stands Logan U. Reavis's often reprinted tome, *St. Louis: The Future Great City of the World* (1870; St. Louis, Gray, Baker and Co., 1875). For a general picture of booster literature, see J. Christopher Schnell and Katherine B. Clinton, "The New West: Themes in Nineteenth-Century Urban Promotion, 1815–1880," *Bulletin of the Missouri Historical Society* (hereafter cited as *BMHS*) 30 (1974): 75–88; as well as Daniel J. Boorstin, *The Americans: The National Experience* (New York: Vintage, 1967), 113–68.

11. In William G. Bek, "The Followers of Duden," *MHR* 15 (July 1921): 686. See also William G. Bek, trans., "Gottfried Duden's 'Report,'" *MHR* 12 (1917): 1–21, 81–89, 163–79, 258–70; and 13 (1919): 44–56, 157–81, 251–81; as well as the summary of that report and its impact on Missouri immigration in Charles Van Ravenswaay, *The Art and Architecture of German Settlements in Missouri: A Survey of a Vanishing Culture* (Columbia: University of Missouri Press, 1977), 23–29.

12. Edmund Flagg, *The Far West, or a Tour Beyond the Mountains*, 2 vols. (New York: Harper, 1838), 1: 117.

13. Glen Holt, "The Shaping of St. Louis, 1763–1860" (Ph.D. diss., University of Chicago, 1975), 61.

14. William Carr Lane to "Children," 14 November 1836, W. C. Lane Papers, MHS Archives.

15. *Missouri Republican*, 1 February 1843 (2:1).

16. Holt, "The Shaping of St. Louis," 283 (fig. 10), and Richard Smith Elliott, *Notes Taken in Sixty Years* (St. Louis: R. P. Studley and Co., 1883), 177.

17. *Missouri Argus*, 2 September 1836 (3:4), 22 April 1836 (3:6).

18. *Journal of the Board of Public Improvements*, 1878–1879 (St. Louis: Woodward, Tiernan, and Hale, 1879) (hereafter cited as *BPI Journal*), 266.

19. In its earliest stages, this encouragement consisted simply of providing the legal means by which the process could take place. In 1831, the board of aldermen passed a law allowing the annexation of any adjacent subdivision upon the petition of two-thirds of its residents, subject to the subsequent approval of three-fifths of the city's voters. This carrot was hardly sweet enough for anyone to bite. Two years later, the city relaxed its conditions by demanding the assent of only a simple majority, both of petitioners and voters. Unnumbered ordinance, 15 January 1831, in *The Ordinances of the City of St. Louis* (St. Louis: George Knapp, 1856), 58–59; unnumbered ordinance, 16 January 1833, in ibid., 59–60.

20. "An Act to Incorporate the Inhabitants of the Town of St. Louis," 26 February 1835, in ibid., 66–67.

21. Ibid. Hartog, *Public Property and Private Power* (169), attributes New Yorkers' ready consent to benefit damages to the fact that street improvements there were carried out in accordance with the Commissioners' plan of 1807. St. Louis had no such guidelines with which the City might assure property owners of the inevitable rise in the value of their land that would follow street improvement.

22. Unnumbered ordinance, 19 January 1836, in *The Revised Ordinances of the City of St. Louis* (St. Louis: Missouri Argus, 1836), 175.

23. Much of the information on subdivisions found throughout this paper depends on an invaluable but unpublished document: Norbury Wayman's "Chronological Index-List of Subdivisions to the City of St. Louis since 1816," which is keyed to a set of maps held in the MHS Photographs and Prints Collection. While cross-checks of Wayman's maps with the detailed survey books kept by the Pitzman's Company of Surveyors reveal occasional small discrepancies, Wayman's labor has created a document remarkably reliable for something of its scope and complexity; scholars of the morphology of the city will be indebted to it for years to come. Holt's count of twenty-five subdivisions between 1836 and 1840 may have been based on a less complete review of local subdivision activity that appeared in the *St. Louis Globe-Democrat* on 2 April 1882 and was reprinted as part of an article entitled "St. Louis Real Estate—In Review" that appeared in the MHS *Glimpses of the Past* 4 (1937): 119–77.

24. As determined from the paving ordinances listed in Elliott C. Bennett, ed., *Index—St. Louis City Ordinances from Incorporation to 1903* (St. Louis: William H. O'Brien, 1904) (hereafter cited as *Index*).

25. *Index*, and "An Act to Incorporate the City of St. Louis," 8 February 1839, in *Ordinances* (1856), 83.

26. James Neal Primm, *Lion of the Valley: St. Louis, Missouri, 1764–1980*, 3d ed. (St. Louis: Missouri Historical Society Press, 1998), 146.

27. "An Act to Reduce the Law Incorporating the City of St. Louis, and the Several Acts Amendatory Thereof, into One Act, and to Amend the Same," 8 February 1843,

in *Revised Ordinances of the City of St. Louis* (St. Louis: Missouri Argus, 1843), 49–66.

28. "An Act to Amend 'An Act to Incorporate the City of St. Louis,'" 15 February 1841, in *Ordinances* (1856), 95; "An Act to Reduce . . . " in ibid., 113.

29. *Index*.

30. "An Act to Reduce . . ." in *Ordinances* (1856), 114.

31. *Index;* Ordinance 1880, 30 August 1847; Ordinance 2233, 16 July 1849.

32. The history of this influential family is detailed in William E. Foley and C. David Rice, *The First Chouteaus, River Barons of Early St. Louis* (Urbana: University of Illinois Press, 1983). See also Jay Gitlin, "'Avec bien du regret': The Americanization of Creole St. Louis," *Gateway Heritage* 9(4) (1989), 2–11.

33. The names of the persons responsible for each subdivision are derived from an inspection of the records originally compiled by City Surveyor Julius Pitzman and kept in the files of the Pitzman's Company of Surveyors. Addresses and occupations were taken from St. Louis city directories for the year in which each subdivision was granted. For more information on John Daggett, see Chapter 3. The case of St. Louis, which has always looked to a conspicuous group of older families in influential positions, is usefully compared with the similar case of Pittsburgh, as described in Joseph F. Rishel, *Founding Families of Pittsburgh: The Evolution of a Regional Elite, 1760–1910* (Pittsburgh: University of Pittsburgh Press, 1990). For a historical account that emphasizes the importance of newer, Eastern-based capital and family ties in the antebellum economy, see Jeffrey Adler, *Yankee Merchants and the Making of the Urban West: The Rise and Fall of Antebellum St. Louis* (Cambridge: Cambridge University Press, 1991). For a wider perspective on the relation of family identity, wealth, and political power in antebellum America, cf. Edward Pessen, *Riches, Class and Power Before the Civil War* (Lexington: D. C. Heath, 1973).

34. On national trade networks, cf. Adler, *Yankee Merchants.*

35. Based on a comparison of subdividers' names with a list of city officeholders since 1823, printed in *The Revised Code of St. Louis* (St. Louis: Woodward and Tiernan, 1912), ii–xix. Rishel, *Founding Families,* describes a similar convergence of social and political power around this time, although his analysis is unrelated to landowning or subdivision *per se.*

36. "An Act to Incorporate the City of St. Louis," 8 February 1839, in *Ordinances* (1856), 74.

37. John F. Darby, *Personal Recollections of Many Prominent People Whom I Have Known and of Events—Especially of Those Related to the History of St. Louis—During the First Half of the Present Century* (St. Louis: G. I. Jones and Co., 1880), 242.

38. For more information on this artist and his work in St. Louis, see John W. Reps, *Saint Louis Illustrated: Nineteenth-Century Engravings and Lithographs of a Mississippi River Town* (Columbia: University of Missouri Press, 1989), 29–51.

39. See Morton J. Horwitz, *Transformation of American Law, 1780–1860* (Cambridge, Mass.: Harvard University Press, 1977), 43–47, on the general shift in nineteenth-century American law from an earlier regard for the primacy of older, traditional claims on land, to a more proactive concern for protecting its highest possible productive value. Hartog, *Public Property and Private Power,* 8, discusses more specifically the ethos by which public lands were considered best left in the hands of private enterprise.

40. "Abstract of Proceedings, Resolutions, Ordinances, Reports, and Compromises in Relation to the St. Louis Common," Henry Williams Collection, MHS Archives, 7 January 1837, n.p.

41. Ibid.

42. "An Act to Authorize the Sale of the St. Louis Commons," in *The Ordinances of the City of St. Louis* (St. Louis: George Knapp, 1856), 69–72; Ordinance 307, 26 January 1836.

43. "Abstract of Proceedings," 22 August 1837, n.p.

44. Ordinance 315, 25 March 1836. On Lafayette Square's history, see John Albury Bryan, *Lafayette Square* (St. Louis: Lafayette Square Press, 1962).

45. "Abstract of Proceedings," 2 April 1836, n.p.

46. For a brief profile of Russell and his estate, see Primm, *Lion of the Valley* 112, and John Rodabaugh, *Frenchtown* (St. Louis: Sunrise Publishing Co., 1980), 24–28. The full text of Allen's and Russell's contract, dated July 6, 1842, appears in the archives of the First American Title Company, Clayton, Mo. (File 26,826). In addition to guaranteeing semi-annual allowance payments to Ann Russell, Allen agreed to apply any profits from the sales of his new assets "to the same uses, subject to the same conditions, limitations, and provisions" that had characterized the original property. Russell clearly expected Allen to manage his inheritance in the most conservative manner possible; the significance of this conservatism in light of the changing landscape of the early-nineteenth-century city will become clearer in the course of this chapter.

47. Thomas Allen Account Books, vol.9, "Real Estate Holdings, 1848–1864," MHS Archives, 7.

48. Ibid., 21, 1. The Allen account book is also the general source on which the preceding discussion is based. The "Dutch" to whom Allen referred were German immigrants.

49. Ibid., 1–2.

50. Ibid., 3, 13, 21.

51. *Eleventh Census of the United States*, vol. 1, *Population* (Washington: Government Printing Office, 1890), 370–71.

Chapter Four

1. Slaveholding and slave trading were by no means insignificant elements of the St. Louis economy of the 1850s. Despite the strong Eastern roots of many newly arrived entrepreneurs, as documented in Jeffrey Adler's *Yankee Merchants and the Making of the Urban West: The Rise and Fall of Antebellum St. Louis* (Cambridge: Cambridge University Press, 1991), the long-entrenched tradition of urban slavery remained central to the worldview and material well-being of a good portion of the city's political and economic élite. For two vital documentaries of slave life in St. Louis, see William Wells Brown, *Narrative of William W. Brown, a Fugitive Slave, Written by Himself* (Boston: Anti-Slavery Office, 1847), and Elizabeth Keckley, *Behind the Scenes, or Thirty Years a Slave and Four Years in the White House* (New York: Oxford University Press, 1988). That said, it is nevertheless true that the ratio of free to enslaved African Americans in the city had increased steadily through the 1800s,

until by 1860 the two groups—together comprising roughly 2 percent of the entire population—were roughly equal in number.

2. The best architectural review of the post-fire city is contained in Lawrence Lowic, *The Architectural Heritage of St. Louis, 1803–1891: From the Louisiana Purchase to the Wainwright Building* (St. Louis: Washington University Gallery of Art, 1982), 69ff. Some of the buildings that stood downtown in 1850 are among those discussed in John B. Kouwenhoven, "Downtown St. Louis as James B. Eads Knew It When the Bridge was Opened a Century Ago," *BMHS* 30 (1974): 181–93, a detailed discussion of the architecture of the central city as of 1875. The St. Louis waterfront's utilitarian, mid-century commercial architecture would, incidentally, be lionized later as a missing link in the history of modern architecture by Swiss architectural historian Sigfried Giedion in his influential work *Space, Time, and Architecture: The Growth of a New Tradition* (Cambridge, Mass. Harvard University Press, 1941). The story of Giedion's introduction in the 1930s to these soon-to-be-demolished commercial blocks is spelled out in his correspondence with Charles Peterson, preserved in the archives of the Jefferson National Expansion Memorial in St. Louis. On St. Louis's Eastern financial ties in the 1850s, see Adler, *Yankee Merchants.*

3. *State v. Joe*, 19 Mo. 223; *Reeves v. Larkin*, 19 Mo. 192; *Benoist v. City of St. Louis*, 19 Mo. 179.

4. Samuel R. Curtis Diary, 23 April 1851, Journals and Diaries Collection, MHS Archives.

5. *Report of the Celebration of the Anniversary of the Founding of St. Louis* (St. Louis: Chambers and Knapp, 1847). The Chouteau narrative is reprinted in John F. McDermott, ed., *The Early Histories of St. Louis* (St. Louis: St. Louis Historical Documents Foundation). At stake in the subtly differing accounts of one after another nineteenth-century commentator was more than a question of historical trivia. Through their fur-trading operations, the Chouteau clan dominated a significant portion of St. Louis's economy well into the nineteenth century; they also proved invaluable to Thomas Jefferson, William Clark, and other American officials for their extensive connections with Western Indian nations. Yet the Chouteaus' reasonable claim to being St. Louis's founding family remained clouded, in this heavily Catholic city, not only by the subsequent arrival of new wealth but by the illegitimate relationship between Auguste's mother—Marie Thérèse—and Pierre Laclède who, while not her legal husband, lived with her and fathered Auguste's four younger sisters and brothers. In addition to hiding the nature of this common-law relationship, some family descendants went so far as to re-carve the birth date on Auguste's headstone in the fall of 1921, during one of the periodic public bouts of doubt as to his ability to have founded the city as an adolescent (*St. Louis Globe-Democrat*, 15 August, 1921). For more on the Chouteaus, see William E. Foley and C. David Rice, *The First Chouteaus, River Barons of Early St. Louis* (Urbana: University of Illinois Press, 1983). For the question of the authenticity of the Chouteau "Narrative" and its relation to the changing power structure of the antebellum city, the author is indebted to an unpublished article by historian William Leckie Jr., "'Easy, Swift-Reading Rhetoric': The St. Louis Historical Documents Foundation and the Urban Romance of Western History."

6. Wyatt Belcher, *The Economic Rivalry Between St. Louis and Chicago* (New York: Columbia University Studies in History, Economics, and Public Law, no. 529,

1943). Belcher's thesis, still a commonplace of amateur and professional historians, is taken to task in James Neal Primm, *Lion of the Valley: St. Louis, Missouri, 1764–1980,* 3d ed. (St. Louis: Missouri Historical Society Press, 1998), 223–26. For an overview of the Civil War's impact on the city, see William C. Winter, *The Civil War in St. Louis: A Guided Tour* (St. Louis: Missouri Historical Society Press, 1994).

7. Philip J. Ethington, *The Public City: The Political Construction of Urban Life in San Francisco, 1850–1900* (Cambridge: Cambridge University Press, 1994), 8.

8. American urban historians are inordinately fond of periodizing the growth of the nation's cities. For influential examples of temporal frameworks based on changing modes of manufacturing and transportation, see Warner, *The Urban Wilderness: a History of the American City* (New York: Harper 7 Row, 1972), as well as John R. Borchert, "American Metropolitan Evolution," *Geographical Review* 57 (1967): 301–32. David Ward's *Cities and Immigrants: A Geography of Change in Nineteenth-Century America* (New York: Oxford University Press, 1971) puts the evolution of cities in terms of their shifting positions in relation to the geographical concepts of core and periphery. Barbara Sanford, "The Political Economy of Land Development in Nineteenth-Century Toronto" (*Urban History Review* 12 [1987]: 17–33), offers an example of how such periodization might be applied to the city-building process, although she offers nothing comparable to the period of dispersal that will be described in St. Louis. Common to all of the various approaches to urban chronology is the recognition of a break between two types of urban order taking place around 1870. That break corresponds roughly to the division described between the first two phases mentioned above.

In terms of the building industry itself, the phases described here bear a general similarity to periods described in greater detail elsewhere, both for the nation as a whole and for particular regions or cities. See Albert Farwell Bemis and John Burchard 2d, *The Evolving House,* 2 vols. (Cambridge, Mass.: MIT Press, 1933), as well as Gwendolyn Wright, *Moralism and the Model Home: Domestic Architecture and Cultural Conflict in Chicago, 1873–1913* (Chicago: University of Chicago Press, 1980), and Catherine W. Bishir et al., *Architects and Builders in North Carolina: A History of the Practice of Building* (Chapel Hill: University of North Carolina Press, 1990).

9. "Abstract of Proceedings . . . ," 31 June 1836.

10. Ibid., 26 January 1837, 11 July 1837, 15 May 1838.

11. William Carr Lane to Mary Lane, 11 July 1842, William Carr Lane Papers, MHS Archives. Ordinance 719, 6 February 1841; ordinance 1077, 5 September 1842.

12. Ordinance 1199, 20 July 1843; ordinance 1226, 21 August 1843; ordinance 1570, 6 November 1845.

13. Ordinance 3126, 3 February 1854.

14. Ibid. A growing awareness of the need to alter the city's practices in relation to the Common had survived the partisan seesawing of city government in the 1850s. As early as 1850, comptroller George Budd had cursed the "evil hour" when the city foolishly disposed of so much in return for so little—by Budd's accounting, less than $164,000 had actually been collected from a cumulative total of $425,000 worth of land. Budd and his boss, Mayor Luther Kennett (a Whig), argued that the land would be assessed higher if it could be sold in individual lots; this same notion was adopted by Kennett's successor, Democrat John How, and at last realized in the legislation of 1854. *Mayor's Message and Accompanying Documents . . .* (St. Louis: Missouri Republican, 1850), 12; ibid. (1853), 4.

15. *Missouri Republican*, 26 October 1854 (2:1), and 27 October, 1854 (2:1). The marketplace, never actually built, was to have been located on Indiana Avenue between Wyoming Avenue and Cherokee Street. As an amenity designed to speed up real estate sales, it would have followed the example of markets already established by Thomas Allen and the Soulard family in their own South Side additions. See Chapter 6 for more on the subsequent history of Soulard Market.

16. *Missouri Republican*, 2 May 1855 (2:8),ibid. 12 May 1855 (2:5).

17. James Clemens Jr. to Henry Boyce, 21 February 1852, Mullanphy Family Collection, MHS Archives; John Hogan, "Thoughts About the City of St. Louis," *Missouri Republican*, n.d. (c. 1854), in *Glimpses of the Past* 3 (1936): 176.

18. Ibid., 169; Curtis Diary, 23 April 1851.

19. Walter B. Stevens, *St. Louis, the Fourth City*, 3 vols. (Chicago: S. J. Clarke, 1909), 1: 792–93; *Missouri Republican*, 8 and 11 January 1853, quoted in Glen Holt, "The Shaping of St. Louis, 1763–1860" (Ph.D. diss., University of Chicago, 1975), 367–69.

20. Hogan, "Thoughts About the City of St. Louis," in *Glimpses*, 155.

21. James Mulholland to Jonathan Darby, 26 February 1853, Jonathan Darby Papers, MHS Archives.

22. P. Dexter Tiffany to Hamilton Gamble, 11 December, 1854, Tiffany Family Papers, MHS Archives. The city's right to assess a benefit tax against the owners of land appropriated for streets (rather than simply paying such owners outright for the cost of the land) had been restored in Article 6, Section 5, of the Amended Charter of 23 February 1853, *Ordinances* (1856), 158.

23. The Kaysers, who owned land beside the projected course of Grand Avenue, were among the sponsors of the promotional "Map of St. Louis with Proposed Extensions," prepared by E. and C. Robyn, 1853 (Illustration 4-3). For more information on this family, see *German Engineers of Early St. Louis and Their Works* (St. Louis, c. 1915), 16ff.

24. Half of those developers who lived somewhere on the South Side were involved in the handful of small subdivisions at the far northern end of the study area, between Lafayette Avenue and the Petite Prairie fields. These subdivisions were always distinct, socially and physically, from those to the south; Lafayette led past the stylish Lafayette Park area to the high grounds around the water company's Grand Avenue reservoir, in the northwest corner of the Common, where a number of substantial estates were located. The majority of South Side subdivisions, however, were made in the more distant and less socially desirable areas around the Third Common Subdivision, or in the Petite Prairie south of Allen's lands.

25. Thirty-two of the forty-three subdividers were traceable in city directories of the time. Nineteen lived within the central corridor. Of the twenty-five developers listed by occupation, fourteen were merchants or attorneys.

26. Walter Stevens, *St. Louis, the Fourth City*, 1: 791; Richard Smith Elliott, *Notes Taken in Sixty Years* (St. Louis: R. P. Studley and Co., 1883), 258. The implications of "real estate" as a professional and conceptual structure for ordering land have yet to be fully explored in historical literature. For classic definitions of the practice and definition of the real estate trade, see Morton Bodfish, "Real Estate," in Edward R.A. Seligman, ed., *Encyclopaedia of the Social Sciences*, 15 vols. (New York: Macmillan, 1937), 13: 135–40; also George Bloom, Arthur M. Weimer, and Jeffrey D. Fisher, *Real Estate*, 8th ed. (New York: Wiley, 1982). For a more analytical work exploring the meaning

of land development in a historical context, see Richard M. Yearwood, "Land Subdivision and Development: American Attitudes on Land Subdivision and Its Controls," *American Journal of Economics and Sociology* 19 (1970): 113–26. Marc Weiss's *The Rise of the Community Builders: The American Real Estate Industry and Urban Land Planning* (New York: Columbia University Press, 1987) offers an insightful look at real estate practices in a later period than the one considered here. A general guide to the literature of land development in North America can be found in Michael Doucet, "Urban Land Development in Nineteenth-Century North America: Themes in the Literature," *Journal of Urban History* (hereafter cited as *JUH*) 8 (1982): 299–342.

27. Harry S. Gleick, "Banking in Early Missouri, Part II," *MHR* 62 (1967): 34–35; James Neal Primm, *Economic Policy in the Development of a Western State: Missouri, 1820–1860* (Cambridge, Mass.: Harvard University Press, 1954), 68–71; Wilber Clarence Bothwell, "History of Banking in Missouri from 1875 Until the Establishment of the Federal Reserve System" (M.A. thesis, Washington University, 1933), 3ff.

28. "Account Book of Henry Hagan, 1843–1861," Account Books Collection, MHS Archives, n.p.

29. "Soulard Deeds," 1 October 1842, 29 October 1842, Soulard Papers, MHS Archives. For a comparison of the practice of in-kind payment to builders, see Bishir et al., *Architects and Builders*, 154. Construction practice in St. Louis was far slower to develop than it was in a larger city like New York, where a pronounced specialization and subdivision of activities had already become evident by the 1830s. See Sean Wilentz, *Chants Democratic: New York City and the Rise of the American Working Class, 1788–1850* (New York: Oxford University Press, 1984), 132–34.

30. *Missouri Republican,* 20 May 1840 (2:4). Wilentz, in *Chants Democratic,* describes the origins of similar labor sentiments in New York, several years earlier, as the birth of a uniquely American radical tradition (238–48, 254). As Wilentz points out, the workers' demands were not for the abolition of private property, but for a renewed commitment to the opportunity for self-improvement that was theoretically guaranteed to all Americans. In the case of St. Louis, then, we can see that the journeyman carpenters were struggling with some of the same issues of justification that faced the members of the committee on the Common at the same time. In either case, opportunity and liberty were colored by social standing and self-interest. That self-interest called for quite different paths toward a commonly articulated goal.

31. *Missouri Republican,* 23 May 1840 (2:2).

32. For more information on the early years of labor in St. Louis, see Russell M. Nolen, "The Labor Movement in St. Louis Prior to the Civil War," *MHR* 34 (1939): 158–81, and Walter R. Houf, "Fifty Years of Missouri Labor, 1820–1870" (M.A. thesis, University of Missouri, 1958).

33. Thirty-two names appeared within city directories; of these, twenty-three were listed by occupation. Sixteen lived within the bounds of South St. Louis as defined by this study. Only nine were described as merchants of one kind or another. See Michael B. Katz, "Occupational Classification in History," *Journal of Interdisciplinary History* 3 (1972): 63–88, on the difficulty of drawing conclusions on social change from nineteenth-century job titles. While the occupational shift noted here among local subdividers may not reflect directly on changes in either class or wealth, it nevertheless indicates a change from the highly professionalized, politically connected, and socially well-established clique that dominated development activity in earlier years.

34. S[ylvester] V. Papin and Brother, "A Review of the Real Estate Business of St. Louis in 1877, Causes of Decline and Prices, and When Activity and Advances May Be Looked For" (St. Louis, 1877), 13.

35. Ordinance 10,389.

36. Bothwell, "History of Banking," 11, 25, 42; Stevens, *St. Louis, the Fourth City,* 1: 320ff.

37. *Missouri Republican,* 29 March 1855 (1:8).

38. *Western Building and Loan Journal* 1(2) (15 September 1893): 8; "By-Laws of the Park Building and Loan" (St. Louis, 1890). For a good introduction to the building and loan industry, see H. Morton Bodfish, ed., *A History of the Building and Loan in the United States* (Chicago: U.S. Building and Loan League, 1931), and William Frank Willoughby, *Building and Loan Associations* (Boston, 1900).

39. *Building Association Record* 1(1) (15 June 1891): 4; ibid. 1(4) (25 September 1891): 14.

40. Missouri Bureau of Statistics of Labor (hereafter cited as MBSL), *Fifteenth Annual Report* (St. Louis, 1893), 145, 160; *Building Association Record* 1(1) (15 June 1891): 2.

41. MBSL, *Sixteenth Annual Report* (St. Louis, 1894), 390; Superintendent of Building and Loan Associations of the State of Missouri, *First Annual Report* (Columbia: E. W. Stephens, 1896), 170. For estimates of the relation between mortgage size and purchase price, see Sam Bass Warner, *Streetcar Suburbs: The Process of Growth in Boston (1870–1900),* 2d ed. (Cambridge, Mass.: Harvard University Press, 1978), 200.

42. "Minutes of the St. Louis Architectural Association," 14 March 1858, John S. Bowen Papers, MHS Archives.

43. The primary professional organization for architects, the American Institute of Architects, was chartered in New York in the previous year. See Henry H. Saylor, *The AIA's First Hundred Years* (Washington, D.C.: American Institute of Architects, 1957). For examples of the early organization of the profession in other cities, see Bishir et al., *Architects and Builders,* 162–75, and Wright, *Moralism and the Model Home,* 22ff. Architects in Missouri were by no means immediately successful in their efforts to establish professional exclusivity. In their article, "The A. B. Cross Lumber Company, 1858–1871," *MHR* 80 (1985): 14–32, George Ehrlich and Peggy E. Schrock demonstrate the ease with which one trained architect switched his professional affiliations during his residence in Kansas City, before the period in which architects had established a firm foothold in local building practice.

44. Based on an inspection of St. Louis city directories for 1870, 1880, 1890, 1900, and 1910. At the start of that period, thirty-eight architects practiced in the city; by the end, there were 160.

45. Charles Jones Account Book, 1875–76, Charles Jones Papers, MHS Archives. See also the specifications for the T. S. Noonan house, Peugnet Collection, MHS Archives.

46. *Building Trades Journal* 3(1) (January 1886): 5ff.

47. MBSL, *Eighth Annual Report* (St. Louis, 1886), 253; Russell M. Nolan, "The Labor Movement in St. Louis from 1860 to 1890," *MHR* 34 (1940): 157–81; David T. Burbank, *Reign of the Rabble: The St. Louis General Strike of 1877* (New York: Augustus M. Kelley, 1966).

48. The *Annual Reports* of the MBSL through the 1880s provide a good record of these strikes; see especially the annual synopsis of labor actions contained in the

Ninth Annual Report (St. Louis, 1887), 262–93. In the spring of 1886 alone, there were six construction strikes in the city.

49. One key aspect of the transformation of building trades from an artisan-based craft to a complex industrial process is the tension between a drive for progress, improvement, and rationalization, on the one hand, and a sometimes conflicting desire to protect traditional cultural or occupational values, on the other. An awareness of this tension characterizes Elizabeth Blackmar's fine account of the "rationalization" of the construction trades in New York, in *Manhattan for Rent, 1785–1850* (Ithaca, N.Y.: Cornell University Press, 1989), 183–212; see also Thomas J. Surbuhr, "The Economic Transformation of Carpentry in Late-Nineteenth-Century Chicago," *Illinois Historical Journal* 81 (1988): 109–24. Among the number of works that address the larger question of the function of organized labor in relation to the changing modes of production of the late nineteenth century, see David M. Gordon, Richard Edwards, and Michael Reich, *Segmented Work, Divided Workers: The Historical Transformation of Labor in the United States* (New York: Cambridge University Press, 1982); Jeffrey Haydu, *Between Crafts and Class: Skilled Workers and Factory Politics in the United States and Britain, 1890–1922* (Berkeley: University of California Press, 1988); Susan E. Hirsch, *Roots of the American Working Class: Industrialization of the Crafts in Newark, 1800–1860* (Philadelphia: University of Pennsylvania Press, 1978); and David Montgomery, "Workers' Control of Machine Production in the Nineteenth Century," *Labor History* 17 (1976): 485–509. What applied to other trades, however, did not necessarily hold for the construction industry. For an analysis of the differences between the organization of the construction industry and the rest of the economy, see Donald R. Adams Jr., "Residential Construction in the Early Nineteenth Century," *Journal of Economic History* 35 (1975): 794–816.

50. MBSL, *15th Annual Report*, 63.

51. According to the Merchants' Exchange of St. Louis, 300 million bricks were produced in St. Louis in 1892; by 1904 one company alone (Hydraulic-Press Brick) produced that number annually. Merchants' Exchange, *Annual Statement of the Trade and Commerce of St. Louis, 1892* (St. Louis, 1892); *Brick* 20(5) (1 May 1904):235. On the brick industry in St. Louis, see Esther Louise Aschemeyer, "The Urban Geography of the Clay Products Industries of Metropolitan St. Louis" (M.A. thesis, Washington University, 1943), as well as *Brick* 20(5) (1 May 1904): 217–40. Early brick construction laws include ordinance 418 (28 May 1839), and ordinance 3461 (7 December 1855), which followed the disastrous fire of 1849. For examples of prevailing wages, see MBSL, *Fourteenth Annual Report* (St. Louis, 1892), 45, and *Fifteenth Annual Report*, 63.

52. Bricklayers Local 3 "Minutes," 22 March 1889, 12 October 1888, 18 April 1888, collection Bricklayers Union, Local 1, St. Louis.

53. Ibid. 7 October 1895.

54. Ibid., 10 November 1897, 1 June 1898, 8 June 1898, 13 April 1898, 8 August 1898.

55. Bricklayers' Union Executive Committee notes, 27 February 1897, collection Bricklayers' Union Local 1, St. Louis; Minutes, 11 October 1898, 5 February 1899, 15 June 1898. The issue of banning German had provoked a major citywide political fight in the context of the city schools, where German instruction was discontinued in 1888. See Audrey Olson, *St. Louis Germans, 1850–1920: The Nature of an Immigrant*

Community and Its Relation to the Assimilation Process (New York: Arno Press, 1980), 91–106.

56. On the Building Trades Council and its political conservatism, see Gary M. Fink, *Labor's Search for Political Order: The Political Behavior of the Missouri Labor Movement, 1890–1940* (Columbia: University of Missouri Press, 1973), 2. The conclusion that changes in the union were not indicative of a conscious concern for class-based issues contradicts Surbuhr's thesis in "The Transformation of Carpentry" regarding the case of the Chicago carpenters in the same period. It seems more logical, as Haydu notes in *Between Craft and Class,* that inter-trade organizations like the BTC did not so much reflect class consciousness as encourage it (6). Indeed, the rather mechanistic notion that changing modes of production and straitened circumstances led workers to view their self-interest in radically altered terms has come under increasing question. For a cogent account of how an essential social conservatism overlapped with the growing need for trade solidarity, see John Bodnar, *Workers' World: Kinship, Community, and Protest in an Industrial Society, 1900–1940* (Baltimore: Johns Hopkins University Press, 1982), as well as Herbert Gutman's influential article, "Work, Culture, and Society in Industrializing America, 1815–1919," *American Historical Review* 78 (1973): 531–87.

57. Ordinance 12,027, 1 April 1882.

58. Ibid.; ordinance 18,964, 7 April 1897; ordinance 22,022, 7 April 1905.

59. Master Builders' Association, "Articles of Incorporation," 25 March 1896, collection Associated General Contractors of St. Louis.

60. These figures were determined by an inspection of the business listings in St. Louis city directories for the years 1880, 1890, 1900, and 1910. While city directory listings do not necessarily provide the most accurate information in terms of the actual numbers engaged in a given occupation, the question at hand is the changing manner in which people defined their occupation. A cross-check of listings of bricklayers and carpenters in the 1880s and 1890s with the membership rolls of Bricklayers' Local 3 and Carpenters' Local 5 (the two South Side–based union locals) reveals almost no overlap. This suggests that only contracting bricklayers or carpenters (who could not belong to the union) bothered to place listings in the directory. Thus, the results of the city directory search reveal more about professional nomenclature within the contracting field than they do about the structure of the entire building industry. Taken on those terms, however, they suggest the increasing division between job titles that implied manual skills and those implying managerial and professional skills.

A further perspective on the significance of this shift, not only for contractors but for other members of the building professions, can be obtained from Magali Sarfatti Larson, *The Rise of Professionalism: A Sociological Analysis* (Berkeley: University of California Press, 1977). Larson draws on sociological tradition (particularly as it is represented in the work of Talcott Parsons) to emphasize the importance of formalized social controls in defining new communities for which existing primary, personal relationships have not been sufficiently established. For a perspective on Larson's work in the context of the literature of professionalism see Michael Schudson's review essay in *Theory and Society* 9 (1980): 215–28.

61. See "100th Anniversary of Connecticut Mutual's Agency in St. Louis" (St. Louis, 1948), in Insurance Papers, MHS Archives. James Russell was a brother of

Thomas Allen's father-in-law, William Russell and, incidentally, the grandfather of the artist Charles Russell, who spent his boyhood years on the family estate.

62. There were comparable shifts in development and construction practices in other cities around the same time. See Wright, *Moralism and the Model Home*, 40–44, on Chicago's Samuel E. Gross; and Bishir et al., *Architects and Builders*, 264–72, on Jacob Holt and other prominent North Carolina developers. Consolidated developers were not new to the 1890s; rather, they simply acquired a greater and more visible share of the urban housing market. Anne Bloomfield's "The Real Estate Associates: A Land and Housing Developer of the 1870s in San Francisco," *Journal of the Society of Architectural Historians* (hereafter cited as *JSAH*) 37 (1978): 13–33, offers an example of a similar developer operating a generation earlier.

63. St. Louis Merchants' Exchange, *Annual Statement of the Trade and Commerce of St. Louis, 1900* (St. Louis, 1901), 52.

64. *St. Louis Builder* 12(7) (July 1905): n.p.

65. *Building Association Record* 1(4) (25 September 1891): 13; Bothwell, "History of Banking," 96; Supervisor of Building and Loan Associations of the State of Missouri, *Eighth Annual Report* (Warrensburg, Mo.: Star Press, 1903), 10.

66. *Eighth Annual Report*, 10.

67. *St. Louis Builder* 12(7) (July 1905): n.p; 8(9) (November 1901): n.p.

Chapter Five

1. St. Louis *Daily American*, 7 April 1847, in Walter Otto Forster, "Saxon Lutherans in Missouri, 1839–1847: A Study of the Origins of the Missouri Synod" (Ph.D. diss., Washington University, 1942), 33. German immigrants accounted for more than one-quarter of St. Louis's population in 1850; their percentage in South St. Louis wards was considerably higher. For a general introduction to the German presence in St. Louis, see Audrey Olson, *St. Louis Germans, 1850–1920: The Nature of an Immigrant Community and Its Relation to the Assimilation Process* (New York: Arno Press, 1980); on their concentration in South St. Louis, see the analysis in Frederick Anthony Hodes, "The Urbanization of St. Louis: A Study in Urban Residential Patterns in the Nineteenth Century" (Ph.D. diss., St. Louis University, 1973). For a more recent interpretation of the local immigrant community in the context of their transatlantic origins, see Walter D. Kamphoefner, *The Westfalians: From Germany to Missouri* (Princeton, N.J.: Princeton University Press, 1987).

2. Ethnicity has occupied a central place in American urban social history, perhaps because it seems one of the clearest criteria available for measuring isolation, assimilation, and community, all of which have been key to the long line of works that have come out of the liberal social tradition of interwar historians like Oscar Handlin; see Handlin's *Boston's Immigrants (1790–1880): A Study in Acculturation* (1941; rev. ed., Cambridge, Mass.: Belknap Press of Harvard University Press, 1979). That historical tradition in turn owes a debt to the breakthroughs (and shortcomings) of the sociologists gathered around the University of Chicago in the 1920s and 1930s, who focused on ethnicity as a key component of the social structure of the city. Works like Paul F. Cressey's "Population Succession in Chicago, 1898–1930," *American Journal of Sociology* 44 (1938): 59–69, helped set the agenda for sociologists and urban historians

alike well into the last generation; for an example of the resonance of Cressey's thesis to later scholars, see Humbert S. Nelli, *Italians in Chicago, 1880–1930: A Study in Ethnic Mobility* (New York: Oxford University Press, 1970), 43–53. The broad assumptions that they made as to the primary significance of ethnicity were eventually brought into question by historians like Nelli and by later sociologists like Gerald Suttles, who found them simplistic and deterministic; see Suttles, *The Social Construction of Communities* (Chicago: University of Chicago Press, 1972), 25–29. More recently, urban historians have begun to look more specifically at ethnicity's interaction with different circumstances at different times. For two articles that suggest ways of placing ethnicity within a larger social context, see Kathleen Neils Conzen, "Immigrants, Immigrant Neighborhoods, and Ethnic Identity: Historical Issues," *Journal of American History* 66 (1979): 603–15, and Olivier Zunz, "Residential Segregation in the American Metropolis: Concentration, Dispersion, and Dominance," *Urban History Yearbook* (1980): 23–33.

The ethnicity issue in St. Louis is addressed more fully in Olson, *St. Louis Germans*, as well as in Gary Ross Mormino, *Immigrants on the Hill: Italian-Americans in St. Louis, 1882–1982* (Urbana: University of Illinois Press, 1986), and Margaret LoPiccolo Sullivan, *Hyphenism in St. Louis, 1900–1921: The View from the Outside* (New York: Garland, 1990). Relatively less has been written about the historical development of African American communities within the city, despite the fact that their growing concentration—primarily, within the industrial belt on either side of the Mill Creek Valley—offers a useful contrast with the more dispersed German and Irish communities in the matter of the complex relation of ethnic consciousness to geographic clustering. A suggestive start to that study is represented by the fascinating details included in Cyprian Clamorgan's *The Colored Aristocracy of St. Louis* (St. Louis, 1858); for a more recent review of the geography of early African American settlement, see Lawrence D. Christenson, "Black St. Louis: A Study in Race Relations, 1865–1916" (Ph.D. dissertation, University of Missouri, 1972).

3. This choice of forms is a simpler version of the six-frontage "clusters" that Olivier Zunz studied in his work on Detroit, *The Changing Face of Inequality: Urbanization, Industrial Development and Immigrants in Detroit, 1880–1920* (Chicago: University of Chicago Press, 1982).

4. In the case of areas 1 and 4, all building lots face on the long sides of the block; thus every building on these blocks is included in the study. Areas 2 and 3 each have a smaller number of buildings facing the short ends of their blocks. While the significance of this altered block form will be discussed below, the additional lots in question are not discussed specifically.

5. For more on the place of ethnic-based institutional life in the neighborhood, see Olson, *St. Louis Germans*. The equation of common traits with a sense of solidarity rests on the longstanding assumption of the primacy of kinship ties that informs the work of early social theorists like Durkheim and Weber, and that was extended to ethnicity, occupation, and other contemporary markers of identity in the works of American urban sociologists. See Robert E. Park, Ernest W. Burgess, Roderick D. McKenzie, eds., *The City* (1925; Chicago: University of Chicago Press, 1967), or for a more extended examination of ethnicity and religion as the basis for understanding the community, see Louis Wirth, *The Ghetto* (1928; Chicago: Phoenix Books, University

of Chicago Press, 1962). However, even where earlier assumptions of ethnicity have been seriously questioned, as in Conzen, "Immigrants," or Zunz, "Residential Segregation," the simple fact that common ethnicity means *something* (or something more than nothing) is never argued; rather, it is the degree of generalization drawn from that concept that is at issue.

6. The history of Lucas Place is examined in detail in Richard Allen Rosen, "St. Louis, Missouri, 1850–1865: The Rise of Lucas Place and the Transformation of the City from Public Spaces to Private Places" (M.A. thesis, University of California, Los Angeles, 1988). For a briefer synopsis in the context of the history of private-place development in St. Louis, see Charles C. Savage, *Architecture of the Private Streets of St. Louis: The Architects and the Houses They Designed* (Columbia: University of Missouri Press, 1987), 13–17.

7. James Neal Primm, *Lion of the Valley: St. Louis, Missouri, 1764–1980*, 3d ed. (St. Louis: Missouri Historical Society Press, 1998), 219–20; William Hyde and Howard L. Conard, *Encyclopedia of the History of St. Louis: A Compendium of History and Biography for Ready Reference* (St. Louis: Southern Book Company, 1899), 1: 16–17.

8. Except for the three central blocks leading up from the river, Laclède's blocks were 240 feet by 300 feet each.

9. There were, of course, the deed restrictions mentioned in Chapter 1, but these were common enough throughout the city, even as early as the 1850s.

10. Ordinance 4551, 6 December 1859; ordinance 6230, 2 July 1867.

11. Details on these and all other land transactions described in this chapter are derived from the records of the First American Title Company, St. Louis. Deeds referred to in subsequent notes will be listed by their book and page number in the official city records where they are known, and where they not, by their file number in the First American (hereafter cited as FA) archives. See Blackmar, *Manhattan for Rent*, for a comparison of long-term ground lease practices in another city.

12. Theodore Dreiser, *A Book About Myself* (New York: Boni and Liveright, 1922), 93; see also Charles Dickens, *American Notes* (Boston: Fields, Osgood, 1867), 359, on the city's "crazy old tenements."

13. For more information on Compton and Dry's remarkable *Pictorial St. Louis*, which assembled large-scale bird's-eye views of every block in the city, see John W. Reps, *Saint Louis Illustrated: Nineteenth-Century Engravings and Lithographs of a Mississippi River Town* (Columbia: University of Missouri Press, 1989), 126–53. Their surprising detail and accuracy make these views particularly useful for historical research. If any general fault might be found with them, it would be their vertical distortion, which caused buildings to appear taller than they actually were.

14. Patricia L. Jones, "Whatever Happened to Bohemian Hill?" *Gateway Heritage* 5(3) (Winter 1984–85): 22-31; *Messenger of St. John Nepomuk Parish, Diamond Jubilee Number* (St. Louis, 1929).

15. Saloon and grocery addresses were derived from the city directory of 1880. These two categories were chosen as examples of commercial uses that had a daily utility in the lives of neighborhood residents, and might therefore be expected to reveal more about the character of the neighborhood in their location.

16. Arthur Proetz, *I Remember You, St. Louis* (1916; St. Louis: Zimmerman-Petty Company, 1963), 56–57.

17. *Fath v. Tower Grove and Lafayette Railway*, 105 Mo. 537.

18. Deed 730/310, 16 June 1884; deed 339/252, 8 June 1867. The occupational categories described here and elsewhere in this chapter are based on those developed by Kathleen Neils Conzen, in her *Immigrant Milwaukee, 1836–1860: Accommodation and Community in a Frontier City* (Cambridge, Mass.: Harvard University Press, 1976), 234–37.

19. Information regarding builders, owners, and dates of construction is drawn from building permit abstracts on file at the city's building department. Because the original permits are inaccessible, and because of the variations in the manner in which permit information was recorded on the abstracts, this information is less complete and consistent than it might be. Records dating from after 1900 are more complete and include the name of the contractor and, where applicable, the architect.

20. The urban rowhouse plan in a number of cities other than St. Louis has received a great deal of attention in the literature of architectural history. See Mary Ellen Hayward, "Urban Vernacular Architecture in Nineteenth-Century Baltimore," *Winterthur Portfolio* 16 (1981): 33–63; Sarah Bradford Landau, "The Row Houses of New York's West Side," *JSAH* 34 (1975): 19–36; and William John Murtagh, "The Philadelphia Row House," *JSAH* 16 (1957): 8–13. On the peculiarity of St. Louis's detached rowhouses, see R. Rosen, "St. Louis," 103–12.

The Creole house plan is less well-documented, particularly as it appears in urban settings. For an early analysis of the type within its "cultural hearth," see Fred B. Kniffen, "Louisiana House Types," *Annals of the Association of American Geographers* 26 (1936): 179–93. Recently, Kniffen's work has been expanded by Jay Edwards, who also focuses more on the original diffusion of the type than its subsequent transformations. See "The Origins of the Louisiana Creole Cottage," in Michael Roark, ed., *French and Germans in the Mississippi Valley: Landscape and Cultural Traditions* (Cape Girardeau, Mo.: Center for Regional History and Cultural Heritage, 1988), 9–60, as well as "The Complex Origins of the American Domestic Piazza-Veranda-Gallery," *Material Culture* 21(2) (Summer 1989): 3–58. An account of the type as it appeared in the early years can be found in Charles Peterson, "The Houses of French St. Louis," in John Francis McDermott, ed., *The French in the Mississippi Valley* (Urbana: University of Illinois Press, 1965), 41–58. For a contemporary account of the urbanized-Creole plan in St. Louis (and still nearly the only account to date), see C. E. Illsley, "St. Louis," *The American Architect and Building News* 3 (25 May 1878): 184.

21. Charlotte Rumbold, *Housing Conditions in St. Louis* (St. Louis: Civic League of St. Louis, 1908), 48. Rumbold was describing an area of the near North Side that was developed at approximately the same time as the Menard area.

22. Information on the particular and aggregate characteristics of neighborhood residents comes from the manuscript enumeration tables of the Tenth, Twelfth, and Thirteenth Censuses of the United States (1880, 1900, and 1910).

23. Rumbold, *Housing Conditions*, 30.

24. The theory that family structure and size is the essential determinant of residential choice is central to Martin Cadwallader's "A Unified Model of Urban Housing Patterns, Social Patterns, and Residential Mobility," *Urban Geography* 2 (1981): 115–30. A detailed study of the determinants of residential stability and mobility was carried out for the purposes of our study, but time and space demands have prevented

it from being recounted in full here. Essentially, however, the study (based on a chi-square analysis of the various social traits of household heads in relation to residential location ten years prior and subsequent to their census listings) revealed that, except for home-ownership, no single trait predicted stability at the same address as well as the mere fact of having lived at that address before. In other words, ethnicity, occupation, family size, and so on all had less effect on residential choice than what we might call the inertial pull of place. This finding contradicts the thrust of much of the urban mobility literature of the 1960s and 1970s, although it is in keeping with the geographer James W. Simmons's definition of "propinquity" in residence patterns—simply stated, that "the best single factor to predict location of a new residence is the location of the former house" (Simmons, "Behavioral Bases of Changing Social Space: Individual Mobility and Waves of Succession," in Brian J. L. Berry and Frank E. Horton, eds., *Geographical Perspectives on Urban Systems, with Integrated Readings* [Englewood Cliffs, N.J.: Prentice-Hall, 1970], 405). Other findings from my own mobility analysis, particularly those that help to clarify the differences between the four study areas, will be mentioned where they are worthy of note.

25. See, for example, deed 1505/191, 5 April 1899; deed 1596/260, 23 April 1901; deed 2020/74, 26 February 1907.

26. Ordinance 5870, 7 July 1866; ordinance 6230, 2 July 1867.

27. In their scale and layout, the blocks of the Barsaloux Addition may well have provided Cozzens with his model for the layout of the blocks of the Second and Third Subdivisions of the St. Louis Common, drawn two years after the initial dedication of Daggett's land.

28. Deed 388/368, 11 August 1869.

29. *Diamond Jubilee, St. Francis de Sales Parish, St. Louis, Missouri, 1867–1942* (St. Louis, 1942), n.p.

30. The broad directional patterns of late-nineteenth-century mobility in the city are analyzed in Hodes, "The Urbanization of St. Louis," 150ff.

31. Deed 522/180, 29 May 1875; deed 1985/550, 9 April 1907; deed 2106/178, 1 March 1908.

32. Deed 153/202, 19 June 1854; deed 156/90, 19 June 1854; deed 156/124, 19 June 1854.

33. Pape's fortune was listed in the 1870 census enumeration manuscript—the last census in the nineteenth century to list personal worth.

34. See, for example, deed 1516/441, 26 May 1898; deed 1883/153, 16 August 1905; deed 2054/456, 11 December 1907.

35. Similar functional and symbolic interpretations of this type of domestic space can be found in Gwendolyn Wright, *Moralism and the Model Home: Domestic Architecture and Cultural Conflict in Chicago, 1873–1913* (Chicago: University of Chicago Press, 1980), 34, as well as Margaret Marsh, "From Separation to Togetherness: The Social Construction of Domestic Space in American Suburbs, 1840–1915," *Journal of American History* 76 (1989): 506–27.

36. The distinction that separates the placement of Pennsylvania homes within the streetscape from the buildings of either Menard or McNair might be considered a matter of yards dominating the street, rather than vice versa. The significance of that distinction, originally posed by the geographer Wilbur Zelinsky, is one subject

of Paul Groth's "Lot, Yard, and Garden: American Distinctions," *Landscape* 30(3) (1990): 29–35.

37. Carolyn Hewes Toft and Jane Molloy Porter, *Compton Heights: A Historical and Architectural Guide* (St. Louis: Landmarks Association of St. Louis, 1984), 3–11.

38. Hyde and Conard, *Encyclopedia*, 2: 996–97; Primm, *Lion of the Valley*, 198–200.

39. FA files 11,739, 30,765, 37,489. "Tower Grove" was originally the name of St. Louis merchant Henry Shaw's country estate, just west of Grand Avenue. It eventually became the name of the large public park that Shaw donated to the city, and that stretched just west of Steedman's property.

40. Deed 1523/42, 2 June 1899.

41. Missouri Corporate Records no. 28-78, in FA file 37,489. Because it had long served as a lender to developers, Connecticut Mutual naturally had access to a great deal of land. The incorporation of Connecticut Realty made official a sphere of interest already well-established in the company's history.

42. Deed 1826/14, 8 February 1905.

43. Hyde and Conard, *Encyclopedia*, 1: 350–51; Frederick E. Billon, *Annals of St. Louis in Its Territorial Days* (St. Louis, 1888), 117, 133, 231.

44. FA file 13,817.

45. The practice of taking in boarders was far more common and widely accepted as of 1910 than it has since become; inferring the significance of that practice from our contemporary perspective is, therefore, fraught with difficulties. Without excluding other interpretations, I will consider one vital function of taking in boarders in the Halliday area to have been the financial assistance that it offered homeowners working to pay their mortgage. For a fuller discussion of the phenomenon and its significance in American domestic life, see John Modell and Tamara K. Hareven, "Urbanization and the Malleable Household: An Examination of Boarding and Lodging in American Families," in Tamara K. Hareven, ed., *Family and Kin in Urban Communities, 1700–1930* (New York: New Viewpoints, 1977), 164–86.

46. The cultural implications of homeownership in the United States have come under increasing question by historians. See Daniel D. Luria, "Wealth, Capital, and Power: The Social Meaning of Homeownership," *Journal of Interdisciplinary History* 7 (1976): 261–82; Carolyn Tyirin Kirk and Gordon W. Kirk Jr., "The Impact of the City on Homeownership: A Comparison of Immigrants and Native Whites at the Turn of the Century," *JUH* 7 (1981): 471–98; Matthew Edel, Elliott D. Sclar, and Daniel D. Luria, *Shaky Palaces: Homeownership and Social Mobility of Boston's Suburbanization* (New York: Columbia University Press, 1984); and Richard Harris, "Working-Class Home Ownership in the American Metropolis," *JUH* 17 (1990): 46–69. While it may be true, as these and other writers have maintained, that the marked propensity among immigrant and working-class families to become homeowners should not be seen as a simple acceptance of mainstream, middle-class values, the St. Louis census data suggest that we take care not to assume, on the contrary, that homeownership was a form of financial servitude. The overwhelming majority of homeowners listed in all four of the study areas during each of the census years indicated that their homes were fully paid, rather than still under mortgage. Inspection of the more detailed records contained in the First American Title Company files reveals a few cases of owner-occupied buildings that were apparently sold in order to pay off the steep lump-

sum principle due at the end of the mortgage term (in other words, the principle was past due and was not recorded as having been repaid until the day of the sale). On the other hand, the title records reveal a far greater number of cases in which the original term of the mortgage was extended, and repayment was not received until long after the original deadline.

47. In their study of a comparable population in Chicago at the same time, Hartmut Keil and Heinz Ickstadt have noted the replacement of "interaction across class boundaries within the ethnic group . . . by interaction across ethnic boundaries within the same class." See their "Elements of German Working-Class Culture in Chicago, 1880–1890," in Hartmut Keil, ed., *German Workers' Culture in the United States, 1850–1920* (London: Smithsonian Institution Press, 1988), 90.

48. This is not to say that the general outlines of the findings suggested by the evidence presented here necessarily diverge from those arrived at by urban historians in the past. Instead, we should consider the focus on creating and experiencing neighborhood spaces as a complementary (and necessary) adjunct to a theoretical framework already well developed but still insufficiently anchored in, as Zunz once phrased it, "the concrete bedrock of time and place" (*The Changing Face of Inequality*, 9). For a viewpoint that is particularly well suited to the one suggested here, see Michael Frisch, *Town into City: Springfield, Massachusetts, and the Meaning of Community* (Cambridge, Mass.: Harvard University Press, 1992). Especially useful in the context of this chapter is the author's explanation of the transition from a sense of community "as a strong and meaningful personal reality" to the "more abstracted conception" that the term represented by the end of the nineteenth century (49). Frisch also concentrated on spatial decisions as the key to that transition, but he concerned himself primarily with changes made at the gross, citywide level rather than exploring the full range of the public and private landscape.

Chapter Six

1. Sam Bass Warner Jr. *Streetcar Suburbs: The Process of Growth in Boston (1870–1900)*, 2d ed. (Cambridge, Mass.: Harvard University Press, 1978), 117ff. See Hendrik Hartog, *Public Property and Private Power: The Corporation of the City of New York in American Law, 1730–1870* (Chapel Hill: University of North Carolina Press, 1983), 174–75, for a similar interpretation of the manner in which streetmaking "clarified" the dichotomy of private and public space in the American city. On sewerage, which because of its highly dispersed structure had a similar history in St. Louis to streetmaking, see Katharine T. Corbett, "Draining the Metropolis: The Politics of Sewers in Nineteenth-Century St. Louis," in Andrew Hurley, ed., *Common Fields: An Environmental History of St. Louis* (St. Louis: Missouri Historical Society Press, 1997).

2. The idea of using the history of public works to gain new insight into the social and political culture of cities has developed most rapidly in the last twenty-five years, particularly since the publication of Joel Tarr, ed., "The City and Technology," special issue, *JUH* 5 (1979). Particular articles that have proven useful for the purposes of the current study include Clay McShane, "Transforming the Use of Urban Space: A Look at the Revolution in Street Pavements, 1880–1924," *JUH* 5 (1979): 279–307,

which considers "shifts in the cultural and political climate" of cities as factors that helped to spur technological and scientific advances (302), and Christine Meisner Rosen, "Infrastructural Improvement in Nineteenth-Century Cities: A Conceptual Framework and Cases," *JUH* 12 (May 1986): 211–56, which deals with the political limitations that hampered the efficient or equitable provision of public services in the American city. For a broader review of relevant works, see Clay McShane, "Essays in Public Works History," *JUH* 10 (1984): 223–38. The best encapsulation of the political ramifications of the debate between centralized and dispersed, or "segmented," services in the city comes from Robin Einhorn, *Property Rules: Political Economy in Chicago, 1833–1872* (Chicago: University of Chicago Press, 1991).

3. See, for example, Ann Durkin Keating, *Building Chicago: Suburban Developers and the Creation of a Divided Metropolis* (Columbus: Ohio State University Press, 1988).

4. The experience of the St. Louis Common is usefully compared in this respect to other public land sales occurring at the same time. See Elizabeth Blackmar, *Manhattan for Rent, 1780–1850* (Ithaca, N.Y.: Cornell University Press, 1989), 247, on the disposition of common lands in New York in the 1850s.

5. "Report of the City Engineer," *The Mayor's Message, with Accompanying Documents, to the City Council of the City of St. Louis* (hereafter cited as *Mayor's Message*), St. Louis, 1861, 13; James Parton, "The City of St. Louis," *Atlantic Monthly* 19 (1867): 657–58.

6. Samuel R. Curtis Diary, 7 January 1851, Journals and Diaries Collection, MHS Archives.

7. Ibid.

8. *Missouri Republican*, 2 March 1851 (3:1).

9. "Report of the Street Commissioner," *Mayor's Message* (St. Louis, 1872), 4; "Report of the Board of Public Improvements," *Mayor's Message* (1881), 162; *Journal of the House of Delegates* (St. Louis, 1881), 87–88. Excessive as St. Louis's commitment to street paving had come to seem, the city still boasted less than half of the total paved street mileage of Chicago at the same time. See Arthur Meier Schlesinger, *The Rise of the City, 1878–1898* (Chicago: Quadrangle Books, 1971), 89.

10. "Report of the City Engineer," *Mayor's Message* (1872), 9; ibid. (1874), 21; *Journal of the House of Delegates* (1881), 87–88.

11. "R. C." to "Mother," 9 May 1881, and Theodore Sandberg diary entries, 13 and 14 January 1897 (all in St. Louis History Papers, MHS Archives).

12. Paving expenditures are extracted from the "Report of the City Engineer" printed in the *Mayor's Message* for the years in question.

13. "Report of the City Engineer," in *Mayor's Message* (1870), 185.

14. In 1870, the First Ward had a population of approximately 34,000—roughly the same as the population of the Eleventh Ward, and nearly 75 percent larger than that of the Twelfth. *Ninth Census of the United States*, vol.1, *Population* (Washington: Government Printing Office, 1870), 194.

15. "Report of the City Engineer" (1871, 1875), Tables 1 and 2; *Edwards' St. Louis Directory* (1870, 1871); *Gould's St. Louis Directory* (1874, 1875).

16. "Report of the Board of Public Improvements," in *Mayor's Message* (1878), 200–203.

17. "Report of the City Engineer," in *Mayor's Message* (1871), 155.

18. Ibid. (1875), 6.

19. State Act of 16 January 1860, in *The Revised Ordinances of the City of St. Louis* (St. Louis: George Knapp and Co., 1871), 292.

20. "Abstracts of Damages and Judgments Awarded in Streets and Alley Openings," 18 April 1856, Microfilm C-3689, City of St. Louis Archival Library.

21. In *The Revised Ordinances of the City of St. Louis*, 96.

22. "Abstracts of Damages," c. August 1871; n.d. (c. 1872); n.d. (c. 1876); n.d. (c. 1870s). All of these accounts are found on Microfilm Roll C-3689 at the St. Louis City Archives; the poor quality of the microfilm reproduction compounds the problem of finding dates or consistent page numbers on these hand-drafted documents.

23. *BPI Journal*, 3 June 1878; *Journal of the House of Delegates of St. Louis*, 1894–95, 492.

24. Ordinance 6905, 14 June 1869.

25. Based on an examination of street opening and improvement ordinances listed in *Index* for those blocks included in the Benton Park neighborhood, as defined by the Landmarks Association of St. Louis. These blocks, which comprise the heart of the study area, have been the focus of historical research carried out by Landmarks; therefore, they provide a good basis on which to build further study.

26. On Lucas Place and the private streets in general, see Richard Allen Rosen, "St. Louis, Missouri, 1850–1865: The Rise of Lucas Place and the Transformation of the City from Public Spaces to Private Places" (M.A. thesis, University of California, Los Angeles, 1988); Charles C. Savage, *Architecture of the Private Streets of St. Louis: The Architects and the Houses They Designed* (Columbia: University of Missouri Press, 1987); and Scot McConachie, "Public Problems and Private Places," *BMHS* 34 (1978): 90–103. These and other accounts of the private-street phenomenon in St. Louis have tended to focus on the streets' value in shielding residents from noxious uses or undesirable neighbors. In so doing, they underplay the extent to which restrictive covenants were already commonly applied to public streets as well. More recently, David T. Beito and Bruce Smith, in "The Formation of Urban Infrastructure Through Nongovernmental Planning: The Private Places of St. Louis," *JUH* 16 (1990): 263–303, have placed the issue in the political perspective that it demands, by considering it as a response to the particular inefficiencies and shortcomings of the city's public improvements process. Beito and Smith's thorough account would be further enhanced by a discussion of the City's own attempt to emulate private-street creation in the Boulevard Law of 1891.

27. "An Act to Extend the Limits of the City of St. Louis, and for Other Purposes," 5 December 1855; in *Ordinances of the City of St. Louis* (1856), 180. Despite the fact that it went unheeded, the 1855 call for a city plan was relatively prescient. New York had followed a detailed street plan since early in the century, but other cities were generally slow to follow; Boston, for example, had no such law until 1891 (Warner, *Streetcar Suburbs*, 122).

28. *Scheme for the Separation and Re-Organization of the Governments of St. Louis City and County and Charter for the City of St. Louis* (hereafter cited as *Scheme and Charter*) (St. Louis: Woodward, Tiernan and Hale, 1877). The standard reference to the charter remains Thomas S. Barclay, *The St. Louis Home Rule Charter*

of 1876, Its Framing and Adoption (Columbia: University of Missouri Press, 1962). See also E. Terrence Jones, *Fragmented by Design: Why St. Louis Has So Many Governments* (St. Louis: Palmerston and Reed, 2000), Ch. 1; and Jon C. Teaford, *The Unheralded Triumph: City Government in America, 1870–1900* (Baltimore: Johns Hopkins University Press, 1984), 112–17.

29. Silas Bent quoted in *St. Louis Globe-Democrat*, 4 May 1876, in Barclay, *The St. Louis Home Rule Charter*, 48; Barclay, 53. For an introduction to the history of St. Louis's German newspaper industry, see Harvey Saalberg, "Dr. Emil Preetorius, Editor-in-Chief of the *Westliche Post*, 1864–1905," *BMHS* 23 (1968): 103–12; George S. Johns, "Joseph Pulitzer," *MHR* 25 (1930–31): 201–18, 404–20, 563–75; and Steven Rowan, ed., *Germans for a Free Missouri: Translations from the Radical Press, 1857–1862*, introduction by James Neal Primm (Columbia: University of Missouri Press, 1983).

30. *Scheme and Charter*, 78, 91–92, 95.

31. *Scheme and Charter*, 45–46. Although the city had had a bicameral legislature from 1839 to 1859, and again for a single year in 1866, members of both houses were elected in these years by ward or district. The 1876 charter was the first to include any kind of provision for the citywide election of representatives. Howard Lee Hibbs, "The Governmental History of St. Louis Before 1876," (M.A. thesis, Washington University, 1931), 114ff.

32. *Scheme and Charter*, 91.

33. Barclay, *The St. Louis Home Rule Charter*, 41–42; Catherine V. Soraghan, "The History of St. Louis, 1865–1876" (M.A. thesis, Washington University, 1936), 30–31.

34. *Scheme and Charter*, 89.

35. See Christine Meisner Rosen, "Infrastructural Improvement in Nineteenth-Century Cities: A Conceptual Framework and Cases," *JUH* 12 (1986): 211–56, as well as Terrence J. McDonald, *The Parameters of Urban Fiscal Policy: Socioeconomic Change and Political Culture in San Francisco, 1860–1906* (Berkeley: University of California Press, 1986), xi, for a fuller exploration of that fiscal philosophy as it related to public improvements. The broader implications of this developing complex of social and political attitudes in the late nineteenth century are discussed in Robert H. Wiebe, *The Search for Order* (New York: Hill and Wang, 1967), 133–35.

36. *Scheme and Charter*, 89.

37. *BPI Journal*, 12 March 1878.

38. *BPI Journal*, 15 August 1878.

39. "Report of the Board of Public Improvements," *Mayor's Message* (1878), 199.

40. "Report of the Street Commissioner," *Mayor's Message* (1878), 248; "Report of the Board of Public Improvements," *Mayor's Message* (1881), 160; ibid. (1883), 166.

41. *BPI Journal*, October 1877–February 1880.

42. *Scheme and Charter*, 90. The "majority" clause of the charter's public improvements section was sufficiently ambiguous that the board could interpret it as the occasion demanded. At times, it was interpreted as referring to a majority of the total number of affected landowners; at other times, to that group of landowners (however small in number) owning a majority of the affected land. See *BPI Journal*, 29 November 1877, 12 December 1877, 21 January 1879.

43. *BPI Journal*, 25 November 1878, 13 January 1880.

44. Ibid., 21 January 1879. With the charter, the city had been divided into twenty-eight wards, as it continues to be today; the Ninth and Eleventh lay in the heart of South St. Louis.

45. Ibid., 11 February 1878.

46. Ibid., 19 November 1877; 3 September, 3 January, 29 January, and 11 February 1878. Cf. Teaford, *Unheralded Triumph*, 17ff., on the increasingly localized function of aldermen in American cities during this period.

47. *BPI Journal*, 3 January 1878.

48. Ibid., 21 October 1879. The effects of landfill on streets already occupied by houses can still be seen on Lemp Avenue north of Cherokee Street, where the first stories of older buildings are entered below street level.

49. William T. Sherman, letter to John Eaton Tourtelotte, 7 September 1884, Sherman Papers, MHS Archives.

50. *Scheme and Charter*, 95.

51. "Report of the Board of Public Improvements," *Mayor's Message* (1880), 175.

52. *BPI Journal*, 14 January 1878.

53. Ibid., 13 October 1879.

54. Ibid., 16 November 1877. The denial of this sidewalk petition was actually among those overturned by the subsequent pleadings before the board of Councilman Nicholas Berg.

55. To some extent, portions of every American city suffered from this cycle of caution, neglect, and disrepair. A similar case is described in Carl V. Harris, *Political Power in Birmingham, 1871–1921* (Knoxville: University of Tennessee Press, 1977), 154–55.

56. Based on a review of Norbury Wayman's unpublished "Chronological Index-List of Subdivisions to the City of St. Louis since 1816," for the years 1877–1886.

57. "Report of the Board of Public Improvements," *Mayor's Message* (1878), 207.

58. *BPI Journal*, 3 February 1880.

59. Walt Whitman, letter to "Lou" (Hannah Louise Whitman), 11 October 1879, Whitman Family Papers, MHS Archives. Whitman wrote to his sister while in St. Louis to visit his brother Jeff, a prominent engineer in the city.

60. "Report of the Board of Public Improvements," *Mayor's Message* (1878), 203.

61. In the year before the passage of the charter, St. Louisans paid a total of 1.42 percent in taxes (including separate assessments for police, sewer construction, streets, water service, and harbor maintenance), plus another two-thirds of 1 percent earmarked for the service of municipal debt. After the charter, the debt assessment rose to three-quarters of 1 percent, while the general property tax was limited to 1 percent total (Ordinance 9503, 18 June 1875; *Scheme and Charter*, 78). The frustration of City officials with this marked decline in revenue was evident from the outset: see, for example, "Report of the City Engineer," *Mayor's Message* (1877), 6.

62. Samuel Nicolson, *The Nicolson Pavement, Invented by Samuel Nicolson, of Boston, Massachusetts* (Boston: Dutton and Wentworth, 1855). Wood blocks were considered useful as much for the fact that they cut down considerably the ubiquitous noise of horseshoes as for their relatively untested durability. See also McShane, "Transforming the Use of Urban Space," 288–89.

63. "Report of the Street Commissioner," *Mayor's Message* (1872), 4.

64. "Report of the Board of Public Improvements," *Mayor's Message* (1878), 203; "Report of the City Engineer," *Mayor's Message* (1875), 10; ibid. (1874), 17.

65. "Report of the Street Commissioner," *Mayor's Message* (1884), 212.

66. Soraghan, "History of St. Louis," 68; "Report of the City Engineer," *Mayor's Message* (1875), 10; ordinance 6649, 4 December 1868; ordinance 6678, 16 December 1868.

67. "Report of the City Engineer," *Mayor's Message* (1875)ibid. Among the problems that asphalt use posed in early years were the expense that resulted from patents applied to its manufacture and application, and the fact that street-sprinkling operators persisted in treating it like macadam—in spite of the fact that below-freezing temperatures turned sprinkled asphalt streets into sheets of ice. See "Report of the Board of Public Improvements," *Mayor's Message* (1878), 202; *Journal of the House of Delegates,* 31 October 1884.

68. Telford pavement had a surface of macadam, but this surface lay atop a 12-inch bed of stone and sand, and was therefore less susceptible to settling than simple macadamizing. "Report of the City Engineer," *Mayor's Message* (1874), 24. The first ordinance calling for Telford paving within the study area dates from 1878; but the technique did not predominate in South St. Louis streets until well into the 1890s (based on a study of paving ordinances listed in *Index*).

69. League of American Wheelmen, *Good Streets: The Ways and Means of Attaining and Preserving Same* (St. Louis: Cordner Publishing Co., 1896), 44.

70. "Report of the Street Commissioner," *Mayor's Message* (1904), Table 5, 79; Soraghan, "History of St. Louis," 70.

71. "Report of the Board of Public Improvements," *Mayor's Message* (1878), 203; ibid. (1880), 173.

72. "Report of the City Engineer," *Mayor's Message* (1877), 6.

73. *Mayor's Message* (1881), x. As in other cities, the idea that personal improvement assessments might benefit downtown landowners would not take hold in St. Louis until the last decade of the century. See Harris, *Political Power in Birmingham,* 178–79.

74. "Report of the Street Commissioner," *Mayor's Message* (1881), 207; ibid. (1904), Table 5, 79.

75. *St. Louis Globe-Democrat,* 2 April 1882, in "St. Louis—In Review," *Glimpses of the Past* 4 (1937): 120.

76. "Report of the Street Commissioner," *Mayor's Message* (1882), 177; ibid. (1883), 167.

77. "Report of the Street Commissioner," *Mayor's Message* (1904), Table 5, 79. This table contains a complete record of street reconstruction, listed by year and paving type, in the city.

78. Savage, *Architecture of the Private Streets,* 13, 22. Beito and Smith, in "The Formation of Urban Infrastructure," address the legal basis of the private streets more in terms of general land-use restrictions than in regard to their more unusual restriction of traffic within the roadway.

79. Ordinance 12,509, 4 August 1883.

80. See especially the Missouri Supreme Court's ruling in *Glasgow v. City of St. Louis,* 87 Mo. 678 and 15 Mo. App. 112. In *Glasgow,* the court overturned the City's decision to turn over a public right-of-way (Papin Street) to the Shickle, Harrison, and

Howard Ironworks for the company's private use. The justices determined that "the streets of the city are held by it in trust for the public."

81. St. Louis Merchants' Exchange, *Annual Statement of the Trade and Commerce of St. Louis* (St. Louis, 1893), 68. The idea of a wide "system" of landscaped parkways was considerably promoted by the city of Boston's experience in creating a series of connected roads through the drained fens, from the Charles River to Franklin Park. The notion went as far back as the 1860s, when the landscape architect Frederick Law Olmsted (designer of Boston's system) planned parkways for Brooklyn and Buffalo. See David Schuyler, *The New Urban Landscape: The Redefinition of City Form in Nineteenth-Century America* (Baltimore: Johns Hopkins University Press, 1986), 128–33.

82. "Report of the Street Commissioner," *Mayor's Message* (1887), 266; *A Discussion of the Boulevard System, as Proposed in the City of St. Louis* (St. Louis: Continental Printing Co., 1892), 5; *Missouri Laws* (Jefferson City, 1891), 47; Ordinance 16,206, 24 June 1891.

83. "Report of the Street Commissioner," *Mayor's Message* (1887), 266.

84. The only exception to this rule came in the following year, with the designation of the streets of the new Compton Heights Subdivision as boulevards. This subdivision is too often seen by historians as another of the private places.

85. William Hyde and Howard L. Conard, *Encyclopedia of the History of St. Louis: A Compendium of History and Biography for Ready Reference* (St. Louis: Southern Book Company, 1899), 1: 200–201; *St. Louis Post-Dispatch*, 1 March 1897 (3:4), 2 March 1897 (7:4). The law was revived, in slightly modified form, in the city's 1901 charter (ordinance 20,144, 31 July 1901).

86. "Report of the Board of Public Improvements," *Mayor's Message* (1896), 452.

87. Edward V. P. Schneiderhahn Diary, vol. 5, 4 September 1900, Journals and Diaries Collection, MHS Archives.

88. Ordinance 20,444, 31 July 1901.

89. "Report of the Street Commissioner," *Mayor's Message* (1892), 234.

90. Isaac H. Sturgeon, "What Can the City Do in a Financial Way for the Streets?" in *Good Streets*, 11.

91. *Laws of Missouri* (1893), 59; "Report of the Street Commissioner," *Mayor's Message* (1893), 218; "Report of the Board of Public Improvements," ibid., 206.

92. Anonymous diary, 21 January 1897, St. Louis History Papers, MHS Archives; *Twentieth Annual Report of the Health Commissioner* (St. Louis, 1898), 283.

93. "Report of the Board of Public Improvements," *Mayor's Message* (1896), 454.

94. Based on a yearly analysis of expenditures listed in the *Mayor's Message* for the years 1870–1904.

Chapter Seven

1. Details on this busy day in the life of the South Side are drawn from the *Missouri Republican*, 21 March 1910 (7:1), 22 March 1910 (3:3).

2. *Labor*, 29 April 1893 (1:6).

3. Scot McConachie, "The Big Cinch: A Business Elite in the Life of a City, St. Louis, 1895–1915" (Ph.D. diss., Washington University, 1976), 200, 60ff. For a comparison

of a similar change in the organizational structure of another city's elite, see Joseph F. Rishel, *Founding Families of Pittsburgh: The Evolution of a Regional Elite, 1760–1910* (Pittsburgh: University of Pittsburgh Press, 1990), 187–88. In terms of the broader connection between industrial consolidation and the rise of the progressive mindset, see the well-worn but still compelling interpretations given in Samuel P. Hays, "The Politics of Reform in Municipal Government in the Progressive Era," *Pacific Northwest Quarterly* 55 (1964): 157–69; and Robert H. Wiebe, *The Search for Order* (New York: Hill and Wang, 1967), 181–85.

4. McConachie, "The Big Cinch," 206ff; Jack Muraskin, "St. Louis Municipal Reform in the 1890s: A Study in Failure," *BMHS* 25 (1968): 46–48. Ironically, Harrison had something of a South St. Louis connection: his father, James, had owned the Common land that became the Halliday area (see Chapter 3).

5. *St. Louis Post-Dispatch*, 6 November 1898 (12:3).

6. The proposed charter changes are enumerated in Ordinance 19,365 (16 April 1898); see also *St. Louis Post-Dispatch*, 21 June 1898 (4:3). If Ziegenhein, in supporting the amendments, did not act the familiar part of the "boss," that fact may suggest that we alter our notion of what motivated political bosses, rather than that we figure out the nefarious intention behind his seeming inconsistency with our externally imposed image. It was the latter option, however, that reformers and newspaper editors chose to follow, and it is their interpretation that historians have inherited.

7. *Missouri Republican*, 10 July 1898 (8:1); *St. Louis Post-Dispatch*, 11 July 1898 (4:3), 14 June 1898 (6:2).

8. For information on sectional support for Walbridge, see James Neal Primm, *Lion of the Valley: St. Louis, Missouri, 1766–1980*, 3d ed. (St. Louis: Missouri Historical Society Press, 1998), 350.

9. *St. Louis Globe-Democrat*, 13 July 1898; *Missouri Republican*, 13 July 1898 (5:1).

10. Lincoln Steffens, *The Shame of the Cities* (1905; New York: Sagamore Press, 1957), Chs. 2 and 4.

11. Ibid., 20, 25–26.

12. McConachie, "The Big Cinch," 214. On South Side violence, see *St. Louis Post-Dispatch*, 12 May 1900 (2:2), 21 May 1900 (1:6). For a general account of the strike, see Clifton D. Hood, "The Workers' Struggle for Organization: The St. Louis Street Railway Strike of 1900" (undergraduate honors thesis, Department of History, Washington University, 1976).

13. Ordinance 20,444 (31 July 1901). The 1901 amendments appropriated virtually the complete wording of Ordinance 19,365. There were two differences in those sections that concerned landscape improvement. First, the new bill established specific ways of measuring the area around proposed street improvements to be designated and assessed as a benefit district. The earlier bill left the determination of each district's boundaries to the board of public improvements. Second, the new bill maintained the existing requirement that damages to private property be assessed "without reference to the projected improvement," rather than on a basis of the future, higher value of the land.

14. *St. Louis Post-Dispatch*, 21 October 1901 (1:2), 23 October 1901 (1:7), 20 October 1901 (6:2).

15. Ibid., 22 October 1901 (1:6), 23 October 1901 (1:7, 6:2). The shape that that "public welfare" would take was clear from the day of the election, when Street Commissioner Charles Varrelman announced that the new amendments would allow him to order reconstruction of streets from Laclede Avenue north to Franklin Avenue, as far west as Union Boulevard: the central corridor.

16. Ibid., 23 October 1901 (9:1).

17. Dwight F. Davis, *Some Municipal Problems* (St. Louis: Round Table, 1907), 3.

18. *Missouri Republican*, 31 January 1911 (8:2).

19. Ibid., 25 January 1911 (8:2), 27 January 1911 (6:2). The drive toward citywide council elections was a common feature in early-twentieth-century urban reform politics, though in at least one city—Seattle—changing demographics eventually led reformers to urge a return to ward-based elections. See Lee F. Pendergrass, "Urban Reform and Voluntary Association: The Municipal League of Seattle, 1910–1916," in Michael H. Ebner and Eugene M. Tobin, eds., *The Age of Urban Reform: New Perspectives on the Progressive Era* (Port Washington, N.Y.: Kennikat Press/National University Publications, 1977), 63.

20. *St. Louis Post-Dispatch*, 1 February 1911 (9:1). Organized labor, including the Building Trades Council, had aided the cause against the amendments with its strong opposition. That opposition would change to support when a new, compromise package was voted on in the following year. See Gary M. Fink, *Labor's Search for Political Order: The Political Behavior of the Missouri Labor Movement, 1890–1940* (Columbia: University of Missouri Press, 1973), 37–39.

21. There are few precedents in the literature of the City Beautiful movement to which we can look for guidance in finding an approach that considers the strengths and weaknesses of that movement in the full light of the ongoing dynamic of forms that preceded and followed it. A number of works from within the last generation (see especially M. Christine Boyer, *Dreaming the Rational City: The Myth of American City Planning* [Cambridge, Mass.: MIT Press, 1983] and Giorgio Ciucci, Francesco DalCo, and Mario Manieri-Elia, *The American City: From the Civil War to the New Deal* [Cambridge, Mass.: MIT Press, 1979]) have critically and successfully considered the political context of city-beautiful reforms. In taking at face value the claims of planners, however, they have unwittingly perpetuated the "historical idealist view," as Richard E. Foglesong calls it (*Planning the Capitalist City: The Colonial Era to the 1920s* [Princeton, N.J.: Princeton University Press, 1986], 9), that characterized progressive reform in the first place. More recently, William Wilson (*The City Beautiful Movement* [Baltimore: Johns Hopkins University Press, 1989]) has tried to find a middle ground between approving and skeptical, or aesthetic and political interpretations of the period. Wilson's interpretation avoids the excessive simplicity of accounts that presume the "coercive" power of planning reformers (81); nevertheless, he shares the *prima facie* belief that the movement did indeed represent a radically different notion of order, one whose origins can be traced along a well-documented, self-conscious series of landscape improvements in America and Europe through the nineteenth century. More recently, the essays collected in Mary Corbin Sies and Christopher Silver, eds., *Planning the Twentieth-Century American City* (Baltimore: Johns Hopkins University Press, 1996), suggest the range of new interpretations made possible by close reassessment of particular case studies in city planning history.

For recent studies of Progressive Era and City Beautiful reform in St. Louis, see Tom Martinson, "The Persistence of Vision: A Century of Civic Progress in St. Louis," *Places* 6(4) (Summer 1990): 22–33; Edward C. Rafferty, "Orderly City, Orderly Lives: The City Beautiful Movement in St. Louis," *Gateway Heritage* 11(4) (Spring 1991): 40–62; and Mark Abbott, "Déjà Vu All Over Again? St. Louis Master Plans and the Dream of the Democratic Community," *Gateway Heritage* 19(4) (Spring 1999): 4–19.

22. Ordinance 20,760, 12 July 1902; ordinance 21,226, 28 September 1903.

23. Julius Pitzman, letter to George Kessler, 5 October 1902, George Kessler Papers (hereafter cited as Kessler Papers), Box 4, MHS Archives. Pitzman was the single most influential person in the laying out of St. Louis's streets in the half-century after the Civil War. Best known for laying out virtually all of St. Louis's private streets from Benton Place (1868) to Parkview (1905), he was perhaps even more influential in his capacity as the official city surveyor during these years; as such, he laid out many of the city's public streets as well. Pitzman's power in the shaping of the city was ultimately greater than that of most elected officials; by 1912, according to one visiting journalist, he was "so well established in the confidence of the bankers that no one can finance a real estate project unless Mr. Pitzman surveys it" (John L. Mathews, "The Alarm Clock in St. Louis," *Boston Evening Transcript*, 22 June 1912).

24. *Report of the Kingshighway Commission* (St. Louis, March 1903), 38.

25. Ibid., 8. The perception that "everyone" was moving west, a common notion at the time (as it is today), was based on the assumption that "everyone" lived in the central corridor, which was the one part of the city to which that perception applied.

26. Ibid., 33.

27. Civic League of St. Louis, *Yearbook* (St. Louis, 1911), 36.

28. Civic Improvement League Papers (hereafter cited as CIL Papers), 18 September 1902, MHS Archives.

29. "Constitution" (11 February 1902), in *Yearbook* (1911), 38; Civic Improvement League, *First Annual Report* (St. Louis, 1903), 11; CIL Papers, 23 May 1902.

30. CIL Papers, ibid.23 and 27 May 1902; Civic Improvement League, *Second Annual Report* (St. Louis, 1904), 26.

31. CIL Papers, 3 June 1902; *First Annual Report*, 11.

32. CIL Papers, 18 September 1902.

33. "Constitution of the Civic Improvement League of St. Louis," CIL Papers, 6 March 1905.

34. CIL Papers, 25 February 1904 and 22 March 1905.

35. Civic League, *A Year of Civic Effort: Addresses and Reports of the Civic League* (St. Louis, 1907), 11; CIL Papers, 13 February 1906. While no proof of a cause-effect relation exists, it is worth noting that just prior to these changes, in March 1905, the realtor John Gundlach had joined the executive board of the League. Gundlach was instrumental in lending to the general civic improvement effort in St. Louis a more businesslike cast. For a comparable case of the impact of volunteer groups on progressive reform in the beginnings of the post–City Beautiful era, see Pendergrass, "Urban Reform and Voluntary Association."

36. CIL Papers, 26 September 1905.

37. *A City Plan for St. Louis* (St. Louis, 1907), 9, 11, 8. That the actual text of the plan was aimed at a quite specific readership is suggested by the fact that only 2,500

copies were printed. On the uncertainties of the "dynamic of support and opposition between planners and businessmen," see Foglesong, *Planning the Capitalist City*, 231. The potential for conflict between those two seemingly common-minded groups has remained an issue in the formation of a reform agenda for St. Louis to this day.

38. *City Plan*, 24, 80.

39. Ibid., 100–104, 97. St. Louis, as the plan proudly pointed out, ranked ninth out of the nation's ten largest cities in per capita debt. Its 5 percent maximum compared with higher rates in other major cities, ranging as high as 10 percent in New York (97). The idea of excess condemnation to ensure the value and character of a public improvement had ample precedent in European cities, to which the plan alluded. It would not gain solid grounding in American case law for a number of years to come (*White v. Johnson*, 148 S.C. 488, 146 S.E. 411 [1929]).

40. Ibid., 39; *St. Louis Post-Dispatch*, 3 February 1907 (4:3).

41. *City Plan*, 37. The civic centers committee acknowledged its debt to the example set by Chicago park planners, although the example included in the plan— of Chicago's Armour Square (38)—was a strictly recreational park without the public buildings of the St. Louis centers. Absent from the committee's proposed list of neighborhoods were any of the poor and increasingly crowded African American neighborhoods confined to the blocks of the Mill Creek Valley, west from Twelfth Street toward Grand Avenue.

42. Ibid., 49. Only a small amount of literature details the geographic and social characteristics of turn-of-the-century ethnic communities in St. Louis; the best overview of the subject is contained in Ruth Crawford, *The Immigrant in St. Louis* (St. Louis: Studies in Social Economics, 1917). For a more subjective, but more compelling, contemporary description of the North Side slums, cf. Theodore Dreiser, *A Book About Myself* (New York: Boni and Liveright, 1922), 219–20.

43. *City Plan*, 37.

44. In the sense that I have treated it here, the political paradigm within which Ziegenhein and his supporters operated may indeed have had the intermediate effect of making the government work to abet personal gain. More fundamentally, however, it was an example of the "balanced system of municipal decision making" that, as Jon C. Teaford has shown, was particularly susceptible to criticism at that point in the development of American political culture (*The Unheralded Triumph: City Government in America, 1870–1900* [Baltimore: Johns Hopkins University Press, 1984], 308). Teaford's insight into the manner in which a viable, alternative view of urban order might be retold by its opponents as "at best a tale of fragmentation and confusion" (3) echoes the reminders of urban sociologists like William Foote Whyte that the problems of an outlying or underprivileged portion of the city likely reflected "not a lack of organization but the failure of its own social organization to mesh with the structure of the society around it" (*Street Corner Society: The Social Structure of an Italian Slum*, 2d ed. [Chicago: University of Chicago Press, 1966], 273). In the period covered in this chapter, meshing with that larger society had become increasingly necessary. It is all the more important, therefore, that we see that for all their eventual differences, Ziegenhein's appeal shared common roots with the appeal of the Civic League.

45. Henry Wright, ed., "City Plan Association Report" (1 April 1911), 3.

46. Civic League, *Yearbook* (1911), 18; George Kessler, unidentified ms., 26 March 1913, in Kessler Papers, Box 3; *Civic Bulletin* 1(8) (20 March 1911), n.p.

47. "City Plan Association Report," 4.

48. Ibid., 14, 1.

49. Ordinance 25,745.

50. The salient features of the ordinance are described in *Forward St. Louis* 2(9) (9 November 1914), 2.

51. On Shaw and his properties, see William Barnaby Faherty, *Henry Shaw, His Life and Legacies* (Columbia: University of Missouri Press, 1987).

52. George Kessler, letter to John Gundlach, 19 June 1911, Kessler Papers, Box 3.

53. Unidentified notes, n.d., in John Gundlach Papers (hereafter cited as Gundlach Papers), MHS Archives.

54. Unidentified ms., n.d., Gundlach Papers.

55. Mayo Fesler, letter to Gundlach, 9 March 1915, Gundlach Papers.

56. John Gundlach, "City Planning and the Industrial Future," *The St. Louis Idea* 1(2) (October 1916), 13; "Do You Ever Give a Thought to the Growth of Your City?" *St. Louis Times*, 7 August 1919; letter to August Busch, 22 February 1916, Gundlach Papers. For an instance of the kind of contemporary real estate advice literature that preached the virtues of predictable land use, see Richard M. Hurd, *Principles of City Land Values* (New York: Record and Guide, 1903).

57. *St. Louis Post-Dispatch*, 24 June 1914 (4:3), 29 June 1914 (1:4), 30 June 1914 (1:1).

58. Ibid., 1 July 1901 (2:1, 2:2).

59. Walter B. Stevens, letter to George Kessler, 3 July 1912, Kessler Papers, Box 3; City Plan Commission, *St. Louis Central Traffic-Parkway* (St. Louis, 1912), 5–6.

60. *Mayor's Message* (1915), 3.

61. On the Business Men's League, see *Forward St. Louis* 2(6) (31 August 1914), 6. Abbott quoted in Rafferty, "Orderly City," 56.

62. *Missouri Republican*, 7 June 1915 (4:3). Citywide assessment was, in fact, precisely the kind of situation that charter supporters had promised would be avoided; cf. *St. Louis Post-Dispatch*, 28 June 1914 (3:3). For the UWA remarks, see Rafferty, "Orderly City," 56.

63. *Missouri Republican*, 4 June 1915 (5:1), 9 June 1915 (1:1). The one-quarter African American ward in which the improvements were scheduled to be made voted in favor of the project; see Rafferty, "Orderly City," 57.

64. Norman J. Johnston, "Harland Bartholomew: His Comprehensive Plans and Science of Planning" (Ph.D. diss., University of Pennsylvania, 1964), 121; Mary Seematter, interview with Harland Bartholomew, 14 July 1983 (hereafter cited as "Bartholomew Interview"), MHS Archives, 7.

65. *St. Louis Post-Dispatch*, unidentified article (c. October 1916) in Kessler Papers, Box 4; George Kessler, letter to Nelson Cunliff, 6 November 1916, in ibid.

66. Gundlach to Busch, 22 February 1916; Kessler, letter to Dwight Davis, in "Annual Report of the Park Commissioner," in *Mayor's Message* (1913), 13.

67. The preceding episodes are described in detail in Johnston, "Harland Bartholomew," 85–121.

68. City Plan Commission of St. Louis, *Problems of St. Louis* (St. Louis: City Plan Commission, 1917), iii.

69. Unidentified manuscript (c. December 1914) in Kessler Papers, Box 3.

70. *Problems of St. Louis*, xxii, xv (original emphasis).

71. Ibid., 65, 66, xviii, 20, xv.

72. Ibid., 12. Such reassurances smoothed over the fact that a few of the commission's proposals actually veered far from "generally accepted" opinion: for example, the proposal that the city's debt ceiling be doubled, from 5 to 10 percent.

73. The City Plan Commission reports include: *The River Des Peres Plan* (1916); *Recreation in St. Louis* (1917); *The Kingshighway* (1917); *A Major Street Plan for St. Louis* (1917); *St. Louis After the War* (1918); *Zoning for St. Louis: A Fundamental Part of the City Plan* (1918); *The Zone Plan* (1919); *A Public Building Group Plan for St. Louis* (1919); *Twelfth Street, St. Louis' Most Needed Commercial Thoroughfare* (1919); *The St. Louis Transit System, Past and Future* (1920); *Ten Years Progress on the City Plan of St. Louis, 1916–1926* (1927); *A Plan for the Central River Front* (1928); and *A Plan for the Northern and Southern River Front* (1929).

74. *Annual Report of the City Plan Commission, 1916–1917* (St. Louis, 1917), n.p.; ordinance 29,463, 7 February 1917.

75. *The Zone Plan*, 17; *Annual Report of the City Plan Commission, 1917–1918* (St. Louis, 1918), n.p.

76. Ordinance 30,199 (28 June 1918). St. Louis's was, as Bartholomew liked to boast, the second comprehensive zoning ordinance in the country, after that of New York City.

77. *The Zone Plan*, 14, 63.

78. Ibid., 11, 30 (emphasis added).

79. Ibid., 60–61.

80. Ibid., 34, 28.

81. Ibid., 11.

82. Nor was Bartholomew above having recognized representatives of that *status quo* instruct him in what the "natural processes of growth" in St. Louis were: when August Busch—whose help John Gundlach had solicited not long before—objected to the restrictive zoning proposed for the blocks around his brewery (specifically, the area bounded by Lynch, Wyoming, Thirteenth, and Second Streets), Bartholomew and the commission quickly reversed their initial decisions and declared the neighborhood an unrestricted zone.

83. The first zoning ordinance was never enacted; it was immediately challenged in court and was at last struck down by the state supreme court in November 1923. In July 1925, the state legislature passed an enabling act, which the high court eventually affirmed as being in keeping with the federal Supreme Court's landmark decision in *Village of Euclid v. Ambler Realty Co.* (272 U.S. 365). The state law led to a second zoning ordinance, effective 26 May 1926, which resembled the first but substituted a "Multiple Dwelling" designation for the old "Second Residential" district and provided greater flexibility regarding building heights.

84. Bartholomew Interview, 3.

85. City Plan Commission of St. Louis, *A Major Street Plan for St. Louis* (St. Louis, 1917), 18.

86. Most conspicuous among these gaps were connections from Twelfth Street to North Florissant Avenue (which continued through the North Side beyond the city

limits) and, on the south, to Gravois Avenue, which at the time dead-ended at Eighteenth Street and Russell Avenue.

87. *A Major Street Plan*, 8.

88. Ibid., 53–57, 67–69.

89. *Annual Report of the City Plan Commission, 1916–1917*, n.p.; *Problems*, 9.

90. See, for example, City Plan Commission of St. Louis, *St. Louis After the War* (St. Louis, 1918).

91. Ibid., 5.

92. *St. Louis Post-Dispatch*, 12 May 1920 (1:7, 2:1).

93. Bartholomew interview, 2.

94. Ibid.; "The St. Louis General Improvement Bond Issue, and Why You Should Vote for It" (c. 1923), MHS Archives, 7.

95. John Gundlach, "The Courthouse Site" (c. October 1924), n.p., and "Reasons for Keeping Courthouse on Broadway" (c. October 1924), n.p., Gundlach Papers. Gundlach lost the fight, and the new structure arose as part of a larger public-buildings group around Twelfth and Market Streets. See Martinson, "The Persistence of Vision," on the subsequent history of the site.

96. W. C. Bitting, letter to John Gundlach, 27 October 1924, Gundlach Papers; *St. Louis Post-Dispatch*, 5 November 1924 (19:8). The plaza site was rejected in Wards 3, 4, 5, 6, 7, and 9. The potential contradictions that create tension between business and planning interests forms one of the central concerns of Foglesong (*Planning the Capitalist City*). For an analysis of similar tensions in another city at the same time, see Carl V. Harris, *Political Power in Birmingham, 1871–1921* (Knoxville: University of Tennessee Press, 1977), 271. Neither of these accounts, however, discusses the kinds of geographical and spatial factors that might realign one or another of those power elites with different areas of neighborhood support.

97. See City Plan Commission of St. Louis, *The River Front, Possible Municipal Ownership of a Riverway from Chain of Rocks to River des Peres, with Additional Approach to Municipal Bridge* (St. Louis, 1913), and *Problems*, 59–63.

98. City Plan Commission of St. Louis, *A Plan for the Central River Front, St. Louis, Missouri* (St. Louis, 1928), 28.

99. Ibid.

100. City Plan Commission of St. Louis, *Comprehensive City Plan, St. Louis, Missouri* (St. Louis, 1947), 2.

101. Ibid., 4, 28, 31.

102. The specific impact that terms like blight and obsolescence, as used by the Home Owners' Loan Corporation, had on the housing ownership patterns of St. Louis is discussed in Kenneth T. Jackson, *Crabgrass Frontier: The Suburbanization of the United States* (New York: Oxford University Press, 1985), 199–201.

Chapter Eight

1. Isaac Lionberger, "Glimpses of People and Manners in St. Louis, 1870–1920," MHS Archives, 61, 54–55.

2. Blacks in St. Louis numbered more than 150,000—roughly one-fifth of the city's population—in 1950. For more on St. Louis's African American population in the

interwar years, see Katharine T. Corbett and Mary E. Seematter, "No Crystal Stair: Black St. Louis, 1920–1940," *Gateway Heritage* 8(2) (Fall 1987), 8–15. The specific boundaries of the "negro district" delineated by the Real Estate Exchange can be found on one of the series of St. Louis City Plan Commission maps, c. 1930–35, which are held in the MHS map collection. For an invaluable personal perspective on life in the city's segregated neighborhoods during the 1940s and 1950s, see the audiotapes and written transcripts of interviews conducted for MHS's "Through the Eyes of a Child" oral history project between 1998 and 2000, filed in the MHS Archives.

3. Lewis F. Thomas, "The Geographic Landscape of Metropolitan St. Louis," in Lewis F. Thomas, ed., *Contributions in Geology and Geography* (St. Louis: Washington University Studies, New Series, Science and Technology, no. 7, 1932), 31.

4. Recent demographic changes on the South Side are described in *St. Louis Post-Dispatch*, 19 November 1989 (1:2); see also the series of occasional articles on immigration in St. Louis (much of it centered on the South Side) authored by Philip Dine in the *St. Louis Post-Dispatch:* 21 May 1995 (1B:3), 25 June 1995 (1B:3), 15 October 1995 (1B:2), 17 December 1995 (1B:2).

5. East-West Gateway Coordinating Council, *Transportation Redefined: The St. Louis Metropolitan Area's 2020 Transportation Plan*, Issue Paper: Transportation and Sustainable Development (18 August 1998), available at: <ewgateway.org/html/wphtml/issu8-18.htm>.

6. "A City of Many Neighborhoods," *St. Louis Post-Dispatch*, 15 October 1989 (4B:3). The neighborhoods included within the study area are Dutchtown North, Benton Park, Soulard, McKinley/Fox, Fox Park, Compton Heights, and Tower Grove East.

Index

Italic page numbers indicate illustrations.